THE LETTERS OF LADY PALMERSTON

COUNTESS COWPER

(afterwards Viscountess Palmerston)

aged about twenty-three

From the portrait by Hoppner-Jackson at Firle Place

The Letters of Lady Palmerston

Temple, Amelia Mary (Viscountess Palmerston)

SELECTED AND EDITED

FROM THE ORIGINALS AT BROADLANDS

AND ELSEWHERE BY

TRESHAM LEVER

JOHN MURRAY

Fifty Albemarle Street London

© *Tresham Lever 1957*

Printed in Great Britain by
Butler and Tanner Ltd, Frome and London
and published by John Murray (Publishers) Ltd

To
The Countess Mountbatten of Burma
in gratitude

CONTENTS

ILLUSTRATIONS

PREFACE

'I SHOULD not like Mr Briggs to look over the papers in the Evidence Room—what my brother George gave him leave to publish is quite different, but one cannot be too careful about family papers.' So wrote Lady Palmerston in October 1858 to her agent at Melbourne Hall. I am in whole-hearted agreement with her views about the care that should be exercised about the publication of private papers; therefore, though all the principal persons mentioned in this book have been long dead, I trust that nothing that follows may be found to grieve or offend their descendants who are alive today. With the many hundreds of Lady Palmerston's letters that have been available to me, it has inevitably been a difficult task to decide what to publish and what to omit. I can only hope that my readers will feel that I have exercised my judgment with discretion and discernment. Omissions apart, I have taken few liberties with the text, though I have modernized the punctuation throughout and have reparagraphed many passages; furthermore, here and there I have corrected Lady Palmerston's somewhat unorthodox spelling. But I have made as few amendments as possible, and those I have made are merely designed for more agreeable reading.

Of those who have allowed me the use of manuscripts, I must first and foremost express my great sense of gratitude to Countess Mountbatten of Burma for granting me access to her splendid collection of Lady Palmerston's letters. Some three-quarters of those that follow are in her muniment room at Broadlands: thus it is clear that but for her generosity this book could not be. Furthermore, Lady Mountbatten has allowed me to reproduce some of her paintings as illustrations to my book. For her great kindness I am intensely grateful. I also thank the Broadlands librarian, Mrs Blois, who typed the letters.

My sincere thanks are due to Her Majesty the Queen for her gracious permission to include letters at Windsor Castle; and to Her Majesty's librarian, Sir Owen Morshead, for his advice and

xi

assistance. I must also thank the Duke of Devonshire for allowing me to use letters at Chatsworth, the Marquess of Lansdowne for letters at Bowood, and the Marquess of Lothian for letters at Melbourne Hall. The Hon. Lady Salmond and her sister, Viscountess Gage, granted me access to the papers formerly at Panshanger and now deposited in the County Record Office, Hertford; I am most grateful to them for this permission, and also for allowing me to reproduce their paintings at Henfield Place and Firle. The Melbourne Papers that were formerly at Brocket and were left by Lady Palmerston's younger daughter Fanny (Viscountess Jocelyn) to her grandchildren were deposited on their behalf a few years ago in the British Museum by the late Dowager Countess of Airlie. I have received permission to use certain of these papers, and I wish to express my sincere thanks to Lady Jocelyn's grandchildren or their representatives: the Earl of Arran, K.P.; the late Dowager Countess of Airlie (and her daughter, Lady Helen Nutting, who assisted in my negotiations with her mother, when Lady Airlie was nearly ninety years of age and shortly before her death in April 1956); the Marquess of Salisbury, K.G., and Lord David Cecil, C.H., acting for their mother, the late Dowager Marchioness of Salisbury; and the Hon. James and the Hon. David Smith, acting for their mother, the late Dowager Viscountess Hambleden.

For professional advice I have been fortunate in obtaining the help of Professor A. Aspinall and Professor Jack Simmons both of whom have made many suggestions and criticisms to correct and improve the book. I gladly acknowledge the great debt I owe to these distinguished historians.

For guidance on the illustrations generally I am indebted to Mr Kingsley Adams, Director of the National Portrait Gallery; and for permission to reproduce paintings as illustrations to my book (apart from those already mentioned) I must thank the Earl of Shaftesbury, K.P., Lord Forester, Lord Dormer, Julian Salmond, Esq., and the Trustees of the National Portrait Gallery.

Others from whose advice I have greatly benefited are Sir John Murray, Mrs Bernard Tower, and Mr V. Cameron Turnbull. To all three of them my thanks are due.

T. L.

January 1957

Book One

COUNTESS COWPER

CHAPTER I

Early Years

THE LAMBS were not an ancient family. Indeed, the earliest known to fame were a certain Matthew Lamb, who early in the eighteenth century was for many years a respected attorney in Southwell, and his brother Peniston, who had a highly successful practice at the Bar. Matthew had two sons: Robert, who became first Dean and eventually Bishop of Peterborough; and Matthew, who followed his father's calling. In 1734, Peniston Lamb died unmarried, leaving his considerable fortune to his two nephews; and early in the following year old Matthew also died, bequeathing an estate of some £100,000 to his sons in order of succession. When eventually the bachelor bishop died, leaving his fortune to his younger brother, that brother became a rich man.

But Matthew Lamb was not content to be a wealthy idler; he was in fact an energetic and able man of business, and for long acted as solicitor to the Revenue of the Post Office,[1] and as confidential adviser to Lord Salisbury and Lord Egremont. He also succeeded his father as legal adviser to the Cokes of Melbourne Hall, near Derby, an ancient family descended from Charles I's handsome and showy Secretary of State, Sir John Coke, quizzed by Pope as 'Sir Plume' in *The Rape of the Lock*. With Mr Coke, Matthew Lamb was soon in high favour; with his employer's daughter, Charlotte, he was in high favour too; and in 1740 he married her. In 1746, Matthew Lamb purchased the Brocket Hall estate in Hertfordshire. A few years later his brother-in-law died suddenly, with the result that the Melbourne estate devolved upon his wife. Since 1741 Matthew had sat in Parliament for Stockbridge; subsequently he sat for Peterborough, and in 1755 he was created a baronet. Indeed, Sir Matthew Lamb's life ran a course of steady prosperity, so that when he died in 1768 he left to his son property and ready money to the value of almost a million pounds.

---

[1] Assuming he was the Councillor Lamb of Lincoln's Inn mentioned in the *Gentleman's Magazine*, 1738, p. 547.

This son, Sir Peniston Lamb, was a very different person from his father. Aged twenty-three at his succession and of an easy disposition without any marked talents, he soon fell a prey to the designs of the leading siren of the day, Mrs Sophia Baddeley, in whose memoirs he occupies a distinguished place. He was also much sought after by mothers with eligible daughters, with the result that within six months he found himself the accepted suitor of Elizabeth, only daughter of Sir Ralph Milbanke, 5th Baronet of Halnaby in Yorkshire, one of the ablest and handsomest young women of her day. But if Elizabeth was attractive, she was also ambitious: a mere second baronet of the parvenu Lambs was not good enough for the ancient house of Milbanke, and within a year the fashionable world was felicitating the young couple on the birth of a son, christened Peniston, and on the elevation of the father, who sat in the House of Commons for Ludgershall as a silent follower of Lord North, to the barony of Melbourne of Kilmore. Later he was created an Irish Viscount, and in 1815 an English Peer.

There was not much prospect of domestic happiness for the redoubtable Elizabeth in her union with her weak and rakish lord: and perhaps partly to cloak her sense of frustration, she turned her essentially masculine mind to the mundane object of securing for her family the great worldly position that her husband would certainly never achieve. Thus Melbourne House in Piccadilly, which stood where Albany now stands, was purchased in 1770 from Lord Holland, the father of Charles James Fox. The house, enlarged and redecorated, became a centre of Whig society, a favourite meeting-place of the Prince of Wales and all the leaders of the great world of the day. Some twenty years later Melbourne House, Piccadilly, was at the Duke of York's urgent request exchanged for His Royal Highness's house in Whitehall, 'that grey spreading pile of rusticated stone which is now the Scottish Office'.[2]

But if Lady Melbourne wished to appear as a great Whig hostess she had to meet the potential rivalry of one woman several years younger and of much greater social standing than she, the fascinating Georgiana, Duchess of Devonshire; and such competition Elizabeth was wise enough to realize would be dangerous. She therefore set out to captivate the young Duchess. This fortunately was not difficult, for Georgiana, who was no fool, was not a little bored by the emptyheads who surrounded her. In contrast with them, Elizabeth Melbourne

[2] Cecil, *Melbourne*, pp. 43–4.

4

THE HON. EMILY LAMB

aged sixteen

From the portrait by Sir Thomas Lawrence at Broadlands

seemed an altogether superior person. She took an intelligent interest in art and knew what she was talking about; she studied politics and enthusiastically espoused the Whig cause; furthermore, she was capable of generous friendships. All this was after Georgiana's heart. Unfortunately, the younger woman failed to perceive that her new friend was really a sham, that all her interests were simulated, and that she had in truth but one object at heart, the social advancement of the Lamb family.[3]

As the years passed and the two wives increased their families, the young Lambs spent much of their time in the Devonshire House nursery. And what a nursery it was! There were Georgiana's children, Georgiana and Harriet Cavendish, known as G and Hary-O in the intimate family circle, lacking their mother's looks, but with a charm and vivacity of their own, and baby Hartington—dear, kind, whimsical Hart, everyone's favourite. Then there were the two Foster boys, sons of the Duchess's intimate friend, Lady Elizabeth Foster, who had been an inmate at Devonshire House for several years; and three more children, Clifford, Caroline and Eliza, whose parentage was not discussed, though the observant noticed that the two eldest bore a marked resemblance to Lady Liz. In addition there was the family of the Duchess's sister Henrietta Frances, who in November, 1780, had married Lord Duncannon, now 3rd Earl of Bessborough. Lady Bessborough's children were four, three boys and little Caroline Ponsonby, small and slim with a Puck-like charm, but strange and wild. In charge of this motley assembly was Miss Selina Trimmer, a pleasant, plain young lady of sunny temperament.

It was with this joyous company that the Lamb children, four boys and two girls, grew up. And how soon they were to mature! Only little Harriet Anne, whose merry, laughing face looks at us from the vivid canvas of Sir Thomas Lawrence, was still a child. Emily, two years older, was on the threshold of womanhood and already developing into the beauty she was so soon to become. Of the four boys, the eldest, Peniston, who sat in Parliament first for Newport and later for Hertfordshire, was a gentle, shy, affectionate person. Throughout his short life he cared for only one woman, the lovely Mrs Dick Musters. He was his father's favourite, perhaps because the relations of this delicate young man with his strapping brothers put him in mind of his own relations with his overbearing wife, perhaps because he was the

[3] Marjorie Villiers, *The Grand Whiggery*, p. 16.

5

only one of the family of whose paternity he could feel no doubts.[4] How different were his other sons, William, Frederick and George— big, strong, heavy young men, extremely handsome in a rather bloated way, who ate too much, drank too much, talked too much, and swore too much!

For Christmas and New Year 1801–2 there was a great gathering at Chatsworth of Cavendishes, Ponsonbys and their friends. Among the guests were Lord Granville Leveson Gower, son of Lord and Lady Stafford who, though Tories, had somehow contrived to remain for long on friendly terms with the Devonshires; and Lord Granville's friend, Morpeth, son of Lord Carlisle. Lord Morpeth had for some time been paying particular attention to little 'G' Cavendish, and to everyone's delight this preference was soon to ripen into an engagement. The young couple were married on the 21st of March, and soon afterwards went north to make their home with his parents at Castle Howard.

Thenceforth, Hary-O Cavendish, deprived of her sister's company, became her constant correspondent, and through the eyes of this lively, engaging girl, we see many happenings in the Cavendish, Ponsonby and Lamb families. Thus, within a few months of the Morpeth marriage, she is writing of an 'extraordinary flirtation between William Lamb and Caro Ponsonby', and that they seem 'mutually captivated.'[5] In the following January we hear of the two brothers, William and Frederick, at a party at their mother's, and both had dined out and were very drunk, and William, so Hary-O reported, talked to her all the evening in a loud voice 'of the danger of a *young womans* believing in *weligion*, and *practising mowality*'.[6] And again a fortnight later Tom Sheridan and William Lamb came very drunk to a supper at Devonshire House, and they 'disputed till they almost fought'.[7] About this time too we hear of Earl Cowper, the immensely rich but somewhat stolid lord of Panshanger, a vast castellated Gothic

[4] It was generally believed that Lady Melbourne had imbibed the maxim that a wife's duty was to produce her husband one undoubted heir, and that nobody should look too closely at the features of the younger children. Of these, William was generally believed to be Lord Egremont's son, and George, the Prince of Wales'; whilst Emily's father was a complete mystery.

[5] Lady Harriet Cavendish to Lady Georgiana Morpeth, 'Chiswick, Tuesday (1802)'. *Hary-O*, p. 23.

[6] Lady Harriet Cavendish to 'Miladi Georgine Morpeth, Hotel d l'Empire, Paris. Devonshire House, January 15th, Tuesday morning, 1803'. *Hary-O*, p. 44.

[7] Lady Harriet Cavendish to 'Miladi Georgine Morpeth, Paris. Devonshire House, Jan. 30th. Sunday evening, 1803'. *Hary-O*, p. 49.

6

pile near Hertford,[8] dining with the Devonshires at Chiswick, when Pen and William Lamb were of the party. Hary-O apparently met the newcomer for the first time on this occasion and took a dislike to him because, as she told her sister, 'he seems so very heavy and stupid'.[9] Evidently there came back a warning note from Georgiana, who perhaps had heard rumours that Lord Cowper was paying rather particular attention to Emily Lamb, for later in the year Hary-O returned to the subject. 'Forgive me, dear G, but in spite of your advice I do hope that man of sense, Lord Cowper, will keep away . . .' [10]

Whilst Cowper was wooing his Emily[11] and William Lamb his Caroline, Frederick Lamb was pursuing a less desirable amour. In her entertaining *Memoirs* Harriette Wilson, the fashionable courtesan of the day, tells in her inimitable style how Frederick rescued her from the intolerable inanities of Lord Craven; and, if we can believe her, with the encouragement and aid of his father. At first, so she tells us, much to the indignation of the outraged parent, she was resisting Fred's advances. 'What, not have my son, six foot high and a fine strong handsome able young fellow? I wonder what she would have.' And Lord Melbourne bustled round to Miss Wilson's house to seek an answer to his question. Perhaps his mind was full of the halcyon days of his youth when he had lived with Harriet Powel, who for convenience had called herself Harriet Lamb, and on his marriage had been paid off with a settlement; perhaps he was thinking of the many £200 bills he had lavished on Mrs Baddeley under the very nose of 'his dear Betsy', whom, incidentally, he had only married the previous year. Mrs Baddeley had never had a settlement, in spite of her lover's repeated promises. Maybe she was more extravagant and exacting than Harriet Powel; possibly one settlement was as much as Lord Melbourne felt he could afford; perhaps his dear Betsy was making heavy demands upon him: all we know is that Mrs Baddeley received no settlement

[8] Built between 1806 and 1822 by William Atkinson (*c.* 1773–1839); now demolished.

[9] Lady Harriet Cavendish to Lady Georgiana Morpeth, 'Chiswick, Tuesday morning, August 21st, 1803'. *Hary-O*, p. 56. So printed, but August 21st, 1803, was a Sunday.

[10] Lady Harriet Cavendish to Lady Georgiana Morpeth, 'Bath, Monday morning, Nov. 14th, 1803'. *Hary-O*, p. 72.

[11] She had had, it seems, at least one previous suitor, as in 1803 William Lamb's friend, Lord Kinnaird, had asked her in marriage. Emily Lamb to Frederick Lamb, undated, Lady Airlie, *In Whig Society*, pp. 78–9.

and that she was loud in her complaints, made public in her somewhat vapid memoirs.[12] But whatever Lord Melbourne's thoughts may have been when he visited the recalcitrant Miss Wilson, his remonstrances were effective for she found herself unable to withstand the combined assault of both father and son. And, anyhow, Lord Craven was *such* a bore! So the fair Harriette capitulated and Fred Lamb marched into the citadel. Unhappily, this particular citadel was extremely expensive to maintain. After all, Frederick Lamb was only a younger son without ample means, and Miss Wilson was hardly the woman to make allowances. If only Fred had been more generous, she tells us, her memoirs would have been lost to the world, and what a pity that would have been! As it was, having retired from business, married and settled down in Paris, in 1825 she published her *Memoirs* in which she unmercifully pilloried her admirers. The great success of the first volume brought rumours of a second pending: whereupon everyone took fright, those who had been ridiculed in the first joined forces with those who feared they might be ridiculed in the second; the hat was sent round, and no further memoirs ever appeared. But the fascinating Harriette lived for another twenty years, and during this time she contrived to make herself a nuisance to certain exalted folk ere her day was done.[13]

Meanwhile bereavement overtook the Lamb family. In 1803 merry, laughing little Harriet died of consumption. Then, little more than a year later, the kindly Peniston died of the same disease. When all hope for him had been abandoned, Lady Melbourne summoned Mrs Musters, the love of her son's life, to Melbourne House, and he drew his last breath supported in her arms.[14]

The death of Peniston had a profound effect upon two members of the family. To Lord Melbourne it was an almost mortal blow, and we are told that when his domineering wife tried to secure for the new heir the same allowance that had previously been granted to Peniston, she met with a blank refusal. This was perhaps the sole occasion upon which Elizabeth failed to get her own way with her lord. But, allowance or no allowance, the lot of William Lamb was vastly improved. His engagement to Lady Caroline Ponsonby had somewhat flagged,

[12] *Memoirs of Mrs Sophia Baddeley late of Drury Lane Theatre,* (ed. 1787, Mrs Elizabeth Steele). Six volumes, *passim.*

[13] *Letters of George IV,* III, No. 1263, pp. 177–9; No. 1432, pp. 340–1; No. 1471, p. 368; No. 1570, pp. 465–6; and Appendix, pp. 501–5.

[14] Lady Airlie, *Lady Palmerston,* I, pp. 12, 14.

owing mainly to the hostility of the Bessboroughs. But William the heir was a very different proposition from William the younger son: now all opposition to the match was at an end, and on the 3rd of June, 1805, William Lamb and Caroline Ponsonby became man and wife. A few weeks later, on the 20th of July, Emily Lamb married Lord Cowper. On the honeymoon, Lord Cowper wrote a few lines to assure his mother-in-law that his bride was 'perfectly well'; and the bride added her own tribute to the 'dear dear Mum' who had done so much for her.

As you tell me that I *must* write, here I am writing. But I can add nothing that is not contained in L[o]rd Cowper's short epistle, except that I wish above all things to see you, that Pans-hanger is the prettiest and pleasantest place I ever saw, that L[o]rd C[owper] is kinder than I can express, and that I am hap-pier than any person ever was before . . . only feeling as if I was just awaked from a dream and at last which is the cause of my happiness I begin to believe that he does really love me; and therefore, dear Mama, you will never again be obliged to spend so much breath on that subject. Is not this a relief? I hope to hear from you tomorrow—by the bye that's impossible, and so I shall finish by signing my name within the Circle of the mystical ring that has such unaccountable power.

Yrs. ever affectly, dear Mum

Emily
Cowper

Melbourne Papers
B.M. Add. MSS. 45548–50
Lady Airlie, *In Whig Society*, p. 84

We hear much of the newly-weds during the next few years. In the autumn of 1805 Hary-O was at Brocket when she reported Caroline looking pale and ill but pretty, and William very ugly. Emily Cowper, also at Brocket, told her 'that she was very anxious as it was just barely possible that she might be going to be with child . . .' [15] That

[15] Lady Harriet Cavendish to Lady Georgiana Morpeth, 'Holywell, Wednesday October 9th, 1805'. *Hary-O*, p. 118.

was a little wishful thinking! However, she had not long to wait, and just nine months later, on the 26th of June, 1806, she gave birth to a son and heir, to whom the Prince of Wales stood godfather.[16] But Hary-O Cavendish never liked Lord Cowper and all her remarks about him have a disparaging sting. 'He is never with her and affects the greatest indifference and neglect, though I believe he really cares for her as much as he can for anything, and she seems tolerably contented, though I hear she is reduced to rejoice when he comes home drunk, as he talks more to her then than at any other time' [17] and 'Lady Cowper is very unwell, with a bad cold, and I am afraid he is very inattentive to her. She says he loves her excessively but he is always away from her'.[18] But if Lord Cowper was in some degree a disappointing husband, his young wife had her distractions—her babies, for her nursery was soon filled, and the gaiety of Almack's, where she was on the Ladies' Committee. This committee of women of high rank and influence managed the club and saw to it that no one unworthy of the privilege was admitted within its sacred portals. Admission to the balls at Almack's was by voucher or personal introduction and was highly prized. Among the young men who could be constantly found there on these occasions was the Secretary-at-War, Lord Palmerston, whom Lady Cowper had known from childhood. They called him 'Cupid' for his gay, twinkling eye and jovial air, and he sketched a Cupid in Emily's album: he also wrote her a verse:

> Cease, mortals, to conserve your Prime
> In vain attempts at killing Time.
> For Time, alas, whate'er you do,
> Is sure to end in killing you![19]

These two, it seems, did not kill time. She taught him to waltz. In other accomplishments, more exclusively male, he did not stand in need of instruction.[20]

Meanwhile, poor Lady Bessborough had troubles to face. In the

[16] Mrs Creevey to Miss Ord, '25th August' (1806), *Creevey Papers*, I, p. 82. William and Caroline Lamb's son was christened Augustus Frederick at the same ceremony. The Prince was godfather to this child also.

[17] Lady Harriet Cavendish to Lady Georgiana Morpeth, 'Devonshire House, Friday morning, December 1805'. *Hary-O*, pp. 138–9.

[18] Lady Harriet Cavendish to Lady Georgiana Morpeth, 'Devonshire House, Saturday, 1806'. *Hary-O*, p. 148.

[19] Guedalla, *Palmerston*, p. 72.   [20] Bell, *Palmerston*, I, p. 19.

first place, her beloved sister, Georgiana Devonshire, was gravely ill, and she died in March. But far worse was the anxiety she was made to feel by the eccentric conduct of her daughter. Within a few months of her marriage we hear of Caroline being 'in the *beau milieu* of a violent quarrel with William'—and on the important topic as to whether their maid Betsy should drive to the Abercorns' house in an open or shut carriage.[21] 'It was all so unpredictable. At one moment Caro and William were a loving couple, at the next she was in one of her rages or doing something so indiscreet as to alarm the whole family.' It was this failing in the wild, undisciplined young wife that was so distressing. 'You cannot conceive how anxious Lady Cowper was to make Caroline discreet', Hary-O told her sister, 'how far her endeavours have hitherto succeeded you may judge . . .'[22] The distressing story of Lady Caroline Lamb has been told so often and in such detail that there is no need to tell it again.[23] But the inevitable effect was to divide the families that hitherto had been on friendly terms. Naturally enough, William's mother, Lady Melbourne, took a violent dislike to her daughter-in-law, and Emily, Frederick and George, who conceived that she was ruining their brother's life, did all they could to bring comfort and aid to William. But William was in a curious position: though infuriated and distressed by his wife's antics, he could not help loving her, and at the same time his naturally lethargic disposition made him reluctant to take any positive action. This attitude was peculiarly exasperating to his family. How, they asked, could one help a man who refused to help himself? Who knows? Perhaps he did not want to be helped. But one could not expect his brothers and sister to view things in that light!

And soon others were involved. The reader will recall mention of another Caroline in the Devonshire House nursery. This child, known by the fanciful name of Caroline St Jules, was in fact the daughter of the Duke of Devonshire and Lady Elizabeth Foster; and she had grown into an attractive young woman to whom George Lamb had for some time been showing marked attention. Naturally her mother

[21] Lady Harriet Cavendish to Lady Georgiana Morpeth, [October 26–28?] 1805. *Hary-O*, p. 125.

[22] Lady Harriet Cavendish to Lady Georgiana Morpeth, 'January, 1806'. *Hary-O*, p. 149.

[23] For a beautifully told version of the familiar story, see Cecil, *Melbourne*, *passim*.

was distressed at hearing that the married Caroline had been trying to make mischief between them; and Hary-O Cavendish, who was staying with her cousin Lord Spencer at Althorp, received an eight-page letter from Lady Liz complaining of Caroline Lamb's meddling in her daughter's affairs. 'I am going to dispatch as much contrapoison as I can cram into a sheet of paper', Hary-O told her sister G, 'but you may be sure that I shall not say a word that can set her against Mr Lamb (oh! if you could hear my deep groan) whom I firmly expect will be one of the chosen friends of my bosom before the year is out.' [24] And so it seemed, for when George Lamb dined at Devonshire House that autumn, Hary-O reported to G. Morpeth, 'I will own to you . . . that he looked so very enormous, his hair and face so red and his actions so uncouth, that I felt more strongly than ever all my doubts and fears about Caroline's present and future prospects, with something so perfectly opposite to herself and what I had always fancied she could love. My relief, therefore, was very great at the letter I received from her this morning in which she says . . . that her feelings for him are such as would fully satisfy any person who could doubt the reality of her affection.' [25] And a fortnight later: 'I am quite in spirits about Caro and George. I like him as a companion . . . better every day . . . He seems to love her.' [26] And she seemed to love him; for once, when George could not come, Caroline declared to Hary-O 'that she did not know how she should live through the long evening without him . . .' [27] and when he was ill she was 'almost as bad from agitation. One would think he was a poor emaciated being, to whom every cold must be fatal, instead of which he always shines out after any of these attacks fatter and more blooming than before. He is improved in person I think, and in manners I am sure, and I really think her affection for him is as great as one can wish it.' [28] Yet it was another eighteen months, the 17th of May, 1809, before they married. And on Christmas Eve

[24] Lady Harriet Cavendish to Lady Georgiana Morpeth, 'Althorp' (c. March, 1807). *Hary-O*, pp. 183–4.

[25] Lady Harriet Cavendish to Lady Georgiana Morpeth, 'Devonshire House, Saturday October 31st, 1807'. *Hary-O*, pp. 228–9.

[26] Lady Harriet Cavendish to Lady Georgiana Morpeth, 'November 16th, Monday, 1807'. *Hary-O*, p. 248.

[27] Lady Harriet Cavendish to Lady Georgiana Morpeth, 'Jermyn Street, Thursday morning, November 19th, 1807'. *Hary-O*, p. 251.

[28] Lady Harriet Cavendish to Lady Georgiana Morpeth, 'December the 17th, Thursday morning, 1807'. *Hary-O*, p. 272.

Hary-O Cavendish became the bride of Lord Granville Leveson Gower. 'Adored Granville who would make a barren desert smile,' she wrote as a bride. She was to become the perfect wife, and she brought up the two children that her Aunt Bessborough had borne her husband together with her own.

Early in 1812, William Lamb was offered by the Prince Regent a seat at the Treasury Board, an offer that he saw fit to decline.[29] A few weeks later, on the 10th of March, his father was made a Lord of the Bedchamber. This appointment was a considerable embarrassment to his Whig sons. One cannot help feeling that the ambitious, pushing Lady Melbourne was responsible for the unfortunate appointment.

Whilst his relatives were getting married, Frederick Lamb was idling away his time with the bewitching but expensive Miss Wilson. But as Fred reached the later twenties, it began to dawn upon him that he had better find some work to do. He accordingly entered the diplomatic service. His promotion was rapid. In 1811 he was appointed secretary of legation, and the following year minister plenipotentiary *ad interim* at the Court of Naples and the Two Sicilies. Early in 1813 he was secretary of legation at Vienna, and in August of the same year was appointed minister plenipotentiary *ad interim* pending the arrival of Lord Stewart as Ambassador for the Congress of Vienna the following year. In 1815 Lamb was appointed minister plenipotentiary at the Court of Bavaria. He was destined to remain there for the next five years.

In September 1816 Lord and Lady Cowper left on a continental tour and were abroad until the following June. Before leaving England, Lady Cowper wrote a brief adieu to Hart, who had recently succeeded his father as Duke of Devonshire.

George St. Tuesday August 20th [1816]

... We set off on Friday or Saturday next so adieu dont forget me and if you will not come to Italy at least come and meet us at Paris next Spring tho I do not expect to run such *Dangers* and *Hazards* as we did last year in Devonshire yet I feel rather qualmish at the thoughts of so long a Journey and I really think that I would exchange my Journey with all its pleasures and its

[29] Melbourne to Prince Regent, 'Whitehall, Feby. 26, 1812'. *Letters of George IV*, I, No. 16, pp. 27–8; Lady Airlie, *In Whig Society*, pp. 106–7.

pains for one of our little *perfect parties* either at Chiswick or Chatsworth . . .

Chatsworth Papers, 856.0

In the summer of 1817 the Cowpers were back in England and the family united at Panshanger. For Christmas they went to stay with Emily's friend, Sarah Jersey,[30] at Middleton Park near Bicester. Thence Emily wrote to her brother Fred in distant Bavaria with all the news and gossip from home.

Middleton, Decr. 21st, 1817

I cling to writing 1817, as I feel it will so soon be chased by its successor. It is really alarming and distressing to see how quick the wheel is whirled round and how every year that passes seems to give it an increased velocity.

We have been here a week and are passing what is called a Merry Christmas. Lievens[31] and Esterhazy,[32] who is more boyish than ever and in greater spirits since the absence of his wife,[33] and Nieman,[34] whose pomposity increases in proportion as he thinks his master is wanting in that quality. One runs about, gets so thin that you could draw him through a small ring, and the other swells himself up like the *grenouille qui veut être un bœuf*. Luttrell[35] is also here and Ly Glengall[36] and daughter . . . And

[30] The eldest daughter of the 10th Earl of Westmorland and his first wife, Sarah, daughter of the great banker, Robert Child of Osterley Park, Middlesex.

[31] Count Christopher Andreievitch Lieven (1774–1839), Russian Ambassador in England, 1812–34; created Prince 1826, and his famous wife, Dorothea (1785–1857), daughter of Baron Christopher Benckendorff.

[32] Prince Paul Esterhazy, Austrian Ambassador in England, 1815–42.

[33] Princess Thérèse Esterhazy (1794–1876), daughter of Charles, Prince of Thurn and Taxis. Her mother, a daughter of Charles Louis Frederick, Grand Duke of Mecklenburg-Strelitz, was first cousin of George IV.

[34] Baron Philip von Neumann (1781–1851); First Secretary of Austrian Embassy, 1816–33; Austrian Ambassador, 1841–4; married in 1844 Lady Augusta Somerset, daughter of Henry, 7th Duke of Beaufort.

[35] Henry Luttrell (1765?–1851), natural son of the 2nd Earl of Carhampton, wit and society poet. Introduced to London society through the Duchess of Devonshire.

[36] Emily Jeffreys (1767–1836), daughter of James St John Jeffreys of Blarney Castle, Co. Cork; married in 1793 Pierce Butler, 1st Earl of Glengall.

we have also had Ly Euston[37] who is a nice bouncing milkmaid, married to a hunting brute, little better than his dogs. Ly Worcester and Ld Worcester,[38] who makes themselves too ridiculous in all ways, he in particular, she is even more disagreeable than ridiculous. Did I, in my last letter, mention Humboldt[39] to you, who is a great amusement to everybody who knows him and a great acquisition to the Corps Diplomatique? . . .

When we go from here Brocket is our object, where there is to be a party, but which will all be soured by the Devil, 'Cherubina'.[40] The only chance we have of getting rid of her is by committing murder and getting hanged, of which I think there is some chance, for the page has been hardly any lesson and she stabs as she used to do.[41]

Minny[42] is the delight of all here—she is so drole—so amiable, that one can just bear her getting so big. Mr Luttrell reproached her with being so boyish and said: 'Your brother W[illia]m[43] behaves better than you.' She said: 'If I am a boyish girl, he is a girlish boy, which is worse.'

Broadlands Papers

The next letter, though undated, was clearly written early in the following year.

[Undated]

. . . We have had the Lievens here, and have been very gay this Christmas. George and Caro [Lamb] are gone today, she seems

[37] Mary Caroline, daughter of Admiral the Hon. Sir George Cranfield Berkeley, married in 1812, Henry, Earl of Euston, afterwards 5th Duke of Grafton. Lady Euston's eldest sister was married to Sir Thomas Masterman Hardy, first baronet, Nelson's Hardy.

[38] Henry Charles Somerset, Marquess of Worcester, afterwards 6th Duke of Beaufort, and Charlotte Sophia, daughter of Granville, 1st Marquess of Stafford.

[39] Baron Friedrich Wilhelm von Humboldt (1767–1835), German Ambassador in London 1817.

[40] A family name for Lady Caroline Lamb.

[41] This is a reference to the famous occasion when Lady Caroline very slightly wounded one of her pages and rushed out into the street shouting: 'Oh, God! I've murdered .the page.'

[42] Lady Emily Cowper, at this date the Cowpers' only daughter.

[43] William Francis Cowper (afterwards Cowper Temple), Lady Cowper's second son. The father was possibly Lord Palmerston.

comfortable and I was delighted to see that he has partly got his old Spirits again, so I suppose he is now at his ease.[44] Cherubina bores very much and looks hideous, and makes up to a Scotch Doctor, they have got as a Tutor. He is young, and she says like Lord Byron. He is not well-looking, and seems a plain, unpolished Scotchman, like Samson in *Guy Mannering*, always reading improving himself, and seems not to perceive her . . . and he is astonished and bored with her absurdities, but she makes herself ridiculous in the eyes of others—and her familiarity with him shocks the maids[45] . . .

Minny is doated on by all who see her, she gets more amiable every day and dances beautifully . . .

Broadlands Papers

In a previous letter Emily had expressed some anxiety about her mother's health: now she returned to this subject again.

Monday March 23 [1818]

I wrote you a letter on Friday. I think Mama is very much in the same state, not worse nor I do not think better; she has good nights no Fever and Bailey[46] [*sic*] who was consulted today and

[44] This is a reference to a serious quarrel which George Lamb had had with his wife about eighteen months previously, after which Caroline, much to George's annoyance, had gone abroad with her mother, the former Lady Elizabeth Foster, who had recently married the Duke of Devonshire. There were soon rumours afloat that Henry Brougham and Caroline Lamb were seen together too often for propriety; whereupon Lady Melbourne in her usual forthright way wrote reprovingly to Mrs George Lamb, then in Geneva. For Caroline's reply admitting the friendship with Brougham but saying that she thought her husband had ceased to care for her, see Lady Airlie, *In Whig Society*, pp. 187–8. Caroline did eventually return to her husband, but not for some time and probably not very long before Lady Cowper's letter was written.

[45] For Harriette Wilson's story of Lady Caroline's silk stocking being found at the foot of the doctor's bed, see her *Memoirs*, I, p. 322. It must be remembered, however, that Harriette Wilson had no cause to feel well disposed towards the Ponsonby family, for she had had the misfortune to fall in love with Lady Caroline's brother, William, who at parting from Miss Wilson had treated her as men are apt to treat professional prostitutes.

[46] Matthew Baillie (1761–1823), anatomist; pupil of William Hunter; physician to St George's Hospital, 1787–99; physician extraordinary to George III.

saw her says there is no immediately threatening symptom but that what he fears is weakness and that he thinks the Rheumatism itself does not so much signify but that he thinks it indicates a change of Constitution . . .

Panshanger Papers

Baillie's fears were well founded. On the 6th of April, 1818, Lady Melbourne died at Melbourne House. On her death-bed she besought her daughter Emily to be true—not to her somewhat dull husband, Lord Cowper—but to her gayer and more distinguished admirer, Lord Palmerston; and her son William to have the energy to achieve the great position for which since childhood she had designed him. What were her eldest son's thoughts on his mother's ambitions? No expression escaped him at the time; but as a very old man at Brocket he was once found lost in meditation before his mother's portrait. 'A remarkable woman,' he was heard muttering to himself, 'a devoted mother, an excellent wife—but not chaste, not chaste.' [47]

Some four years after Lady Melbourne's death, in April, 1822, when Lord and Lady Cowper were staying at the Pavilion at Brighton, the King began talking to Emily of his old friend, her mother, saying that during her last illness he had walked across to Melbourne House every day to inquire and sometimes to see her, and that at the last she had died in his arms. But, as Emily told the Duke of Wellington, she had never left her mother's room for the last ten days of her life, so she knew only too well that the Prince Regent had not even sent to enquire! [48]

A year has passed before the next letter; and when writing it, Lady Cowper had just been staying with Lord Cowper's brother, Edward Spencer Cowper, at Digswell, on the Panshanger estate in Hertfordshire.

Thursday April 3rd [1819]
. . . I find William Temple [49] is ordered to go to you. I am afraid this accession of company will not be much to your

---

[47] Cecil, *Melbourne*, pp. 177–8.   [48] *Mrs Arbuthnot*, I, p. 154.
[49] Sir William Temple (1788–1856), Minister plenipotentiary to the Court of Naples, brother of Lord Palmerston.

17

amusement, and it will certainly diminish your stock of wine, for he is always drunk. I believe you led him such a life at F[rank furt] that he was obliged to take to drinking for comfort.

... We all go to Brighton on the 15th. I will give you news from there ...

... Brother George is quite well, but quite grave at his bosom friend, Elliston,[50] having lost his wife. The Theater is his home and his happiness.

Broadlands Papers

In this last paragraph, Emily was poking fun at George Lamb's love of the theatre. Whilst all the Lamb brothers enjoyed amateur acting, the theatre was the absorbing interest of George's life; and though he had been called to the Bar at Lincoln's Inn he soon abandoned law for literature. On the 5th of March, 1807, he had had his two-act comic opera, *Whistle for it*, produced at Covent Garden, where it was performed some three times. It was printed the same year. Though it was far from contemptible, he was jeered at by Byron in his *English Bards and Scotch Reviewers*: and, because as one of the committee of management of Drury Lane he had written some prologues to the revivals of old English plays, the poet likened him to Upton, who wrote the songs for Astley's Circus. He was a great friend of Elliston, the actor, who in 1819 had just become lessee and manager of Drury Lane.

In her next letter Emily Cowper has more fun on the same topic.

London, April 10th, [1819]

... I cannot think why Catullus is kept back so long[51] but George cares for nothing and thinks of nothing but whether there is a full house at Drury Lane. As you say, no one can fight against his destiny, but he makes me laugh. Of course, as you may suppose, he attended Mrs Elliston's funeral—players are all brothers ...

Broadlands Papers

[50] Robert William Elliston (1774–1831), the distinguished actor.

[51] This refers to George Lamb's most important literary work, *The Poems of Caius Valerius Catullus translated, with a Preface and Notes*. This was published in two volumes in 1821 and was subsequently republished in Bohn's Classical Library.

In the election of 1818 the outstanding Whig success had been the return for Westminster of Sir Samuel Romilly over Sir Murray Maxwell and Henry Hunt, the idol of the mob. Upon Romilly's suicide shortly afterwards, George Lamb was persuaded to stand as Whig candidate against the radicals Hobhouse and Major Cartwright, the founder in 1812 of the Hampden Club to work for the securing of universal suffrage. After a contest lasting some fifteen days Lamb was elected, having polled 4,465 votes against 3,861 for Hobhouse and 38 for Cartwright. The last day of the contest was very disorderly. The triumphant Whigs, anxious to chair their candidate and escort him in procession from Burlington House to Brooks's, were warned that any such attempt would be the death of George Lamb; they therefore thought better of it and sent messengers to stop the escort. Unfortunately the messages miscarried, and when the escort arrived, they found Covent Garden blocked by a seething mass of humanity who greeted them with mud, dirt and stones. Meanwhile, Lady Cowper, who had been an active canvasser for her brother, and whose coachman was wearing Lamb's colours in his hat, was pelted with mud as she drove through St James's Square and Pall Mall to Melbourne House on her return from the Ladies' Committee at Almack's; and one large stone almost broke the panel of her carriage just below the glass. Lady Caroline Lamb, who had also taken a prominent part in the campaign, fared no better; her carriage was also attacked in St James's Street and a boy inside was cut on the forehead by a stone.[52]

In the autumn of the same year, William Lamb, who some three years previously had been returned for Northampton, was invited to stand for Hertfordshire. It seems that he showed much irresolution about this, to the disgust and annoyance of both George and Emily.

P[anshanger] Monday Oct. 18, [1819]
I wonder if this will still find you at Paris. Lady West[morlan]d talked of leaving England today and of stopping with you at Frankfort in her way to Italy, *voyez quel bonheur vous attend*. I have a long rigmarole letter from her all about Almacks. She seems crazy upon the subject—by the way she dotes on you. Ly J[ersey] could not think how you had bewitched her, for she

[52] Palmerston to William Temple, 'Stanhope Street, March 12, 1819'. Ashley, *Palmerston*, I, p. 87. *Greville Memoirs* (1874), I, pp. 17–18.

talked of nothing else but you. She and Ly J[ersey] are *enfroid* at present, owing to the promised explanation and Ld W[estmorland]'s knight-errantry who chose to go and sermon the other upon *all* her faults in hopes of opening her eyes and producing a reform. We have just had Motteux[53] here, and Lord Thanet,[54] the latter is reform wild and thinks of nothing but meetings, but he is very gay and agreable. Brougham[55] is on his way to London with the Widow; they say he is grown quite hen-pecked, and that when she is displeased she throws the dishes at his head. I think she did right to *begin* for if she had not perhaps he would.[56]

George has been staying at B[rocket] patting W[illiam] on the back and trying to give him a little courage, but he is quite disgusted with his irresolution and want of decision, having evidently fixed his whole heart upon this business, (why I cannot tell, but so it is). He is in all the nervousness possible, not daring to look the case in the face, not able to summon courage to say he will stand a contest, and has worked and agitated himself quite thin. The fact is that I really believe there is no chance of a contest and he is perfectly safe, but he ought to put a stout face upon it. Why he should desire it so very much, I don't know, but nothing can be so foolish as wishing a thing so much and then not daring to stand up to his tether. My Lord too on this occasion makes no objection to anything, but is hardly nervous at all, and I have heard no *fears* of what his master may say, and he said he was willing to do all he could to help, but Cherubina's husband is a miserable fellow always thinking of the money it may cost . . .

I keep quite well, and we go to Brighton on the 1st of Nov. and return to Town for the Meeting of Parliament, when all these weighty measures will be discussed and probably occupy some

[53] A rich bachelor friend of Lord Cowper, something of a toady and a snob, who owned the Sandringham estate in Norfolk. For Lady Harriet Cavendish's very unfavourable views on him, see *Hary-O*, pp. 199, 222, 244.

[54] Sackville Tufton, 9th Earl of Thanet (1767–1825), nephew of the 3rd Duke of Dorset, a friend of Lord Cowper.

[55] Henry Peter Brougham, 1st Baron Brougham and Vaux (1778–1868): defended Queen Caroline, 1820; Lord Chancellor, 1830–4.

[56] Brougham married Mary Anne, daughter of Thomas Eden and widow of John Spalding. According to the *D.N.B.*, the marriage was in 1821; this letter shows it to have been in 1819.

'MINNY'. LADY EMILY COWPER

(afterwards Countess of Shaftesbury)

From the portrait by Sir Thomas Lawrence at St Giles's House

fortnight or three weeks before the Holidays. I daresay every body will come to Town at that time; they say Govern[ment] will try to carry strong measures and crush any enquiry, but I don't think they could carry it. Every body wants enquiry,[57] even the most moderate, and this keeps them quiet now.

I suppose you heard of Mrs Musters'[58] death. George [Lamb] gets a thousand pounds by it, and I was very glad of it, as it would clear him if he has any debts and make him comfortable. Upon a small income every windfall is such a help. Mrs Musters had, I believe, settled her own thousand upon Master George;[59] this is also good for him . . . My little W[illia]m is getting well and looks like himself again, but I think hardly stout enough yet to go to School . . . Caro George is very amiable indeed. I dreaded that B[rougham]'s arrival should produce any change, but I hope he is now like a spiked cannon, harmless.[60] She is staying in Town keeping P[apa] company and very kind to him.

Broadlands Papers

William Lamb supported Althorp's motion for a select committee to inquire into the state of the country to ascertain the cause of the discontent and distress which had led to the recent disorders.

George St, Nov. 23rd, [1819]

The time draws near, and we are all on tiptoe for tomorrow, and London is very full of men sanguine, oppos[it]ionists reckon

[57] Lord Althorp's motion for an inquiry into the state of the country, in view of the recent disturbances in Manchester, generally known as the 'Peterloo Massacre' when, on August 16th, a large crowd had assembled to listen to an address by 'Orator' Hunt, on parliamentary reform. In the scattering of the crowd with the aid of troops eleven persons had been killed and over five hundred injured.

[58] Mrs Dick Musters, whom Peniston had loved.

[59] Her eldest son, Viscount Fordwich, now thirteen years old.

[60] This is a veiled reference to the association which Mrs George Lamb had had with Brougham a few years previously, to which her mother-in-law, Lady Melbourne, had strongly objected. In the family she was frequently called 'Caro George' to distinguish her from the other Caroline, Lady Caroline Lamb, 'Caro William'.

they shall be above 100. This is a great body, tho' not very useful, as they suppose Govern[men]t will be above 300 . . .

Broadlands Papers

In fact the motion was rejected by 323 votes to 150! Christmas found the whole Cowper family at Panshanger.

Panshanger, Dec. 25th, [1819]

. . . We came down here about a week ago. Ld C[owper] was obliged to leave the House still sitting and to abandon his post at the earnest intreaty of Fordwich, who was in despair at being kept in Town, and grudged every hour he passed there. I was also quite tired of London, and anxious to get down here, and tho' I am perhaps a little inclined to activity and feel more low at this season from various recollections than at any other time of the year, yet I have exerted myself manfully, or I might rather say *womanfully*, to make the dear children pass a Merry Christmas. We have had Snapdragon and games of all sorts every night, and next Friday Emily is to have a child's Ball of all the children and gentry of the neighbourhood—it will be quite a grand affair, and I hope gay, which is better; all the rooms lighted, dancing in the Drawing-Room and Supper in the Dining-Room. She is out of her wits with joy, and Fordwich is as glad as his shyness will allow him, but he is combated between his wish for gaiety and his fear of meeting strangers and being put in any situation for exertion. He is an amiable, dear boy, but I am vexed at his langour and want of briskness, and I think he is too grave for a boy of his age. I wish I could make him more like his sister, who is *Toujours plus charmante*.

. . . W[illia]m [Lamb] and his Lady come here Tuesday for a Hertford Ball. George [Lamb] as soon as he has done with the House sets off to Sessions as he says he has some retainers which he cannot find in his heart to give up.[61] Ld H[olland] says he likes him so much, that he is such a fine indiscreet fellow—I think that such a good account of him. He really is just that, and I think his speech at the Westminster meeting and one or two of his

---

[61] George Lamb was still a barrister, practising on the northern circuit.

Parliamentary ones quite partook of that character, for the first he was run away with by the delight of being applauded. Now he ought to be impressed that, with the Mob, he can never be as popular as Sir F. [Burdett][62] and Hobhouse[63] who will say and do anything, and that therefore his line is the respectable people, and that he is very likely to lose them as he says things to gain the rabble with whom he will never be a first object, while Sir F. [Burdett] and H[obhouse] remain, particularly,—now the latter, is a Martyr to the cause of liberty. However, I am glad to say his incarceration seems to have produced very little, or no sensation, and Ridgway says he never saw people inclined to be so down in the mouth as they are at present . . .

Our P[rince] however, does not vex his head with present disasters or the thoughts of future cares, for I never saw anyone in such spirits as he was at St Carlos's Ball, quite merry and good-humoured as in old times—the scowl quite gone and all sunshine and prosperity, and this I am told is the present disposition—all powerful Love again rules his destiny.

> Tralvia, Tralava, my old love Adieu
> Tralvia, Tralava, I have got me a new.

Ly Conyngham has carried the day completely, and they say the other is quite dished.[64] All this impossibility of going to Brighton is an arranged thing to prevent taking a party, and he hops down continually to see his dear sister, the D[uche]ss of Gloucester, and by the way his dear love, who is settled here. People say she is too foolish to keep him, but she is very handsome, and there is no knowing and any change is for the better, and it is well the old one should be punished for all her misdeeds, and I believe she was the worst sort of person for him, for having no good-humour, she was always morose and telling him how people abused him, and setting him against every body.

[62] Sir Francis Burdett (1770–1844): married a daughter of Thomas Coutts, the banker; M.P., Westminster, 1807–37, North Wilts. 1837–44; imprisoned on political charges, 1810 and 1820.

[63] John Cam Hobhouse, Baron Broughton de Gyfford (1786–1869), friend and executor of Byron, had earlier in the year been sent to Newgate for breach of privilege.

[64] Lady Conyngham had just replaced Lady Hertford as the Prince Regent's mistress.

My Ball is all I can think of just now, so adieu, as details of this would hardly interest you at Frankfort ...

Broadlands Papers

This was a hard winter, but all seems to have been gaiety at Panshanger[65]—shooting for the grown-ups, balls and parties for the children.

P[anshanger], Jan. 4, 1820

... We had a brilliant Ball here last Friday to dance in the New Year, it began with a Ball for Minny, but got extended and grown people and children all danced together, there were nearly 150 people. I had all the neighbourhood, a very handsome supper, and the house and pictures very well lighted up, and the suite of rooms really looked beautiful, for I closed the Ante-Room door, and made every body pass thro the billiard-room which was turned into a tea and refreshment room, and the Drawing-Room was used for dancing. They danced with hardly any intermissions from 8 till two o'clock. Minny was out of her wits with joy and looked beautiful and danced every dance. I had the Salisburys[66] and several London people, who happened to be in the neighbourhood, and Ld and Ly Dacre[67] ... W[illia]m and Ca[roline Lamb] were here, and for a wonder she did nothing outrageous or absurd, but was almost as rational as the generality of people in her behaviour. By the way did I tell you that in London, after her fly out at dinner with George, that I had had an explanation about her with W[illia]m which I was glad of, as being upon terms of communication with him even in ever so small a degree, destroys the effect of her misrepresentations.[68] ...

[65] Lady Cowper to Frederick Lamb, Panshanger, January 17th, 1820. Broadlands Papers.

[66] The Cowpers' Hertfordshire neighbours at Hatfield.

[67] Thomas Brand, 21st Lord Dacre, and Barbarine, daughter of Admiral Sir Chaloner Ogle, whom he had married the previous year. She was a poet, dramatist and amateur artist of distinction, and one of the most accomplished women of her time.

[68] For Lady Caroline Lamb's absurd efforts to have a ball at Brocket following the success of Lady Cowper's at Panshanger, see Lady Cowper to Frederick Lamb, Panshanger, Jany. 22, 1819. Lady Airlie, *Lady Palmerston*, I, pp. 44–6.

I am quite well and shall stay here, till the last day of this month, when for safety I shall settle in London tho' I dont think I shall lye in, till towards the end of Feb[ruar]y, I am not the least annoyed about it, as I feel so stout, and think I shall do very well. Clarke[69] is positively to attend me, which I am glad of . . .

Broadlands Papers

Panshanger, Jan. 22nd, 1820

I suppose I shall hear from you when you return to Frankfort, which I suppose will be soon.[70] If your winter is as bad as ours travelling must be horrible, for the last six weeks with the exception of a day or two, we have had severe frost, and generally a deep snow and now we have a fresh cover again. Lord C[owper] has been shooting the last two days with Irby and quite eager. They killed yesterday thirty head of something or other . . .

Broadlands Papers

A week later, on the evening of the 29th of January, Londoners heard the tolling of the great bell at St Paul's. It announced that the old king, who had been dead to the world for almost ten years, had entered into his rest.

[69] Sir Charles Mansfield Clarke (1782–1857), a noted accoucheur, created a baronet 1831.

[70] *Letters of George IV*, II, Nos. 793, 794, pp. 306–7.

CHAPTER II

Lady Cowper in the New Reign

A T THE ACCESSION of George IV, the Tories were in office and were destined to retain their parliamentary majority for another ten years. The Government, which included such able men as Eldon, Castlereagh and Canning, was led by the colourless Liverpool.[1] But if the Tory party had its stresses and strains, the Whigs were in an even worse case; for the party had splintered into groups—the Granvillites, the Foxites and the 'Mountain', each with their own leaders, over whom the brilliant but erratic Brougham sought in vain to exert a controlling influence.

The great object of the new king at the very outset of his reign was, of course, to rid himself of the hated wife whom he had married in 1795, ten years after his illegal marriage with Mrs Fitzherbert. In 1806 the Government, under pressure from the Prince of Wales and against its better judgment, had instituted an inquiry into the conduct of the Princess; the findings, whilst damaging to her reputation, were to the effect that the more serious charges were not proved. Ten years later, when the King seemed likely to die at any moment and the Regent's health was bad, the probability of Princess Charlotte succeeding to the throne made Caroline's cause full of interesting possibilities. The ambitious Brougham was not slow to observe what might happen and, seizing the chance with both hands, he became the Queen's chief adviser. Unfortunately, however, things did not work out as expected. In 1817 Princess Charlotte died; whereupon Brougham perhaps began to repent of having championed her mother's cause. Be that as it may, he subsequently, without Caroline's knowledge, put forward the suggestion that the Princess's allowance should be increased from £35,000 to £50,000 a year and should be for life, on the express understanding that she should renounce her title and agree never to set foot in England again.[2]

[1] For a recent biography, see that by Sir Charles Petrie.

[2] For all these matters discussed, see Arthur Aspinall, *Lord Brougham and the Whig Party*, pp. 99 *et seq.*

26

In mid-February, however, in spite of all the excitements of the moment, the Cowpers retired to the peace and quiet of Panshanger, whence Emily a few days later announced to her brother her safe delivery of 'a dear little girl'.[3] Very shortly afterwards she and her husband returned to London.

Meanwhile Liverpool had replied to the King's request that divorce proceedings should be instituted on his behalf by hinting that his wife's counter-charges might well go far to discredit the Crown and by more or less accepting Brougham's proposal that Caroline's allowance should be increased on condition she remained abroad. Would she agree, or would her chief adviser persuade her to return to England and claim her rights? If he did, the Government would certainly fall. At first Brougham appears to have hesitated. Then in March he let it be known that he would be more accommodating if he were appointed a King's Counsel, thus enabling him to increase his income by many thousands a year. Brougham's conduct seems to have been equivocal in the extreme, for most of his negotiating was done without the knowledge of his client. Certainly the financial offers were kept from Caroline at first; and when Brougham eventually told her of them he recommended their rejection.

For some time Frederick Lamb was destined to hear a good deal about Emily's nerves, about the new baby, about Minny, the apple of her mother's eye, and about the election in Westminster, where Brother George, who had been elected the previous year, was standing again.[4] His opponents were Sir Francis Burdett and Hobhouse.

[Undated *c.* February–March 1820]

. . . George's election goes prosperous now, and I believe will be successful, but we have been worried . . . It was certainly vexatious to have so few Canvassers, four being away and so many at their own elections, but Ld Sefton and Duncannon have been very stout and Ld C[owper], and there is a very good subscription made and everything is going on now as well as possible.

[3] Lady Cowper to Frederick Lamb, Thursday, 17th February, 1820. Broadlands Papers. Lady Airlie, *Lady Palmerston*, I, pp. 46–7, where the latter is incorrectly dated 1819.

[4] The General Election of 1820 was consequent upon the demise of the Crown.

But I fear the mob will be riotous. However, if it should be so G[eorge] is advised to stay away which I think indeed will be much the best. I will write again very soon.

What a horrible plot this was, makes one shudder, another Guy Faux[5] . . .

Broadlands Papers

Alas! In spite of Emily's optimism, George's election at Westminster was not going well.

March 14th [1820]

. . . My little girl is very well and a nice baby, and as she is to be *my last* Child I chuckle over her, as over a treasure.

This Election worries me a good deal, tho I try not to think of it, but I feel anxious to be doing something, and I have no strength and the least exertion makes me faint. This is the 5th day and Hobhouse is nearly 700 ahead. I cannot say the case is hopeless, but I am not easy about it. We have been so terribly in want of canvassers and the Ministers will do nothing for us: George's Speeches have put them in such pets and Tierney's[6] saying in the House that their support did us harm.[7] I wish you was here with all my heart. George has done very well on the Hustings and made the best of it he could, but it is a terribly awkward situation to be between his two opponents and with so many different interests to manage. W[illia]m is arrived today and Graham[8] and some others and, if they will exert themselves, something may yet be done. For the opinion of the tradespeople seems all in George's favour, but they want stirring up and they want your activity, and we want a spokesman with the Ministers, for they can hardly

[5] The Cato Street Conspiracy, Arthur Thistlewood's plot to assassinate Cabinet ministers when dining at Lord Harrowby's house in Grosvenor Square. Thistlewood and his confederates were convicted of high treason and hanged.

[6] George Tierney (1761–1830): recognised as leader of the Whig Party, 1817–21.

[7] For Mrs Arbuthnot's interesting comment on the Westminster election, see *Mrs Arbuthnot*, I, p. 10.

[8] Sir James Robert George Graham (1792–1861), statesman; M.P. for St Ives at this time.

be so unprincipled as really to wish H[obhouse] to succeed, or at least they cannot well avow this feeling . . .

This Cato Street Conspiracy is horrible, and I fear stretches very far. I am told there were horrible things come out before the Privy Council, and that a very great many are implicated far and wide. I fear we live in bad times.

. . . I mean to go to Brighton as soon as I am strong enough to move . . .

Broadlands Papers

In spite of everybody's efforts George Lamb was defeated.[9] The figures were: Burdett 5,327, Hobhouse 4,882, Lamb 4,436.

So on Friday the 31st of March, off to Brighton went Em, with her ailing old father, and three days later she wrote to Frederick to report progress.

Brighton April 3rd [1820]

. . . We are come here for a fortnight but may stay longer and afterwards I shall probably go to Panshanger . . . I have seen Ld Eg[remont][10] today. It seems that he is often in the P[rince]'s[11] company and he says that the other night he burst forth in a panegyric of you, said C[astlerea]gh has such a high opinion of you and that you was the cleverest diplomat going and that if there was any knotty discussion or negociation to transact that you would be the only person fit to do it. The P[rince] seems to be growing good-natured altogether and said to Lord E[gremont] that he could not think why George [Lamb] cut him when he

---

[9] According to Princess Lieven's story to Metternich, George Lamb had only won the previous Westminster Election because of the efforts on his behalf of his sister-in-law, Lady Caroline; but in this second election Hobhouse had had the foresight to persuade her not to help George—hence his defeat! (Princess Lieven to Metternich, March 11 [1820], *Lieven-Metternich Letters*, pp. 20-1.) But the Princess's statement, in this as in many other instances, must be received with caution.

[10] George O'Brien Wyndham, 3rd Earl of Egremont (1751-1837), patron of the arts, and successful stock-breeder at Petworth.

[11] Presumably force of habit made Lady Cowper still speak of George IV as the Prince.

met him in the street and spoke good-naturedly about him, regretting him having lost West[minste]r, and said also something kind of me; so that you see we are all coming round, and in consequence I have a great mind to subscribe to his statue erecting here, and I think I shall and make Lord C[owper]. They say there is nothing gratifies him so much, and as he appears to be leaving off his *old habits* I think it is a good thing to encourage him . . .

Broadlands Papers

(Taken from a copy made by the late Lord Mount Temple. The original cannot be traced.)

Brighton, April 10th [1820]

I wrote you one letter from here a few days since, but I am indefatigably come again. I find this place agrees very much with me. I walk about quite stoutly and go into the Shower Bath every day . . . Papa likes being here very much, and |so does Ld C[owper] so we are all pleased. Fordwich takes to drawing and dancing with the active little master we had last time, and Emily rides in the riding house, and has learnt to master her fears . . .

The K[ing] certainly disagrees very much with his Ministers, and if he has the nerves to do so will certainly try and get rid of them very soon. His feelings also towards opposition are also considerably changed, and he was particularly pleased with Tierney's speech about the Princess. If they remain prudent and moderate, I really believe some changes will be attempted; this difference in his disposition I know from very good Authority. Whether there may not be too many difficulties in the way is another consideration. His wish to do something about the P[rince]ss may be one reason, but also believe that he is alarmed at the bad spirit in the country, and thinks that a change of Govern[men]t might in part soothe the dissatisfaction and make the distressed part of the community at least think that something might be attempted to be done in their favour, instead of mere keeping down their clamour with the sword. I doubt whether this may do much good for we certainly are in a bad way, and this last affair at Glasgow is far from pleasant.[12] . . .

[12] There had been disturbances in Glasgow, and the rioters had been dispersed by the military.

The King's health is quite re-established. He has still remains of nervous symptoms like mine, but they are things which do not signify and his constitution is quite untouched. The Mar[chione]ss C[onyngham][13] sails about here in great Glory very proud of her situation, and he says that he never was so in love before in his life, that he's quite ashamed of being so boyish . . .

Remember and tell me, who sends you books. I like Ivanhoe[14] in parts, very much; Rebecca is beautiful. The new one[15] is I am told not so good. Ld Egremont is at Petworth, we think of stopping there on our way home . . . George and Caro are at Chiswick[16] where there have been many gay parties, great succession of company.

Broadlands Papers

The reader will have noticed the constant mention in Lady Cowper's letters of her elder daughter Minny, who was obviously idolized by both her parents. Indeed, she must have been a delightful and pretty child, but with so much adoration she would have been scarcely human if she had not been spoiled. In consequence, she did not want for critics. 'Lady Cowper's little girl is by far the prettiest and most spoilt child I ever saw . . .' wrote the not very friendly Lady Bessborough, when Minny was about three, '. . . she is the nautiest little thing I ever saw, and rules the House rather unpleasantly',[17] and some ten years later Lady Granville pronounced her 'absent and *blasé*, but full of grace and *finesse*'.[18] Her father and her grandfather, it seems, were always giving her pound notes; and the letter which follows was probably written when she and her family were at Brighton at about this time, when Emily was some ten years old.

[13] Elizabeth (1769–1861), daughter of Joseph Denison, a wealthy self-made merchant. In 1794 she had married Henry, 3rd Baron and 1st Marquess Conyngham (1766–1832).

[14] Published this year.

[15] The new one must be *The Monastery*, published in March, 1820.

[16] Staying with the Duke of Devonshire.

[17] Lady Bessborough to Lord Granville Leveson Gower, undated (*c.* December 1813). *Leveson Gower Correspondence*, II, pp. 494–5.

[18] Lady Granville to Lady Georgiana Morpeth, 'Bruton Street, January 3, 1824'. *Lady Granville Letters*, I, p. 245.

Brighton, Tuesday

My dear Papa,

I am very much obliged to you for the poundnote you sent me. It is the first you ever gave me and you must change your opinion about my given [*sic*] it back and about Brighton being a place where nobody ever spends any thing, first I shall not give you the pound back and next I have spent two pounds since I have been here. I hope that will prove to you that on the contrary Brighton is a place where nobody ever keeps a penny in there [*sic*] pocket. I must go to dinner so good by my dear papa. I am yours ever

Emily Cowper

Panshanger Papers

On their way back to London the Cowpers paid Lord Egremont a visit at Petworth.

Petworth, April 21st 1820

We came here two days ago in our way to London where I mean to stay a little while, and then push on to P[anshanger] or go to Tunbridge [Wells] for a little while, for I am determined to take care of myself, and I know quiet is the only thing for me . . . I have been at Brighton for three weeks and liked it very much . . . George is come here with us and returns tomorrow with his wife who has remained bathing at Brighton. She is a good soul and she really worried herself ill and thin during the West-[minste]r Election. George is in very good spirits, but I fear there is no place vacant for him to come in for . . . I believe the Law will be the best speculation for him, but as he has no children to work for, I think he should do what amuses him best and Par[liamen]t is certainly what he likes . . .

Broadlands Papers

In London Lady Granville found Emily looking 'thin, pale, nervous and bored'.[19]

[19] Lady Granville to Devonshire, London, May 10th, 1820. *Lady Granville Letters*, I, p. 152.

London, Thursday, May 4th 1820

... I am just returned from Wimbledon where Ld C[owper] and I have been to look at W[illia]m's school which is a very comfortable one and kept by nice people, but I cannot tell you how sorry I am to part with him he is such an amiable boy—and improves every day ...

Ld Thanet has not made known his intentions yet and nobody knows whom he will bring in—I wish it may be George but I dare not flatter myself. George is still at Brighton with Mrs L[amb] ... I have been in Town only a week and think of going again soon either to Tunbridge [Wells] or Panshanger—the latter is a subject of great interest at this time as the new room is half built and I am anxious to see how it looks. People are as mad as ever after Almacks, etc. and plague me with their applications but we have started upon half a score of *new rules* to keep them in order. I believe it is this Almacks Tyranny that moves their bile, and makes them all so feverish and inflammatory. We are threatened with a female Thistlewood and party to storm our Committee.

My little Girl is very pretty and waiting for you to name her. The name I am most inclined for is Louisa—Caroline is a name disgraced. Fanny I like pretty well and also Mary. Eliz[abeth] or Harriet I should in some respects like but the names are not pretty and they make one melancholy but tell me what you think. Dorothy I also think rather pretty ...

Panshanger Papers

Saturday. This letter ended May 21 [Sunday 1820]

... The K[ing] was very civil to all the Whigs at the Levee, particularly so to Ld Holland[20] and Ld Thanet. This moved Ld Angleseys[21] choler who said its too bad ! ! you all think to get something by this but you wont. Ld T[hanet] afterwards had an opportunity of making Ld A[nglesey] angry again for upon

[20] Henry Richard Vassall Fox, 3rd Baron Holland (1773-1840): entertained profusely at Holland House.

[21] Henry William Paget, 1st Marquess of Anglesey (1768-1854): commanded cavalry and horse artillery at Waterloo where he lost a leg; field-marshal.

some mention of Ly H[olland][22] he said I thought that old fat . . . would show us some spirit at least. The K[ing] was very civil to Denison.[23] He took him by the shoulder at the Levee and said my old Friend how do you do . . . I dont think Ly C[onyngham] can last very long she is too foolish and vulgar and when she is driven out I really should not wonder if Mrs F[itzherbert][24] was to come round again. There are more unlikely things than this have come to pass, and she is handsomer now I think than Ly C[onyngham] who looks so fat and as if she was swelled with drinking Curacoa . . .

Panshanger Papers

In her next letter Lady Cowper turned to a more serious subject than Mrs Fitzherbert's charms and Lady Conyngham's bulk. 'The Queen has given us all a fillip,' she told Fred, 'some are sorry, some are glad, but all are on Tiptoe to know the result. I believe the Alderman,[25] fool as he is, hit upon the best thing for her—impudence is mistaken for courage and people admire her dashing into the midst of it all.'[26] Queen Caroline had indeed given them a 'fillip'; three days previously, on the 6th of June, she had entered London in triumph, even the sentries outside Carlton House saluting as she passed. The result was not for long in doubt, for it was clear that proceedings would have to be taken against her; and the air was soon full of rumours as to the form they would take. In these circumstances it is only to be expected that the letters which Lady Cowper wrote to her brother at this time should be full of speculations as to coming events.

[22] Elizabeth Vassall Fox, Lady Holland (1770–1845): hostess at Holland House.

[23] William Joseph Denison (1770–1849), Lady Conyngham's brother: M.P. 1796–1802; 1806–7; 1818–49. Died unmarried and left bulk of his vast fortune to Lord Albert Conyngham, who in 1850 took name and arms of Denison and was created Baron Londesborough.

[24] Maria Anne Fitzherbert (1756–1837), Roman Catholic; wife of George IV: married Prince of Wales 1785; lived with him till 1803.

[25] Sir Matthew Wood, 1st Baronet (1768–1843); Lord Mayor of London, 1815–16 and 1816–17; M.P. for City of London, 1817–43; friend and counsellor of Queen Caroline; created a baronet by Queen Victoria, 1837, this the first title she bestowed.

[26] Lady Cowper to Frederick Lamb, 'London, Friday, June 9th, 1820'. Lady Airlie, *Lady Palmerston*, I, pp. 51–3.

... Amongst impossible and extravagant conjectures, what do you think of mine, that the K[ing] should go mad and she be Regent, with the care of his person? He is in a great state of nervous irritation, as well he may, for he has been *very* ill-used. In the great debate, nobody said a word for him and Ld H[olland] says that people are so angry with him for being guilty of preferring true charges against her. Ld H[olland] says people want to make him out frivolous and vexatious; he is very cross and angry, everybody says ... Ly Conyngham has been very ill and worried, as you may suppose. Mrs Fitzherbert also, they say, is horribly nervous. The Queen wanted to go herself to the Bar of the House to-day, and would have done so if unfortunately they had not determined to hear her Council. The Chancellor[27] was so afraid of her coming there suddenly that he had given strict orders no woman should go in, so that two ladies who meant to sit behind the curtains were refused admittance. We are all in a pretty mess and so, I think, is she, since she refused Wilberforce's[28] terms. The two parties were both bullying and Ministers have been driven to open the bag, which nobody thought they had courage enough for. They should have done it at first, and not have cut such a foolish figure and increased the agitation of the public mind. B[rougham] and Denman[29] are her ostensible advisers, but she has other private ones whom she minds much more. B[rougham] thought she would have taken Wilberforce's terms. Nobody knows who counsels her, or if she follows her own wild head ... Canning's[30] seems the most curious situation. He is to keep his place, but to absent himself from the Cabinet on questions about the Queen—*voilà du nouveau*. His friends say he wanted to resign, but was begged

[27] John Scott, 1st Earl of Eldon (1751–1838); Lord Chancellor 1801–6 and 1807–27.

[28] William Wilberforce (1759–1833); philanthropist; took prominent part in movement for the abolition of the Slave trade. He negotiated with Brougham on terms to be offered to the Queen, but they broke down on the question of the restoration of her name to the liturgy.

[29] Thomas Denman, 1st Baron Denman (1779–1854); solicitor-general to Queen Caroline; afterwards Lord Chief Justice; peerage 1834.

[30] George Canning (1770–1827): was in the Liverpool administration as President of the India Board until his resignation.

to stay as it would perhaps dissolve the Ministry if he withdrew.[31] He has had interviews with the King; people say His Majesty is pleased with his old friends standing so aloof on this question and being so quiet. The fact is nobody knows what to do, and no two people are of the same mind. Ld Grey[32] is come to Town and looks quite hearty and brisk, very much against the Queen which every one must allow is conscientious, but against a private Committee.[33] He prefers scandalising the country *openly* by such details as I believe were never heard before, though I believe they belong more to levity and madness than decided evidence. *Et voilà le malheur!* Nobody can tell what will come of it all. The common people, and I fear the soldiers, are all in her favour and I believe the latter more than is owned—this is natural enough; they look upon her as an oppressed individual, whereas she is oppressing. As for her virtue, I don't think they care much about it, for tho they call her innocent, the Mob before her door have repeatedly called out 'A cheer for Prince Austin,[34] the Queen's son . . .

Broadlands Papers

June 20th [1820]

. . . You are pretty right I think in what you say about the Queen and B[rougham] but I think she is half wild and follows her own head more than any body's. They say the Committee

[31] The Queen was an old friend and had stood godmother to Canning's son who had recently died. Thus when in spite of his strong disapproval the Queen returned to England and his colleagues decided to introduce a Bill to deprive her of her title and to terminate her marriage, Canning felt himself in a very awkward position. He accordingly went abroad early in August before the proceedings against the Queen opened. He resigned in the following January.

[32] Charles Grey, 2nd Earl Grey (1764–1845): opposed the King's divorce. See Trevelyan, *Grey*, p. 193.

[33] Immediately after the Queen's arrival in England it was proposed that a private or secret Committee should consider the charges against her. This was agreed to in the Lords; but the lower House were anxious for time to be granted for further negotiations. It was soon apparent, however, that Caroline would accept no accommodation.

[34] William Austin (1802–49), adopted son of Queen Caroline. She set up a trust for his maintenance after her death. He became insane and was for long in an asylum in Milan, subsequently being brought to a private home in Chelsea.

will not have to sit more than 3 or 4 days. She has an unlimited power of money, but goes about in a miserable equipage to excite compassion. I think her popularity is a little falling, there is but a very small crowd about her door and a very miserable set follow her open carriage with the pair of Post Horses, when she goes out. Yesterday they took them off and dragged her up St James's Street—a miserable set. The soldiers are, I think, most to be feared; those who are behind the curtains say they are so much for her, and so dissatisfied at the K[ing] never appearing amongst them, that they think it is cowardice keeps him shut up. They have also an idea that they swore allegiance to G[eorge] 3d, and owe him nothing, and some of them cried to the D[uke] of G[loucester][35] on parade, 'You ought to be our King'.[36] Now it may all go on smoothly, but should the population rise in her favour will they with their discontents march against them? *Voilà ce qui reste à voir*, and what I feel no security about . . .

Broadlands Papers

The next letter finds the Cowpers 'ruralizing' at Panshanger.

July 27th, 1820

. . . here I am ruralizing—and indeed all my nerves are much better and everything about me looks prosperous, five Children about me all well and amiable, *on serait heureux à moins*. The Gallery is beautiful. the Country Green as in Spring and my Garden and Conservatory beautiful. I have been driving my darling Pony Carriage which has made me late and unable to write more than this short letter, but next post I will make up for it. I drove to Digswell with all the Courage of a Coachman and tomorrow (or next day) I intend to ride . . .

Broadlands Papers

[35] William Frederick, 2nd Duke of Gloucester (1776–1834): son of the first duke, grandson of Frederick Prince of Wales; field-marshal; married his cousin Mary, fourth daughter of George III, 1816.
[36] There had been a mutiny in one of the Guards Regiments a few days previously. According to Mrs Arbuthnot the grounds of complaint were over-crowded barracks, insufficient pay and too much duty. *Mrs Arbuthnot*, I, pp. 23–4.

Emily kept her promise to write a long letter to her brother by the next post; much of it concerns gossip and scandal of no great interest today, but she also had much to say about the sordid affairs of the Queen.

Monday, July 31st [1820]

... Ld Grey went out of Town very cross and vexed and annoyed, which one cannot wonder at, finding all his friends pulling different ways and unable to do anything ...

I am anxious for the day when the evidence will come out, I so much fear it will be weak, that there are things to prove I have no doubt, but to prove it is the difficulty. Italians talk so lightly, they will brodé and then prevaricate and though what they state may be true, they will give it an air of falsehood. I am afraid it will be a terrible scene altogether. It is reported that their best witnesses are two seamen, who looked in at the cabin window. If so, this would tell in the public opinion, but really the feeling is so strong that she is injured and that the K[ing] has taken his own full swing, that I don't think they care about her being innocent or not. They think her justified in anything ...

I have run too much into Politics, but such is the order of the day ...

She then runs into rumours of scandals, which occupy several pages!

... I am quite ashamed of this letter it is so long; I must put two covers. I have somehow had so many things to say to you. The Gallery here is quite beautiful and such an improvement to the house as you cannot believe without seeing it ...

Broadlands Papers

Towards the middle of August Emily and her husband returned to London to enable Lord Cowper to attend the proceedings in the House of Lords on the Bill of Pains and Penalties against the Queen.

CHAPTER III

The Trial of Queen Caroline

O N THURSDAY the 17th of August, the proceedings opened in the House of Lords. All the peers, other than minors and those who could plead indisposition, old age or some other reasonable excuse, were required to attend. Lord Melbourne, now over seventy and in poor health, took advantage of his age to be excused. 'Papa does not mean to attend (as he is exempted by age)', his daughter told Frederick, 'and I really think by all accounts it is much better for him to avoid it.'[1]

The extraordinary excitement aroused and the general fear of rioting is vividly depicted in the letter that Emily wrote to Fred on the opening day of the proceedings.

London August 17th [1820]

The Peers are all gone to the House and had no difficulty in getting in. Details I will give you the last thing tomorrow. I think if there is to be any blow up that it is much more likely to be at the end than at the beginning, but I hope it will all go quieter than is expected. Active measures have certainly been taken in all ways for the preservation of peace. Troops have been marched to London from all quarters, regiments from Hertford marched on to Barnet, and Barnet to London. W[illia]m is ordered to be in readiness with his Yeomanry, and so of course are all the others. He has sent to Ld C[owper] to beg for four horses to be at his disposal in case he should want them. I dined with Huskisson[2] at Whitehall yesterday. He says it is wonderful the terror people are in at a distance from the Metropolis. He says by the letters he gets one should fancy it was all over with us . . .

[1] Lady Cowper to Frederick Lamb, P[anshanger] August 14th, 1820. Lady Airlie, *Lady Palmerston*, I, pp. 54–5.

[2] William Huskisson (1770–1830), statesman. His wife was Elizabeth, younger daughter of Admiral Mark Milbanke, who was a younger brother of Lady Melbourne's father, Sir Ralph Milbanke, 5th baronet.

The Queen and all her violent Radical friends are furious with B[rougham] and say he betrayed her. The Ministers are also abusing him, for they say if he had not persuaded them that he could manage her, they would have sooner proposed measures of conciliation. In short, when a job has been thoroughly mismanaged, of course every body abuses every body. B[rougham] was jockeyed by her, and his vanity made him believe his influence with her to be very great, and she did with him what he intended to have done with her, which was to use her name for his own interest. I think B[rougham] feels that he wants friends very much, for he makes up to me greatly, but I am not his dupe as many others are. Mrs Damer's[3] obstinacy is all engaged in the Queen's cause. I like her for her stoutness, but it is very absurd. She is a great croaker about the state of the country however. She says that in all ages when a country has arrived at its highest pitch of glory, some events happen which make it sink and pass away, and such she foretells is our fate now to be . . .

Friday 18th

All was very quiet yesterday, the Mob quite immense, but in good humour and little said by them. The newspapers will tell you what the L[or]ds do. Huskisson says he thinks that division (of 206 to 40)[4] should do good in the eyes of the country, for as people were all jumbled according to their different opinions, it shows that it is no party question. Ld[s] Grey, Lansdowne,[5] Erskine,[6] Grenville,[7] Fitzwilliam[8] and others were in the majority,

[3] Anne Seymour Damer (1749–1828): noted sculptress; daughter of Field-Marshal Conway, married John Damer, later Lord Milton.

[4] The exact figures were: contents 41, non-contents 206. This was in reply to the Duke of Leinster's motion to rescind the order of the day for proceeding to the second reading of the Bill for depriving the Queen of her title and of all the prerogatives, rights, privileges, etc., as Queen Consort of the realm.

[5] Henry Petty-Fitzmaurice, 3rd Marquess of Lansdowne (1780–1863): supported abolition of slave trade; formed coalition of Canning's followers and section of Whigs and entered Cabinet without office, 1827: resigned 1828.

[6] Thomas Erskine, 1st Baron Erskine (1750–1823); Lord Chancellor 1806–7; opposed Bill of Pains and Penalties against the Queen.

[7] William Wyndham Grenville, Baron Grenville (1759–1834): supported Bill of Pains and Penalties against the Queen.

[8] William Wentworth Fitzwilliam, 4th Earl Fitzwilliam (1748–1833).

and Ld Kenyon[9] and all the Saints in the minority. The Duke of York[10] was much applauded going down, and the Duke of Wellington[11] hissed, which much surprised him. The Duke of York's speech may very likely today *depopularise* him. Brougham's speech was in part good, but the beginning very tiresome and it sent the Queen to sleep. His attack on the Duke of York was very bad; stupid and in bad taste and no argument and very ill received, as he is highly popular with every body just now.[12] Upon all these things being stated at Ly Jersey's I ventured a remark which was not well received either 'that the moral of the story only went to show how very little it signified whether people were hissed or applauded, for it was quite chance and ignorance, and likely every day to change.' Whigs cast an evil eye upon me . . . They pretend to like truth, but it's only some truths they like. It is difficult to see through that future opaque cloud the Queen talks of, but I really believe the Bill will never pass the H[ouse] of Commons, if it does the House of Lords. There is no denying it, the feeling of the people is almost every where in favour of the Queen, not merely the rabble, but the respectable middle ranks. All their prejudices are in her favour. They hate the King, disapprove of his moral conduct and think all foreigners are liars and villains.

How Govern[men]t have got the witnesses to come over, I don't know, but I suppose by power of money, and when this comes out it will still further invalidate their testimony. Besides, I cannot think they will be got to speak, for they are frightened out of their wits. They are confined in Cotton Garden [*sic*] and

[9] George Tyrell-Kenyon, 2nd Baron Kenyon (1776–1855).

[10] Frederick Augustus, Duke of York and Albany (1763–1827), second son of George III.

[11] Arthur Wellesley, 1st Duke of Wellington (1769–1852): Field Marshal; Master General of the Ordnance with seat in the Cabinet at this time.

[12] Lord Holland's lines on the Queen's sleeping in the House of Lords were:

'Here her conduct no proof of the charges affords,
She sleeps not with menials, she sleeps with the Lords.'

In his opening speech for the Queen, Brougham asked the House why, if it was right to bring this bill against his client, no 'bill of degradation' had been brought against the Duke of York in 1809, at the time of the Mrs Clarke scandal.

heard all the hurra and noise yesterday, which terrified them out of their senses. They thought the Mob was breaking in and coming to murder them. A messenger, who was very hot, comes into them wiping his throat, which they took for an explanatory gesture in lieu of the Italian language, to inform them they were going to have their throats cut. Think what a state of terror they must be in, and how they will shiver and shake and prevaricate in the House. If the thing goes on we shall have shocking work in the Winter with all this Mob on the long dark nights. Now they are good-humoured, but one cannot trust to its lasting, and all the time one thinks what a pity it is to see the country embroiled for a thing that signifies so little, merely to gratify the King's angry feeling and to enable Ministers to keep their places, which, however, I believe they will manage to do in any event. Really, when one thinks of it, the whole thing is too absurd and all brought on by the Litany omission, which, in fact, nobody cares about, and she has got herself hampered, and fighting to remain in this country, which is, in fact, the thing she would dislike most. Her manner was very good on entering the House, but she lay lolling in her arm chair in a ridiculous way and her head did not appear above the bar. She had a white veil over her face, which was the colour of brickdust ... Ld Archibald[13] says on his conscience he believes the Queen guilty, but that he should still vote for her acquittal, because he thinks the K[ing] has no right to a divorce or to embroil us in a Civil War for a thing which signifies so little, and this I daresay, is the feeling of many other members of the House. The Q[ueen] has subpoenaed Ld Granville,[14] Somerset, Rogers and in general all the men who were in Italy in her time. They are not called upon to say hearsay evidence, and as of their own knowledge they can know little, she will expect the country to look on that as evidence in her favour; besides, she wishes it to appear that while they call foreigners, her witnesses are respectable English. The point of Bergami being behind her chair first and afterwards at dinner is

[13] Lord Archibald Hamilton (1769–1827), son of the 9th Duke of Hamilton and 6th Duke of Brandon; M.P. Lanark. His sister, Lady Anne Hamilton (1766–1846), acted as Lady-in-Waiting to the Queen.

[14] Lord Granville Leveson Gower had been created Viscount Granville in 1815. In 1833 he was created Earl Granville.

what they all can speak to,[15] but that point she gives up as of no importance, I suppose.

Papa is quite well, but I think was right to give up the House (tho some Peers older than him attend). It is wiser for him to be away, and it is very fatigueing and being a little deaf is another reason. The House is better ventilated than was expected.

Broadlands Papers

Sunday August 20th [1820]

... the Queen, the Queen, and nothing but the Queen is heard of. Her impudence surpasses every thing, and one requires great command of temper to keep within bounds, for the folly of people and the absurdity they talk outdoes any thing you can conceive ... W[illia]m [Lamb] is coming to Town Monday, when business is expected in the House. George [Lamb] I saw today; he came up from Richmond. He looks very well and stronger on his legs than I expected. Ld Byron is reported to be arrived in Town, but I don't believe it ...

The Queen is tired out by her Advocates' long speeches and bored to death, so she did not go yesterday. I believe she knew Saturday was a bad Mob day and did not like to see herself ill-attended, so she has saved herself for Monday. She said to Tommy Twyrrit t'other day, as he handed her in, 'Tell the King I am very well, and that I shall live some years to plague him.' One thing surprises me that B[rougham] told Ld C[owper] she had never had the curiosity to look into a newspaper since she came to England. This must, one should think, be design, but he said it was a want of interest on her part to know what was said. Wood, the foolish Alderman, has at last found out that his proper place when he goes in her carriage, is to sit backwards, so he has accounted for his arriving in London by her side on the score of his stomach,[16] so Henry Fox[17] heard a woman say in Hammer-

[15] In his opening address the following day, the attorney-general made the point that whereas hitherto the Courier Bergami had stood behind Caroline's chair at meals, in August 1815 he for the first time was admitted to a seat at her table.

[16] Wood had been much criticized because, when he drove with Queen Caroline upon her entry into London in June, he sat beside her, allowing Lady

smith the other day, 'Poor dear Alderman, how sick he looks sitting backwards.' The Queen's colour is white, the Symbol of purity, so you see some white cockades in the street on some of the rabble—tis laughable! ! One hardly knows what to wish should be the result. I should much like to see her clearly convicted for being so impudent. At the same time, if the Lords would throw out the bill, it would save a great deal of trouble and perhaps danger, and the carrying it thro' can do no good. I assure you the rabble look in a very unpleasant manner at the Peers' Carriages. I sometimes wish my royal crown was off the arms.[18] It is such a foolish hobble to have got into, and if it goes on I do think we shall have blood shed before it passes the Commons. A Bill of Pains and Penalties is an awkward name, it sounds to the ignorant as if she was going to be fried or tortured in some way.

Broadlands Papers

At the date of Lady Cowper's next letter the proceedings in the House of Lords had occupied seven days. After various preliminaries and Counsels' opening speeches, the House had examined one Theodore Majocci, who had been engaged as a servant in the Princess's household during her wanderings abroad in 1815 and afterwards. His examination in chief had been very damaging to Caroline's reputation; but Brougham's severe cross-examination had done much to discredit the witness. Indeed, so often did he reply *non mi recordo* (I do not remember) to the questions put to him by the Queen's Counsel, that these words came to be bandied about as a token of evasion and falsehood. Furthermore, when Brougham elicited from Majocci that he had been in England about a year previously, when he had spoken of the Princess in favourable terms—'Of her conduct I always said that she was a good woman, but she was surrounded by bad people'— much of the damaging effect of his examination-in-chief had been removed.

The other three witnesses, mentioned by Lady Cowper, were

Anne Hamilton, the lady-in-waiting, a duke's daughter, to sit with her back to the horses.

[17] Henry Stephen Fox (1791–1846), diplomatist, a son of General Henry Edward Fox and grandson of Henry Fox, 1st Lord Holland.

[18] Lord Cowper was a Prince of the Holy Roman Empire.

Caltuno Peturzo, mate, and Vincenzo Garginlo, owner and master, of the polacca engaged to take the Princess and her party from Augusto to Innis and Greece, and Franciso Birollo, the cook, all of whom testified to the Princess and Bergami having slept together under a tent on board deck during the voyage.

Friday August 25th [1820]

I wrote in haste yesterday[19] having imagined it was Post day, which I found out to be a mistake after I sent my letter. Nothing new has occurred; the three last witnesses did not go so far as Theodore [Majocci] though the foundation of his story is evidently quite true, yet has managed to act and to answer so that I should not be surprized if he was prosecuted for perjury, and one thing he seems to have awkwardly concealed, that he was in England about a year ago. This is, in my opinion, a great pity for the effect on the country, as doubting the credibility of any witness, tends to throw doubt also upon the others, and as the whole story is so evidently true and the case so strong, that the *bill cannot* be thrown out, the only thing would be for the evidence to be perfectly clear and decisive, and to leave no loop hole to doubt upon any body's mind . . . Ld Liverpool says the evidence on the part of the King will be over in about three weeks, then it is doubted whether she will go on directly or take time to send for any witnesses. They say she wants to Subpoena the Patriarch of Jerusalem, that she would like to do it for fun! Before the Attorney General had stated his case, she went to the House in a street carriage, and had a double thick veil over her face, but since the long list of horrid improprieties, he states, she has cast off the veil entirely and goes boldly into the House. She must be mad! ! . . .

Broadlands Papers

In her next letter Emily Cowper had some shrewd remarks to make on the respective advocacy of Brougham and Denman. Many people would be inclined to agree with her view.

[19] Letter not found.

... I got a long letter from you yesterday which delighted me very much, for I do now begin to see what you think upon various subjects and I pretty much agree with you in all, except that I think one cannot call Ld H[ollan]d a wrong-headed man tho' he is apt to take fancies, and that B[rougham] is surely a powerful advocate tho' in this case he has failed on the one instance of making people believe that *he thought* his client innocent, which would have been more use to her than all his arguements, but this his Vanity forbid for he would not appear so thickheaded. Now Denham has either done so on principle or has really been bamboozled by the Queen, for he has made everybody think that he is perfectly convinced of her entire innocence. I don't know him myself, but the strength and cleverness of his Speeches are amazingly praised and I do not think it likely therefore that he should be such a dupe ...

Tuesday [29th] It is believed that B[rougham] will not finish the X. questioning now so that the Attorney General will not be able to sum up, and that the whole will begin again in December. I think B[rougham]'s wish to put it off looks to me like feeling the weakness of his cause. He continues to talk very big, but I dont think he feels so. Barbar Cras[20] (I spell anyhow) he had thought entirely to disprove by showing that she was a person of Bad Character, but Lord Auckland[21] told me last night that he feared he could not do this, and that he now thought there must be two or three women of that name. Ld Grey is very decided I see still and said yesterday when I met him at Ld Derby's dinner that Sir W[illia]m Scott[22] felt not a doubt that the facts had all been proved tho Theodore and Mlle Dumont[23] had

[20] Meidge Barbar Kress, previous to her marriage, had been a chambermaid at the Post Inn, Carlsruhe, where the Princess of Wales stayed. She was a witness for the prosecution; and, according to Lady Granville, had been sent over by Frederick Lamb. Lady Granville to Lady Georgiana Morpeth, London, August 22, 1820. *Lady Granville Letters*, II, p. 160.

[21] George Eden, 1st Earl of Auckland (1784–1849), succeeded his father as 2nd Baron Auckland, 1814; Governor-General of India 1835–41; created Earl 1839.

[22] William Scott, Baron Stowell (1745–1836), judge of the High Court of Admiralty, 1798–1828; brother of Eldon, the Lord Chancellor.

[23] Louisa Dumont, another witness for the prosecution, had been in the Princess's service as first *femme de chambre*.

in part broke down and that the evidence of yesterday *alone* was enough to give anyone a divorce.[24] It is believed however that the Bishops are conscientious and will not vote for a divorce and that Ld Liverpool means to leave that out of the bill ...

Broadlands Papers

A week later, on Saturday, the 9th of September, the House adjourned until Tuesday, the 3rd of October. This enabled the Cowpers to return to their beloved Panshanger, whence most of the news was domestic.[25]

Panshanger, Sept. 25th [1820]

... George and Caroline are here. He seems pretty well, much better than he was, but I am very anxious to make him more regular in his way of life and eating and drinking. ... W[illia]m is also here, Caroline confined with a cold at Brocket. Agar-Ellis was off today to Ld Granville's and we expect him to be replaced by Luttrell ...

Our building goes on famously, the Gallery will be beautiful, and we are quite grieved to be obliged to leave it next week when Lord Cowper's holidays expire. Papa seems to have set his heart upon passing all the month of December at Brocket and thinks of nothing else. Of course I encourage him for I think anything good that is any amusement to him—and that helps to pass the time. I believe his chief object is to rescue poor Brocket from the aspersions of stingyness under which it labours,[26] and I fear his residence will be a rare source of squabbling, and as far as I am concerned, you can easily believe how much I dislike the thoughts

[24] On the previous day, Saturday, August 26th, the chambermaid Kress had given some very intimate and unpleasant details of the state of the sheets of Bergami's bed in the Carlsruhe Inn, which it was her duty to make. Mrs Arbuthnot took the same view as Lady Cowper that this evidence was sufficient to procure anybody a divorce. *Mrs Arbuthnot*, I, p. 35.

[25] Lady Cowper to Frederick Lamb, Pan[shanger], September 18th, 1820. Broadlands Papers. Lady Airlie, *Lady Palmerston*, I, pp. 65-6.

[26] William and Lady Caroline Lamb were living at Brocket and there were rumours that the servants and tradesmen were hard put to it to get their dues from Lady Caroline!

of the whole thing, but I have promised to go there and to take the Children to make it comfortable for him. It would certainly be a good thing for him if he could get to feel an interest in the place and like to be there again, it would break the winter for him, and make a variety for him, instead of always coming here, tho I think he is more comfortable and more satisfied here this time than I ever saw him; but tho he pretends not to care he certainly was a good deal annoyed at all the stories of W[illia]m and Caro's way of going on, and wants I believe to set them a *brilliant example* . . .

Broadlands Papers

(Taken from a copy made by the late Lord Mount Temple. The original cannot be traced.)

And so early in October Lord Cowper's holidays did expire, for the House was due to meet on the 3rd.

The proceedings commenced with an exceedingly powerful opening speech for the defence by Brougham. Thereafter, a number of witnesses were called on Caroline's behalf. These included Lord Guilford[27] and his sister Lady Charlotte Lindsay[28] (son and daughter of the famous Lord North who shortly before his death had succeeded his father as 2nd Earl of Guilford); Keppel Craven[29] and Sir William Gell,[30] who had acted as Chamberlain to the Princess; and Dr Henry Holland, her doctor. All these witnesses swore that they had never seen any impropriety between the Princess and Bergami. Unfortunately, Lady Charlotte's evidence was marred by the admission extracted from her that she had retained her position in order to earn some money to assist her worthless and spendthrift husband and that she had finally

[27] Frederick North, 5th Earl of Guilford (1766–1827).

[28] Lady Charlotte North (1771–1849), youngest daughter of Lord North, 2nd Earl of Guilford; married the Hon. John Lindsay, spendthrift seventh son of James Lindsay, 5th Earl of Balcarres; Lady-in-Waiting to the Princess of Wales.

[29] The Hon. Keppel Richard Craven (1779–1851), third son of William Craven, 6th Baron Craven, and his wife Lady Elizabeth Berkeley, daughter of Augustus Berkeley, 4th Earl of Berkeley, afterwards Margravine of Brandenburg-Anspach and Bayreuth; Chamberlain to the Princess of Wales.

[30] Sir William Gell (1777–1836), archaeologist and traveller; Chamberlain to the Princess of Wales.

resigned on the written advice of her brother. She could not find his letter; but when pressed to say what reason Lord Guilford had given for tendering this advice, she was bound to admit that, whilst she could not positively swear to it, she thought it might have been owing to the ugly rumours that were afloat as to her Royal Highness's conduct. Further, according to Mrs Huskisson, who was likely to know, in spite of his evidence, Lord Guilford only a week previously had told William Huskisson 'that the Queen was so infamous a character that he could not account for it otherwise than to suppose that it was a disease . . .' [31] Altogether the general effect of the evidence of these witnesses was that, though Caroline had undoubtedly been Bergami's mistress, it was not possible to prove her guilt. That was Lady Cowper's view.

Tuesday, October 10th [1820]

. . . You will see by the papers the turn the evidence has taken, and there is every probability of the bill being given up. It was reported yesterday that some of the Ministers had been to the King to get him to comply. The fact is that tho the impression must remain very much the same upon all rational minds, yet there is not evidence to convict her, or at least so many parts of the evidence being disproved and the character of the witnesses taken in, and added to this the expediency of throwing out the Bill, and so many of their own Lords are of this opinion that, should the Ministers persist, I am told they would most probably be beat. The Polacca [story] is still uncontradicted, but parts remain open—Mannochi, etc. who is clearly proved to have lied about the masquerade and the Opera night at Naples.[32] Brougham says he will be obliged to allow by his witnesses that they both slept under the tent in the Polacca—and this I think for a month, which is awkward, but they were both dressed upon two beds, and this is not sufficient to pass the Bill upon them.

The Queen has a strange luck in her favour; the worse she behaves, the *more* it redounds to her credit. The only *good* I see in the turn affairs have taken, is that the Radicals are furious, and

[31] *Mrs Arbuthnot*, I, p. 40. See also *Letters of George IV*, II, No. 855, pp. 370-1.
[32] Evidence had been given that the Princess had gone to a masquerade in a very indecent dress that exposed her breasts.

Cobbett[33] makes a violent attack on Brougham for lukewarmness, and for having spared the King in his speech. The fact is that the Bill being thrown out is death to their hopes. . . . B[rougham] has certainly shown uncommon talent in the conduct of the whole business and what he is not in general famous for, great prudence and *temper*, except with a few exceptions . . .

. . . (*entre nous*) I believe most of the Queen's witnesses are more or less perjured, but it is very different swearing to what you believe and what you know. The Queen is in high glee, but bored with it all, and they say when the whole thing is settled will *certainly* go abroad . . . The Queen says she pities the King for having such *foolish* people about him; that if she had wished to get up a thing of this sort, she would have done it better. She says it is true she did commit adultery once, but it was with the Husband of Mrs Fitzherbert. She is a drôle woman . . .

Broadlands Papers

Wednesday [October 11th 1820]

. . . After all this, how impossible it will be for any man to divorce his wife for the next 20 years, after such philippics as are daily uttered against spies and informers, and above all, servants' evidence, as if any body had ever objected to it before in any common case. We are really growing enlightened . . . The most shameful thing that has appeared in the whole transaction is Col[onel] Lindsay having sold to Govern[men]t Ly Charlotte's letters written to him from Naples, and it was upon these that her cross-examination was founded. Did you ever hear of such a thing? She has satisfied nobody. The anti-Queens believe she told very great lies, and the Queen's friends think she did not do it boldly enough. They say if she had made up her mind to say a thing, she should not have hesitated . . .

I believe the Almanac recommends, spring and fall, a little blood letting and a cooling diet. However, I now wish the bill to be thrown out. After all this evidence it is the only thing to do. The King might make his Party good by saying he was glad to find he had been deceived by false reports. The Bill being thrown

[33] William Cobbett (1762-1835), essayist, politician, who wrote strongly in favour of Queen Caroline.

50

out and the Queen well used, is death to the hopes of the Radicals, and may save us much unpleasant work. What does it signify letting her have a little Court and establishment? Her being received as Queen will disgust the Radicals of her, and no decent person will have any more to do with her than just leave their names. It is the idea of injustice that gets her so many partizans and raises a cry, for all know what to think of her, and I believe there are none who would trust her, perhaps excepting Denman, who is quite a fool on that subject. She has completely bamboozled him, and I believe made him in love with her. It is unlucky for Mannochi that he should have fixed on the Masquerade for the indecent dress, as in fact, it seems the only time in her life when she was dressed decently . . .

Two days later Lady Cowper continued her letter.

Friday Oct. 13th [1820]

The reports now are these:

Tho it is difficult to have a résumé, as the two sides see things in so different a light, the Queen's Court fancy the Bill will be thrown out, but somehow with a vote of censure attached. Ministers are in doubt what to do, they were very low before Flinn[34] and Howman,[35] but these have given them much to say and to lay stress upon, though I think there is not much to find fault with in the latter's evidence, tho he spoke evidently with a strong bias in her favour. Flinn is quite a mad Irishman, bother-headed and wild, with a neck cloth, which Lord Erskine says must be the sail of the Polacca, but as B[rougham] laid much stress upon small inaccuracies destroying the whole weight of the evidence of a person, this applies very much to these two witnesses, and he seems to feel it so and to be out of sorts. Many Peers who before said the Bill *must* be thrown out, are now in doubt . . . Many Peers are against passing the Bill who would yet vote her guilty. Therefore Ld Grey thinks Ministers will

[34] Lieutenant John Flinn, R.N., in command of the polacca, a witness for the princess.
[35] Lieutenant Joseph Robert Howman, a witness for the princess.

somehow or other have first a vote upon whether she is guilty or not, which would commit them as to what they would next propose. I heard of Lord Sidmouth[36] saying yesterday that their places were twenty per cent better than they were on Monday. This is the only view in which they look at the question, though I have no idea that in any turn the affair had taken they would have gone out, for they would certainly have found some saving clause by throwing it all on the King. I hear the Duke of Y[or]k told the King on Saturday that the Bill must be thrown out. I am all on this side of the question now. I think so many witnesses having failed . . . and told evident and disgusting lies ought to vitiate the whole. I believe her *nearly* as guilty as ever I did, but it will not do to pass such a Bill in the teeth of such witnesses as Ly Charlotte and Gell and H. Craven and her respectable maître d'hotel, and upon the evidence of such liars . . . it is neither just nor expedient, for I am sure it would put the whole country in a flame. They don't consider that these witnesses speak but to a few weeks after Bergami's appearance, and cannot weigh the real state of the case—and it appears at first sight such an evident injustice. If the Bill goes to the House of Commons, we shall have dreadful scenes I do believe. This Bill never ought to have passed without the evidence being quite clear and decisive and untouched, so as to leave no doubt on one's mind. It will not do to force it on some points and quite failing on others. The Polacca is now what Govern[men]t mean to lay stress upon. I believe they have quite given up Naples, and the Polacca will not be strong enough, for it is just possible two people may lye in a tent on two beds in their cloathes, *en tout bien tout honneur*. One thinks it an *odd* proceeding, but it is not proof . . . I think B[rougham] did well in his speech by not retaliating upon the King or putting in any offensive matter he could avoid, and really it is for every bodies interest now to keep up the Monarchy, for it is in a sad low state. I always fear that B[rougham] will lose his temper, and that if M[inister]s force the Bill, they will drive him to it.

Broadlands Papers

[36] Henry Addington, 1st Viscount Sidmouth (1757–1844): Speaker of the House of Commons 1789–1801; first Lord of the Treasury and Chancellor of the Exchequer 1801–4; President of the Council and Home Secretary at this time.

... Papa is determined to pass December at Brocket, so that he has no wish this November for Brighton, which is lucky, as I shall wish to be a little at home somehow, and it is a difficulty between this London work and December, which I have promised Papa. I expect to have rare bothering work between him and Caro at that time, so it is good to be in nerves preparatory to it. She let out one of her secrets comically the other day, and it amused me though it was nothing *new*. I was at that moment in high favour, so she was praising me, and said: 'I was saying yesterday to W[illia]m that there never was anybody so amiable and so good-natured as you,' and he answered: 'If so, why do you so often abuse her?'

This affair of Rastelli[37] and the supposed bribes may very likely put an end to this whole Queen business, at least people think so yet others think the Ministers will try to pass the Bill, or if not will try to prove the preamble and then be satisfied with that, which would leave us all in a strange situation. I am all for the Bill's being thrown out, I think many of the disgusting details having failed, and considering the exaggeration of ordinary low Italians, one may look upon her case as one of no particular horror, and it merely remains with her having taken a Courier for her Lover, which Lover, if he had been a gentleman, she had, in my opinion, a good right to have, without anybody objecting, (if he did not). She is a coarse low-minded woman, I have no doubt, but it is hard on her to have such disgusting details invented about her, and they really must have done so in many instances, for they say the Attorney General's opening speech was not a third part up to his brief, and there are many people ready to swear to stories of the green bag, ten times more extraordinary, which they did not bring forward from thinking them impossible. Two witnesses on oath were ready to prove they had seen her dance naked before an open window, and many other

[37] Giuseppe Restelli had acted as courier for the Commissioners at Milan. He was brought to England to give evidence against the Queen; and afterwards on the advice of John Allan Powell, a solicitor of Lincoln's Inn and one of the members of the Milan Commission, he was sent out of the country, presumably in the hope that he might collect further evidence. Brougham's complaints put the Government in a difficulty. Furthermore, there had been allegations of the bribery of witnesses against the Queen.

things of this sort. Ld Erskine says the only good of this Bill is to separate everybody. The Queen cannot see Bergami; the King cannot see Ly Conyngham. He is obliged to pass his time alone and bored at the Cottage, and she is going to Spa. Brougham's quotation from Milton[38] is very good, and came very appropriately—it was given him while he was standing there by young Percival.[39] Canning cuts a miserable figure, loitering about at Paris,[40] to see what turn affairs will take . . .

Broadlands Papers

And so the proceedings dragged on through the autumn. 'The Peers are going on much in the same bother, and may sit a month or two longer till they are all ill,' wrote Emily to Fred, 'two or three drop off with excuses every day. Brougham looks ghastly, and the Chancellor is really ill, my doctor tells me.'[41]

It was almost another week before Emily wrote again and then it was to congratulate her brother. On the 5th of October the Foreign Secretary, Castlereagh, had sent a dispatch informing Frederick Lamb, plenipotentiary at the Court of Bavaria, that the Queen's legal advisers were anxious to call as a witness for their client Baron d'Ende, a Chamberlain in the service of the Grand Duke of Baden who had been assigned to attend upon the Princess of Wales during her visit to Carlsruhe in 1817, and that the Baron had agreed to come to London

[38] Brougham pleaded to know for whom the solicitor Powell had been acting. 'I know nothing about this shrouded, this mysterious being,' he told their lordships, 'this retiring phantom—this uncertain shape—

> "If shape it might be call'd, that shape had none,
> Distinguishable in member, joint or limb—
> Or substance might be called—that shadow seem'd,
> For each seemed either. . . .
> . . . What seem'd his head
> The likeness of a kingly crown had on".'
> Milton, *Paradise Lost*, Bk. 2, ll. 666–73.

[39] Spencer Perceval, M.P., eldest son of the Prime Minister who had been assassinated in the House of Commons in 1812. He was twenty-five at this time.

[40] He resigned from the Government in December 1820. Petrie, *Canning*, pp. 153–4.

[41] Lady Cowper to Frederick Lamb, Friday, October 20th [1820]. Broadlands Papers.

for this purpose if the Grand Duke could be induced to consent. Accordingly, Lamb was instructed to take prompt measures to try to overcome the Grand Duke's apparent reluctance. The plenipotentiary's reply from Carlsruhe a few days later showed that he had been completely successful in gaining the Grand Duke's consent; but that the Baron, on the plea of ill-health, now declined to come. The whole correspondence relative to the matter had been laid on the Table of the House of Lords, and on the 23rd of October the motion of Lord Holland had been read to the House. It was generally agreed that Lamb had done everything possible in the matter, and his sister was naturally delighted at his success.

Thursday night, October 26th, 1820

Everybody is in admiration of your letter to Benstead[42] [*sic*]. Denman's Speech was very fine everybody agrees. I think he would have done better if he had spared the King more, all that abuse is of no use whatever, Ld Essex[43] calls Carleton House, *Nero's Hotel*. Leopold has been today to call on the Queen;[44] this looks as if the Bill would not pass. Ly J[ersey] is *toujours comme un cheval qui prend le mors aux dents*, when the Queen is mentioned. Ministers and their friends say the bill will certainly be carried through and that the King is so set on it that he would urge it on if he thought to have only *one* majority. They say Ld Ellenborough[45] carried a sort of proposal to Ld Grey that Ministers would let the bill be thrown out if there could be a means hit upon of saving the Ministers, but he said he could hear of no arrangement of that sort, that he had come unprejudiced, listened to the evidence, and should act accordingly without any arrangement. I don't see what should drive them from their places even if they were to be beat, which is not likely. The King dare not, they would only say it was his act and not theirs. In Denman's

---

[42] His letter to the minister, Berstell, dated Carlsruhe, October 11, 1820.

[43] George Capel, 5th Earl of Essex (1757–1834).

[44] Prince Leopold was the widower of Princess Charlotte, George IV's daughter, so the Queen was his mother-in-law.

[45] Edward Law, 1st Earl of Ellenborough (1790–1871): eldest son of the 1st Baron Ellenborough, the Lord Chief Justice; Governor-General of India, 1841–4; Earldom 1844.

speech[46] there is a violent attack on the Duke of Clarence,[47] who has been about in an indecent manner abusing the Queen which is not so bad as his abuse of Howman and Flinn,[48] saying *I shall take care* they shall never rise in the Navy. The Duke of York is also violent. The Duke of Gloucester for her stoutly; this is not so much believed to be his generosity as he pretends for former friendship, as the Duchess's doing to prevent the Queen fulfilling her threat of Publishing Memoirs of herself and the rest of the Princesses. By the way such a threat as that shows what a degraded person the Queen is, yet people are so blinded now [that] if she were to do such a thing they would reckon it all fair.

I am much better, but going to Brighton tomorrow, where I shall be in *rude health* directly, but this dirty town, at this nasty time of year tries my convalescent state too highly... Caro G[eorge] is very kind and good and does all she can. By the way I never said I think she was for the Queen violently; she is rational enough, but of course has rather a leaning that way out of former affection for B[rougham.]. There is very little left now but of course great admiration, and this is excusable now for he gets uncommon praise for his talents and one must own he to a degree deserves it for he has managed this whole business uncommonly well and with a degree of prudence which does not usually belong to him...

Broadlands Papers
Lady Airlie, *Lady Palmerston*, I, pp. 71–3

So Lady Cowper took her old father to the sea, and when she next wrote to Frederick a week later they were comfortably installed in

---

[46] Denman's speech on behalf of the Queen lasted from October 24th to October 26th, the day Lady Cowper was writing to her brother. His most pointed attack, however, was not on the Duke of Clarence but on the King himself, for he likened George IV's treatment of Caroline to Nero's treatment of his wife, Octavia!

[47] William, Duke of Clarence and St Andrews, afterwards William IV (1765–1837); third son of George III.

[48] Who had given evidence on the Queen's behalf. Lady Airlie calls the latter Fleurs (*Lady Palmerston*, I, p. 72), but his name was Flinn. See note 34.

Lord Egremont's house at Brighton. All was well, except that poor old Lord Melbourne was failing, and this was giving his daughter much anxiety.

> Brighton, November 2nd 1820
>
> ∴ We are in Lord Egremont's House and very comfortable and Fanny has been with me. Ld C[owper] will come as soon as the House permits . . . Ministers will carry the Bill by a few it is expected, and Ly J[ersey] is going to see the Queen. I am glad I am out of it all by being here. Shabby Leopold and foolish wild Ld Fitzwilliam! can anything be more improper than for a Judge to go and see the accused before he has given his Judgment? I am sure the Dog Star rages! Ld Grey has been trying all he could to keep people back, at least till the Trial is over. The King is very much vexed, but well in health, tho he has lost three Pounds in the last week or fortnight . . . The King says Opposition on the whole have behaved well, but he hears every joke and is always angry. He was furious with Brougham's quotation and more so with young Perceval for giving it to him, shapeless Mass is an unfortunate epithet.[49] I think the Attorney General's Speech very good, and great part very true and well put, in short *fact*.

> Broadlands Papers

(*Taken from a copy made by the late Lord Mount Temple. The original cannot be traced.*)

At the close of the proceedings on Monday, the 6th of November, the second reading of the Bill of Pains and Penalties was passed by a majority of twenty-eight. At the opening of the proceedings on the following morning, Lord Dacre informed the House that he had received a formal protest from Queen Caroline, who positively asserted 'before God' that she was wholly innocent of the crime laid to her charge. Lady Cowper's next letter to her brother was written a few days later.

[49] Brougham's quotation from *Paradise Lost* (see note 38), and its obvious reference to George IV's ungainly figure.

Brighton, November 1820

I am afraid I must have alarmed you by my last account of Papa. The fact is that I believe I said more than the case warranted, altho' less than I felt upon the subject, for he was in such a state of debility and nerves when he came down here first that I was quite alarmed and he shook so of a morning that I really feared there was something of Palsy in it. All that is now gone and he is quite himself again, certainly older than he was six months ago to a certain degree but healthy, and his Pulse, and Stomach and Spirits very good . . .

You want to know about Ld L[iverpool]'s proposal. It was not made public*ally* [*sic*], but as I understood, hinted I suppose to B[rougham] to know if that arrangement would be satisfactory.[50] Ly H[ollan]d first told me of it upon which I mentioned it to Ld Cowper, and he said, 'Oh you have heard of that have you? I was told it as a great secret and promised not to tell;' and as far as I remember he was so close that he did not tell me the person who had confided in him but to satisfy your curiosity I wrote to him by the Post in London today and desired him if he remembered about it to write you word the particulars. Ly H[ollan]d you know is always *boutonée* and will never tell who has told her a thing. She thinks I suppose that Mystery adds to the weight of Her Oracles. Ld C[owper] is still in London dividing away and I doubt not talking nonsense, as I know he is acting foolishly, for he writes me word he has been to see the Queen. What folly— and what a preposterous act judges going to see the accused before they have pronounced their judgment . . . I wrote him word that I was not surprised for that no one can live with mad Dogs without being bit. I like to row him a little, but it's all the better for him that he should agree with his friends and it's a good thing to be eager about Politics or anything else, so that he is amused and interested . . . I have a letter from Fanny, saying that Huskisson is with them and very low, and says if Ministers do not carry the bill they must go out, and that he knows in this

[50] So far as is known, no formal proposal was put to Brougham by the Government. But the attitude of the populace, very much in the Queen's favour, made Liverpool increasingly anxious to bring the proceedings to a timely end. He probably therefore made informal suggestions for financial grants to try to satisfy the Queen's cupidity.

case Ld Liverpool intends to resign. She says Ld E[gremont] is strongly against the bill, says it should fail and never ought to have been thought of. Ly J[ersey] is still wild and with her *Tête Montée*, thinking the Queen innocent, the best Joke is to hear people reprobate the idea of ser[van]ts' evidence and saying what a horror it is and how ungentleman like to listen to it as if this was quite a new case, and as if every ser[van]t in every House did not believe it to be part of his duty to watch his Lady.

I am rather glad to have been out of Town at this time for I should have been worried to go and see her and now I am clear of the whole thing. Her protest[51] shocks me beyond measure it is so atrocious so wicked and so unprincipled to volunteer such an Oath when she cannot be innocent; a Woman may be found to do such a thing and may be wretched at it, but reconcile it to her conscience by saying yours is the sin for forcing me to do it, but here it is mere wickedness uncalled for: it sets me ten times more against her, for it is quite horrible.

Broadlands Papers
Lady Airlie, *Lady Palmerston*, I, pp. 74–6

But the sands were running out. On Friday, the 10th of November, only four days after the passing of the Second Reading of the bill, the Prime Minister, recognizing that the Bill would certainly not pass in the Commons, brought the unhappy proceedings to an end.[52]

Sunday, November 12th [1820]

... The whole affair was over Friday, so Ld C[owper] came here yesterday, and now we are all very comfortable. The account of the whole public matter will be in the papers, so I have nothing to say about it, but all parties, Ministers and all, are glad the Bill is withdrawn, for they knew it would not have passed the Commons. Besides, now they can manage to keep their places, tho people imagine there may be some shuffle amongst them.

[51] The Queen's formal protest to the House of Lords against the proceedings.
[52] Lord Liverpool's views are very fully set out in the letter he wrote to Wilberforce a few weeks later. 'Fife House', November 29th, 1820. Petrie, *Liverpool*, 246–8.

Had the Bill passed in the Lords and been thrown out in the Commons, every body says they must have gone out ... Par[liamen]t meets on the 23rd, and I suppose there will be some management proposed, her name restored to the Liturgy, and allowance made on condition of her going abroad, which it is thought she will accept, as she is heartily tired of being here, and they say bored with the whole thing. Her sprinkling of visitors has been very small. I am surprised at its being so small considering how people are blinded by Party ...

The following day Lady Cowper finished her letter with an account of reactions at Brighton.

Monday
There is great exultation amongst the Mob in Town, and Sir Mathew[53] is in great taking here. He thinks they will insist on lighting up tonight, which shocks him very much, under the very nose of his Majesty. It is rather a shame, I think, that this place should be so averse as it is to him, considering that he has really been the making of it ...

Broadlands Papers

Thus ended the proceedings against Queen Caroline. They had lasted for just three months.

[53] Sir Matthew John Tierney, 1st Baronet (1776–1845); the noted physician practising at Brighton. He was physician to both George IV and William IV. He attended the Cowper family when there.

CHAPTER IV

Mainly Domestic

DURING THE MONTHS immediately following the dropping of the Bill of Pains and Penalties, Lady Cowper's thoughts were much with her family. Of course she enjoyed with the rest of the fashionable world the luxury of speculating on what the Queen would do next. But she was sorely preoccupied with her ageing father's health; with the personal problems of her brother George; with the tragedy of the married life of her elder brother and his wife, 'Lady Lamb' as she at times sarcastically called her; and the still greater tragedy of their son, poor feeble Augustus.

Throughout November the Cowpers remained at Brighton, though Emily was anxious to return as soon as possible to Panshanger, where she had left her 'little bantlings' whom she had not seen for several weeks.

Brighton, Thursday Novr. 16th, [1820]

. . . I know nothing of news, but it is expected Parliament will be prorogued, some say by proclamation without meeting; this sounds awkward, and will create discontent, but I suppose they think that better than facing the House of Commons and having addresses to the King to remove his Ministers and to reinstate the Queen's name in the Liturgy, and to make a provision. It seems to me their object is to gain time, that she may be bored and go off abroad. Brougham says she is very much inclined to go. I suppose she is now divided between her spite and her ennui. I think she must be disappointed at so few ladies having been to see her . . .

An attempt was made to illuminate here, but it did not succeed. Tierney was furious. At Worthing many windows were broke. What asses people are! ! ! The King should reign here if nowhere else after all he has done for Brighton. He is expected down early next week . . .

Broadlands Papers

Brighton, Novr. 20th [1820]

Here we are still, and think of staying a fortnight longer, then to Town for 3 days and then on to Panshanger . . .

The King is expected here, but he is put to it to know how he can manage to have Ly C[onyngham] here at this moment. It would have such a bad effect, and this is what stops him, but he is wanting to come. Report says also that Ly Hertford[1] has sent to take a House . . .

Ly Lamb[2] wanted to come here, but I hope I have poked her off; it would be insupportable, yet I think Papa would like it; it gives him an employment to abuse her and quarrel with her. George and Caro are in Town. Lloyd[3] got his windows broke for not lighting up on the Queen's night, and so did several others. He is in a proper passion, as you may suppose.

Broadlands Papers

About the middle of the month Frederick Lamb wrote in some anxiety to his sister about their father's health. Clearly her reports on Lord Melbourne's state had alarmed him. But towards the end of November, after they had been at Brighton for some three weeks, she was able to send more reassuring news of his condition. If only she could keep the old man from 'boozing'!

Brighton, Novr. 23rd Friday[4] [1820]

. . . the life he had led for three weeks in London was enough to have killed a horse, never walking or taking any exercise, but just driving up to me between 5 and 6, and all day and night in a state of complete drunkenness, drink at dinner, which put him to sleep till 12, and then drink again till 2 or 3 o'clock in the morning, and then all the next day continual and repeated glasses of

---

[1] Isabella Anne Ingram Shepherd, daughter of Charles Ingram, 9th Viscount Irvine, and second wife of Francis Seymour, 2nd Marquess of Hertford.
[2] Lady Caroline Lamb.
[3] A wealthy neighbour of the Cowpers in Hertfordshire.
[4] So written, but November 23rd 1820 was a Thursday.

sherry. But what shows the strength of his constitution is the way he has rallied here with a different life . . . In a fortnight we shall go from here to Town and so on to Panshanger. I want very much to get a sight of my little children, whom I have not seen these two months, and I want to be at home for Christmas for Fordwich and William, but should I not feel so well at home as I do here, we shall return in Jany or Feby, as the sea air is so good a thing for me. Ld C[owper] does not dislike being here, and he puts no other object in competition with my health— there never was so good a person . . . The King *wants* to come here, but *has not* the face to bring Ly Conyngham or the heart to come without her, so that he remains suspended . . .

Broadlands Papers

In her next letter Lady Cowper had some shrewd things to say on the attitude both of the Government and of the Opposition on the Queen's case.

Monday Decr. 3rd[5] [1820]

. . . The Opposition have some of them been foolish, and Ld[s] Lansdowne and Grey began better than they ended, but I cannot admire Ld Liverpool, he should never have engaged in the business without more enquiry and knowing the real state of the case, he should never have *prejudged* the question by leaving her name out of the Liturgy, which has made the great cry against them. In short, all thro' I never saw a business so mismanaged, and all parties are open mouthed against him. When they saw how the thing went, they had better have given it up, unless they meant to go through with it, but to force it thro, and then give it up is absurd . . . and now I think it means they are *bitching* the question. They should do something or other and make some proposal, some arrangement, for this sort of trick of dissolving Par[liamen]t is miserable . . .

I shall only stay a day in Town and hurry on to Panshanger. Papa seems undetermined, he hates leaving this place and dislikes the thoughts of Brocket . . . he is really very well and Tierney

[5] So written, but December 3rd 1820 was a Sunday.

tries hard to break this wine habit which is the only thing that does him harm. I second him all I can, tho it grieves me to deprive him of his only real enjoyment. Lord C[owper] is gone for two days to Petworth to enjoy Ld E[gremont] and the range of the House, which he so much admires . . .

I don't go out here of an evening, or but little, as there is so much junketing and if I go to one I must to all, but Ld C[owper] is quite gay and goes about playing *petits jeux* and acting Charades, and is reckoned the very best of *Papa's*, for he has taken Minny out to two Balls as her Chaperon, and was as proud of her beauty and as pleased at taking her, as she was to go to the Ball, which is saying a great deal. I never saw a man hardly so fond of a Child.

The King is still at the Cottage, *plus épris que jamais*. Lady Co[nyngha]m drives over from Denison's to see him and they say he watches like a boy for the sound of her carriage. He will not come here tho he wishes it because he could not manage to have her here just now. It would make such a bad effect . . .

Broadlands Papers

Ten days later, Lord and Lady Cowper arrived at their house in George Street, but only for two or three days' stay, and then on to their beloved Panshanger.

The family was full of trouble. Lord Cowper had been for several days suffering from sciatica; William Lamb had been down with a bad cold; his wife had pretended to have a fever; and Lord Melbourne was quite affected at the thought of his drunkenness. He had recently taken his young connection, Jack Milbanke,[6] to live with him, and Emily was hopeful that this 'good-natured fellow' would be a help and companion to her father, who was firmly resolved never to take 'above one glass of Negus at supper'. Meanwhile her brother George was in London, much employed arranging for his edition of Catullus to be

[6] John Ralph Milbanke (1800–1868), the late Lady Melbourne's nephew, afterwards Sir John Ralph Milbanke-Huskisson, 8th Baronet, authorized to take additional surname of Huskisson and to bear the arms of Huskisson and Milbanke quarterly.

published—'it is an amusement to him and I hope will do him credit besides putting money in his pocket'.

In London there was constant talk of what the Queen would do next and frequent discussion as to whether the Liverpool Ministry could or could not remain in office. Much of this is set out in Lady Cowper's first letter to Frederick Lamb on her arrival in London;[7] and in the letter she wrote to him three days later.

George St. Decr. 18 [1820]

... The Ministers and the King all quarrel, but he is in their hands and cannot help himself. He insisted upon Par[liamen]t meeting and having the thing settled. They said if so they would resign, upon which he gave way. I believe this is certain. They say if she is restored to the Liturgy or has a palace, they must go out and without these concessions the popular ferment never will be allayed. Nothing, in my opinion, is so foolish as the Ministers' conduct, it even beats the Opposition's. In their place, having gone so far, I would certainly have forced the Bill thro', or having once given it up, they should now give up everything, give her an income, Hampton Court and her name in the Liturgy. She would then have nothing to ask for and soon get tired of the thing, as people would get tired of her. Now the battle keeps her alive, and she is wise enough to know (as Archibald Hamilton[8] says) that if she was to go she would go hissed out of the country, and never be able to set foot in it again. Now (tho [she] might prefer being abroad) her time passes well. She has a dozen Italians about her, plenty of society, and always fresh events to interest her. She is in very good spirits, he says ...

We go to Panshanger tomorrow, Tuesday. Next Monday is Xmas Day, and the Monday after my ball—my annual. I feel quite well and comfortable about myself and I have such very delightful children that this alone ought to make me happy ...

Broadlands Papers

[7] Lady Cowper to Frederick Lamb, George Street, Friday, December 15th, 1820. Broadlands Papers, Lady Airlie, *Lady Palmerston*, I, pp. 78–81.
[8] Lord Archibald Hamilton.

Over Christmas at Panshanger Emily Cowper was kept busy with the arrangements for her Ball on New Year's Day.

Thursday, Decr. 28 [1820]

I have not written much lately, as I am not so fond as I used to be of the action of writing, and I have had many notes to write for my Ball, which is to be the 1st of January on Monday. It will be a grand affair. George and Caro are here, and Papa and Jack[9] and Nugent and Ld and Ly Ossulston[10] are just arrived. Ld C[owper] has suffered dreadfully from the rheumatism, acute rheumatism in the thigh sciatic nerve, but he is better now, and I am pretty well . . .

Broadlands Papers

Meanwhile, though old Lord Melbourne was keeping rigidly to his one glass of Negus, as prescribed by Sir Matthew Tierney, his daughter had to admit that 'he manages *somehow or other to be drunkish*'; adding strangely that she supposes it 'must be the fog that makes him so'.[11]

In Emily's next letter, we are given a charming picture of the Cowper family at Panshanger.

Jany. 15 [1821]

You must wish me joy of getting well, for I am at least grown courageous, and ride every day, which is sure to set me up . . . I am mounted capitally upon Fordwich's little mare, whose knees Will Moore broke, but for me she is none the worse and is very pleasant, tho' perfectly quiet. Fordwich rides my mare or any horse that happens to come: Minny is mounted on Frisky and William on the little grey Pony, so there you see the Cavalcade, full gallop. I have no fear and enjoy it very much, and we have had delightful open weather the last week, and quite warm . . .

---

[9] Jack Milbanke.

[10] Charles Augustus, Lord Ossulston, son of the 4th Earl of Tankerville, and Corise de Gramont, daughter of Antoine, Duc de Gramont.

[11] Lady Cowper to Frederick Lamb, December 1820. Broadlands Papers. Lady Airlie, *Lady Palmerston*, I, p. 81.

The very day I wrote George word you advised him not to print his name, the advertisement appeared, so one can only hope now it will be so good as to do him credit; a good translation of Catullus is said to be wanted, and nothing sells without a name. I am in hopes Murray[12] has given him a sum for it . . .

We shall go to Town for a few days . . . The Duke of York is a gay widower,[13] goes visiting about; I was asked to meet him at Gorhambury[14] next week, *mais je ne le puis*—home is the only place for me, but I am getting quite well, cured by riding, and a mutton chop for Breakfast . . .

Broadlands Papers

The general confusion brought about by the sordid affairs of the Queen is well illustrated by the letter Lady Cowper wrote to her brother on the 1st of February:

Finished Thursday, Feby. 1st
begun before posts [1821]

. . . Politics are fallen very flat, high expectations have been disappointed. The Whigs are low and out of temper; the Ministers are abused and consequently peevish; the landholders are all poor and get only two-thirds of their rents. In short, every body has a grievance, and I alone am in spirits, for I am glad to find myself *perfectly* well. My nerves are gone as they came. I suppose they have at last been as tired of me, as I was of them . . . The Peers, who all came to Town exulting and triumphant from their country meetings, cheered and drawn and huzza'd, found the scene in London horribly flat . . . This Queen's subject is detestable, for one thing that it moves the calmest people to choler; nobody's temper can stand it. One party thinks the other fools, idiots, and madmen, and the compliment is returned with the epithet of base, ungenerous and time serving. Nobody is allowed

[12] John Murray (1778-1843), the publisher.

[13] The Duchess of York (Frederica Charlotte, eldest daughter of Frederick William II of Prussia) had died universally regretted on the 11th of August 1820.

[14] Seat of the Earl of Verulam, near St Albans.

an inbiassed opinion. There never was such an Apple of Discord as that Woman has been to the public and private families. As for me, I think it all fun, for I am in spirits and that makes all the difference of one's view of events.

Mrs Hope[15] has parties every Tuesday. Duke of Devonshire starts tonight with his Thursdays, and I am off tomorrow for the country to pass about 10 days. The Opera is going to revive, it is said, and Papa wants a box . . . He is very well indeed, but drinks too much at night, that's the worst of it. Jack [Milbanke] does all he can to stop it—his being in the house is a fortunate thing, for he is a good boy. . . . There is certainly a change in popular feeling about the Queen, the Theater shows it, and the difference is remarkable. On the Accession Day 'God Save the King' was received with rapture and waving of hats and encored, a few hisses quite drowned and when they called for 'God Save the Queen' they were hissed down directly. . . . *John Bull*[16] has had some amazing droll things in it, Brougham is quite furious at it . . .

. . . I know nothing else to write, so adieu. I may perhaps add something tomorrow morning before I go. Adieu.

George Street Friday morning [February 2nd 1821]
I have nothing to say, but I am setting off . . . The debate in the House of Commons last night certainly went very much against the Queen—so says Tierney, and W[illia]m who came home at nine o'clock hungry as a hawk. He cannot quite get rid of his lumbago, Caroline makes a great bother about it, as you may imagine. He is very good humoured and amiable. The Queen seems to me *dished*, yet I think Ministers had better have her put in the Liturgy, as I am told for certain the King has no objection—it seems to me to signify so little . . .

Broadlands Papers

[15] Probably wife of Thomas Hope (1770–1831), of Deepdene, Surrey. He collected marbles and sculpture; caricatured with his wife by Dubost as 'Beauty and the Beast'; author of *Anastasius*, *Household Furniture*, and other works.

[16] A notorious Sunday newspaper which violently attacked the Queen and her supporters.

Meanwhile Emily had sent a copy of the newspaper *John Bull* to her brother and was anxious to know what he thought of it.

> P[anshanger] Wednesday [*c*. February 1821]
>
> Tell me if you received the 'John Bull' and if it amuses you—there are certainly very good things in it, and I believe it will drive B[rougham] mad if it goes on, for he is very thin-skinned . . . The 'John Bull' is amusing, for you see it is not written by a common hack, but by some man who knows society. Theodore Hook[17] denies it, but is strongly suspected and they say Croker[18] gives articles. It's true enough that some of the Whigs have been so foolish as to talk of making a subscription, but I hope it will be dropped—*cela prête trop au ridicule* and how foolish they would look after it was done—if she was off with it to Bergami when it was done and live publicly with him, of which nothing is more probable. . . .
>
> Broadlands Papers

For some time, Emily Cowper, who like her mother was something of a matchmaker, had been trying to find a suitable wife for her bachelor brother; and towards the end of 1820 and in the early months of the following year, she was busy singing the praises of a certain Miss Jones. The reader may be somewhat taken aback at Lady Cowper contemplating such an obscure person as a suitable bride for her favourite brother; but the young lady was a niece of Lady Tierney,[19] wife of the eminent Brighton doctor who was doubtless in Emily's good books for having to some extent cured her nerves and her parent's unfortunate addiction to drinking. Be that as it may, in February she was certainly urging Frederick to come to England and have a look: 'She is', she told him, 'very young and probably may be formed to anything, has a good temper and has been very regularly,

---

[17] Theodore Edward Hook (1788–1841) was in fact the founder and editor of *John Bull*.
[18] John Wilson Croker (1780–1857), politician and man of letters.
[19] Lady Tierney was Harriet Mary, daughter of Henry Jones of Bloomsbury Square.

strictly and religiously brought up . . .'; furthermore, she had a fortune, not quite what Sir Matthew stated it to be, perhaps, but a good one, and 'no train of vulgar relations'. Altogether, Miss Jones was worth a visit to England!

Other family news was that George was tired of going on circuit in the North of England and was anxious to leave the Bar in order to devote his life to writing and the stage: '. . . his heart is in Drury Lane, and he thinks of nothing but plays and epilogues, and prologues,' wrote Emily. 'This may be idle,' she added sagely, 'but what is there better than being happy in one's own way . . .' To all this Papa had to be reconciled and that reconciliation his daughter was determined to achieve.[20] Meanwhile brother William was being foolish in the House of Commons. On the 13th of February a member named John Smith had moved for the restoration of the Queen's name in the Liturgy. Lamb had replied with an inconclusive speech that satisfied no one. In his view a Queen Consort had an inherent right to have her name put in the Liturgy; however he thought that the Queen should have conceded the point so as to allay present animosities. Indeed, the Crown, the Queen and the House ought each to concede something in the cause of peace. Nevertheless, William expressed his determination in deference to the opinion of a large majority of the people to vote for the motion.[21] Emily had no use for that sort of 'splitting hairs', as she told Fred two days later.

Panshanger, Thursday Feby 15th [1821]
. . . I don't like W[illia]m's speech (on Mr. Smith's motion), it is twaddling and foolish, speaking on one side and voting on the other, splitting hairs. I am not for the Queen, God knows, but I think he has run aground about it. When you differ with *your party* about trifles, it is better to hold your tongue; the other side look to great questions and not slight differences or else 200 people would not have been found to say that it was a pity the Ministers acted so hastily about the Liturgy, when you will hardly find ten of them in private who will not say it was ill-advised and that it would have been better to leave it alone.

[20] Lady Cowper to Frederick Lamb, Panshanger, Feby 12th [1821]. Broadlands Papers.
[21] There was a majority against the motion of 120.

Ld C[owper] and I and George went Tuesday to Hatfield, a party given for the bride[22] to make her appearance. She is pleasing mannered and tolerably well-looking but clumsy . . .

Broadlands Papers

At the opening of Emily Cowper's next letter, she begins by laughing at the antics of her brother George,

London Friday February 23rd 1821

. . . who enters so warmly into B[rougham]'s quarrel as to be furious with me his own blood for *reading* 'the John Bull', altho I proved to him I had nothing to do with Papa's taking it in (and never heard of it), and that it was better for me to read it and burn it, than to let the servants at Whitehall keep it. *C'est comique*, George's vehemence. B[rougham] would have done anything to annoy him (if the Devil in the shape of Mrs B[rougham] had not cut his claws) and now George is frantic and furious at his getting a little well deserved abuse in a public paper for his public conduct which he himself owns is rather doubtful, and this with heart and soul and *real* feeling on the subject, he fears B[rougham] will *shoot himself*. All my eye and Betty Martin, taking abuse and gain altogether, he has made a very good bargain, a silk Gown and 3,000 a year. Who would not stand a little fire for such a return . . .

Papa is very well, but hankers after the King and longs for Brighton: he rides me more tightly than did the Old Man, poor fainting Sinbad, and gets drunk without falling off which is worse. After three weeks entire seclusion at Pan[shange]r, I came to Town at length, when Papa has the conscience to meet me and propose going to Brighton for a month—*figurez vous*—I utter a piercing shriek like that exhibited on the stage in a scene of horror. No, thought I, let me remain and ruin myself in London like a gentleman (I mean in money matters) for everybody cries misere and Ld C[owper] talks pathetically sometimes on that tack, but the truth is that we are very well off—there are arrears certainly,

[22] Frances Mary Gascoyne, daughter of Bamber Gascoyne of Childwall Hall, Lancashire, had married Viscount Cranborne, afterwards 2nd Marquess of Salisbury, on 2nd February, 1821. They became the parents of the Prime Minister.

but he has such resources and all the balance is restored by omitting to put money in the sinking fund, which is really nonsense for a person with such expectations as he has ... Canning's object, some people say, in going abroad, was to make Ministers feel the want of him—if so, they say he has competely succeeded.[23]

Broadlands Papers

[Tuesday, February 27th, 1821]

... Ld Normanby[24] also called upon me. He is lately come from Brighton, and says that Court is too comical. Ly C[onyngha]m giving herself airs, and throwing herself about like Dolalotta, and the King épris like a boy and walking about between her and P[rince]ss Augusta.[25] The Queen is going to take Cambridge House, Leopold having at last refused her Marlborough House. He has kept her in suspense three months, and now writes her word it would offend a certain Personage,[26], as if he cared about that when he went to see her, that's the shabbiest Ass! ![27] ...

Ld Gower[28] tells me a report today that the Queen had seen some Physician, I think Baillie, and that he said hers was a dangerous time of life, and that he thought she ought to take care of herself, and had advised her going *to Spa*. This looks to me like a preparation, I believe you will have her at Frankfort before long. The thoughts of a Whig subscription[29] was quite

[23] Canning had gone abroad to avoid being involved in the Queen's affairs. He had resigned from the government in December 1820.

[24] Constantine Harry Phipps, Viscount Normanby (1797–1863), succeeded his father as 2nd Earl of Mulgrave, 1831; created Marquess of Normanby, 1838.

[25] Princess Augusta Sophia (1768–1840): daughter of George III.

[26] The King.

[27] That is not quite fair, for after all Queen Caroline was Leopold's mother-in-law and he might well wish to call on her out of respect to his late wife, Princess Charlotte.

[28] George Granville Leveson Gower, Earl Gower (1781–1861), succeeded his father as 2nd Duke of Sutherland, 1833.

[29] Earlier in the month, the 'Big-Wigs' had suggested the setting on foot of a voluntary subscription on behalf of the Queen, by which it was thought that several hundred thousand pounds would be raised. In view of this Brougham advised Caroline to decline the provision, but she was naturally mortified on learning that the Whig subscription meeting was a hopeless failure, and blamed Brougham for tendering bad advice. A week or two later she made up her mind to accept the parliamentary provision that she had just refused. Aspinall, *Brougham*, p. 120.

given up. It was absurd, impossible. I give the D[uke] of D[evonshire] great credit for having refused the proposal at once. *Il a du Caractère*, I really think, and is much improved lately, very decided in Whig Politics, but not mad. He is acting very well now, giving parties once a week, and dinners continually, and civil to every body . . . When the King was at the play, [illegible] Jokes were attempted, one man in the front of the Pit cried out how is Lord Conyngham, your Majesty. The Opera is likely to be brilliant, all the old subscribers taking boxes, and the King to have a State Box always kept for him, where our old Box was, and his Private Box underneath, I suppose for Lady C[onyngham] to sit in . . .

Broadlands Papers

Tuesday, February 28th [1821][30]

Our Queen has taken Cambridge House, and means to try an establishment and parties. Leicester Stanhope[31] is off again, but the decided acceptances are—Duke of Roxburgh[32] Master of the Horse, a man 78 years old, residing in Scotland, and Lord Hood[33] is her Chamberlayn, and Lady Hood[34] one of her Dames d'Honneur, these are settled; *nous verrons*, who else she will have. B[rougham] is gone out of Town, wretched at *John Bull's* attacks, he seems to have no philosophy on the subject . . .

Broadlands Papers

Meanwhile a letter had been written on the King's behalf to the Queen suggesting that she should be granted a yearly income of £50,000 on the express condition that she did not call herself Queen of

---

[30] So written, but the 28th of February, 1821, was a Wednesday.

[31] The Hon. Leicester Fitzgerald Charles Stanhope (1784–1862) in September 1823 offered to go to Greece on an English Committee in aid of Greek Independence; joined Byron at Missolonghi, January 1824; returned to England in June 1824, bringing back Byron's body; succeeded his brother as 5th Earl of Harrington in 1851.

[32] James Innes, 5th Duke of Roxburghe (1736–1823). His age in 1821 was therefore eighty-five, not seventy-eight.

[33] Henry Hood, 2nd Viscount Hood (1753–1836).

[34] Jane, daughter of Francis Wheler of Whitley.

England or assume any title attached to the English royal house, and further that she should never return to this country. Though this offer was subsequently declined, Caroline at first returned a foolish, ill-written letter of thanks, that covered her with ridicule. As can be imagined, Emily Cowper was soon writing to Frederick about it.

Friday March 9th [1821]

... Everybody is here talking of ... the Queen's letter. The Ladies are coming down from their High Horses. The Queen's letter is quite ridiculous and absurd, as far as I hear stated, for a copy I have not yet been able to see. They say it is not at all of a piece with her late proceedings, all low and thankful, obliged to the King for the money, obliged to the people and, *by the way*, hopes he will put her name back in the Liturgy. In short, the substance comes out much to this. Her friends look blank, and it's all her own doing and writing, ill-spelt and without help or consultation; *elle est folle voilà tout! ! !* The other news is that Tierney wants to give up the lead, says nobody minds him, and he is sick of politics. People beg him to continue for want of a better, but he says he cannot.[35]

Broadlands Papers

From Emily's next letter it is clear that what she had written about Lady Tierney's niece had interested Frederick sufficiently for him to have asked for further details. Again she urged him to come to England for an inspection. When at Brighton, the two families frequently dine together; when in London, the Tierneys and Miss Jones go to all the Almack's Balls on Lady Cowper's list; so in either case a meeting could very easily be arranged. Then she turned to other topics of the hour; Sir Walter Scott's latest novels, Lady Jersey's folly in visiting the Queen, and lastly the tragedy of William and Caroline Lamb's only child, Augustus, who though now in his teens remained mentally a child; and a child with embarrassing habits, for he was wont to romp half-dressed into the drawing-room when the nurse or a maid was setting it to rights, tumble her over and sit upon her.[36] It was indeed a sad case.

[35] In fact, George Tierney did not give up the leadership of the Whig party until the following year.   [36] Cecil, *Melbourne*, p. 193.

. . . I like Kenilworth,[37] tho' part of the things you say are true; the end is horrible—I cried my eyes out . . . I will order Ivanhoe[38] for you, but I think you must have had it. Papa has agreed to George leaving the Law, and he has handsomely given him his Chambers. G[eorge] seems quite happy and says he will be quite well off and comfortable. He means to be a *Littérateur* or I believe as you say a bad manager, but what can people do better than be happy?

I must say that I cannot be sorry to see the Queen so fallen, and Ly J[ersey] hampered with having visited her, '*cela me fait rire*'. She will be obliged to appoint a time for going there as soon as she comes to Town, which she has been trying to avoid all this time, and then of course she will be invited to dinner, and made much of. She put off going last time she was in Town by saying she was ill, and thinking *many* people would have called there before her return; but in this she has been disappointed. However she says nothing to me about it . . .

Augustus certainly goes on in a bad state, and Lee[39] has a bad opinion of his case, but I have not mentioned him lately, because I think they none of them know anything about it, and whether he may recover or die, or live and be an idiot, is quite uncertain. The last would be the worst effect, and I think appears to my mind the most probable, but it also is very possible that any day a fit might kill him. His fits have been lately rather less violent owing to the treatment they pursue with him, hardly any meat and leeches upon his head every tenth day; but in the end this must hurt his constitution . . .

Broadlands Papers

Tuesday March 13th 1821

. . . Papa is very well and comfortable . . . W[illia]m does not look well and is not well. He has had a Lumbago a good while and that foolish wife makes him be cupped continually which does not cure the Lumbago but makes him look fat and white. I am sure it cannot be good. How can he be such a fool, as ever to

[37] Sir Walter Scott's novel, published this year.
[38] Published in 1820.   [39] The doctor attending the boy.

be doctored by her? I would manage my own health, if I let her have her way in everything else. The Fool has a Man to magnetise Augustus every morning. The Man who is the greatest Charlatan I ever saw has persuaded her that he shall conjure his fits away, and draw off the obnoxious fluid which produces them with Metallic Tractors; she and Lee quarrel about it every day, but he is a miserable wretch and stays on in spite of everything.

We think of going to Brighton for a fortnight at Easter to please Papa, I should like meeting you at Paris much better but there are difficulties . . .

Broadlands Papers

(Taken from a copy made by the late Lord Mount Temple. The original cannot be traced.)

In her next letter to Frederick, Emily made fun of the eccentric Lady Jersey, whose enthusiastic espousal of the Queen's cause was a source of amusement to many of her friends.

. . . Ly J[ersey] is in a state of sub-irritation, but we keep on good terms. She has been to see the Queen, and from her own statement seems to have talked a deal of nonsense to her—but it don't signify. The King was at the Opera yesterday and highly applauded (Papa in attendance),[40] he sat between the Dukes of York and Clarence, to the latter of whom he never addressed a word. I am just opposite, so that I commanded his position . . .

Broadlands Papers

1821 March 27th

. . . I sadly fear Madame De Lieven is going, I cannot really say how sorry I shall be to lose her, she is so clever and agreeable. I have no fancy for Princess Esterhazy, she is so odd, says such strange things and appears so improper, which I cannot endure . . .

[40] He was a Lord of the Bedchamber.

I must fill my letter with another story. Ly Harrington[41] wrote to the D[uche]ss of Bedford[42] for her Play Box. She sent the note down to the Duke, he wrote for answer 'The Old Cat cant have it.' The Ser[van]t took it to the D[uche]ss's door, who could not let him in just then, so she said to the ser[van]t, take the Duke's answer to Ly Harrington, so it went just as I tell you. How comical! Johnny [Bedford] should not be so jocular. What excuse can be made?

Broadlands Papers

What made things worse was that Tavistock, the Duke's eldest son by his first wife, had married the Harringtons' eldest daughter! What excuse could be made, indeed!

Tuesday [c. March 28th 1821]

... The Queen is a sad drab, there is no doubt, but the whole business on the part of the King has been terribly mismanaged. I suppose it will not last long now. However, I am not personally so interested, as I am off for Brighton Wednesday. I find this staying in London at this bad time of year made me ill and nervous, so the best thing is to be off directly. Ld E[gremont] has good-naturedly lent me his house, and Papa will be all the better for it, as he has been having lately one little ail after another, all produced, I verily believe, by London in this season. Ld C[owper] will follow so soon as he is free ... Minny goes with me ...

Broadlands Papers

So off went the Cowpers with old Lord Melbourne to Lord Egremont's comfortable house in Brighton, where they stayed for about a fortnight, returning to George Street early in May.

[41] Jane, daughter of Sir John Fleming, Bt., of Brompton Park, wife of the 3rd Earl of Harrington.
[42] Georgiana, daughter of the 4th Duke of Gordon, second wife of the 6th Duke of Bedford.

London, May 3rd [1821]

Returned to Town as you see and also this morning from Court, and tonight we are going to a party at Carleton [sic] House, and Ld C[owper] went to the Levee yesterday, so you see we are quite Courtiers. The King is uncommonly gracious. Many people say he is only civil to Opposition to frighten Ministers; this may be an object, but I don't think it is the whole. I really think he is grown quite happy and good humoured and some of it overflows towards his old friends, and I believe he really feels gratefull towards any of the Opposition who have not been to see the Queen . . .

Ly Conyngham evidently has the greatest influence and is indefatigable. She always talks of herself as of an Opposition lady and says, my friend Lord Grey. Besides this every womanly feeling is roused to vengeance for I find some time ago Ly Cas[tlerea]gh[43] refused to receive her, I suppose to invite her, saying she could not think of receiving the King's Mistress. Now this was absurd, for whatever Ly Hert[for]d was to the King, Ly Conyngham is, and it is nonsense to try and make a distinction because the former was her relation.[44] I suppose Ly Cas[tlerea]gh judged ill of the different interests and thought the former would still preponderate, or else, which is possible, that she acts too much from impulse and temper to be a Courtier, even if she would. This Mde de Lieven told me and I never heard it till the other day.

Friday Morning [May 4th]. The ball at Carleton [sic] House was very brilliant, and very dull, as such things are, nothing enlivening but the two rival Ladies Hert[for]d and Conyngham meeting and bristling up, and the King trying to carry it off.[45] Every body on the watch to see something, the Ministers all cross. The King very civil to all, there seems to be a general amnesty, for Leopold was there, and the D[uche]ss of Bedford tho' she had been to the Queen. I believe she forced herself upon him at the drawing room today. Ly Conyngham magnificent, never

[43] Lady Amelia Anne Hobart, daughter of John Hobart, 2nd Earl of Buckinghamshire, and wife of Robert, Viscount Castlereagh, afterwards 2nd Marquess of Londonderry.

[44] Lord Castlereagh's mother was Lord Hertford's sister; she was Lady Sarah Frances Seymour, daughter of the 1st Marquess of Hertford.

[45] For Mrs Arbuthnot's account of the ball and the King's absurd behaviour with Lady Conyngham, see *Mrs Arbuthnot*, I, pp. 91-2.

were such jewels, and the family pearls which she talked of last
year have increased greatly, the string is twice as long as it was,
and such a diamond belt, three inches wide, with such a sapphire
in the centre. By the way I must tell you the history of it. The
Cardinal York[46] left it to the King to be added to the jewels of
the Crown. The K[ing] in a fit of parental fondness gave it to
P[rince]ss Charlotte; when she died, he sent to Leopold for her
jewels, saying they belonged to the Crown. Leopold, *qui n'aime
pas rendre les bijoux*, as Mde de L[ieven] says, answered that he
could not bear to part with anything which had belonged to her.
The K[ing] insisted, upon which Leo[pol]d gave in, said he
would present them *au Roi comme un Hommage*. The King saying
that in particular he must have this stone for his Coronation as it
was to go in the Crown—when lo and behold here it has appeared
in Lady Conyngham's waist, *la ceinture de Venus* . . .

By the way, I am very glad to find Ld Palmerston[47] has done
himself such credit by the talent, discretion, and temper he has
display'd during all this time and if Hume[48] has not managed to
reduce the estimates, he has at least reduced the Secretary at War,
for he has grown as thin again as he was.

The Queen has written a letter with her own hand to the King,
asking him what dress she is to wear at the Coronation, applying
to his known taste and she leaves him in doubt whether she
means to appear as Queen or as a spectator.[49]

Broadlands Papers

Lord Palmerston had been having a trying time at the War Office
where he had had to withstand Mr Creevey's economy campaign, and

[46] Henry Benedict Maria Clement, Cardinal Duke of York (1725–1807),
second son of Chevalier de St George or 'James III' and Princess Clementine,
daughter of Prince James Sobieski. He bequeathed the Crown jewels, which
James II had taken with him to France in 1688, to the Prince of Wales, afterwards
George IV.

[47] Henry John Temple, 3rd Viscount Palmerston (1784–1865), Secretary at
War at this time.

[48] Joseph Hume (1777–1855), Radical M.P.

[49] 'The impudence of this woman is beyond belief. It would have been well to
have sent her word to appear in a white sheet.' *Mrs Arbuthnot*, I, p. 92.

the onslaught of Joseph Hume, who had forced the appointment of a Committee to enquire into the disproportionate cost of collecting the revenue. This had much embarrassed the Government, for the Committee had reported in Hume's favour. It may well be that the Secretary at War, thus pestered, had not been much seen at Almack's recently: but even if that were so, Lady Cowper, 'with a bright, attentive eye for his career'[50] had evidently not forgotten him when she expressed her joy at 'the credit' he had done himself 'by the talent, discretion and temper he has display'd during all this time . . .'

But the news from London was not exhilarating: Emily had a heavy cold; Augustus had had a bad fit; George had unspecified complaints that worried him; and William had the gout and was far too fat. But Papa was the worst of them all, for he had been taken ill from eating too much 'sturgeon and Cutlets with onion sauce', and also, one suspects, from the wine that had washed them down; furthermore, he had been very much put out by his doctor ordering him to dine at seven o'clock and go to bed at twelve—'and today I told the brute that I had no appetite and could only eat for my dinner two wings of a chicken and a piece of plum pudding and he said it was quite enough!!'[51]

Friday May [should be June] 8th 1821

. . . We are just returned from Salt Hill. I am better for my jaunt, and Papa is a little better for the change of air, but not much. He is certainly weak and ill and in very low spirits. He is broken within the last few months, there is no concealing from oneself, yet he had so strong a constitution that one hopes he may pick up again. Tierney don't think him ill to signify, but I am afraid he is no great conjuror. The number of deaths we have had lately too affect Papa's spirits and make him think ill of himself . . .

The King is quite well, wonderful man as to constitution.[52] The Courtiers say the Coronation will be the 10th of July and that afterwards he will go to Ireland. The King dines with D[uke] of Devonshire on the 14th and so do I and Ld C[owper] and the 13th the King has a Child's Ball, to which Minny and I go, and Ld

[50] Guedella, *Palmerston*, p. 106.

[51] Lady Cowper to Frederick Lamb, London, Tuesday, 22nd [May 1821] and May 28th, 1821. Broadlands Papers.

[52] George IV had recently had a nob cut out of his forehead.

C[owper]; but think of the impudence of Her Majesty giving a party that same night, and has invited me and numbers of people who like me have never visited her. What a fool she is to subject herself to receiving such rebuffs for nobody will go. The Card is written by Lord Hood, and I suppose Wood's wise head conceived the plan.

Broadlands Papers

Emily's pessimistic accounts of her old father's health evidently alarmed her brother, for a few days later she wrote to reassure him. Then she passed on to other topics.

Tuesday, June 12 [1821]

... The Coronation is at last fixed for the 19th of next month and the Household have received their orders to follow the King to Ireland afterwards ... Ly C[onyngha]m has taken Lady Heathcote's box so as to be exactly opposite to him whenever he goes to the Opera, never was such love before! *c'est touchant*, he never takes his eyes off her! only eats what she eats and drinks out of the same glass, but I think I told you this before. He is perfectly well again and his head healed up.

I shall take Minny and W[illia]m to the Childs' Ball Wednesday, and Thursday dine at D[evonshire] House ...

I hope you like George's Catullus,[53] we admire it here very much and the Litterati compliment him highly. I think he is delighted with its reception, and it has cured all his little ills and aches. Some of the verses are very pretty and the notes show so much variety of reading and really he has managed very well to step lightly over improprieties. Ld C[owper] admires it all very much and only regrets he did not take a little more time to look over some of the verses here and there and change a word for one which would have sounded better. ...

Broadlands Papers

[53] George Lamb's translations of the Poems of *Caius Valerius Catullus* had just been published in two volumes. It was to be savagely attacked in *Blackwood's Magazine* in August (ix, pp. 507-16).

In the next letter we hear of the Duke's great dinner to the King at Devonshire House.

Friday, June 15th [1821]

I hear from Ld C[onyngha]m that leave is sent to you, but perhaps you may not come yet, as I see they are afraid of too many foreign Ministers being here at one time. As far as Papa goes there is no reason for your hurrying, as I am quite easy about him, for the present . . .

Yesterday was the long expected dinner at D[evonshire] House. It went off remarkably well and was very brilliant, the King in excellent humour and spirits but suffering from the gout. He made a great fuss with [illegible], was very kind indeed, made me sit by him the whole time and made Ly Cas[tlerea]gh, Ly Harrowby and many others envious.[54] He asked a great deal about you, said he was afraid you found Frankfurt dull and so forth. I was rarely bored between him and the D[uche]ss of Kent[55] but I was pleased to provoke Ly Salisbury[56] and many others. The whole set out of the Duke's was very magnificent, quite in princely style. The King said my William was a remarkably pretty boy and Minny beautiful. His Childs' Ball was the day before and was a very pretty sight and very well managed.[57] I am grown quite to doat upon the K[ing] he said so many kind things about Mama, with tears in his eyes. The Queen had her party on Wednesday, and was in high spirits—Lady Jersey, Tavistock,[58] and Milton[59] represented the Aristocracy, and the first of these

[54] As wives of ministers, they would look askance at the King's marked favour to a prominent Whig lady. Lady Harrowby was Lady Susan Leveson Gower, daughter of Granville, 1st Marquess of Stafford and wife of the 1st Earl of Harrowby.

[55] Victoria Mary Louisa, Duchess of Kent (1786–1861), widow of Edward Augustus, Duke of Kent, mother of Princess, afterwards Queen, Victoria.

[56] Lady Emily Mary Hill, daughter of Wills, 1st Marquess of Downshire, wife of James Cecil, 1st Marquess of Salisbury. She was burned to death when the west wing of Hatfield was destroyed by fire on the 27th of November, 1835.

[57] For Mrs Arbuthnot's account, see *Mrs Arbuthnot*, I, p. 101.

[58] Lady Anna Maria Stanhope, daughter of Charles, 3rd Earl of Harrington, married in 1808 Francis, Marquess of Tavistock, afterwards 7th Duke of Bedford.

[59] Mary, daughter of 7th Lord Dundas, married in 1806 Charles William Viscount Milton, afterwards 5th Earl Fitzwilliam.

said she looked remarkably well, *so well dressed*, but she is very sore on the subject and has got [in] a sort of mess with the Duke of D[evonshire] because he would not let her come to his party last night. The Queen said a comical thing, that the King's party and hers were like two rival Inns on the road, the George and the Angel. Report says, but I don't know how true, that she has written to the King to say that she acknowledges that she has no right to be Crowned unless he likes it, but that she has a right to sit at the Banquet, and that nothing but force shall keep her away . . .

The King said he hoped I would not go to Brighton till he was there, and make a point of coming when he was. He said he thought to be there late in the Autumn—see what favour I am in!! . . . Ld C[owper] he was very civil to also, to George and Mrs Lamb I think a little distant, and W[illia]m and Caro I did not see him speak to. He says since his operation he finds it is a very great happiness to be free from pain . . .

Broadlands Papers

Meanwhile, preparations for the Coronation went ahead, though many, including William Huskisson, doubted if it would take place this year.[60] But, when Lady Cowper went to see the preparations for the banquet and in the Abbey, she felt convinced, as she told Frederick, that it would take place in spite of anything that the Queen could do. She was also full of the party at Devonshire House; and presumably her brother was still interested in Miss Jones, for she was careful to tell him: 'I got the D[uke] of D[evonshire] to ask Sir Mathew and Lady T[ierney] and Miss J[ones] to his party last night which delighted them. She is really a nice girl but I hate the little Doctor, he is so pushing.'[61]

And now the King was to show his favour to the Cowpers in a form they would be certain to appreciate, for he appointed their eldest son, Lord Fordwich, to be one of the Pages of Honour to hold his train at the Coronation. Indeed, if the Tory and obviously biased Mrs

[60] Lady Cowper to Frederick Lamb, June 19th, [1821]. Broadlands Papers.
[61] Lady Cowper to Frederick Lamb, George Street, June 22nd, 1821. Broadlands Papers.

Arbuthnot is to be believed, all the pages were chosen from Opposition families: 'and all selected by Lady Conyngham'. This latter statement is almost certainly untrue, though it does seem that some families were affronted at being approached by the Sovereign's mistress instead of by the Sovereign himself.[62]

George Street, June 26th, [1821]

It is a very nice thing for a boy, an epoch in his life, and a way of seeing the whole thing with perfect safety. I found every place was to be applied for and that the K[ing] reckoned it as a Compliment; so, as he has been so excessively courteous to me lately, I was glad to pay him a compliment also. I wrote an official letter to Bloomfield[63] to be laid before his Majesty, who as he answered was much gratified. I only state all these particulars to show that I do nothing thro' la Conyngham. I think that base and you know me however well enough to make this explanation unnecessary. Ld C[owper] is delighted, which would surprise you (knowing his former radical ideas) if you did not also know his extreme pride in his Children and pleasure in everything that shows them off.

Papa is quite overjoy'd and H[enry] Cowper is delighted. I wish I could dress up Minny in Fordwich's Cloathes and send her to personate him; she would be sure to do the thing so well and to be always in her place.

Since I have seen all the forward preparations in West[minste]r Hall and the Abbey, I can have no doubt of the thing taking place, but there is still an idea of that sort about. It will certainly be very fatigueing but the King is stronger than they think . . .

I cannot make out what the Queen will do, but her friends talk big and say her rights she will stand by, and so forth. If she stands out I suppose they will be obliged to appoint some box for her to see the whole thing and this would be a good way of getting rid of the business. I am told she is going to give another party . . . The Queen falling in amongst us has been quite an apple of discord. The Ministers, as you may suppose, abuse us all mightily and say we court Ly C[onyngham] in forgetting their

[62] *Mrs Arbuthnot*, I, p. 199.
[63] Benjamin Bloomfield, 1st Baron Bloomfield (1768–1846): Keeper of the Privy Purse and Receiver of the Duchy of Lancaster, 1817; Irish peerage, 1825.

courting of Lady Hertford!—and run at the King whenever they have an opportunity. It's a comical world we live in! . . .

Broadlands Papers

George St., Tuesday June [should be July] 10th, [1821]
. . . This is what I make out from Tierney of the King's plans. The Coronation on the 19th early in the next week, a Levee, Drawing-Room, and a Grand Ball, and a day or two afterwards to Brighton; from thence he will sail to Ireland. His horses (in number 25) are already gone. This Irish Journey will take no more than three weeks and then they will all come back again and I suppose go to Brighton.

Sir M. and Ly T[ierney] and 'X' dined yesterday at Whitehall, a very fine dinner for really Papa does manage his dinners better than anybody in London. The Girl is very pretty and was much admired and a very very nice gay little thing, not the least vulgar. They keep her monstrous strickly [sic] and I think she seems to look forward with great pleasure to this Irish Jaunt and to having three weeks of balls and racket. I have a *little party* on Thursday next and have invited them—tho' I think him so odious, I hate his vulgar figure, medically proud, and, I think, ignorant.

Ld and Ld Gwydir [sic] are charming; he is so amiable and good-natured and has got such credit for his liberality and all his arrangements. I am sure the whole thing will be a dreadful bore and I wish it were well over, but it is impossible not to go and see it. I cut the Peeresses and go in Ld Gwydir's [sic] box, where we shall have every convenience of accommodation and each Lady may bring a Knight which is better than sitting all day next to some strange Peeress one never saw before. I have chosen George Fortescue[64] for my attendant which is a great favour for places are much in request. I believe we are to embark at Vauxhall in full dress, Feathers and Diamonds and streaming ringlets, and to land in Cotton Garden and so slip into the Abbey, but to get out will I am told be the difficulty.

Lambton is just returned from Paris. He says poor Napoleon's

[64] Perhaps George Matthew Fortescue (1791–1877) of Boconnoc, Cornwall and Dropmore, Bucks., second son of Hugh, 1st Earl Fortescue and Hester, daughter of George Grenville and sister of George, 1st Marquess of Buckingham.

death[65] seemed to make no sensation; without approving or admiring the Man there is something very melancholy in the close of his career—after such a brilliant situation as he might still have been in. He appears to have behaved with great patience and fortitude. Tierney says it is not an unusual disorder, that he has known several people die of it.

Broadlands Papers[66]

Friday, 20th [July 1821]

The Coronation was yesterday and we are all delighted with it. We found it very fatigueing and the whole might very easily have been curtailed one half; but, however, we have outlived it and so has the King, but he looked more like the Victim than the Hero of the Fete. I really pitied him from my heart, several times he was at the last Gasp, but then came a cheering draught in the shape of a look from Ly C[onyngha]m who sat near me, and it revived him like Magic or Ether. I was in the line of fire so I had a full view. When he put on the Ruby ring he cast up a most significant look at her, but I could not well make out whether the look meant, I will wear it for your sake, or, after the Ceremony I will give it you *pour tenir Compagnie au Saphir*, which was in full display, and must have nearly put out Leopold's eye when the sun shone upon it. I rather imagine this last was the true interpretation.

The great sight was truly beautiful both in the Hall and Abbey, perhaps more from the brilliancy of the Spectators than from the sight itself, but the whole thing was indeed very handsome in the Procession and the variety and beauty of the dresses had a very fine effect. Much of the Ceremony in the Abbey was Monkish and twaddling and foolish and spun out, but the music and applause had a grand effect. He was very well received everywhere, and seemed much gratified and had a complete victory over the Queen, who if she could have been lower than she was before would have made herself so by her miserable attempt of yesterday. Even the Mob and Spectators hooted her away after

[65] Napoleon had died at St Helena on the 5th of May. He died of cancer, which is certainly now not 'an unusual disorder'.

[66] A letter similar to this in parts is quoted by Lady Airlie in *Lady Palmerston*, I, pp. 92–4.

she had been refused at every door and had walked thro' the mob with only Ly Anne [Hamilton] and jostled by all the lowest rabble. Think what a degradation for a Queen, if Queen she can be called. Even Ly Jersey has left her, and the King, who wishes to make an end of all feuds and perhaps from a less fine motive to slap his Ministers' faces by his civility to their enemies, took Ld Jersey's two boys into his train of Pages. So there is a reconciliation. Ld Lansdowne he also made a place for as Constable of Ireland which offends all the Irish, and the Duke of D[evonshire] carried the Orb. If his only motive was to have no more quarrels and to keep well with all parties it would be very wise and right.

Ld Gwydyr has pleased everybody by his good nature and civility to everybody. She is a little too courting of the reigning favourite. I cannot bear the least appearance of that, but I like her much.

Think how stout I must be. I had the night before but three hours sleep between the Bells ringing and the noise. I was in the Hall at 7, and staid there till the end, with hardly any refreshment or rest; there is nothing like my strength after all. I boast to you for I know you think me a weedy thing still.

I am writing in haste so adieu I have no time to say more as my letter will miss the post and I am going to ride with Lord C[owper].

Broadlands Papers

Lady Cowper continued her account of the Coronation a few days later.

Sunday, July 22nd [1821]

I wrote you a very hurried account of the Coronation the next day after it and it is still the general subject of conversation . . . It was indeed a very grand sight, as much perhaps from the brilliancy of the Spectators as from those who were in the procession. The old Prince Esterhazy and the Ambassadors' box was [sic] dazzling with brilliancy, and the P[rince]ss Esterhazy fainted away twice, which Fordwich who was standing next to her in true boyish language reports to have been a *regular sham*; and I rather believe it was for effect, as she never changed colour. A great deal of the Ceremony was very beautiful such as the Champion riding in; but part in the Abbey was flat and tiresome, and I thought it rather shocking mixing up the Sacrament and the Gravest Ceremonies of the Church with all the Vanity and the Jokes and the *Oëillades* and the ring, and the Kiss which he thought he sent her *unseen*.[67] . . .

Tuesday, July 22nd [should be 24th]

We went to a breakfast at Cray[68] yesterday, I carried Ld and Ly Jersey and George Fortescue. It was a good party and gay enough tho' we had several Showers and the day was not very favourable. The Foreigners were in great force as you may suppose . . . conceive the King a week ago having a great dinner of all the Foreign Ambassadors and not asking with them any one of his own Ministers not even Ld Castlereagh,[69] I don't approve that sort of way of proceeding; it is miserable to show petty slights. The K[ing] is to go to Esterhazy's Thursday after the Drawing-Room,[70] and on Friday to dine with the Duke of Wellington, and afterwards to go to the Duc de Grammont and Lady Ossulston's grand Ball at the Almacks Room, where there is to be a magnificent supper in the rooms below stairs and the King to have a Supper in our Tea-room[71] . . .

I see nothing but an Embassy for you and so far when I talked to him at D[evonshire] House I said what a bore F[rankfur]t

[67] For Mrs Arbuthnot's much fuller account of these events, see *Mrs Arbuthnot*, I, pp. 106–9.

[68] Lord and Lady Londonderry had a house at North Cray.

[69] Castlereagh had in April succeeded his father as second Marquess of Londonderry. It was presumably force of habit that made Lady Cowper still use the title by which he was so widely known.

[70] The Drawing Room was on Thursday, 26th July.

[71] 'At night the King dined with him [Duke of Wellington], was in high good humour and afterwards went to a magnificent ball given at Almack's by the Duc de Grammont, the French Ambassador Extraordinary. Nothing could be finer; the ladies had all nosegays given them as they went in, and everybody was dressed in their finest clothes. The Duke of Wellington wore his *St Esprit* given him by the King of France, which is said to be worth 25,000£ and Lady Londonderry told me she was worth 24,000£. The King again spent the whole evening by Lady Conyngham's side.' *Mrs Arbuthnot*, I, p. 112.

was. He will go off on the 29th or 30th to Brighton and from thence sail to Ireland which will not make an absence of more than four or five weeks. After that he returns to Brighton and then he said he hoped I would come there, and this would very well suit our arrangements, or I would make it suit them, if you liked it, otherwise we should not naturally go there till Oct[obe]r or Nov[embe]r. I hope in your next letter to hear *when* you come exactly . . .

Papa is quite well and as stout as he was two years ago . . . I am very well, and very flourishing, and stood the fatigue of the Coronation better than almost any body . . .

Broadlands Papers

Wednesday [July 25th 1821]

. . . The Children going to Panshanger two days ago had the trunk cut from behind the Carriage somewhere near Essendon . . . One is sorry to see the state of demoralization spreading so far from London. We are consulting Lavender and hope to get at the offenders; three men who live near Barnet and are supposed to be the same who cut off Johnson's trunk. It is supposed that the post boy was in league with the Thieves . . .

Parl[liamen]t will not be up till the 9th. Ld Gwydyr is to attend on the King at Holyrood House, and she[72] goes in a lodging at Edinburgh. The K[ing] will be accompanied by the same suite he had in Ireland, with the exception of the Chamberlain.

Thursday July 25th [should be 26th]

. . . I hope you will not move from Frankfort at present and that you will have received my other letter in which I announced the Duke of W[ellington]. He goes early in next month as soon as Parl[iamen]t is up, and promised to write to you to let you know of his coming[73] . . . People are very much going out of Town. However we shall have one more Almacks. Ecarté is played everywhere and in the small room at Almacks; it is good

[72] Lady Conyngham.
[73] The Duke left London for a Continental tour on 3rd August.

enough in itself but it hurts Society and I think people play too deep.

Broadlands Papers

Monday July 29th [1821][74]

... The Duke of W[ellington] whom I saw last night at Ly Glengalls says he expects to set off about the 8th.[75] On his return we have made an engagement that he should come and see us at Panshanger and meet the Countess.[76] This should be about the end of Sept[embe]r or beginning of Oct[ober]. We have given up all our plans of tours and intend to remain there till Nov[embe]r, when we go to Brighton; but next Spring Ld C[owper] says positively that we shall go to Paris, so bear this in mind ... Papa saw the King the day before yesterday who was very kind to him and asked a great deal about us all, and Papa had the opportunity of saying *what we settled* which was so far so well and was answered as I expected with civil speeches and so forth and nothing positive;[77] he was very good natured to P[apa] but is I am told in general rather in a bad temper and hates the idea of this Scotch trip ...

This book of O'Meara's[78] as you may suppose makes all the Ministers furious and they and Chateaubriand swear it is full of lies—this I don't think. Of course there is a strong bias in the Doctor, and Buonaparte was angry and irritated, but I daresay the foundation of the whole is true and that all the conversations did take place. There is a sort of Character in what B[uonaparte] says which could not have been imitated and which must be original tho he may perhaps in transcribing have given more

[74] So written, but July 29th, 1821, was a Sunday.

[75] As already stated, he actually set out on 3rd August.

[76] Madame de Lieven.

[77] Old Lord Melbourne and all the Lamb family were anxious to get Frederick an Embassy.

[78] Barry Edward O'Meara (1786–1836) had acted as surgeon to Napoleon at St Helena until he was dismissed in 1818 for intrigues with the prisoner. Subsequently he wrote pamphlets against Sir Hudson Lowe, and had just published a book entitled *Napoleon in Exile; or A Voice from St Helena*, recording conversations with Napoleon and attacking both Lowe and the Government for their treatment of him. It naturally created a profound sensation.

force to some of the things or to a degree altered them. Whatever it is, *c'est un livre qui fera du bruit dans L'Europe et du mauvais sang*; evidently B[uonaparte] talked to him on all these subjects with a view to publication and knowing that he kept a Journal . . .

We went yesterday pleasuring to Richmond and dined at the Castle—a family party, George and Caro and Papa who enjoy'd it very much. He is in very good spirits and quite well, all but weakness.

Broadlands Papers

Tuesday, July 31st [1821]

. . . The King sails immediately as it is said to Ireland, and talks of Hanover afterwards but I hardly think this journey can take place this year. He ought to have delay'd going and have given us a Grand Fête or two in honour of the Coronation for I think it is not handsome towards the foreigners who came here to give them nothing, and that the only two fêtes given on this occasion should have been by two foreign Ministers, Grammont and Esterhazy.[79]

. . . I am afraid this will be a bad time for you to talk of retiring, you had better have an Embassy first [illegible], the Hague or even Madrid—*qu'en pensez vous*—but we shall have time to think of all this now I hope to see you so soon . . . Caro G[eorge] goes tomorrow to Spa with the Duke to meet the D[uche]ss of D[evonshire].[80] She is to stay there a little while and then go to Paris with her. The K[ing] wanted the Duke to go to Ireland but he turned a deaf ear which I think was wise (as I told him). I am not for people being too coming; *Let the Whigs be civil* and nothing more—I say—it is far wiser and looks better not to be too courting.

Broadlands Papers

No letter from Emily Cowper to Frederick Lamb can be found for the next six weeks. No doubt she was constantly expecting her brother's return. In the interim Queen Caroline died and it is much to

[79] Esterhazy's ball had been on July 26th, and Grammont's on the 27th.
[80] Her mother.

be regretted that we have no comments from Lady Cowper on this momentous event.

Her last letter of the year was written in late September.

Pans[hange]r Thursday September 19th [1821][81]

... Papa was fidgetty today, and I was obliged to give up my own barouche and [illegible] this fine day to go poking in his Chariot and pair; and moreover he was determined to be an hour too late, but I bear his whims with great equanimity, thinking all the time what a good lesson it is for the Children, and does them more good than a Sermon an hour long. I really think there is no practise so good for Children as that of humouring an old Man. Caroline was as usual full of bother. W[illia]m very amiable, but I think not happy ... Augustus looks very ill and strange. I am sure his intellects are affected ...

Broadlands Papers

Shortly after this, no Embassy as yet being forthcoming, Frederick Lamb arrived in England for an extended stay. In consequence there were no more letters from his sister until early in the following year.

[81] So written, but September 19th, 1821, was a Wednesday.

CHAPTER V

The Lambs, the Conynghams
and the King

IN MID-DECEMBER 1821 the Cowpers were guests of the King at the
Pavilion;[1] before the month was out they were at Panshanger for
Christmas and the New Year. In January, Emily gave her annual
Ball, which as she wrote to Fred on the 17th, 'went off delightfully and
Minny's dancing was much admired'.[2] Later in the month the whole
Cowper family returned to Brighton; and there, according to Madame
de Lieven, there was a *contretemps*, for one of the Conyngham sons
who was engaged to an heiress with £40,000 a year had the temerity
to fall in love with Minny Cowper. That was indeed awkward! 'She
likes the young man', the Princess told her friend, Prince Metternich;
'but she is afraid to encourage him, because that would upset the marriage and put her out of favour at Court. The young man, too, is
anxious not to annoy his Mother. So, on both sides there is a struggle
between love and discretion.' [3]

What truth, if any, there was in Madame de Lieven's tattle, we cannot say; but Lady Emily Cowper returned heart-whole from Brighton,
and no son of Lord and Lady Conyngham was married that year!

In February the George Lambs went to Ireland, for he was about to
stand for the Duke of Devonshire's borough of Dungarvan in Co.
Waterford. The kindly Hart had lent them his Irish seat, Lismore
Castle . . . ' Being now in full possession of your Castle,' wrote George
gaily soon after his arrival, 'I think a line or two due to you to tell
you how pleasant it is after a journey, and how well I should be if I
had not drunk a whole bottle of port on my arrival which has given

---

[1] *Greville Memoirs* (1874), I, p. 49.

[2] Lady Cowper to Frederick Lamb, Panshanger, Thursday [January 17th,
1822]. Broadlands Papers.

[3] Princess Lieven to Metternich, the 26th [January 1822]. *Lieven-Metternich
Letters*, p. 149.

me a little goutishness. This however I shall soon get rid of. I got here at a little after seven last night, not quite easy at travelling in the dark, which was occasioned by a wheel coming off . . . We have now a prospect of everything smooth at Dungarvan . . .' [4]

This spring the Cowpers were constant visitors to the Pavilion, where Frederick was also a frequent guest.[5] In April Fred left for Paris, where he anxiously awaited the Embassy to which his diplomatic services certainly entitled him.

Brighton, April 26 [1822]

Here we are all in favour *mon ami Gil Blas tu es bien á la Cour*! Our party the other night was hot and dull as may be, but when one basks in the smiles of the Sovereign what more can be wanted! He was very gracious to us all, to me in particular—and to Lord Lansdowne. He talked to him a long while and I thought Wellesley Pole[6] looked very glum. He was the only Minister amongst all the Whig lords and ladies. Today we are invited to dine with the King to Papa's great delight. I see L[o]rd Harrowby's [illegible] come down here. I suppose he is come to see what is going on, for I dare say the idea of L[o]rd L[ans]d[own]e's being well with the K[ing] is very alarming to Ministers, tho' nothing is likely to come of it now. He may when an opportunity presents take advantage of it. At all events I dare say the K[ing] likes to coquet and to frighten his Ministers as he is angry with them for having refused a Prebend to Sumner[7] one of the Conyngham tutors. L[o]rd Liverpool came down here to remonstrate and the K[ing]

---

[4] George Lamb to Duke of Devonshire, Lismore Castle, Sunday, Feby. 9th 1822. *Chatsworth Papers*, 815, 1.

[5] *Mrs Arbuthnot*, I, pp. 147–8, 150.

[6] William Wellesley-Pole, 1st Baron Maryborough and 3rd Earl of Mornington (1763–1845), son of 1st Earl of Mornington and brother of the Duke of Wellington, took additional name of Pole on succeeding to cousin's estate; Master of the Mint with seat in Cabinet, 1814–23; created Baron Maryborough, 1821; succeeded to Irish Earldom of Mornington, 1842.

[7] Charles Richard Sumner (1790–1874); tutor to sons of the Conynghams who presented him to the King: George IV offered him in 1821 a Windsor canonry, to which Liverpool refused to agree. On this issue the Government threatened to resign. Sumner subsequently became Bishop of Llandaff and Dean of St Paul's, 1826; Bishop of Winchester, 1827. His brother, John Bird Sumner (1780–1862), was made Archbishop of Canterbury in 1848.

slapped [*sic*] the door in his face. To make the case better they gave it afterwards to a friend of his, Stanier Clark.[8] But this he did not care about and he was much affronted for he had already given it and they made him retract.

I am in rude health, always out in the air, but I don't like the idea of a hot dinner and a hot evening after it. The Band plays beautifully and for a thing in bad taste one must also allow that the rooms lighted up are very handsome—all the gold and glitter and bright colours makes it[9] look like an enchanted palace.

Broadlands Papers

During Frederick Lamb's stay in England before his departure for Paris, he had had ample time to meet and become acquainted with his sister's protégé, Miss Jones; and it must now be regretfully recorded that the young lady had not found favour. Indeed, the gay Ambassador had formed quite other plans for his future by showing a marked preference for one of far more exalted station than Lady Tierney's niece, none other in fact than Lord and Lady Conyngham's daughter, Lady Elizabeth: so Emily, undaunted by her past failure, now resolved to do everything possible to promote this suit.

Sunday night May 12th [1822]
You will be surprised at my delay in writing, but I always hoped to have had something to tell you, and that I should have had some conversation with the Lady, but the beauty is surrounded by Dragons, like the heroines of old, there is no getting near her or speaking to her. Sunday I gave her your letter, which evidently she was delighted to receive. Monday I could not get a word, but she squeezed my hand. Tuesday she did not appear. I was to have rode with her, but the day was bad. Wednesday the old one wrote me word that she was going to Almack's so I went, but they never appeared. I found afterwards that the young one was ill and she has never been out since—it was the nettle-rash. I have seen her today but always surrounded by her Dragons, so

[8] James Stanier Clarke (1765?–1834), domestic Chaplain to the Prince of Wales, 1799; Canon of Windsor, 1821. Wrote naval history and Lives of Nelson and James II.   [9] The Pavilion.

that we could not say a word, but evidently she feels in great kindness with me, and I told her I should go and see her again in a day or two—and as soon as she is permitted to go the first fine day, we shall ride together . . .

The King is not well but a good deal better. He has still, however, pain in his arm, though the quantity of Wilson[10] he has taken is extraordinary. He talks of going on Wednesday and Friday to Drury Lane and Covent Garden. She[11] has behaved rather kinder to him lately, and been often to see him, *un peu de froideur* now and then is not perhaps amiss, par[ticularl]y as he has no resources at hand. He talks soon of removing to the Cottage . . . Caroline [Lamb] had been so long restrained by your presence that she burst forth like a volcano as soon as you was gone, and has kept burning on ever since. There have been nothing but storms with her servants and one day with Papa, but nothing to signify; it only made him nervous and she was ashamed of herself. William went into the country with her Saturday, so he wont have a pleasant time of it. I had no idea that your presence had been such a restraint to her. Jack [Milbanke] and she had one quarrel, and he said that he thought she would have beat him. The *charming* Doctor Roe has left the house, never to return; she kicked his door open, threw a looking glass at him, and a bottle and poured a jug of water over him. Her ser[van]ts say she has been quite drunk for a week. I fancy it is all because people do not come to visit her and do not praise or think about her novel. One mad freak I thought rather comical. She heard on Friday that Mrs Fox Lane was brought to bed, so she came home and strewed her ante-room with straw, at least desired the ser[van]ts to do so. When W[illia]m came home he began damning and swearing, upon which she came out and said: 'Mrs F. Lane is brought to bed, and why should not I'—think of the joke it has been to all the servants! Was there ever such an absurd person? . . .

Broadlands Papers

Unfortunately the pursuit of Lady Elizabeth Conyngham was rendered the more difficult by the fact that she was not well, so the persistent Emily was forced to penetrate to her bedroom.

[10] Possibly a medicine or powder prepared by James Arthur Wilson (1795–1882), physician to St George's Hospital, 1829–57.   [11] Lady Conyngham.

... She says she likes you very much, and thinks you the most agreeable person she knows, but that she had not thought of you marrying, that her Mother had spoken to her sometimes about her encouraging you and saying she ought to take care what she did, but that she had always answered that she liked you very much, and thought you very agreeable but nothing more. In short this is my view of the subject. I think she certainly likes you but is afraid of her family and therefore there is nothing to do but to wait and leave it to time. She was rather shy at speaking to me as you may suppose and we were interrupted in a very few minutes by the arrival of the old one[12] and during those few minutes we had Francis's[13] head at the door and Ld Cony[ngha]m like a boxer in his shirt and breeches only, so you may suppose what a flying conversation it was, but I hope to hear more from her when we ride together ... I wish I could have had a few minutes more with her but I shall go on next time we are together. I go to the play with the Madre[14] and her excellency[15] tonight to see the King, and again on Friday; so I think what a Courtier I am. The Girl is not able to come out yet but will in a day or two.

No sooner had this much been written than there arrived a letter from Frederick, anxiously asking for news of Lady Elizabeth. But Emily had none and, continuing her letter the next day, she turned to other topics.

Friday [May 17]
... We are all to go down to Richmond for 2 or 3 days at Witsuntide and Ld Cowper says he will be of the party and Ly C[onyngha]m will come for a day says she. The King is sighing for the Cottage and anxious to bring in the Opera House ball next week, that he may not be delay'd by it. A King sighing for a Cottage sounds like a moral reflection—here it is not *exactly*

---

[12] Lady Conyngham.
[13] Lord Francis Conyngham, afterwards 2nd Marquess Conyngham, Lady Elizabeth's brother.
[14] Lady Conyngham. [15] Presumably Madame de Lieven.

that. I hope he may go soon, and then he will get tired of that and be more anxious to go abroad. For your sake I wish this *very much*. I believe almost as strongly as Mde L[ieven] does—for the advancement of her ambitious passion, I should say quite, only that I believe her whole heart and soul are wrapped up in it as much as if it was real love and not make-believe. Mrs Lamb resides chiefly at Richmond with a Parrot and other animals—out of harm's way, *bonne petite* but not amiable.

Panshanger Papers

Two days later Emily was able to report that Elizabeth Conyngham was 'a little better' but looking 'thin and pallid and is not strong enough to go out much . . .' [16] and on the 23rd she turned to other topics.

Thursday, May 23rd [1822]

. . . The King has a grand dinner today for the Prince and P[rince]ss of Denmark.[17] There is a party in the even[in]g we are asked and I suppose it will be large for Ld and Ly Jersey have a Card. Mde Lieven thinks of nothing but the Country and Richmond; we are all going there for Whitsuntide. Ld Cowper Duke of Wellington &c . . .[18]

Panshanger Papers

Early in June the Cowpers were with the Conynghams guests of the King for Ascot races, and this gave Emily another opportunity of a further talk with Elizabeth Conyngham.

Thursday, June 6th [1822]

We returned today from *the Cottage* or as they call it now the *royal Lodge*. It is a beautiful place and I think the drive we took

[16] Lady Cowper to Frederick Lamb, Sunday [May 19th 1822]. Panshanger Papers.
[17] Prince Christian of Denmark (1786–1848) and his second wife, Princess Caroline of Schleswig-Holstein-Augustenberg (1796–1881). *Mrs Arbuthnot*, I, p. 174.   [18] *Mrs Arbuthnot*, I, p. 165.

yesterday for three or four hours in Windsor Park and by Virginia Water the most beautiful thing I ever saw, it is like the Cumberland Scenery, all the plantations feathering down into this great Lake which spreads in various directions. Monday we went down, Tuesday our whole day was wasted away in the Ascot race stand, yesterday was very pleasant indeed and today we walked about a little before we set off. Ly C[onyngham] and daughter did not go to the race[s] today but she forced the K[ing] to go very much against his inclinations, who wanted to pass the day as yesterday driving her about in a little Poney Chaise; but I think as he was expected on the course it was perhaps better to make him show himself there again; but I dont wonder he prefer'd yesterday for the Poney Chaise was charming, so convenient and so pretty and such pretty little Poneys . . .

The King is in good spirits and very good humour and I think looks happier than at Brighton but any thing *so tender* as he was the first day I never saw before. Mde de L[ieven] was as usual very courting and bustling. The K[ing] has a Ball on Friday the day after the Drawing room. He looked very well but he still complains of gout and is not free from pain.

We had one quarter of an hour conversation but as usual provokingly interrupted. She[19] asked me what I had said to you. I said that I believed I had nearly said what she desired and that I supposed it had not pleased you for that you had sent me another letter to deliver to her which I had no opportunity of doing for some days and that then upon the *receipt* of *mine* you had written to desire me not to give it at all. I said that I wished she would write a few lines herself, which I think she seemed half inclined to do, but said she did not know what to say, and that she thought now you was at Paris that you very likely thought no more of it. I said quite the contrary that you wrote me word that you *thought* of nothing else but her. Now we were interrupted but I was glad to have got in that little bit of conversation. She is really a very nice Girl. I also said to her that perhaps if she could not make up her mind to write that she might soon have an opportunity of seeing you on the Continent and explaining herself. She said she was afraid not, but whether this was a doubt about the Journey altogether or of seeing you I had not time to ask.

[19] Lady Elizabeth Conyngham.

Friday [June 7th]

... The K[ing] returns to Town Monday. Thursday there is a D[rawin]g room and Friday a Ball. Shall I send you Walter Scott's book the fortunes of Nigel,[20] there are many Characters well drawn—but I think it is not interesting.

Panshanger Papers

Meanwhile the pleasure-loving King was anxious to make a tour on the Continent, mainly for his own amusement, a plan of which the Liverpool government strongly disapproved.

Tuesday, June 11th [1822]

... I believe the K[ing] is expecting *every day* his Courier from Vienna to hear the Emperors plans and to fix his own upon it.[21] Francis [Conyngham] says he really dont know what to say about it, that one day he thinks it will take place and that the next he thinks it will not. One thing I believe is certain that the Ministers are rather against it, disliking the money part of it and thinking he will only go abroad to make a fool of himself.

Panshanger Papers

Friday, June 14 [1822]

... I have heard nothing more of the Journey, but it is quite clear that Ministers are much against it and therefore I think it will be prevented somehow or other. The Duke of Wel[lingto]n told me Wed[nesda]y at Almacks that he thought at this time of distress that it would have the worst effect possible for the King to go spending his money on the Continent part[icularl]y as his object was only amusement and that he would not go to Hanover[22] ...

The Drawing Room yes[terda]y was tolerably brilliant and I should say rather thin. The King seemed quite well. There is a

[20] *The Fortunes of Nigel* was published in 1822.
[21] Relative to the conference that was to be held on the Eastern question.
[22] The King had been to Hanover in the previous year.

party tonight at Carleton House [*sic*][23] and we expect that on Monday there will be a Childs' Ball. After these I believe he returns to the Cottage. If he does not go the Voyage, I suppose he will take a Sail pour passer le tems [*sic*] . . .

W[illia]m dined with us on Wednesday with the Hollands. He seems in better spirits and very amiable. She[24] is odious and ill, always rageing or fainting, and Aug[ustu]s is in a state worse than ever; he was in fits all yesterday and they called in all the doctors in London. The critical time seems to be coming on and very awkwardly too. She is frightened about it . . .

Panshanger Papers

George St., June 30th, 1822

. . . We dine tomorrow at Carlton House and are to have Mathews[25] after dinner at nine o'clock, when Minny is to come with the Gwydyr Children and Maria Cony[ngha]m . . . I fancy his Majesty is not in a very good temper. I suppose he don't know what to do this Summer, but I have no idea of there being even a chance of the Voyage still taking place tho' Mde L[ieven] contrives to flatter herself. She is grown rather tiresome with her perpetual trips to Richmond . . . She cut us upon the Water Party last Friday an hour before we set off, and I have not forgiven her yet, as we had the D[uke] of Wel[lingto]n on purpose for her, and it would have been quite awkward if fortunately when we were all prepared and going to start I had not bethought myself of sending off for Mrs Arbuthnot, who instantly put on her bonnet tucked up her petticoats and came off to us in Clanwilliams[26] Cabriolet.[27]

. . . Tuesday [July 2nd]—Carlton House was pleasant enough. Mathews excellent. The K[ing] very much amused with several

[23] *Mrs Arbuthnot*, I, p. 165.   [24] Lady Caroline Lamb.
[25] Charles Mathews (1776–1835), comedian. He was noted for his amusing mimicry of other actors in various parts.
[26] Richard Francis Meade, 3rd Earl of Clanwilliam (1795–1879): Private Secretary to Castlereagh 1817–19; Foreign Under Secretary 1822.
[27] For her description of this water party, see *Mrs Arbuthnot*, I, p. 170.

of his mimickings. We staid there till half past one. The Chol-
mondeleys[28] were there and Strathavon. Eliz[abe]th looks thin
and delicate. Ly C[onyngha]m says in August she shall take her
to the sea somewhere entirely for her health, and live quiet, either
Worthing or Hastings. I had the *innocence* to propose the Isle of
Wight, and I should not wonder if this was the end of the plan of
retirement . . . The K[ing] was very good-humoured, but looks
out of spirits, and I think not very well. I think he is vexed with
being in London and not seeing as much of his Lady as he would
wish, but still I see it rains Bracelets and Jewels and Side Tables.
I took Lady C[onyngha]m yesterday to call at H[olland] House,
which pleased Ly H[ollan]d very much and we had a very agreeable drive . . .

Caroline is more mad and drunk than ever. She had a Consultation of Six Physicians to Augustus because of some plan she
had heard of from France of burning the skull. I believe to please
her they agreed to try it, but with Caustic, upon which she turned
them all out, flew into a rage, abused them all, and threw every
thing in the room at Dr Roe . . .

Papa mismanages himself terribly; ate pickled Salmon for
Supper the other night. There is nothing really wrong about him,
but these continual attacks of Stomach and then dosing must in
the end be very bad for him, and certainly weakens him very much
—It is very vexatious that he will not think a little of his health.

                                              Broadlands Papers

When in July Government opposition forced the King to abandon his
plans for a holiday abroad, he determined to go instead to Scotland.
Emily Cowper suspected that this idea originated in the fertile brain of
Lady Conyngham, anxious for some leisure to take her daughter to the
sea.[29] At the same time there was much speculation in the Lamb family
as to whether the Foreign Secretary would or would not go to the
Verona Congress, for if he did, it was certain that Frederick Lamb,
who this year was sworn of the Privy Council, would be wanted; so

[28] George James, 4th Earl and 1st Marquess of Cholmondeley (1749–1827),
and Georgiana Charlotte, second daughter of Peregrine, 3rd Duke of Ancaster.
Her sister was the wife of Lord Gwydyr.
[29] Lady Cowper to Frederick Lamb, July [13th 1822]. Broadlands Papers.

he must on no account leave his post at Frankfurt where he was Minister Plenipotentiary to the German Confederation. Furthermore, Emily had encouraging news for him relative to Lady Elizabeth Conyngham.

London, Friday July 19th [1822]

... I cannot make out for certain whether Ld L[ondonderry] will go but from all I hear I believe the probabilities are that way, altho' it is not yet completely settled. Mde L[ieven] *thinks* he will, so does ...[30] By the way I sat by him at dinner the other day at Mde L[ieven]'s, and he ... said he should go as soon as the H[ouse] was up, about the 1st or 2nd week of Augt ...

The Girl[31] is certainly anxious to go abroad, and I am sure is very fond of you. She will go out no where and asked me yesterday whether you still thought of those you had left in Engl[an]d, and if you had seen your old Frankf[ur]t favourite, and if you mentioned anything of her in your letters ...

Broadlands Papers

It was about this time that Lady Cowper had a great idea: she would enlist the help of an influential friend to advance Frederick's matrimonial projects. Madame de Lieven should speak to Lady Elizabeth Conyngham on his behalf. At first the plan met with no success but patience was needed!

Friday, Augt. 2nd [1822]

... Last Courier I sent you Tull's Husbandry[32] and little Johnny's new [book][33] but that stupid Ridgway did not send Adam Blair in time. I wish you would tell me what you think of O'Meara for you must have got it long ago. It is amazing how angry it makes all the Ministers and Ld Londonderry is going to

---

[30] Deleted in MS. [31] Lady Elizabeth Conyngham.

[32] Jethro Tull (1674–1741), agricultural writer. The book referred to is *Horse-Hoing Husbandry*, published in 1733.

[33] Presumably Lord John Russell's *Essay on the English Constitution*, published in 1821.

prosecute him for a libel in saying that he was bribed with 30 millions of franks [*sic*] which went to pay for an estate in Ireland. He may be right in prosecuting, but I don't think it signified at all for nobody would believe that, whether he took notice of it or not. Ld Bathurst is very sorry about it and was furious with Ld H[ollan]d for what he said about it in the House of Lords upon the question of the Aliens Bill. They and Chateaubriand[34] and all who are abused in it cry the book down and say it is all lies . . .

This sound project of the Countess[35] has had the same fate as the first as you will have seen long ago by my letters. It is unlucky, but I should not wonder still at something starting up, or the Lady going to Spa or some event, so pray be patient, and do not start away or do any thing in a hurry, only a little patience. They are now in the Country but the Countess will have an opportunity of speaking next Tuesday. She is very friendly and very eager.

Ld L[ondonderry] is going to Paris very soon and Clan-[william] with him. He says they will *not* go on to Vienna, but this I suppose is false. Gwydyr goes with the King in his steam boat. Lady G[wydyr] is gone to Edinburgh to wait for them. Ly O[ssulston] and O[ssulston] are at Worthing and will come to meet me at Brighton in Nov[embe]r. . . .

Broadlands Papers

At last Madame de Lieven found the opportunity to speak, not to Lady Elizabeth, but to her Mother. The result was inconclusive.

Friday, August 10th 1822[36]

. . . Mde L[ieven] had a long conversation with the Lady[37] the other day. She brought it on very adroitly, saying that she had heard from me, that you was much attached to her. The Lady pretended she could not believe it was serious, praised your

---

[34] François-Auguste, Vicomte de Chateaubriand (1768–1848); French statesman and writer; Ambassador in London, 1830–4.
[35] Madame de Lieven.
[36] So written, but August 10th, 1822, was a Saturday.　[37] Lady Conyngham.

talents and agreeable qualities, and so forth, but objected to your morals; said a person who had led that sort of life, could not have a real attachment. The other was up to all that, said that she liked a Husband who had seen the World, that they always made the best Husbands, and this very beaten subject was canvass'd in all its bearings. Then she said that she did not think E[lizabeth] had any idea of your having the least preference for her ... Now, therefore, it appears to me, that there are but two things to be done, either to let it rest for the present, or for you to write a proposal to E[lizabeth] not implicating her, but merely making an offer which she may show to her Mother, and then it will bring the subject to the point. The Lady took her opportunity of talking high morality to Mde de L[ieven], but my idea is that she so wants a greater parti and that she has not courage to say so, and therefore puts it on a false ground ...

Broadlands Papers

With the King's departure for Scotland, the Conynghams made hasty preparations to take Elizabeth for her much needed holiday by the sea.

Monday, Aug 12th [1822]

... The girl was very amiable but does not look well, and they are now going to the sea quietly for a week or two till the K[ing] returns. They have not quite fixed where, but the object seems to be for the girl's health and to be quiet. When he returns they all go to the Cottage, and then afterwards to Brighton. Pray don't be impatient and dont think of giving up your place at present, you keep me in hot water by always talking of it. I am sure it is so imprudent at this time, and if you only wait a little while I feel so sure that you will have the offer of some other. It would really be a pity to throw away your chance ...

L'accoucheur[38] is appointed privy purse and I am afraid his influence increases daily. The Lady is afraid of him and does not

---

[38] Sir William Knighton (1776–1836) was a doctor and had been physician to George IV when Prince of Wales. In 1822 he was appointed Keeper of the Privy Purse. He was created a baronet in 1812.

like him in her heart. This the C[ounte]ss says she has found out for certain. The K[ing] looked very well and in high spirits at the Greenwich embarkation and everybody says it was a beautiful sight, but I did not go to see it for I had promised that day to go with Ld C[owper] to see the building at Panshanger and he did not like to change the day . . . The K[ing] expects to be back in less than a fortnight . . .

Broadlands Papers

With the King in Scotland, the Conynghams about to set out for the seaside and the Cowpers at Panshanger, one might anticipate a little peace and quiet for these busy restive people in the sleepy month of August. But it was not to be. On the very day the last letter was written, a tragic event threw the whole political world into a ferment, prevented Lady Conyngham from taking Elizabeth away, and made Lady Cowper 'nervous as a cat'. On the 12th of August, the Foreign Secretary cut his throat with a penknife and fell dead into his doctor's arms.

CHAPTER VI

No Embassy for Frederick Lamb

THE SUICIDE of Castlereagh[1] led to an important change in Canning's fortunes. In March he had been nominated Governor-General of Bengal, and in August was on his way to Liverpool to bid his constituents farewell when he first heard of the sad news from Cray. It was at once clear that he was the only living statesman with the necessary qualities to succeed to the Foreign Office and that the King's reluctance to such an appointment must at all costs be overcome.

Lady Cowper, like all the great world, was much shocked at the sad death of the Foreign Secretary. But she was also anxious to see what advantage her brother might gain from the ministerial changes.

Thursday Aug 15th [1822]

This horrid event has shocked everybody and really one can think of nothing else. As for me I have been as nervous as a Cat ever since, and I am always thinking of the horrid situation of that poor Lady L[ondonderr]y who was doatingly attached to him. The account you see in the papers is all or nearly all correct. His friends had all perceived him to be deranged for the last fortnight and in a dreadful state of nerves, dreading conspiracies and so forth, but I think great blame appears to attach to Bankhead[2] for not having watched him more closely and for not having taken more blood from him, but it is always a very difficult case to manage. . . .

We only returned to Town yesterday and there is hardly anybody in Town to see or to know anything from. Mde L[ieven] returns from Richmond today and I am going now to call on Lady C[onyngha]m . . .

[1] Lord Londonderry, but I use the title by which he is best known.
[2] Charles Bankhead, M.D., Londonderry's personal physician.

I saw Ly C[onyngha]m and her daughter, they go tomorrow to Dennisons, where they intend to remain quietly instead of going to the Sea. She seems very eager to come to Pans[hange]r and I have promised to let her know as soon as we are settled there. She says it is quite true that the King thought him mad in his last interview with him and told him so, felt his pulse and said he was in a raging fever, and he promised him to see Bankhead. He talked to the King quite wildly about conspiracies against himself (Ld L[ondonderry]) and reports and plots, and when the King told him he was mad, he requested of him not to tell it to any of his colleagues. Therefore either this poor man cut his throat under the immediate influence of pressure on the brain or from the horror of feeling his intellects going and seeing that people perceived it. It is really a most shocking case! She said the K[ing] never slept the night before he went, from the horror he had on his mind after this interview, and was quite miserable. She does not know, or will not tell what the K[ing] means to do, but I suppose Ld Liverpool will try hard for Canning, and the Duke of York, Wellington etc. for Peel . . .

Friday morning [August 16]
I saw Mde de Lieven last night, she came and passed a couple of hours with me, in great grief, as you may suppose. She is really very miserable and unaffectedly so, regrets his loss very sincerely on every account, but says that lately she has perceived several times a strangeness of manner and an excessive absence which she says he did not use to have. She says the Duke of W[ellington] is expected in England either today or tomorrow.[3] . . .

Pray have a little patience and remain quiet. I am so sure something will turn up for you, and I am so afraid of your giving up your place in a pet or in a hurry and then have to repent at leisure . . .

Broadlands Papers

Lady Cowper's next letter to her brother was written a month later. Her great friend, Madame de Lieven, was setting out for Vienna, where

[3] Wellington went to the Congress in place of Londonderry.

she would see Frederick Lamb and discuss his future. At home Lord Liverpool had stood firm and insisted on the appointment of Canning to the Foreign Office in spite of the opposition of the King.[4]

Pans[hange]r Monday Sepr. sixteenth [1822]

... This appoint[men]t has been done for Canning in a way as little flattering as it was possible, coming in alone and without a step for any of his friends. The way it was managed was in a letter from the K[ing] to Ld Liverpool in which he said he would take him into grace and favour, as if he had been offended and forgave.[5] Canning kicked at this, said he would not be received on those terms, said it was as if the Ladies of Almacks were to give him a ticket and then write at the back, 'Let the rogue pass'! His friends were frightened, soothed him and persuaded him to come off his high Horse and not to stickle about terms, for says Mde L[ieven] had there been any further explanations asked of the King, he would certainly have thrown the whole thing over. This fact is all kept secret, so you must not repeat it nor to Mde L[ieven] unless she tells you first. I suppose she had this detail from the Duke [of Wellington] but I don't know ... But the D[uke of Wellington] was the person who finally prevailed and it was not till after the K[ing] saw him that he made up his mind. He was very anxious of course, as thinking it was the only way of keeping in the present Ministers.[6] He wanted a patch, and there was no other *patch* to be had ...

The K[ing] is very well in health, but has been a good deal worried about all this—he is much quieter now. I am afraid Knighton's influence increases daily—he has given up all practice. ... The K[ing] is now going on to the Cottage and will be at Brighton about the middle of Oct. The Lady and her daughter[7] promised to come to me here in the course of the next fortnight. I don't know whether they will be able to do so, but I thought they both seemed to wish it. Mde L[ieven] tries all she can to give

---

[4] His ministers were much divided on the subject.

[5] The King hated Canning, whom he believed to have had adulterous relations with the Queen.

[6] *Mrs Arbuthnot*, I, pp. 186–92; *Wellington Dispatches*, I, pp. 273–6, 277, 284.

[7] Lady Conyngham and Lady Elizabeth Conyngham.

the Mother a little nerve and Character, which is what she wants so much. If she had any courage she would place herself in a much better light in the world and at the same time make herself and the K[ing] much more comfortable; but this perpetual attempt at saving appearances, and a fear of what may be said, makes her conduct irresolute and foolish and more open to censure. Mde L[ieven] gave her some advice about this, which pleased the K[ing] very much, and she expects that he will talk to her about it in her audience of leave which she is to have soon. They think Canning will get quite a favourite with the K[ing]. Others who know him say not, that he has no manner, no dexterity, nothing courteous, and all his jokes are suited to a *Clique*, who laugh before the words are out of his mouth, and that he is particularly deficient in tact as well as in prudence. I tell you all the different opinions that you may take what you like ...

Broadlands Papers

In her next letter Lady Cowper mentioned for the first time her anxiety for her brother-in-law, Spencer Cowper, who was 'ill and in a weak state of health',[8] and was ordered to winter in Nice. At the same time old Lord Melbourne was causing them anxiety again, 'constantly drinking white wine and slopping broth', until his doctor 'reduced him to three glasses, allows no slops';[9] whereupon the invalid promptly recovered! Spencer Cowper's indisposition had an unfortunate effect; Lord Cowper was so upset at his brother's illness that Lady Cowper was compelled to put off the Conynghams who had proposed themselves to Panshanger for early October.

Pans[hange]r Octr. 7th, 1822

... This was very unlucky as I should have liked very much to see them quietly here and to have heard all the news. Reports are everywhere afloat that she[10] is quite out of favour and her influence entirely on the decline. Mde L[ieven] will tell you what

[8] Lady Cowper to Frederick Lamb, Pans[hange]r, Sept. 26th, [1822]. Broadlands Papers.

[9] Lady Cowper to Frederick Lamb, Pans[hange]r, Sept. 30th, [1822]. Broadlands Papers.   [10] Lady Conyngham.

she thinks about this, but 1 am not inclined to believe it. I think he may complain of want of attention and so forth during the London months, but the country sets it right again, and besides he is so shut up, that he has no other resources, and She knows her interest too well, ever to let him quite slip away. I think the general report of the loss of her favour and influence arises from Canning's appoint[ment] which the world believes she was against, and therefore argue that she can have no power; but this is nothing, for she was certainly for it, and was anxious he should keep these people in from thinking any change would be laid to her door, and that she would get all the abuse of it . . .

W[illia]m came over here the other day and talked to me more openly and more freely about Caroline than he had ever done before; he says he is quite miserable, and does not know what to do about her, that he never has a day's peace, and that her violence increases so much that he is always afraid of her doing some serious mischief to some of her Servants, and that he has written to W[illia]m Ponsonby[11] to say something must be done. He says she is the greatest bore in the world, and that there never was such a temper, because her fits of passion instead of being succeeded by a calm, are only changed for the most eternal crossness and ill humour. He is a *great* ass, for having borne her as he has done, but one cannot help feeling for him just part[icularl]y when it appears that he is not blinded about her, and that he really sees her as she is, for he said a great deal more on this subject, and upon the injury she has been to him, which is too long to write . . .

Broadlands Papers

Meanwhile Lady Cowper had been doing her utmost to advance her brother's prospects—not with any great success, it would seem!

Panshanger Thursday Octr. 17th, [1822]
I am rather in despair about your affairs. I hear Canning is so beset with his own friends and with Lord Londonderry's engagements that he told Ward[12] it was impossible to appoint him to

[11] Lady Caroline Lamb's brother.
[12] John William Ward, 4th Viscount Dudley and Ward and 1st Earl of Dudley (1781–1833); Foreign Secretary 1827–8; friend of Canning.

any mission, which was what he wished. The place of under Secretary appears to be going begging. Lord Binning[13] first refused it because he could not bear to deprive the House of his company, and now Ward after taking a fortnight to consider and asking the advice of all his friends and *no* friends has refused it also. Ld Clanw[illia]m they also want to provide for out of respect to Ld Lond[onderr]y. There is some story about the K[ing] asking C[annin]g to think of him or others say C[annin]g asked the K[ing] if he might be allowed to think of him the first thing, but the result is that they say when they have bullied Rose[14] into sending his resignation Clan[william] is to have it. Now it would have been more fair to have offered it to you and given Clan-[william] Frankfurt, but I suppose he would not have taken it and Berlin is a place I should think you would not like at all . . .

Broadlands Papers

In spite of all the efforts of the Lamb family, Frederick was only offered an Under-Secretaryship, which of course would have necessitated his return to England. His sister wrote anxiously to know how he would receive the offer. Then she turned to other matters.

Pans[hange]r Oct. 24th, 1822

. . . Lady C[onyngha]m and her daughter had appointed to come here last Tuesday, but I believe the K[ing] delayed leaving the Cottage so soon and stopped them. She wrote me some rigmarole of an excuse about Denison going into Yorkshire. George and Mrs L[amb] have been here some time and he has taken such flings at the Wine that I am sorry to find he has got a little gout this morning, but I hope it is nothing to signify. Spencer Cowper has got as far as Paris on his way to Nice, and he is better . . .

Broadlands Papers

[13] Thomas Baillie Hamilton, Lord Binning, 9th Earl of Haddington (1780–1858); Tory M.P. 1802–6; 1807–12; 1814–27; a supporter of Canning; Lord-Lieutenant of Ireland, 1834–5; First Lord of the Admiralty, 1841–6; Lord Privy Seal, 1846.

[14] Sir George Henry Rose (1771–1855), diplomatist; M.P. Christchurch, 1818–44.

To Emily's delight Frederick remained determined not to accept an appointment at home; he was resolved upon service abroad and was anxious for an ambassadorship.

Whitehall, Saturday Nov. 9th, [1822]
. . . I find every body knows of the offer and the refusal, two hours after the Courier arrived . . . I am glad of the offer because I think many people think it a great thing, and that refusing it places you the higher and brings you more into notice as a person whose abilities they would be glad to call into their service . . . Then I hope it will make the K[ing] speak to me on the subject and perhaps give me an opportunity of poking in a useful word and saying what is your real object.

We came to Town yesterday and go off tomorrow to Brighton to Lord Egremont's House for a day to prepare accommodation for Papa and the Children . . .

Broadlands Papers

As soon as Fred heard that his sister was going to Brighton he bade her speak to the King on his behalf.

Brighton Monday Novr. 18th [1822]
I was very glad to get your last letter of the 5th of Nov[embe]r. I always like to be told specifically what to do. I approve your plan and shall certainly do what you desire, but I prefer'd waiting a few days rather than fire upon the K[ing] directly. He is remarkably well and better in health and spirits than I have seen him these two years, and so good-humoured and kind to me that I don't feel the least awkward or nervous at the idea of saying what you wish; for so shy a person as I am, it is astonishing how bold and determined I can be when it is worth while. This makes as odd a mixture as what the K[ing] said of me the other day when I could not fix my attention on his Cards or mark for him right. 'I never saw before such an *indolente* active person' . . .

Broadlands Papers

For a time Emily had no opportunity of speaking to the King of Fred's future, though the Cowpers and Lord Melbourne were frequent guests at the Pavilion.

Novr. 25th, [1822]

... Papa looks very well in the face but he is terribly infirm. ... He has been once to dinner and once of an evening to the Pavilion, and think what he told me he was near doing, meaning to make the agreeable to Ly C[onyngha]m he said, 'Has your Ladyship walked today.' This was all well, but he told me it was at his tongue's end to say, 'Has your Majesty walked today.' The idea of it has made me hot ever since, for we were standing in a circle with Aberdeens,[15] Binnings, and several strangers. Think what the Lady's confusion would have been, as she is so sensitive. She is very amiable, and the Girl always delightful—thin, but in great good looks ...

Broadlands Papers

And when at length the chance of speaking to King George came, Emily did not get any very satisfactory answer, for she was side-tracked by the wily Sovereign.

Tuesday Novr. 26th, [1822]

I had my conversation with the K[ing] yesterday, and I cannot say I am satisfied with it, yet I certainly said all I could say and I hope I did some good. Ly C[onyngha]m to whom I told my intention of asking the K[ing] to speak to me, said it was arkward, and would be so formal to have an audience, and it would be put in the papers and so forth. But she said she would manage it for me in the even[in]g, and she would go away and talk to somebody. She is a good-natured, amiable soul, and did just as she said, and I had half an hour's conversation at least with him. I began by saying that you was anxious to know his opinion of your refusal,

[15] George, 4th Earl of Aberdeen (1784–1860) and his second wife, Harriet, daughter of the Hon. John Douglas, widow of James, Viscount Hamilton, and mother of the 1st Duke of Abercorn.

and that if you had been in England and had time you would certainly have consulted him. He said 'I was quite sure of it—only ask Francis [Conyngham] and he will tell you that I said so' . . . and I said . . . I was anxious that he should speak to C[annin]g as I thought there was no one who had greater claims than you from the kind intentions he had expressed about you for so many years, and all he said to my Mother.

He said this was quite true, that he had first induced you to go into that line, that he liked you, of all things that he wished to see you in a more comfortable appoint[ment]: that he first introduced you to Ld Londonderry, who was very partial to you afterwards on your own merits, and that he could not but think that your refusal had partly been produced by your liking to him, that you felt an unwillingness to owe anything to his adversary, and that *he* could not help always feeling very strongly upon that subject . . . He said he had talked to Canning about you, and said how much he was interested about you. Whether this is true or not, I don't know, but I think it possible. I shall talk to Lady C[onyngha]m upon the subject and put her in our interest by telling her what it is you want. She is a good-natured creature and I think likes us both . . .

Broadlands Papers

Frederick Lamb was evidently dissatisfied with this account of his sister's conversation with George IV, for in mid-December she wrote suggesting that he came over to England directly, when he could see the King and say what he liked.

Brighton Decr. 12th, [1822]

. . . The King never mentions Canning and I think he and his Ministers seem willing to see as little of each other as possible. I expect Mde L[ieven] will be of great use to us, for I never saw anything like her favour. The K[ing] talks of her, longs for her, sighs for her, and seems to think no party and no society can go on well without her; his only dread is her removing to Vienna . . . I think the idea of any new people always worries him—his greatest enjoyment is when we five are squeezed up together at one little table with one candle, one pack of cards, not half counters enough, and hardly any room to stir, *voilà le vrai bonheur*. 2 out of the five stand for four—the other three are thin enough for two—Ly Gwydyr, Francis[16] and I—cannot you fancy us. . . .

Lord Tankerville is dead, so the little o's are as you may suppose in a great bustle[17] . . . Lady El[izabeth Conyngham] appears to have no admirer unless Lord Bingham[18] should turn out to be so . . .

There then follows a postscript:

Since I wrote this I have seen Francis, he says the King talked to him about you, seems dissatisfied with Canning for not having made you a more decided promise, said it was very odd, and Francis seems convinced that he will not let any opportunity escape of talking to Canning about you, and doing something. This being the case I think the affair stands as well as it can do.

Broadlands Papers

On the 16th of December Lady Cowper announced their departure from Brighton on the following day, to the regret, she felt sure, of the King and Lady Conyngham. 'She is a very amiable person', she yet again assured her brother, 'and whenever one is alone with her she has such an abandon—without this I can love nobody . . .'[19] From Brighton the Cowpers went to Panshanger where they stayed until the 11th of January; and from Hertfordshire Emily reported an absurd

[16] Lord Francis Conyngham.

[17] Lord Ossulston had succeeded his father as 5th Earl of Tankerville on December 10th, two days before this letter was written. Lord and Lady Ossulston on account of their lack of inches were generally known as the little o's.

[18] George Charles, Lord Bingham, afterwards 3rd Earl of Lucan (1800–1888), married in 1829 Lady Anne Brudenell, daughter of the 6th Earl of Cardigan. The brothers-in-law became notorious in the Crimean War. Cecil Woodham-Smith, *The Reason Why*.

[19] Lady Cowper to Frederick Lamb, Brighton, Decr. 16th [1822]. Broadlands Papers.

rumour that the King was about to marry Lady Elizabeth Conyngham himself, adding a shade maliciously that she believed she would 'end by being a Vieille Fille instead . . .' [20]

In mid-January, Lord and Lady Cowper were guests of their old friends the Jerseys at a house-party to meet the Duke of York. From Middleton Emily sent Frederick all the news and gossip she could gather from every source.

Middleton, Jany. 13, [1823]

Here we came the day before yes[terda]y, a party for the Duke of York . . . The Duke is very good-humoured and talks by the hour without anyone being much the wiser for such a flux of paroles . . .

My Ball was so beautiful, and has made such a sensation you cannot think. I am sure you will hardly believe how magnificent the room looked, with three large gold Candelabras, and the rich gold coloured damask curtains and Furniture, it is such a good mixture with crimson . . .

The report here is that Bragge Bathurst is out,[21] I suppose to make room for Huskisson.[22] My idea is that if Canning can seat himself fast, he will get out Ld Liverpool, and all that part of the Cabinet and perhaps join Ld Wellesley and the Whigs or some of them. He hates the Chancellor[23] and Peele,[24] but there is no depending upon him in any way. Whatever happens D[uke] of Wel[ling]ton is always sure to be in power, and so he ought for he is far the best of them; but I am told Canning dreads the idea of the Meeting of Parliament and [is] alarmed at the attacks that will be made upon him . . .

Mde L[ieven] writes me word the K[ing] doats upon me. I

[20] Lady Cowper to Frederick Lamb, Panshanger, Tuesday, Jany. 7th [1823]. Broadlands Papers.

[21] Charles Bragge-Bathurst was Chancellor of the Duchy of Lancaster.

[22] William Huskisson became Treasurer of the Navy and President of the Board of Trade, 1823–7.

[23] Lord Eldon.

[24] Sir Robert Peel, 2nd Baronet (1788–1850), Home Secretary. The reader will notice that for some time Lady Cowper persists in spelling the name with a final 'e', and so it was spelt in the family until dropped by the statesman's grandfather because 'it was of no use, as it did not add to the sound'. Lever, Peel, p. 23.

expect that after the meeting of Parl[iamen]t, he will send for us down there. I think he would do so now but that he thought it would worry us, and he is right enough there for so it would. We have, I am sorry to say, worse accounts of Spencer Cowper, not enough to be alarmed, but enough to make one anxious, he has a boil gathering . . .

The Duke of York will not go to Wherstead, he cannot bear the Cannings.

Broadlands Papers

Middleton, Jany. 16th, 1823

. . . Tomorrow we go to Cashiobury[25] and Sunday we shall be at Panshanger. The Duke of York went from here on Wed[nesda]y very good humoured, very gay, and very full of prejudices. He is rather *en froid* with the King, since these new appoint-[men]ts and will not hear of Canning. Ly Granville I suppose to court him had invited him for the 25th but he will not go. 'No, Ma'am I will not go there, Lady Granville is very clever—people say—far too clever for me Ma'am'—this was his speech to Lady Jersey. I wished the Duke of W[ellingto]n to come and meet Mde Lieven next week, but he says that he cannot come as he is obliged to be in town . . . He sent an excuse here for this time, but people say he is more in love than ever with Mrs Arbuthnot. I wish Ly Jersey would make a diversion for she is an odious little woman. The Duke has been unlucky at Wherstead; he peppered Lord Granville's face with nine shots, fortunately he miss'd his eyes, but it has given him a great deal of pain . . .

Broadlands Papers

A few days later the Cowpers were back at their beloved Panshanger, whence Emily wrote to Frederick on two succeeding days. Lord Clanwilliam, who had been Castlereagh's private secretary, and more recently an under-secretary, had just been appointed minister-plenipotentiary at Berlin, a post which it seems Frederick had hoped to be offered. Furthermore, the Government had refused the pension to

[25] The Hertfordshire seat of Lord Essex.

which he considered himself entitled and were fobbing him off with a lesser sum. Naturally both brother and sister were indignant at this treatment.

Pans[hange]r Sunday Jany. 19th. [1823]
We have just got home again from Cashiobury and Middleton; the first was very agreeable, but not so the latter . . . The Lievens come here Wed[nesda]y and stay till Saturday, when they go with a *partie Ministerielle* to Strathfieldsay.[26] I am much delighted to see her as I want very much to talk to her upon your affairs, and to hear what she has to say—as she is too cautious to write much, but she tells me that she said to Ly C[onyngha]m that C[lan-william's] appointm[en]t was a great injustice to you. It appears to me that the best course to pursue is not to be angry, or make any fuss, but to shew that one thinks it a great shame and feel it as a *pass over*. I really don't see that there is anything to be done just at this moment . . .

Broadlands Papers

Panshanger Jany. 20th, [1823]
. . . Today is post day so I am obliged to write, otherwise I should defer it till I see Mde L[ieven] on Wednesday, when she comes here, as she says that she has much to say which her caution prevents her writing, and she mentions having said to Ly C[onyngham] . . . that you was very ill used. She is the best person to employ, as they are all so fond of her . . . I really think it quite a shame that in the face of such a list as you send me, they can refuse the larger pension. I suppose they are so driven for money that they hardly know what to do, but the difference to Gov[ern]m[en]t between the lesser and larger sum is quite a trifle. Ought they not to make you a Knight of the Bath? Tell me what you think of this. Of course you and I think the same on those trumpery distinctions, but might it not be of use as a mark of favour and raise your rank for a future Embassy . . .

Broadlands Papers

[26] Seat of the Duke of Wellington, near Reading.

Let us hope that Madame de Lieven made use of her visit to Panshanger to give Emily all the information which her caution prevented her from writing, for she found her stay anything but comfortable. Her room, she told Prince Metternich, was so cold that she could not hold her pen and she could not write in the drawing room as it was always full of people![27]

Towards the end of January Lord Francis Conyngham visited Panshanger, and Emily then had the opportunity of discussing her brother's prospects with one who really knew what was in the King's mind. As a result she told Frederick that she felt less annoyed both with George IV and with Canning for not having done more for him.

Panshanger, Monday Jany. 27 [1823]

Lord Francis . . . says the latter [Canning] is tormented to death to adjust the different claims and expectations and withal has the pension list full so that he can do nothing which is to burthen that. He says the misfortune is having given Clanw[illia]m Berlin, which has made everybody angry . . . Francis said Knighton was certainly a friend of his, and might have spoken to the King but his Mother or he had not; and that he himself (Francis) thought it much more than he had a right to expect and that it was a great pity he should have it as it made all this difficulty and he is very much inclined to think with me that the promise is *ben trovato* and a Lie . . .

He says Canning speaks very well of you and of your talents and says he wishes that he could have done something for you, but that really his hands were tied. One thing I think you are imprudent about and that is asking for leave to go to Italy, in case you remain at Frankfort, for it is just the thing for C[annin]g to take hold of, and he said to Francis: 'What can be the use of a place which Lamb has been away from so long at home, and at Verona, and then, when the diet is going to meet, he asks for five months leave of absence. . . .'

Lord Cowper thinks you had better get your pension and come home: 1,700, you certainly ought to have after such a list as you sent me, but then the times are altered and the cry of economy

[27] Countess Lieven to Prince Metternich, Strathfield-Saye, January 26 [1823]. *Lieven-Metternich Letters*, p. 226.

is so great . . . Therefore he thinks you would do better to take your pension and come home par[ticularl]y as you have no chance at this moment of any other thing presenting itself: *voilà ce qu'il dit*, and you can *faire des économies* while you are living in Papa's *House*—besides a fair prospect for the future, to look to, if you like. I don't like the idea of you trotting off to Italy now, it would be better to come home and settle and explain all this, and see Lady Eliz[abe]th who I am sure likes you very much. If you think I can help your 1,700 by speaking to the K[ing] I am quite ready to do it, and I have a great idea that we shall be asked there very soon . . .

Broadlands Papers

In February came bad news of Spencer Cowper's health. He 'had broke an ulcer on his lungs' and 'is probably not alive at this time', as Emily told Fred on the 7th. This was correct: Spencer had died on the 1st of February, and his brother was so afflicted by the loss that Emily packed him off to Holland House to prevent him from moping. The death of Spencer Cowper also deranged her plans, as she was engaged to dine with the Lievens to meet the Conynghams and the Duke of Wellington.[28] A few days later, however, the Duke, just back from the Congress, called on Lady Cowper, who seized the opportunity to forward her brother's cause.

Monday, [?10 or 17 February] 1823

. . . He looks much better than I expected, a little thin, but nothing particular, and his deafness I thought nothing. He talked a great deal about you, very kindly, and of C[anning] with his usual frankness; said it was a pity he did not know you better and had not more opportunities of appreciating your talents . . . He said Canning did not know what use might be made of Frankfort with a clever person there to send home accounts, said he advised you to stay on there, that he was sure you might as long as you liked, and that with your talents you were quite sure to have promotion the first opportunity . . . He pricks up his ears at

[28] Lady Cowper to Frederick Lamb, Friday Feby. 7th, [1823]. Broadlands Papers.

the idea of a Brighton party and is evidently very anxious to go there, which amuses me so much it is so very Childish! I said I hoped I should be asked—and with him . . .

Broadlands Papers

(Taken from a copy made by the late Lord Mount Temple. The original cannot be traced.)

Towards the end of February the Cowpers went to Brighton, where the King's head was pronounced to be 'full of politicks, affairs of Spain etc. . . .' so that he never so much as mentioned Frederick Lamb's name![29] Early in March they were back in London,[30] where there was much ill-health; and as old Lord Melbourne was suffering from one of his periodic bowel complaints, Emily determined on an early return to the pure sea air.[31]

Brighton Thursday, March 27th, 1823

. . . We are very comfortable in Lord Eg[remon]t's House, and expect Papa the end of this week . . . We came here on Tuesday and have brought all our Children. The place is very full, and they talk of the Pavilion being gay. The King is to have a Ball on Monday, and a party on Saturday . . .

I have desired Ridgway to send you Caroline's new novel *Ada Reis*,[32] it is a strange farrago; but you may think it worth fifteen shillings to satisfy your curiosity . . .

Broadlands Papers

In mid-April the Cowpers were still at Brighton, but contemplating an early return to London.[33] A week later they were back in the

[29] Lady Cowper to Frederick Lamb, George Street, Thursday March 6th, 1823. Broadlands Papers.

[30] Countess Lieven to Prince Metternich, the 5th [March, 1823]. *Lieven-Metternich Letters*, p. 241.

[31] Lady Cowper to Frederick Lamb, Friday March 14th [1823]. Broadlands Papers.

[32] Lady Caroline Lamb's third novel, *Ada Reis: a Tale*, had just appeared.

[33] Lady Cowper to Frederick Lamb, Monday April the 14th, [1823]. Broadlands Papers.

Capital, where they found considerable political excitement. Canning had for some time suspected, probably rightly, that Lieven, Esterhazy and de Polignac, the Russian, Austrian and French Ambassadors, had been intriguing with Lady Conyngham and Sir William Knighton, who had recently been appointed Keeper of the Privy Purse, to thwart his policy by playing on George IV's antipathy to him; and earlier in the month he had delivered two trenchant speeches in the House of Commons which had evoked sufficient enthusiasm in the Country to disconcert his enemies at Court.[34] Lady Cowper was not slow to report to her brother on these events.

London April 22nd [1823]

... I find people in London all very eager about Politicks. Canning's friends, excusing his Violence in the House, by saying the gout made him irritable. Every body seems sorry for it, except I suppose the Chancellor and Peele [sic]. Our friends are sorry because it makes a breach and they wanted good fellowship and his own friends are very sorry, because shewing this excessive irritability has lowered him very much in the opinion of the House. ...

My Children are all well and so I am myself. That month at Brighton has made me fat, and I intend to take great care of myself to keep well ... Papa is quite well, Caroline more termagant than ever. George more reasonable than usual, but says W[illia]m's speech the other night was bad, such milk and water. I wish he would join one side or the other ...

Almacks is in as great request as ever: there is a dressed ball there after the Draw[in]g-Room tomorrow, but there are few dinners and parties and the Town shows melancholy symptoms of economy. Mde. Lieven gets into Ashburnham House Friday, and intends to have *des petits bals*. Esterhazy has one next Thursday, and the Duke of D[evonshire] on Friday[35] ...

Broadlands Papers

[34] Petrie, *Canning*, pp. 174–5; *Mrs Arbuthnot*, I, pp. 227–8; Ilchester, *Lady Holland*.

[35] The Duke of Devonshire gave a coming-out ball for his niece Harriet Howard, third daughter of Viscount Morpeth, afterwards 6th Earl of Carlisle, who had married the Duke's sister, and for Mary Fox, only daughter of the 2nd Lord Holland. *Mrs Arbuthnot*, I, pp. 229–30.

The reader who has followed sympathetically Lady Cowper's efforts to arrange a match between Lady Elizabeth Conyngham and her brother will understand her annoyance at the absurd rumour that the lady in question was going to marry the King. But judge of her chagrin on learning a fresh rumour which was soon all over the town, that Lady Elizabeth was about to marry the Duke of St Albans' son, Lord Burford who, according to Mrs Arbuthnot, was 'all but an idiot and has been confined!' [36] The outraged match-maker wrote of the report in scathing terms.

Sunday, May 25th [1823]

I am sorry to say that I think this Burford marriage will take place. There is nothing I believe settled at present but I think all they say and do looks like it. The Girl looks pale and out of Spirits, but she sees her Mother wish it strongly and the King too and I suppose she is half persuaded to consent. I am really sorry on her own account for she must repent it some time or other and at present she will be dreadfully abused. Every body says he is very nearly an idiot. I only know him just to speak to and he appears half silly. If she should accept of him we certainly can have no cause to regret it as we must have been mistaken in the opinion we had of her, but I am really sorry on her own account, for she did seem such a nice Girl, but after all the young birds generally turn out like the old ones and having always seen her Mother so interested and so worldly what could one expect? The King is, they say, very anxious indeed for it; he only thinks of her being the *fourth* Duchess in the Peerage and has never seen the Man. I think when he does that he will be a little surprised. I really feel very sorry on Eliz[abe]th's own account, for she must feel ashamed of such a Man, and she never can like him. But without persuasion or compulsion there is so much influence produced on a good heart by seeing the wishes of those you are fond of.[37]

The King is in better health and going very soon to the Cottage he cannot stand on his Leg but [the] Duke of W[ellingto]n is

[36] *Mrs Arbuthnot*, I, p. 237.
[37] See also Countess Lieven to Metternich, the 25th [May] [1823]. *Lieven-Metternich Letters*, pp. 266-7.

very much against the idea of this marriage he says it is a loss of Caste. I cannot express how fond I am of that Man. There is always something so honest and straightforward in all he does and says . . .

Tuesday May 27th

I believe Eliz[abe]th's marriage is settled. I have not seen her for the last three days but I am told she looks pale and low spirited and had tears in her eyes yesterday at dinner at Ly Maryboroughs,[38] yet it is her own doing for except the influence of seeing the wishes of her Mother there is no other employ'd—*il faut qu'elle manque absolument de caractère*—people say they will have only 2,000 a year to live on at present, so that she will really have sold herself to a fool for an empty title—did one ever hear of such a thing . . .

How very glad I shall be when you have your pension and return here to settle, married or unmarried. We shall be so comfortable. I think there is nothing much in the book way . . . Now I am going to order for you Quentin Durwent[39] [*sic*], Tooke on high and low prices[40] and Blakes book on political economy.[41] They are only pamphlets and I am told there are many good things in them and those subjects I think interest you. Blake is a clever Man and our neighbour at Welwyn . . .

Panshanger Papers

Friday May 30th [1823]

Lady Eliz[abe]th's marriage with Lord Burford is quite settled. Every body abuses it but I as a friend take her part. I said if so

[38] Catherine, daughter of Sir James Tylney-Long, 7th baronet of Draycot, Wilts., and wife of William Pole-Tylney-Long-Wellesley, 1st Baron Maryborough, afterwards 3rd Earl of Mornington.

[39] Sir Walter Scott's novel *Quentin Durward*, published in 1823.

[40] Thomas Tooke (1774–1858), economist, follower of Ricardo, Horner and Huskisson, published *Thoughts and Details on the High and Low Prices of the last Thirty Years* in 1823.

[41] Possibly William Blake, *Observations on the Principles which regulate the Course of Exchange, and on the present depreciated state of the Currency*, published in 1810.

sensible a girl could have made up her mind to marry Lord B[ur-ford] I must believe till I know more of him that he is better than he appears. The fact is that he is not an innocent or an idiot but a very raw uncultivated strange Cub, very shy very awkward and odd, but I believe not a bad kind of person. He was good to his Mother and goes out driving with three or four of his Sisters in a shut up Carriage. Lady C[onyngham] looks uncomfortable and ashamed and is aware of how much she is blamed which worries her. But I suppose she was persuaded by seeing the wishes of her Son, of the K[ing] and of Dennison, and Francis [Conyngham] says that he thinks she will give up going out and retire alto-gether, not liking to exhibit him and thinking that he is a sort of person who would like to be quite at home—in short it seems to me a sad concern altogether. Francis is annoy'd at it tho he tries to see the best side and he says his Sister is quite *amused* at Lord Burford's odd matter of fact way of saying things and laughs all the time he is with her. Lady C[onyngham] says that one advan-tage with such a Man is that Eliz[abe]th *sera maîtresse chez elle*. The K[ing] is enchanted at it, but he has not yet seen the Man, only his picture which he says is the image of all the Stuarts for-getting Nell Gwyn[42] poor soul altogether. I suppose he is so pleased at the idea of being no longer worried by Ly C[onyng-ham]'s obligation to go out for *Eliz[abe]th's sake* or by complaints of her prospects having been ruin'd by courtly favour. Lady Bathurst did all she could to break off the marriage and drove Ly C[onyngham] half wild the day it was settled by going and telling her [what] all the world said. I was very glad she did this, tho I should not have liked to do it myself.

The first person Ly C[onyngham] told of the proposal and several days before it was settled was the Duke of D[evonshire]. I suppose she was in hopes to bring him on by it and he told me that if he had not made up his mind *never* to *marry*, that he cer-tianly should have married her, for he admired and liked her better than any Girl he ever saw. He is quite angry at this affair and says, it lowers her completely in his estimation. The Duke of W[ellingto]n also and all their friends in general are shocked. They will have only 2,000 a year to live upon at present so that

[42] The Dukes of St Albans are, of course, descended from an illegitimate son of Charles II by Eleanor Gwyn.

really the advantages are not so very great as to bribe one to bear with such a Man. The Duke of St Albans is of course much delighted to get such a nice Girl to act as Bear Leader to his Cub, and tho there is now only 4,000 a year settled with the Dukedom, he has agreed to settle ten upon taking her fortune which I believe they subscribe for and make out £30,000 or £40,000—where this comes from I cannot make out, but I believe chiefly from the great person.[43] If it was Dennison's there would be no reason for not saying it and the Madre[44] told Mde L[ieven] it was a sum left her by her Grandmother. Now this Grandmother (as Lady Glengall tells me she knew very well) died having collected together a sum of *one* thousand pounds *pour tout potage*, and one little trumpery diamond necklace, so that all the pearls belonging to her and so forth are only other incidents in the farce. . . .

I dined yesterday with Ly C[onyngham] and Eliz[abe]th at the Aberdeens without her *futur* and we are to dine at the Lievens on Saturday with them again without the *Cub*. Ly C[onyngham] refused to let her invite him; does not this shew how ashamed they are of him since they cannot bear he should be seen. One really feels quite sorry to think of such a nice girl getting into such a mess and being *persuaded* to do a thing so disgraceful, and which will certainly make her unhappy all her life. I am besides told that he has by no means a good temper to crown the brightness of her prospects . . .

Panshanger Papers

Meanwhile Frederick Lamb had applied for leave. As appears from the next letter, his sister did not approve that course, but it is doubtful whether she knew the facts. A little time before, Frederick had written to the Duke of Wellington giving him the substance of a dispatch to the allied Courts from the Minister of the King of Hanover, which voiced very different views from those supposed to be held by the King of England. In this dispatch, so we are told, approval was given to the invasion of Spain and the outrageous statement was made that English policy was much hampered by Parliament, but that there might all the same be even greater risk in dismissing the Ministers than retaining them. In these circumstances, it is hardly surprising if the

[43] The King.   [44] Lady Conyngham.

envoy was 'much dissatisfied with the situation'[45] and anxious to return.

Having voiced her disapproval of her brother's action, Emily turned to the burning question of the Burford engagement.

London June 2nd [1823]

... Mde Lieven invited Lord Burford to dinner Saturday in consequence of which Eliz[abe]th had not courage to appear, but they both sent excuses. I really pity her even as much as I blame her, for it must be terrible to have been persuaded into such a thing and then not have courage to make the best of it. Francis [Conyngham] is evidently a good deal vexed at the whole affair, but says the thing is done and therefore they must try to make the best of it, so he laughs at his follies, and tries to improve him. He has got his hair cut, and has persuaded him to leave off a scarlet velvet neckcloth, he used to wear, and to take a red lining out of his Cabriolet. If these oddities were unaccompanied by worse things it would be well, but people say he is very ill tempered besides and is sometimes three days without speaking to any of his family. If so they will be easily disappointed for she and her Mother reckon *at least* upon her having her own way in every thing. They should know that sometimes fools are the most difficult to manage. I think it lowers the Girl terribly in every bodys estimation, to think that she should have consented to such a disgraceful arrangement. People say it has been a good deal managed by Knighton who has always attended the Duke and the late Duchess [of St. Albans].[46]

Broadlands Papers

London Friday, June 6th, [1823]

... Canning has not sent you his leave yet, but he probably will soon ...

The K[ing] is getting quite well and goes to the Cottage Sunday. I am told we are to be invited there Monday or Tuesday,

[45] *Mrs Arbuthnot*, I, p. 238.
[46] Maria Janetta, daughter of John Nelthorpe of Little Grimsby Hall, Lincolnshire She had died the previous year.

also Mde Lieven, Lord Burford and I don't know who else. The K[ing] has seen him and instead of saying as I expected Christ God what a man! is quite pleased with him and thinks him very handsome. I suppose he was quite *determined* to be pleased . . .

Broadlands Papers

Soon rumours were afloat that Lady Elizabeth Conyngham would not marry Lord Burford after all;[47] and within ten days Emily was joyously announcing to Frederick that the Burford marriage was definitely off.

London June 24th, [1823]

. . . Francis [Conyngham] tells me your leave is gone off to you, and Frankfurt given up. So I shall now be anxious to know your next move. I hope it will be homewards, as soon as you can, tho I feel there is a magnet which will attract you towards Florence . . .

The Burford Marriage is publickly declared off. His friends and his Father are excessively angry . . . but the world in general are all delighted. I cannot think how so many people should come to care so much about it. Francis hardly knew what to do, or say, at a great dinner at the Duke of Wel[lingto]n's, when everybody came up to him to wish him joy of its being off, as if it would have been a complete sacrifice of his Sister. Denison is glad and the Mother's glad, and what one wonders now is how the Devil it ever came on, since there seems but one opinion on the subject. The World as they are called are a strange Set, first abusing her and saying she would find no husband, then abusing this Marriage as not worthy of her, and all open-mouthed against him, and nobody knows why, for nobody knows him, and instead of his being an idiot and a fool, it appears he is more of the sharper than the fool, but obstinate, ill tempered and underbred, thinking only of getting Money, and the Duke, they say, tried to cheat them about settlements to take her £40,000 and give them only 800 a

---

[47] Lady Cowper to Frederick Lamb, Saturday June 13th [should be 14th, 1823]. Broadlands Papers.

Year, taking them to live in his own den, with all his Wild Girls. The King is in great health, rides and walks, and is quite recovered, he is still at the Cottage. I have not seen La Madre et La Figlia, since this great event, tho they were in town one day on their way to Denisons from whence they are going back to the Cottage. I think anybody who has a fancy for her now, has a fine opening for a proposal . . .

Broadlands Papers

In spite of the 'magnet' expected to attract Frederick Lamb towards Florence, whoever she may have been, he was in fact bent on returning to England; and, as Lady Elizabeth Conyngham was at last free from her entanglements, perhaps the gay diplomat might avail himself of the 'fine opening for a proposal'. And what of Lord Burford? In 1825 he succeeded his father as 9th Duke of St Albans. Two years later he married Harriet Mellon, the former actress, the immensely rich widow of Thomas Coutts, the banker. Perhaps he was not quite so mad after all!

CHAPTER VII

Lady Caroline Lamb

DURING Frederick Lamb's stay in England of over a year, one event profoundly affected at least a single member of the Lamb family. On the 20th of March, 1824, the Duchess of Devonshire—the former Lady Elizabeth Foster—died in Rome. Fortunately her stepson, the Duke of Devonshire, was with her at the time, and he wrote what words of comfort he could to the Duchess's daughter, Caroline, who was at The Hague with Lady Georgiana Morpeth at the time.[1] Her husband, George Lamb, wrote gratefully to dear good-natured Hart for his 'judicious letter', which had 'a soothing effect upon her mind'.

Whitehall, London, April 12th, 1824

... She has this morning had a better night and though very very unhappy and I am afraid likely to continue so is calm and reasonable. I hope that you will not be delayed by F. Foster so as not to be able to attend at Derby, for I think from some few words that poor Caroline dropped to me she would take some comfort from your being present there.[2] ... Caroline has this morning received a letter from Ld Bristol[3] who in common with all the poor Duchess's friends feels the greatest comfort from your having been there at the time this melancholy event happened ...

Chatsworth Papers 815.2

[1] Lady Granville to Lady Georgiana Morpeth, The Hague, April 15th, 1824, May 1824 and to Devonshire June 15th, 1824. *Lady Granville Letters*, I, pp. 276, 297, 298.

[2] At the funeral in the Cavendish family vault in Derby.

[3] Frederick William, 5th Earl and 1st Marquess of Bristol (1769–1859), the Duchess's brother.

Most of Fred's time in England was spent with his father either at Melbourne House in London or at Brocket. In April his sister wrote to him from Brighton, where she had been pushing his interests.

Brighton, Wednesday [April 21st 1824]

... Our visit [to the Pavilion] went off very well. The King, ill at first with a cold, but cured by a bleeding, and very good-humoured, but the brute did not mention you once. John[4] was all smiles and Lies. She hardly told me a word of truth all the time I was there, tho she was by way of being very amiable and confidential. The Girl I like much for she *sometimes* tells truth. She asked me if you had been offered Spain, as she had heard this was likely ...

Broadlands Papers

Lady Elizabeth Conyngham's question about Spain proved to be a bull's-eye, for very shortly afterwards Frederick Lamb was in fact appointed Envoy at Madrid. Meanwhile, his suit seems to have ebbed and flowed. In May Mrs Arbuthnot recorded Elizabeth's engagement to a 'good-natured rattle', Lord Strathavon;[5] in June that she had rejected him. In August she expressed the view that Lady Elizabeth would end by marrying Frederick Lamb.[6] But Madame de Lieven took a contrary view, as she told her friend Metternich at the time of Frederick's arrival at Brighton this August, '... Talking of him', she wrote, 'I regard his romance as over. The lady is simply a coquette. As I rather suspected this, I advised Lamb to bring things to a head and find out where he stood. The test worked. She wants him to adore her; but she does not want to marry him. As his adoration was somewhat lukewarm, it will not be difficult for him to stop adoring her altogether. So he will be going to Spain; but not for two months.'[7] In September

[4] John in MS., but this clearly a mistake, Lady Conyngham is obviously intended.

[5] Charles Gordon, Lord Strathavon (1793–1863); became Earl of Aboyne upon his father succeeding his kinsman George Gordon, 5th Duke of Gordon, as 9th Marquess of Huntly, 1836; succeeded as 10th Marquess of Huntly, 1853.

[6] *Mrs Arbuthnot*, I, pp. 317, 322.

[7] Countess Lieven to Metternich, Brighton, August 18 [1824]. *Lieven-Metternich Letters*, p. 326.

'CARO WILLIAM'. LADY CAROLINE LAMB

From the portrait after Hoppner at Henfield Place

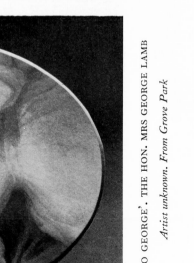

'CARO GEORGE'. THE HON. MRS GEORGE LAMB

Artist unknown. From Grove Park

Mrs Arbuthnot was busy recording that Lady Elizabeth had finally refused him because her family would never consent, even though she liked him better than any one else.[8] How this must have infuriated Emily! So the Lambs were not good enough for the Conynghams, indeed! And who, pray, was Lady Conyngham but the King's mistress and the daughter of a self-made merchant? What a woman to give herself airs!

So ended another of Emily's matrimonial projects for her brother; first Miss Jones and now Lady Elizabeth. The fates seemed unkind to his marriage ventures! But there were other troubles to distract the brother and sister at this time. For many months the married life of their brother William had been gradually deteriorating and things in his household seemed to be coming to a climax. Ever since that unhappy July afternoon in 1824 when Lady Caroline accidentally met Byron's funeral procession on its way to Newstead, her mind had become unhinged to such a degree that at last even her indulgent husband could stand it no longer. A separation seemed the only solution.

The inevitable result was much bad feeling between the Ponsonbys and the Lambs, which the kindly Devonshire did his utmost to dispel. But the task of peacemaker was not easy as a letter that George Lamb wrote to the Duke at this time shows.

London Friday, April 15th, 1825

I cannot help writing you a few lines in consequence of the representation, which I find she [Lady Caroline] has made of your interview with her.[9] We found her on our arrival quite changed from the unhappy reasonable creature which you had represented her, for she had resumed her natural character of violence and threats of all sorts, and now says she is determined to agree to nothing unless William comes back. Of course the only safe method is to believe not one word she says, otherwise Frederick would certainly have some reason to complain of the speeches she has put into your mouth.

You seemed to think it cold that William had gone away and left nobody authorized to settle it.[10] Certainly it would have been

[8] *Mrs Arbuthnot*, I, pp. 332, 336-7.
[9] For Lady Caroline's letters to her cousin, the Duke of Devonshire, written at this time, see *Lady Bessborough*, pp. 282-5.   [10] The Deed of Separation.

so, if he had, but the fact is he left Frederick fully authorized to arrange the whole, and we now I think have much reason to complain that William Ponsonby[11] puts off the whole himself and will not facilitate any settlement. If we are at last forced to take forcible steps the blame will all be on the heads of her own family. The suddenness of William's determination arose from a proposition which had been made her by him and which she was requested to think of at leisure being answered by a letter full of the grossest abuse. It is a [? weird] thing for poor Caroline[12] to be brought from her usual retirement into such a turmoil, but it was impossible not to come up to the assistance of one's family when so sorely harassed and beat . . .

Chatsworth Papers 815.3

For the next few months Lady Caroline remained in her father-in-law's house in London or at Brocket, where, at Frederick's suggestion, some female mental nurses had been engaged to look after her. It could not have been a happy household.

In May, Fred Lamb left England to take up his post in Madrid. He was much missed by his fond sister.

Thursday May 12th, [1825]

. . . Everything goes on at Whitehall as when you left us, no tidings of W[illia]m. Caroline has now turned again to the sickly mood, and says she shall not live and has not eat for four days. However it is very easy to rouze all her energy's by merely disagreeing with her. Dunc[anno]n[13] tells Ly Jersey that W[illia]m Ponsonby is nearly as absurd and as mad as she is. The night before last she went down to the Women and offered them a Guinea if they would show her the straight waistcoat, but they would not hear of it. What an odd thing it is the sort of hankering she appears to have for the Women. I suppose she wants to cajole them. Papa will not hear of their going away, and would I am sure be quite uncomfortable if they were removed . . .

Broadlands Papers

[11] Lady Caroline's brother.   [12] Mrs George Lamb.
[13] Lady Caroline's eldest brother, afterwards 4th Earl of Bessborough.

In June the Cowpers were commanded to Windsor. On her return to London Emily wrote to Fred of the pending separation of William and his wife and of the financial arrangements made for Caroline.

London Tuesday June 7th [1825]
... We went to the Ascot Course Thursday, and then remained till Sunday. Nothing could be more gracious than the King, or more amiable than all the party. He is in greater health and spirits than I have seen him a great while, and in the best humour, with no complaint except a little lameness. Friday we went to the course again, and Saturday to see Windsor Castle, the alterations of which are done in the best possible taste and will make the place very comfortable and quite beautiful. They have introduced large *Hatfield bows* and Gothic windows, which are quite in character with the place, and will look like the oldest part of the building, which is saying all one can in its favour, and a large Gateway just opposite the long walk which has a most beautiful effect ...

There is certainly to be a Drawing-Room Thursday, and I intend to go. I suppose it will give the K[ing] a little gout, but he is very well now. He asked me a great deal about Caroline; as you may suppose, Halford[14] had told him everything. William wrote to you last post and has this, so I suppose he has told you of the arrangement Ld C[owper] and the Duke [of Devonshire] had come to, 2,500 now, and three hereafter and 2,000, for setting out. It is certainly a great deal more than she deserves, but I always think it better to be handsome about money, and it puts everybody on your side—and then it may settle the thing (and quietly too) which is a great advantage and Papa can afford it. The Duke is as amiable and fair as possible, talks of nothing but the liberality and handsomeness of the settlement, and his anxiety to see it all arranged, and that she should go abroad, or make some plan for herself. She has been very unwilling to sign and giving one reason or another, illness or objections, but at last she seems inclined to do so. So that I really think this great work

[14] Sir Henry Halford (1766–1844), physician attached to George IV, William IV, and Queen Victoria. Created baronet 1809.

will at last be achieved, and probably without anything being published. . . .

Broadlands Papers

In spite of these financial arrangements, which certainly seem generous in the circumstances, Caroline was in a chronic state of hesitation that kept all the Lambs on tenterhooks.

London June 15th [1825]
. . . W[illia]m's affairs go on prosperously, but Caroline has not yet signed tho she still says that she will do so. Ld Althorp[15] seems likely to be one trustee, and the Duke of D[evonshire] the other. This would I think be better than W[illia]m Ponsonby . . . She is in a strange state, good-humoured, but always muddled either with Brandy or laudanum. She is very willing to go from Whitehall but cannot fix her plans or her thoughts, one day she will go abroad, or to the Sea, or have a Cottage near London at Chelsea ferry because of the [illegible], and because she has found a Capt[ain] and his wife there who will take her in and nurse her. Or sometimes she talks of going off to you at Madrid, as you are the only person she likes. In short it is melancholy to see anyone in such a state . . .

Broadlands Papers

London June 21st [1825]
. . . W[illia]m's affair is not yet settled, but he looks well and comfortable, and I suppose some day she will march out of Whitehall. I have no fears left on the subject. She talks now of going to Paris, but continues to look at Houses in the Regent's Park, and Chelsea and Brompton. She seems to have given up all hopes of preventing the separation. Trustees are the difficulty still . . . I believe the arrangement might just as well be made without Trustees, and W[illia]m then pay her during pleasure, instead of settling the allowance for life. This would leave her more in his

[15] John Charles Viscount Althorp, afterwards 3rd Earl Spencer (1782-1845), Lady Caroline's cousin.

136

power, and I think answer as well, for W[illia]m says he is determined not to give her such a large allowance for life, without the Trustees exonerate him from her debts . . .

Broadlands Papers

London July 7th, [1825]

. . . W[illia]m's affair is not yet settled, but I think it will be so now, for Duke of D[evonshire] is returned to town and says he will keep her to her agreement, but he may fail and in this case W[illia]m has no alternatives but to take a House in some street and order her into it. This is much better than Shilly-Shally, trying to get her to keep to any one plan for two days together. She is irresolute, and changeable, and drunken, but I think there is method in all these variations, she hopes to tire every body's patience to get hold of W[illia]m and to remain where she is. But this there is no chance of; he is completely stout and completely disgusted, and aware of her tricks, and he has made Papa through Cookney give her notice to go, which produced a violent turmoil for two days, but nothing more (thanks to the Women). Never was there such a House, as that one . . .

Broadlands Papers

London July 14th [1825]

. . . She has written Papa word that she would be out of the House by the 1st of Aug[u]st. She tries to resist having a House, and wants only to take a lodging at Thomas's Hotel, and move about to the Sea or to Paris. This is what she said yesterday, but her plans vary every hour, and she trusts to time bringing back W[illia]m into her power, and she thinks the best chance of this is to avoid all regular separation, and to rely upon him to arrange everything for her, so as never to leave him in peace. In this case no doubt *his* best way is to go off on a Journey as soon as she is safe, and out of my father's House, for he has not strength and decision to resist this sort of warfare.

The King goes to the Cottage today or tomorrow, and all the family are to go on Saturday . . . Duke [of] W[ellington] is to

137

dine with us on the 22nd, and to toad out him [*sic*], I have invited
Mrs A[rbuthnot]. There is nothing I would not do to please him,
he is such a love. . . .

Broadlands Papers

Tuesday [26th July 1825]

Augustus [Lamb] is come to Town, looking stout and strong,
but his fits as bad as ever, they say the warm weather has made
them worse. She made a great push to get down to dinner, but
did not succeed, sent Aug[ustu]s to Papa to say that he could
not come without his Mother, upon which Papa was stout for
once, and said he was sorry, in that case that he could not see
him . . .

Broadlands Papers

Monday, August 1st [1825]

Still in London, but talking of going as soon as Caroline is off;
till then I am obliged to mount guard, but all preparations are
making, and I really think now that she will be off in a day or two
to Paris. W[illia]m has no regrets and all goes on smoothly. The
settlements on her are much *too large* for her deserts, but it was
worth while to get rid of her, and she would not have gone without, and in this case force would have been difficult if she had
been determined to fight every point; now the separation is
regularly drawn up, so that I hope it is now done, and for ever.
William has been to Kent for three days with Lord Cowper, gay
as a lark; what an easy Man he is to live with, and what a foolish
Caroline she is to have so thrown away such Cards . . .

Broadlands Papers

At long last, later in the month of August, Caroline Lamb left
Melbourne House for Paris,[16] where her cousin, the kindly Lady
Granville, wife of our Ambassador, made ready to receive her. 'I am

[16] Lady Cowper to Frederick Lamb, Sunday August 14, 1825. Lady Airlie,
Lady Palmerston, I, pp. 122–4.

disinterested enough to be sorry that Caroline is thinking of returning *fra voi*,' she had told her sister a month previously, 'she would not be beyond a mark troublesome to me, but to Lady Cowper, Mrs Lamb, etc. she is a calamity . . .' [17] And now the 'calamity' was descending upon her in Paris. Meanwhile, Emily, freed from the anxiety of Caroline's presence at Melbourne House, was able to join her family at Panshanger, where there were 'no plagues but the harvest bugs, and you have no idea how those imperceptible wretches torment us': adding that 'The House at Whitehall was all put into a state of preparation to maintain a siege, but it is much better to be avoided, these scenes, par[ticularl]y as she went off in peace and Christian Charity with us all. . . .' [18]

> London August 23rd
>
> We are come up to Town for a day . . . William is at Melbourne[19] with George and Caro, very glad to have got rid of one of his incumbrances, but still rather worried by the other, I mean Augustus. Caroline says he can never be left alone, and nothing interests him but games . . .

Emily's statement that Caroline had gone 'in peace and Christian Charity with us all' was soon to prove singularly optimistic; for early in September the traveller wrote to her husband from Calais a strange, incoherent and terrible letter, which seems to come from a mind unhinged and a soul in Hell.

> Calais, September 8th [1825]
>
> . . . Thank you for keeping the boy so much with you. I always told you it would be better for him than sending him to stupid places where to remain with women and children [he] learns nothing and grows silly. My conduct, spirit and pride shall prove

[17] Lady Granville to Lady Georgiana Morpeth, Paris, July 18, 1825. *Lady Granville Letters*, I, p. 352.

[18] Lady Cowper to Frederick Lamb, Panshanger, Saturday, August 19th [1825]. Broadlands Papers. So written, but August 19th, 1825, was a Friday.

[19] Melbourne Hall, near Derby.

to you that I deserved more mercy at your hands than you have shown. Y[ou]r cruelty will one day recur to your mind and may my curse bitter and entire fall upon the rest. As for you I never will curse you but if it be permitted me to return I will come and look at you even as L[o]rd Byron did at me. The more I think of the mean barbarous manner in which I have been sacrificed the less I can understand how *you* could bring yourself to sanction it. I still maintain that the proceedings have been as illegal as they were cruel, that taking advantage of my long and severe illness with the assistance of the basest and most Hypocritical of men, by intimidation and every sort of unkindness I was forced from your fathers House. Lady Cowper upon her bed of death and Frederick Lamb and that abhorred scoundrel Jack Milbanke *shall* remember me—and when my memoires appear with all my faults clear in this work, some will pity me. . . . The only alleviation you can now make to the agonising sufferings you have heeped upon y[ou]r victim is to write—do so then. . . .

Farewell, you may trample upon me as much as you please, I would not be you for all y[ou]r present momentary Happiness— cruelty even in this world is ever punished—and you are cruel, cowardly, and selfish . . . remember me to my own sweet kind boy, no one wrote to me on his birthday.

Panshanger Papers

When Caroline had gone to France she had had a rough crossing. 'She will, I trust,' exclaimed Emily, 'have been so sick as to feel little anxiety to cross the water again directly.' Vain hope! Early in October she was back at Dover, 'whence she wrote to all and sundry giving a heartrending picture of the poverty-stricken state to which she was reduced.' 'William', she declared, 'is enchanted at the prospect of giving me nothing.' [20] By the middle of the month she was in London, as Emily reported to her brother on the 17th.

Panshanger Octr. 17th [1825]
. . . We have had a great succession of people here, and some very gay parties, which were agreeable to us, and I think par-

[20] Cecil, *Melbourne*, pp. 197–8.

[ticularl]y good for Fordwich, and brother William. By the way he [Fordwich] is so much in the *non si muova* line that I begin to be afraid he will not go off to you. He would like it much, but I think he wants courage to set off . . . She [Lady Caroline] is riding about in London and looking for Houses, and I am afraid will take one in Conduit St., which would be a great bore for me, as I shall have great difficulty in keeping her out of my House, but it can't be helped, so I must take my chance . . .

Broadlands Papers

Hitherto, William Lamb had been, much to the annoyance of his family, listlessly indolent, irresolute as to what course to adopt and even visiting Caroline at times in order to keep her in a good humour. But now at last, convinced of his wife's insanity, he took prompt action: she must be confined. Emily thus reported thankfully to Frederick.

London Ocr. 27th [1825]

. . . W[illia]m is at Whitehall in great glee having I really believe done (at last) the right thing about Caroline. He has placed her with Mrs Peterson, Doctor Goddard and the Woman who inhabited the long room at Whitehall. She got so outrageous, so wild, that it was really a disgrace to allow her to go about, and this Dr Goddard has persuaded him to take this course. He is perfectly convinced of her insanity, and put it to W[illia]m as a *Cas de Conscience* to put some restraint upon her. Since this move she has been quite quiet and resigned, but W[illia]m says irritable with him when he sees her, and now always entreating that she may go back to Calais but he intends to take Mrs Peterson's House at Wimbledon for her, and there to keep her. Before this move she was always rioting and driving about the Streets showing off . . . and in short outrageous in every way, driving a Pony Chaise with four bay Ponies in hand and her Horses following her and a Mob at her Heels. Goddard says he thinks her reason might be restored if wine was kept away, and everything she has been accustomed to, that even getting on her Mare drives her wild from different associations, and she is therefore sent to Brocket, and he says she ought not to be allowed to see any of the people she has been accustomed to. In this state of things of course W[illia]m must remain on the spot, but I very much regret on your account that he should not be able to go to you. He is in great spirits and seems very comfortable, cottons very much to us, and seems to like being at Panshanger, and I should think would very likely come to us at Brighton . . .

Broadlands Papers

But Emily Cowper was not the only one to report on Caroline Lamb's strange doings at this time for George Agar-Ellis,[21] who had married one of Lady Georgiana Morpeth's daughters, reported her as living in Phoenix Yard, near Oxford Street, 'attended by two of Sir George Tuthill's[22] women, whom she drives in an open carriage about the streets—she herself driving four ponies in hand—evidently with the design of breaking their necks'.[23] No wonder poor William gave up the unequal struggle at last!

By the end of November Emily was at Brighton with her old father.[24] On her way back from the Coast, she stopped with the Hopes at Deepdene in Surrey, whence she wrote the news to her younger brother.

Thursday, Decr. 15th, [1825]

We are now at the Hopes' on our way to London . . .

My Ball will I think be about the 9th or 10th. The Lievens are to be there, and Tankervilles, and Emma and Ossulston,[25] which will be a great pleasure to Minny. How I do wish that *you* was to be there . . . W[illia]m is visiting about in Herts. Of her [Lady Caroline] I hear and know nothing. I hope it is not the calm before a storm. I see '*Granby*' a novel advertised in all the papers. I wonder if it can be hers.[26] I always feel suspicious when I see one

[21] George James Welbore Agar-Ellis, 1st Baron Dover (1797–1833).

[22] Sir George Leman Tuthill (1772–1835), physician to Westminster and other hospitals. Knighted 1820.

[23] Agar-Ellis to Lady Holland, November 13, 1825. *Three Howard Sisters*, p. 49.

[24] Lady Cowper to Frederick Lamb, Nov. 30th, 1825. Broadlands Papers.

[25] Lady Corisande Emma Bennet and Lord Ossulston, daughter and son of Lord and Lady Tankerville.   [26] It was not by Lady Caroline Lamb.

announced with pomp. George and Mrs L[amb] are at Castle Howard. I hope they may be coming back, but I think the latter is glad to keep out of fire. Papa is quite well, all the better for Brighton, and so am I ...

Broadlands Papers

Towards the end of 1825 Frederick Lamb had suggested that his nephew Fordwich, now about nineteen years of age, should pay him a visit in Madrid. Emily was delighted for her son was not doing much good at Cambridge, but she rather dreaded the journey!

London Decr. 22nd, [1825]

... Fordwich is come home, amiable, charming and looking very well, but I am convinced getting no good at Cambridge, reading a few hours in the morning, but no more than he would in his own room at home, and thinking of nothing but hunting ... and I am all for his going off to you by March or April, and this is also his strong desire. The starting him alone, I cannot think of ... So, this is what I propose, we intend to go to Paris in the Spring ... well, then, I would take Fordwich with us, keep him with us for a week or two of play-going ... and then from there start him in some safe way to you. I think I would chuse a Physician to go as far as Madrid, and then return back to Paris, if you did not wish him to remain ... Ld Palmerston went to call upon Fordwich in the course of his canvass,[27] and was quite delighted with him. He says when he knocked at his door, and he said *come in*, he could have sworn to his race only from his ear, his voice, and his way was so exactly like all of us, and he had not seen him for a great while.

Broadlands Papers

In January 1826 Emily had her usual Panshanger Ball, now an annual event.

[27] In the General Election of 1826 Palmerston was re-elected for Cambridge University, the seat he had held since 1811.

Thursday January 19th 1826

I have lived in so much bustle lately with my Ball and people remaining here afterwards, that I have let the post days pass in an unaccountable manner, however now we are alone again and I return to my usual habits. The Ball was very brilliant, and I managed to lodge 26 people and Children . . . Fordwich quite happy to have so many girls to play with, Emma Bennet, and Louisa Beauclerk[28] and Minny getting courage enough to sing duets with Ossulston. Unluckily, and very unluckily she hurt her back by carrying her sister and could not dance at my Ball, which was a great damper, but I took her to Hatfield Tuesday, where she made up for it, and tonight I am going to take her to Mrs Byng's Ball, did you ever hear anything so dissipated, but having Louisa to go with her makes it so much pleasanter . . . All the people here have been shooting a great deal, and there are quantities of game . . . George and Caro always talk of coming up, but cannot persuade themselves to leave Derbyshire,[29] I suppose they will stop here a few days on their way to the meeting of Parl[iamen]t. I hear nothing of the other Caroline, which is a good thing . . .

Broadlands Papers

(Taken from a copy made by the late Lord Mount Temple. The original cannot be traced.)

Indeed, no one was destined to hear very much more of Lady Caroline Lamb. The agitation involved in the separation from William seems to have overstrained her worn-out constitution. Her remarkable vitality at last began to ebb. 'From this time on, in a dying fall, a strange muted tranquillity, her storm-tossed career declined swiftly to its period.' She and her son, poor Augustus Lamb, were given a home at Brocket, where 'in eventless rural monotony' [30] she stayed for most of the short remainder of her mortal span.

[28] Lady Louisa Georgiana Beauclerk, daughter of the 8th Duke of St Albans, sister of Lord Burford who had been engaged to Lady Elizabeth Conyngham.
[29] They had for some time been living mainly at Melbourne Hall, near Derby.
[30] Cecil, *Melbourne*, p. 198.

CHAPTER VIII

A Trip to Paris

IN THE GENERAL ELECTION of 1826 two of the Lamb brothers were involved; George stood for Dungarvan, and William offered himself unenthusiastically for Hertford. Of these events we find echoes in their sister's letters.

On the 1st of February the Cowpers returned from Panshanger to London, where they hoped to stay for the next few months.

London Feb. 2nd, 1826

... Last Saturday at Pans[hange]r we received an invitation *pour nous rendre au Cottage* from Monday till Thursday. I had a cold and felt so much afraid of moving that I could not venture and so sent an excuse. I was sorry not to go, but in any case it was difficult, as we expected George [Lamb] from Melbourne [Hall] and Lord and Lady Sefton, and Ld C[owper] had arranged a *grande chasse* for Monday. They ought to give us longer notice in the country. I fancy it was a party made up in a hurry for the Duke of W[ellingto]n before his departure. He sets off next Monday or Tuesday for Petersburgh[1] with Dr Hume[2] and Fitzroy Somerset.[3] He is very well now, but I am sadly afraid this long journey should make him ill ... Some people say Duke [of] D[evonshire] will be sent at the time of the Coronation; others

---

[1] Ostensibly to convey George IV's congratulations to the new Emperor Nicholas on his succession, but as Russia was believed to be on the verge of declaring war on Turkey on behalf of the Greeks, Wellington's real purpose was to use all his influence with the Emperor in the cause of peace. For results of his efforts, see his *Dispatches* (March 5th, 16th and April 4th).

[2] John Robert Hume (1781?-1857), physician to Wellington in the Peninsula and afterwards in England.

[3] Lord Fitzroy James Henry Somerset, 1st Baron Raglan (1788-1855), youngest son of the 5th Duke of Beaufort; Field-Marshal; married 1814 Emily Harriet, daughter of William, Earl of Mornington, and Wellington's niece.

say Lord Clanricarde,[4] but this I should think hardly possible, the Youth is hardly presentable, has no manners and looks like an Irish Chairman . . .

W[illia]m's election is arkward and will be hard run. I believe he could certainly carry it if he would exert himself, but I never saw such a want of energy, or they say a worse canvasser. He never talks the people over, but takes an answer at once, always seeing things in the view of his opponents, as he did in politicks, and too candid, and doing the thing by halves, and always despairing, even Duncomb[5] told Ly J[ersey] that W[illia]m would lose it by his want of activity. It is a great pity now he ever embarked in it, but there is no retreating, unless some event should give him a reason for doing so. W[illia]m says he has never heard one word of Politicks, the cry is independance, and the aim of our friends custom and advantage of any sort . . . George dreads his election with this 'No Popery' cry, and Lord Palmerston[6] stands upon very ticklish ground and most people think will lose it, tho he has all the Whigs and radicals quite warm in his favour . . .

Broadlands Papers

London this winter was as usual 'never in a more unwholesome state, foggy, thick and muggy' and it made Emily ill; so she hurried off to Brighton where the accommodating Lord Egremont was prepared to lend her his house.[7] Not till mid-March, however, was she fit to travel, when she was still worried about William's election at Hertford: if only he could retire, 'but he cannot give up now without cutting such a foolish figure, unless some event may occur to give him an opening . . .' [8]

[4] Ulick John de Burgh, 14th Earl of Clanricarde (1802–74); married Harriet, only daughter of George Canning, 1825; created Marquess of Clanricarde, 1825; Ambassador at St Petersburg, 1838–41; Postmaster-General 1846–52; Lord Privy Seal, 1858.

[5] Thomas Slingsby Duncombe (1796–1861), radical politician; elected M.P. for Hertford in 1826.

[6] Palmerston was M.P. for Cambridge University from 1811 until 1831, when he was rejected owing to his support for parliamentary reform.

[7] Lady Cowper to Frederick Lamb, London, Friday, Feby. 10th, 1826. Broadlands Papers.

[8] Lady Cowper to Frederick Lamb, London, March 10th, 1826. Broadlands Papers.

Emily remained recuperating at Brighton from about the middle of March until the middle of April, when preparations for Fordwich's departure to join his Uncle in Madrid necessitated her return to London. Meanwhile, the Duke of Devonshire, who had been appointed to represent the King at the Coronation of Emperor Nicholas in St Petersburg, wrote to the Cowpers offering to take their eldest son in his train. This would have been a wonderful opportunity for the young man, but unfortunately plans for his visit to Madrid were too far advanced to be cancelled and Emily had regretfully to decline the Duke's invitation.[9] Meanwhile, brother William resolved to abandon his attempts to win the Hertford seat, as his sister told Fred later in the month.

> George Street, Friday April 21st [1826]
> ... W[illia]m has made up his mind to give up Hertford, and I believe go to you, and I am glad of it as I think a Journey the best thing for him, and it will be very comfortable for you to have him. Bulwer-Lytton[10] is to stand for Hertford and will I suppose have all W[illia]m's votes. Ld C[owper] does not interfere, and thinks it most prudent for future advantage to let them fight it out ... I should think Bulwer-Lytton would not get a return, but he will then try on a petition ...
>
> Broadlands Papers

And so at last her precious son set off, and Emily hastened to send after him anxious instructions to his Uncle Frederick. 'Pray keep a look to him and prevent him going out into the streets at night on foot, which I fancy must be dangerous.' 'I hope there is no play at Madrid for that is the rock on which he splits. . . .' Then the fond mother turned to matters of more general interest.

[9] Lady Cowper to Duke of Devonshire, Wednesday, 19th April [1826]. Chatsworth Papers, 856.2.

[10] Edward George Earl Lytton Bulwer-Lytton, 1st Baron Lytton (1803–73); novelist and statesman. He was only twenty-three at this time and was not successful at this election.

George St. Friday April 28, [1826]

... The D[uke] of Wellington is expected today, and Duke [of] D[evonshire] goes on the 6th. They say he has made magnificent preparations, and even embarked Horses, which however Mdl. L[ieven] says will never get to Moscow. The King is come to town to stay for a month, and is they say quite well. We dined at the Conynghams on the 24th—our annual ...

There is no time for sentiment in London, its all hurry scurry. W[illia]m's giving up Hertford vexed some of his supporters but he has written a very good address explaining his motives, which they say has had the best effect, and quite cleared him from blame.[11] I should think Bulwer-Lytton has small chance of a return, but he may try a petition for bribery—anything is better than letting Tommy Duncombe walk over the course. Ld C[owper] remains neuter and thinks it best for his interest not to interfere ...

Broadlands Papers

On the 9th the Duke of Devonshire and his suite left England for St Petersburg. Soon after his return from Russia on the 27th of April the Duke of Wellington called on the Cowpers in George Street and gave them an optimistic account of his labours.

London May 9th, 1826

... The Duke [of Devonshire] and his suite set off today ... All his preparations are magnificent, and he packed off about ten days ago in a transport 20 horses, with which he may shew off at Moscow if they ever arrive there, but this from all accounts seems doubtful as the roads are horrid and a sea-voyage with 5 hundred miles at the end of it is no trifle.

Duke of W[ellingto]n is in amazing health and spirits delighted with all he has seen and looking quite fat and fresh. I never saw such an improvement in anybody. On his journey he went to bed every night at 8 or 9, and I suppose this is the secret of it. He talks much in praise of Nicholas' moderation etc., but what is to be done with four hundred thousand soldiers, and

[11] Torrens, *Melbourne*, I, pp. 206-15.

148

EARL COWPER

From the portrait by Sir Thomas Lawrence at Little Durnford Manor

when one hears of the state and oppression of the lower orders one cannot well wonder that they should be disaffected and wish for some sort of change. However, he saw Constantine[12] living at his Country House without even a guard before his door. Fitzroy[13] is well also, but thin, and seems to have been much bored at Petersburgh. No Houses open, nothing talked of but Funerals, and no places but Churches opened . . .

The Corn Bill and our own distresses supersede every other subject; one hears of nothing else, and the difficulty of finding any remedy. The landowners are furious at the Corn Bill being brought on at this moment and they say it will not be carried, in fact the distress is want of employment, and has nothing to do with Corn. The Spittlefields [*sic*] Ball[14] is very flourishing and all the sub[scriptio]ns have filled wonderfully.

All the Whigs are furious with W[illia]m for his Speech about Reform, and I think it is a pity that he should always somehow manage to say the strangest things against the people he has left. However, as far as the speaking went all accounts say it was very good, but Canning said I could not say anything after W[illia]m Lamb, for I could not have gone so far, and it is a pity that he should always take the unpopular side.[15] . . .

Broadlands Papers

May 12th [1826]

. . . The Corn Laws, and distress have set everybody in a panic in all parts. Tonight we have the Spittlefields [*sic*] Weavers

---

[12] On the death of Alexander on December 1st, 1825, Constantine had been proclaimed his successor, but had withdrawn in favour of Nicholas under some prior arrangement or disposition of the late Emperor. There had been slight unrest started by Constantine's regiment in St Petersburg, which had been put down only after some loss of life. On Wellington's account to Mrs Arbuthnot of his Russian visit, see *Mrs Arbuthnot*, II, pp. 22–4.

[13] Lord Fitzroy Somerset.

[14] A fancy-dress ball to be held at Covent Gardens on May 12 for the relief of the Spitalfields weavers.

[15] William Lamb had spoken in the House of Commons on April 27th against Lord John Russell's motion for the reform of Parliament. The figures had been: For the motion, 123; against, 247.

Ball,[16] but when there are so many in poverty and out of employ all sub[scriptio]ns and balls etc. are but a trifle.

Duke of D[evonshire] and his suite weighed anchor yes[terda]y ...

Broadlands Papers

At last Emily was relieved to hear of her beloved Fordwich's safe arrival in Madrid. At the same time she sent her brother a little further information of their troublesome sister-in-law now living quietly at Brocket—a fact none of the family had dared to reveal to old Lord Melbourne![17]

In June the Cowpers were the King's guests at Royal Lodge for the Ascot Meeting.[18] Back in London later in the month Emily wrote in increasing anxiety about Caroline at Brocket, because, if Papa got to hear of her presence there, there would be trouble! She also held forth to Frederick on some of the results of the General Election which however had brought no material change in the balance of parties. The triumph of her friend Lord Palmerston at Cambridge was particularly gratifying, for the other three candidates for the two University seats, Copley, Bankes and Goulburn, were all against Catholic Emancipation; and it was whispered abroad that powerful influences, including the King and his brother and the Chancellor, Lord Eldon, were anxious to unseat the pro-Catholic Palmerston.[19]

During this summer Lord Melbourne was causing his family some anxiety, for, though not ill, he was very feeble, and certainly growing by degrees weaker.[20] So when the Cowpers went for a few days to Panshanger, the old man went with them. The change seems to have

[16] According to Mrs Arbuthnot, the Ball raised for the charity over £3,750 clear. She went as Mary Queen of Scots; but to her intense indignation it was recorded in the newspapers that she had gone in male attire! *Mrs Arbuthnot*, II, p. 26; *Arbuthnot Correspondence*, pp. 81-2.

[17] Lady Cowper to Frederick Lamb, London, 26th May, 1826. Broadlands Papers. Lady Airlie, *Lady Palmerston*, I, p. 126.

[18] Lady Cowper to Frederick Lamb, London, June 7th, [1826]. Broadlands Papers.

[19] Lady Cowper to Frederick Lamb, London, June 20th, 1826. Broadlands Papers. Lady Airlie, *Lady Palmerston*, I, p. 132.

[20] Lady Cowper to Frederick Lamb, George Street, July 3rd, 1826. Broadlands Papers.

done him good, for on their return to London his daughter pronounced Papa 'wonderfully recovered'. 'If it is possible to leave him Ld C[owper] and I hold a very strong intention of going for three weeks to Paris, when W[illia]m's Holidays are over about the middle of Sep[tembe]r. I think it would amuse Minny and do us good . . .' [21]

In August she wrote more positively.

George St. August 4th, 1826
. . . Next Monday we go to settle at Panshanger till the middle of Sept[embe]r, and then to Paris, I wish you might come back at that time and meet us there. I am in hopes there is some chance of this. Minny is much better, and I feel more comfortable about her. The new Governess comes today, which is always an awful event . . .

Broadlands Papers

Alas, the new Governess was not a success!

Panshanger August 15th 1826
I thought I had cut all my Wise teeth, and I find to my cost that I am as foolish as ever, and as likely to be taken in; my new Governess, Mlle Dalmas, instead of being a piece of perfection, *remplie de talents*, is nothing more than a little chattering gossiping French Woman, with no instruction, no talents worth mentioning, and no knowledge. What a bore!! She has very good manners, quick, lively and good humoured, *voilà tout* . . . She may do very well at present as she plays with the boys in their Holidays, but I shall take the very first oppor[tunit]y of getting rid of her . . .

We really go to Paris the 15th of September . . .

Broadlands Papers

And so at last Lord and Lady Cowper and their elder daughter Minny were able to set out for Paris. It looked like being a gay party

[21] Lady Cowper to Frederick Lamb, George Street, July 14th [1826]. Broadlands Papers.

in the French Capital. 'Lady Jersey is expected today', wrote Lady Granville to her sister at Castle Howard, 'The Cannings will be here on Friday and Saturday, the Clanricardes on the 23rd. Jerseys and Cowpers are not exactly the people we would have selected to complete the Society, but I have no doubt it will do very well ...' [22] Lord Melbourne was reconciled to their departure by having his granddaughter to stay with him.

Septr. 18th, London [1826]
We are really setting off tomorrow. Papa is wonderfully well, and does not mind our going in the least ... he is so pleased at having little Fanny to live with him, that it engrosses all his attention. His recovery is truly wonderful ...

Broadlands Papers

Hotel De Londres, Place Vendôme, Paris,
Sunday Sepr. 24th, 1826
Here we are arrived *depuis hier au soir*—enchanted to be arrived, beautiful weather, excellent passage with no sickness, charming Journey all the way ... I am very glad to hear you are better, but wish you had not been ill. I hate these *rechutes*—and wish most anxiously to hear of your leaving that odious climate. We met a Courier on the road who told me you had been ill, and Fordwich too, but said you were both better. However I could not help feeling anxious. I am delighted to think that I am so much nearer to you ... and that if you felt uncomfortable about yourself, we could *so well* come on to you (*le voyage n'est rien*), and if you have not good advice, I could bring you a Physician. Keep this in mind if you want me and have no scruple about writing to say so for I would *quite like* to go to you, and I am sure in any case of illness or uneasyness, Ld C[owper] would not be in the least averse to it; as for expense, a fig for it now[23] ...

Broadlands Papers

[22] Lady Granville to Lady Carlisle, Paris, September 11, 1826. *Lady Granville Letters*, I, p. 390.

[23] Lord Cowper had just learnt of his mother's death in Florence on the 5th of September. No doubt he would benefit financially by this event. Lady Airlie, *Lady Palmerston*, I, p. 127.

(Taken from a copy made by the late Lord Mount Temple. The original cannot be traced.)

Hotel de Londres, Place Vendôme, Monday Oct. 2nd [1826]
... The account of Fordwich's illness made me shake, but I am very happy to hear he is safe and well ... Pray tell me what you think is best for Fordwich's plans, and settle it for him ... I think it is a great advantage to him to be with you, and if you should go to any other appointm[en]t, I should like him part-[i]c[ular]ly to move with you. But I can hear nothing of your moves here, nobody seems to know, and I did not like to venture asking Mr C[annin]g but write me word what you think best for him.[24]

Broadlands Papers

Paris October 24th [1826]
... Your Friends here are really too kind to me, and you ought to be very proud, for your name is a complete Passport—its like Open Sesamy, and all hearts and all Houses fly open ... The C[annin]gs all go to England tomorrow, I am very anxious to delay here till Fordwich's arrival, as I think it would be so provoking, that he should arrive here just after us, and he would feel so cast away, so that I am expecting more letters from him, with great anxiety ...

Broadlands Papers

Unfortunately, Fordwich had a return of fever and it was decided to send him to join his parents in Paris as soon as he should be fit to travel.[25] At about the same time the fond mother wrote anxiously to her son to say that she had summoned Dr Verity from England to go to Madrid to decide when he could travel.[26] That accommodating doctor soon arrived in Paris, and he promptly set off post haste to

[24] *Mrs Arbuthnot*, II, pp. 51-2, 61-2.
[25] Lady Cowper to Frederick Lamb, Paris, Novr. 18th, [1826]. Broadlands Papers.
[26] Lady Cowper to Lord Fordwich, Paris, Nov. 21st, [1826]. Broadlands Papers.

Madrid—to Emily's evident satisfaction.[27] His verdict was presumably favourable, for Fordwich's arrival in Paris was soon eagerly expected by his fond mother.

Paris Dec. 5th, 1826

... We reckon that Fordwich is at this time on the road, and we feel of course very anxious to see him arrive ... We await here Fordwich's arrival, and shall then set off directly, that is, as soon as he is rested, which will I suppose take three days. The Parl[iamen]t Meeting is over, and there is nothing now to hurry us, but Ld C[owper]'s affairs and he has many things to settle[28] ...

Broadlands Papers

At last, much to his mother's relief, the precious son arrived in Paris;[29] and later in the month the family were back in London.

London Tuesday Decr. 26th, [1826]

We arrived here last Thursday ... Our Journey was very prosperous, and Fordwich is very much the better for it ... We are now here for three days on our way to Panshanger, where we shall settle for the next two months ...

Papa I find remarkably well. Baby grown, and everything prosperous. W[illia]m gay and well (but Caroline in possession of Brocket); George still a little lame, and looking thin, but I think looking well, and he has left off Wine entirely and seems not to mind this, which I am delighted at it, for it makes the greatest possible difference in him, and he is so good humoured and quiet, instead of being irritable, and disputatious after dinner.

The Duke of York is not expected to live many days, and everybody is sorry ... The King talks of Brighton, but will not go I think, unless he should upon the Duke's death to avoid hear-

[27] Lady Cowper to Frederick Lamb, Thursday, Novr. 23rd [1826]. Broadlands Papers.

[28] Relative to his mother's estate.

[29] Lady Cowper to Frederick Lamb, Paris, Tuesday, Decr. 12th, 1826. Broadlands Papers.

ing the bells of Windsor. The Lievens are at Brighton, so I have not seen her . . .

C[annin]g's speech[30] is praised up to the Skies as the finest piece of eloquence, and they say he looked inspired when he delivered it. His Colleagues whisper that they thought it imprudent, but the peaceable tone of France justifys him or shews there was an understanding. The true way to maintain Peace, is to be ready for War, and War would be very popular here . . . [The] Duke [of] Devonshire has Ld Hastings blue ribbon, and is enchanted . . .

Broadlands Papers

The Garter for good, kindly, affectionate Hart was a fitting reward for his embassy to Russia which he had conducted with unsurpassed magnificence; it was too a fitting last tribute to all that remained of the Devonshire House set.

[30] In the House of Commons on December 12th, Canning made two speeches on the King's Message on Portugal, the Queen Dowager having claimed his Majesty's aid against hostile aggression from Spain. It was on this occasion that he spoke the now familiar words: 'I called the New World into existence to redress the balance of the Old.'

CHAPTER IX

A Fateful Year

THE YEAR 1827 opened with a general expectation that one or other of the two questions that divided the Tory party—either the Catholic question or the Corn Law question—would soon break up the Government, and Lord Liverpool[1] himself, now in poor health, had recently expressed doubts of his Ministry being able to survive beyond the meeting of Parliament in February. Then, early in the new year, tragedy precipitated events. On the 5th of January died the Duke of York, the heir presumptive, the most able and popular of the sons of George III, leaving as heir to the throne the eccentric Duke of Clarence, who was known to be favourable to Catholic emancipation; and only a few weeks later, on the 17th of February, Liverpool had an apoplectic seizure from which it was soon evident that he could never recover. The choice of a successor evidently lay between Wellington, Peel and Canning; but Wellington on the Duke of York's death had accepted the post of Commander-in-Chief of the Army, a position which was thought to disqualify him from the premiership, and Peel, though almost forty, was deemed to lack the experience needed for the highest office in the State. Unfortunately, the sole remaining candidate was most unpopular in his party, both on personal grounds and owing to wide hostility to his foreign policy; so that it was not until several weeks had passed that the Canning Ministry was with difficulty formed. Of the negotiations, intrigues and general political upheaval in the interim we learn much from Lady Cowper's letters to her brother during the spring and summer of this fateful year.[2]

---

[1] Robert Banks Jenkinson, 2nd Earl of Liverpool (1770–1828). Prime Minister 1812–27.

[2] For the whole matter covered by this chapter I am deeply indebted to *Canning's Ministry* (ed. Aspinall) and Temperley, *Canning*, pp. 413–46. In most cases where Lady Cowper's letters are printed by Professor Aspinall I have summarized them in the following pages and referred the reader to the relative passages in his book.

The New Year found the Cowper family at Panshanger where Fordwich was convalescing from his recent illness.

Panshanger Janry. 1st, 1827

... What will happen in the future is a great subject now for speculation. Ld Liverpool ill, the Chancellor declining,[3] Robinson unwilling both from idleness and grief to return to his post.[4] All these things considered, make a coalition with some Members of another party[5] not very improbable. Ld L[ansdown]e[6] stands naturally, Ld H[ollan]d[7] supported by the new heir [to the throne],[8] the only difficulty is the sour Northern power,[9] but as he has often said he had retired he may be taken at his word. Many things more improbable than all this have come to pass, and even Peele [*sic*] is now they say sighing for retirement, so it seems as if every thing settled itself. Brougham is called Seymour's Trumpeter.[10] ...

Broadlands Papers

[3] Lord Eldon's influence in the Government had been declining for some time, but he did not resign until April 12th, after Canning had succeeded Liverpool.

[4] Frederick John Robinson, afterwards 1st Viscount Goderich and later 1st Earl of Ripon (1782–1859). In the previous December, Robinson had expressed a wish to go to the House of Lords and to exchange his post as Chancellor of the Exchequer for an easier office. Neither he nor his wife was in robust health, and they had lost their only child, Eleanor, aged 11, on 31st October. It is not correct to say that he was unwilling to return to his post, because at Liverpool's request he retained his office though on a temporary basis. Yonge, *Liverpool*, III, pp. 438–42.

[5] Presumably the Whigs.

[6] Lansdowne was working for a union between the parties and in April was successful in forming a coalition between a section of the Whigs and the followers of Canning.

[7] Holland was in favour of Catholic emancipation.

[8] The pro-Catholic Duke of Clarence.

[9] Presumably Lord Grey, the third great potentate of the party, whose hostility to Canning presented a standing difficulty in the way of an alliance between Canning and the Whigs.

[10] Possibly Edward Adolphus Seymour, Lord Seymour, afterwards 12th Duke of Somerset (1804–85). Seymour did not enter parliament until 1830, when he was elected for Okehampton, and nothing seems to be known of his activities in 1827 when he was only twenty-three. Later, however, there was a connection between Seymour and Brougham, and in January 1835 when Lord Seymour was

Early in February Emily was busy recording rumours and speculations on public affairs for her brother's delectation. She began by deploring—

Monday Feby. 5th 1827 and finished Tuesday, 6th.

... C[annin]g's long illness[11] which has prevented him for a month from attending to any business, and now the very great struggles that is [*sic*] taking place upon Ld Liverp[ool]'s illness, which of course occupies all thoughts and all intrigues ... H[uskisson] also is in a very sickly state,[12] a constant inflammation of the Trachea, and general derangement, and the moment he gets the least better, and is able to move out of his bed room they come and talk to him about business and lay him up again ... from what I hear now however this arrangement seems most probable: C[annin]g to keep the foreign office which he is par-[ticular]ly fond of, and add it to the Exchequer, and Robinson to have the Treasury. However there are many difficulties in every thing, and I suppose a good deal will depend upon the event of the Catholic question,[13] which is now under discussion. The conclusion may be tomorrow night, or it may go on to Wednesday. The Corn [Measure][14] has I think tolerably satisfied the

contesting Totnes there is an interesting reference to this: 'The Tories are confounded at my arrival and at my address; they say that they are sure that Lord Brougham wrote the address for me at Paris.' Seymour to Lady Seymour, Stover, January, 1835. *Letters and Memoirs of the twelfth Duke of Somerset* (ed. W. H. Mallock and Lady Gwendolen Ramsden, 1893), p. 58. This of course does not prove that Lord Seymour was the person referred to in Lady Cowper's letter or that Brougham was assisting him in 1827, but it is at least an interesting possibility, and I am grateful to Professor Norman Gash for pointing this out to me.

[11] Canning was not well enough to leave Brighton for London until February 27th.

[12] He was laid up at his London house in Somerset Place.

[13] It was becoming increasingly clear that emancipation of the Catholics could not be delayed, as any further withholding of their rights would produce a rebellion in Ireland. Yet the King and majorities in both houses were against any measure of relief.

[14] The proposal was designed to stop excessive fluctuations in the price of corn and to give protection to the farmer when prices were low and to the consumer when they were high. The duty was therefore to vary on a sliding scale round the price of sixty shillings a Winchester quarter. When the price was sixty shillings, the duty was to be twenty shillings; and with every increase or decrease of a shilling in the home price, the duty on imported grain was to be reduced or increased by two shillings.

landed proprietors—at least that great Dragon little o[15] says it is not so bad as he expected . . .

Broadlands Papers

In her next letter Emily had a poor account to give to Fred of Canning's health, as his gout was tending to 'fly to the head'.[16] Some days later she wrote to her brother again on the excitements of the moment.

[? February 18th, 1827]
. . . The friends to Catholics are in great spirits as they say the New House of Commons is so much in favour of it [Catholic Emancipation] that it must now be carried. Mr Canning's illness however is unlucky for them but he hopes to be able to resume his duties in a fortnight, which however considering his state is very improbable. He has certainly been very seriously ill, but more painful than dangerous; at first the pain in his head was treated for gout, and then he got worse, but now it is settled to be Ague or Rheumatism in the head, and they give him quinine. Dr Holland[17] was sent for to him the day before yes[terda]y, which made people think him much worse, but he returned yesterday and said there was no danger, that it was a plain sailing case and merely required time. Sir Mathew [Tierney] attends him at Brighton. Lord Howard[18] told me as a proof [of] how ill he has been, that he had not attended to any business for the last month, and that he never knew him before miss three days together. He caught his cold at the funeral,[19] as almost all the rest did who were there, a number of Dignitaries of the Church have died, the Duke of Sussex[20] has been very ill and Huskisson, the Chancellor

[15] Lord Ossulston, now Lord Tankerville.
[16] Lady Cowper to Frederick Lamb, Panshanger, Monday Febr. 12th, 1827. Broadlands Papers.
[17] Sir Henry Holland, first baronet (1788–1873): physician-in-ordinary to Prince Albert, 1840, and to Queen Victoria, 1853; created baronet 1853.
[18] Charles Augustus Ellis, 6th Baron Howard de Walden and 2nd Baron Seaford (1799–1868), Under-Secretary of State for foreign affairs.
[19] Of the Duke of York.
[20] Augustus Frederick, Duke of Sussex (1773–1843): sixth son of George III.

159

saved himself by standing on his hat.[21] They say 5 of the King's Footmen have died of it, and several of the Soldiers; great blame is attached to the arrangements, there should have been a matting on the stones, or a Warm room to wait in, but there were no precautions whatever . . .

Broadlands Papers

During the month that elapsed between the writing of the last letter and the next the intrigues continued unabated. Canning's determination not to be passed over is made clear from a conversation he had with Princess Lieven at Brighton towards the end of February when he told her plainly that he was resolved either to become the head of the Government or to leave the party, adding that to overcome the prejudice of the King on the matter of Catholic emancipation he would consent to keep it as an open question in the Cabinet.[22] But Wellington's attitude is much less certain. On the 18th of February the Duke had a talk with Croker, when he expressed the opinion that he was in his right place as Commander-in-Chief and seemed to assent to his friend's view that for the sake of party unity Canning must be Premier; but the Duke demurred to Robinson going to the Foreign Office.[23] Yet only a few days later, on the 21st, Lord Colchester[24] reported the refusal of both Wellington and Peel to serve under Canning, and the next day recorded the rumour that the Duke was to have first place.[25] On the 27th of February Wellington's crony Arbuthnot wrote to Bathurst that the Duke 'had been tired out for two years' and would never join a Canning Ministry and that he (Arbuthnot) thought that

[21] The funeral took place late at night in St George's Chapel, Windsor, and it was so cold in the Chapel that many of those present were taken ill immediately afterwards and some died of the effects. The Lord Chancellor, Eldon, was persuaded to stand on his cocked hat and so saved himself from the intense cold of the stone floor.

[22] The conversation must have taken place between February 17th, the date of Liverpool's seizure, and February 27th. Temperley, *Canning*, pp. 418-19.

[23] Croker's Diary under date Sunday, February 18th, 1827. *Croker Papers*, I, pp. 363-4.

[24] Charles Abbot, first Baron Colchester (1757-1829); Speaker of House of Commons, 1802-16; peerage 1816.

[25] Colchester's Diary under dates February 21st and 22nd, 1827. *Colchester Diary*, III, pp. 463-4.

Peel would take exactly the same view.[26] On the 10th of March Arbuthnot wrote to Peel that there were in his view only three choices for the Premiership, Peel, Canning or the Duke, and that Wellington would serve under Peel but not under Canning; at the same time he expressed the 'strong belief' that the Duke 'would be glad to discuss with you what there is for him and against him in respect to the Premiership'.[27] What Peel replied to this, we do not know; but Croker, who dined with the Peels on the 16th of March, came away convinced that his host would not serve under a Catholic Premier, but would like to see Wellington, Bathurst or Melville at the head of the Government.[28]

All this obviously led to much uncertainty as Emily told Frederick on the 19th.

George St. Monday March 19th. [1827]
Still nothing settled with regard to the political arrangements. Ld Liverpool is so far recovered as to be able to walk about, but his mind has never at all rallied, and *they say*, no appoint[men]t will be made till he is well enough to resign. Canning is not strong in health and he wants quiet, but I think a little time will set him right. Huskisson is not in so good a way I am afraid ... I wish he could be persuaded to go out of town and be quiet entirely for a short time. The Duke of W[ellington] is the only person I see about in sound health and spirits—and as gay as if there were no intrigues and no politicks in the world ...

Tuesday, 20th
There is a large party going to the Cottage tomorrow, Ester-hazys, Duke [of] W[ellingto]n, Gwydyrs, and I *suppose* that we are kept for another, with the Lievens Duke [of] D[evonshire] and Granvilles ...

[26] Arbuthnot to Bathurst, Whitehall Place, Feb. 27, 1827. *H.M.C. Bathurst*, pp. 630-1.
[27] Arbuthnot to Peel, Whitehall Place, March 10, 1827. *Peel Papers*, I, pp. 452-3.
[28] Croker's Diary under date March 16th. *Croker Papers*, I, p. 365. On the other hand, Colchester recorded in his Diary on the 19th that 'Within these three days the Duke of Wellington has said that he saw nothing to prevent Canning being First Minister. Peel *is* willing to serve under him.' *Colchester Diary*, III, p. 469. See also Temperley, *Canning*, pp. 420-1.

W[illia]m like a fool is going down to Hastings to see Caroline; when will that child have cut his wise teeth. Aug[ustu]s continues in a sad state, he had a fit the other day just as we were going to dinner, which was dreadful . . .

Broadlands Papers

Before Wellington left for Windsor on the 21st, he received a message from the Duke of Buckingham[29] offering, in the name of Lord Londonderry and other peers who differed upon the Catholic question, support to a Coalition Government that did not include Canning. Wellington could certainly have done with the support of Buckingham and his associates, but all the world knew the cost of assistance from the arrogant, self-important Grenville clan, and he thought it prudent to ignore the letter. Whereupon pressure from other quarters was brought to bear on the Duke to accept the Premiership himself, so that a few weeks later Wellington told his brother Wellesley[30] that, though he had discouraged all attempts to make him Premier, yet on the principle that the King's Government must be carried on there might be circumstances 'under which it would be his duty to accept the situation if he were called upon by the King to do so'.[31]

But he was not called upon by his Majesty; for after a deal of playing off of one party against another and one faction against another, the wily King, who had come to London on the 6th of April, on the 10th received Canning in audience and instructed him to prepare with as little delay as possible a plan for reconstructing the Administration. Unfortunately, Wellington, on receiving a letter from Canning asking for his support, pretended not to know who was to be the head of the Government; and, when Canning wrote a particularly frigid answer to his inquiry, the Duke promptly resigned his office, and the following day the command of the army also. The departure of the great Duke was followed by the resignation of all the leading Tories; only

[29] Richard Temple Nugent Brydges Chandos Grenville, 1st Duke of Buckingham and Chandos (1776–1839).
[30] Richard Colley Wellesley, Marquess Wellesley (1760–1842); Governor-General of India, 1797–1805; Lord-Lieutenant of Ireland, 1821–8, 1833–4.
[31] B.M. Add. MSS. 37297, ff. 272–91. Memorandum of Wellington dated April 14th 1827, returned by Canning to Wellesley, Downing Street, May 24, 1827. *Wellesley Papers*, II, pp. 164–9; Temperley, *Canning*, p. 421.

Harrowby, Huskisson, Robinson and Wynn[32] elected to stand by the new Prime Minister. In consequence, Canning was forced to look to the Whigs for support. 'Sir', said he to the King, 'Your father broke the domination of the Whigs. I hope your Majesty will not endure that of the Tories.' 'No,' came the reply, 'I'll be damned if I do.'[33] Fortunately for him, the section of the Whig party led by Lansdowne had already decided to support him; and though at first negotiations broke down, the hitch was only temporary, and in spite of the opposition of Lord Grey, before the end of May, Lansdowne, Carlisle,[34] Tierney and other Whigs joined the Canning Government.

All this was, of course, watched by Lady Cowper with the closest attention and the formidable difficulties facing the new Premier are vividly described in her next few letters to her brother. In the first, dated the 24th of April,[35] she wrote at length of Lansdowne's change of front brought about by Wellesley staying as Lord-Lieutenant of Ireland and her brother William being nominated Chief Secretary, appointments which gave the Irish Government a distinctly less Orange complexion. Yet Lansdowne, the most retiring of men, was not anxious for office; indeed, he was only persuaded to support Canning in his hour of need by fear of the strong anti-Catholic Cabinet that seemed the inevitable consequence of Canning's failure to form a Government. Meanwhile, the Tories, faced with the prospect of going into opposition, were setting no bounds to the fury of their language; '. . . there's nothing they don't say at White's that the K[ing] ought to be in a s[trai]t waistcoat, and everything personal and violent they can think of against him and C[annin]g'. The one thing to be feared, thought Lady Cowper, was the reluctant Lansdowne refusing office; though even in that event, she reminded her brother, Canning could rely on almost all the Whig support, and the King had received assurances from certain Tory potentates[36] that they would rally to his

[32] Charles Watkin Williams Wynn (1775–1850), President of the Board of Control, 1822–8; Secretary at War, 1830–1; Chancellor of the Duchy of Lancaster, 1834–5.   [33] Temperley, *Canning*, p. 434.

[34] George Howard, 6th Earl of Carlisle (1773–1848), Chief Commissioner of Woods and Forests, 1827.

[35] Lady Cowper to Frederick Lamb, London April 24th [1827]. Broadlands Papers. Printed in *Canning's Ministry*, pp. 176–9.

[36] For example, the Dukes of Rutland (*Canning's Ministry*, p. 41), of Newcastle (*Colchester Diary*, III, p. 466), and of Buckingham and Chandos (*Wellington Dispatches*, III, p. 611).

Government, whatever its complexion might be. 'The fact is', she added, rather unfairly, 'that these people are so shabby, they always must come round to try to get on the right side.'

At least two persons were well satisfied with the changes. William Lamb was 'very much pleased, and even more by the manner of the offer, he was asked as a favour to take it, because the K[ing]'s wish being for a Protestant in that place, his regard and liking for W[illia]m would make him pass over that want of qualification. He is also come into Parl[iamen]t for Newport, the borough C[annin]g has just vacated, on very reasonable terms':[37] and Lady Cowper's old friend Lord Palmerston, 'who is to keep his present place and to have a place in the Cabinet, so that he is very well pleased'.[38] Indeed, there was only one cause for regret, and that was Wellington's hasty and ill-considered resignation of the command of the army; but Lady Cowper rejoiced that the King was keeping this in his own hands so as to enable him to re-appoint the great soldier at the first opportunity. For the Duke's precipitate action she blamed the woman who was popularly supposed to have most influence with him, 'I am *so fond* of him but he has not acted wisely on this occasion,' she told Frederick, 'and if I had been at his elbow, I should have prevented him. What a pity that he was not in love with me instead of Mrs A[rbuthnot]. The moral of this story is that no man should be in love with a foolish woman, if he is ever so clever himself, he is sure to be ruin'd by it . . .'

Three days later Emily wrote to Frederick again.

George St. April 27th [1827]
Last night everything was said to be settled with a few minor points to discuss; this morning I hear the Cabinet places are not to be settled till the end of the Session, but that Ld L[ansdown]e and C[annin]g have come to a right understanding and that Ld L[ansdowne] will take the first Lord of the Treasury's place,[39]

[37] William Lamb was returned for Newport on April 24th, and on his appointment as Chief Secretary for Ireland stood for Bletchingly, where he was returned unopposed on May 7th. *Canning's Ministry*, p. 178 fn.

[38] Palmerston remained Secretary at War, the office he had held since 1809, but he was now promoted to Cabinet rank.

[39] This was very wide of the mark; Lansdowne refused any place until mid-July, when he became Home Secretary.

when C[annin]g goes to the Foreign Office,[40] and the Duke of D[evonshire] to be Chamberlain directly.[41] What W[illia]m will be I don't exactly know but he pro[mise]d he would write to you today; perhaps he may go to Ireland now, but I hope he will eventually be Home Sec[retar]y of State.[42] He and C[annin]g are very thick, and all seems to be going on prosperously; and I am delighted for I see all the people I care about in the same boat, and I feel no doubt that Duke W[ellington] will settle his concerns with the K[ing] and be at the Head of the Army before a year is over. The Tories are outrageous and talk such nonsense it is quite absurd, and abuse the K[ing] in the most indecent manner a thousand times worse than the Whigs ever did. *Ly Jersey aussi fait mille folies*, but nobody cares. Brougham has just been stating the case at Brooks's and says we are for the future to reckon ourselves all one party. I had rather the places and the Cabinet had been settled for it may give time for the K[ing] to think and to find out that he has too many Catholics on board, but however I suppose this arrangement was necessary and Ld L[ansdowne] and C[annin]g are hand and glove and quite satisfied with the arrangement. You never saw anything like the turmoil going on lately, and the eagerness and the violence, it has been quite delightful and made me feel all alive alive oh! I think the old Tories are quite beat and must bid adieu to their places for many years to come. Ld Cowper was very eager for the Junction, and so are all the Whigs, but Lord Grey and a very very few. The Vice Chancellor is Master of the Rolls,[43] and very happy in consequence. W[illia]m is elected for the borough of Newport, which C[annin]g vacated. I am so happy on his account at all this move, he always wanted employment, and was in a *fausse position* about Politicks. Now he has everything open to him and is in his proper station, whether he goes to Ireland or stays at home, and will feel much happier than he has done for a great while. What a happy thing it

[40] Canning did not combine the offices of First Lord of the Treasury and Foreign Secretary as many anticipated he would; but in view of the appointment of Dudley and Ward to the Foreign Office, it was clear that he intended to have a considerable say in foreign policy.

[41] He became Lord Chamberlain.

[42] He became Chief Secretary for Ireland.

[43] Sir John Leach (1760-1834), Master of the Rolls and Deputy Speaker of the House of Lords, 1827.

is that he parted with that Woman, she would have been now like a mill stone round his neck.

Broadlands Papers

On the 1st of May Emily wrote to Frederick again,[44] when she told him of the fury of the Tories at seeing all their hopes frustrated by the Whigs, 'there's so much confusion and splitting amongst families and parties,' she told him, 'that it's quite a service of danger to talk politicks at all, and yet it's impossible to talk of anything else'. A few disgruntled Whigs, led by Lord Grey, were furious with Lord Lansdowne; for they maintained that if the party had only stood aloof and refused any negotiations they would have come in on their own terms. But that was far from being Lady Cowper's view: she held that such action on the part of the Whigs would have merely facilitated the return to power of the Tories, 'who are only now so violent because they see themselves lost. It's very agreeable for us,' she added, 'to see this complete turn of affairs and a short time ago so very unexpected.' She was also able to assure Frederick that William was pleased with his appointment, 'and feels I think comfortable to be fixed in his politicks after having been so long no how'. Canning, it seems, had been speaking highly of him, and only recently had told Madame de Lieven that 'he looked upon him not as one, but as *the* cleverest person going'. But if there was confusion among parties, there was apparently also confusion at Court, when Ministers appeared to resign and be sworn in, 'all the ins and outs shown by mistake into one room, 2 Chancellors, 2 Chamberlains, all in pairs,' recorded Lady Cowper, 'and the K[ing] in such a state of perspiration that it seems as if he would quite melt away. The two last days summer is quite come upon us to account a little for this heat, but I suppose the thoughts of meeting all these people was not very cooling and comfortable.'

In her next letter, written a week later,[45] Lady Cowper forecast that the Government would be quite secure, that the Whig malcontents would soon come round, and that Wellington would very shortly resume his command of the army. Meanwhile, Tory violence was

[44] Lady Cowper to Frederick Lamb, London, May 1st 1827. Broadlands Papers. Printed in *Canning's Ministry*, pp. 206-8.
[45] Lady Cowper to Frederick Lamb, London, May 8th [1827]. Broadlands Papers. Printed in *Canning's Ministry*, pp. 216-18.

unabated, for they 'have so long been in office that taking away their places is counted by them like taking away their *private property*'. Lord Cowper, she was glad to tell Frederick, 'is in good spirits and delighted at the state of things and very decided in his opinion for the present Govern[men]t . . .' Things were certainly looking well for the Whig party.

London, Friday May 11th [1827]

. . . Affairs are settling and I think going prosperously for our side in politicks; every day some new Whigs declare for supporters of the Governm[en]t and all the speaking and talent is on our side. Huskisson's speech[46] was excellent, and has done what few speeches ever do, convinced the hearers. It turned completely round the Mayor of Yarmouth who was in the Gallery, and many who were taking notes to answer him threw them away as he went on. Ld Grey's speech yesterday was eloquent, but will do no real harm and only serves to shew his temper and spite and bad feeling.[47] Several Tories are violent in Opp[ositio]n, Duke of Newcastle,[48] Aberdeen; but many are very shabby and trimming. Ld Lonsdale[49] for instance, and Ld Lowther[50] wants to have the Woods and Forests—and people *say* the cause of Ld Aberdeen's violence is that he wanted an offer himself. The King is stout with C[annin]g and the majority it is supposed will be very great in the Commons. The Lords are more doubtful (and the Bishops have not yet declared), but still people who know say it is safe enough . . .

The Granvilles go to Paris tomorrow. Mde Lieven is gay and pleased, but unwell; it is very odd for so clever a person how stupid she is and childish on the subject of Physic—she will take nothing and expects to get well by stuffing inordinately and going to bed early directly afterwards . . .

Duke W[ellington] says he *likes* being out of office, very well

[46] House of Commons, May 4th, supporting the new Government.

[47] He somewhat violently attacked Canning.

[48] Henry Pelham Fiennes Pelham Clinton, 4th Duke of Newcastle (1785-1851).

[49] William Lowther, 1st Earl of Lonsdale, of second creation (1757-1844).

[50] William Lowther, 2nd Earl of Lonsdale, of second creation (1787-1872): first commissioner of Woods and Forests, 1828; summoned to House of Lords in his father's barony, 1841; succeeded to Earldom, 1844.

to say, but one is not bound to believe; indeed I am quite sure he will return the first moment he can do it with credit, and the present arrangement is full of difficulty but merely kept to for the purpose of letting him in time return to his post. I wish he had never gone, for do what he will, the return will always have a foolish and awkward appearance.

Broadlands Papers

In early May Emily received a letter from Fred in which he expressed his delight at their brother William having an appointment in the Canning Government. She replied on the 15th.

London May 15th 1827

... The Newspapers will tell you the turmoil we still live in, and all the bother produced by this provisional Governm[en]t, if it had not been for this *foolish* arrangement there would have been nothing to say on the other side, but I hope when the Session is over all will be finally and regularly settled. Both Ld L[ansdowne] and Canning are very sincere and therefore one may hope all will go well and without any fresh difficulty. The Governm[en]t is strong in numbers and gain fresh advocates every day; the band who are adverse to the Coalition is small among the Whigs and ridiculous, and the Tory opponents are stupid and absurd, and have no talent amongst them so that they cannot do much. Ld Londonderry[51] makes his friends ashamed every time he speaks and Ld Ellen[borou]gh talks glibly but can make no effect; in short I do think the Tory game is up, if our friends will act stoutly and straight forward. The Duke W[ellington] I am very sorry for. I feel little doubt he will be in again in the course of time, but am afraid not at present. The King is still very angry with him, and with all those who have left him in the

[51] Charles William Stewart, 3rd Marquess of Londonderry (1778–1854), half-brother of the famous Castlereagh, 2nd Marquess, whom he had succeeded in 1822. He attacked the Government in general and Canning in particular in very unseemly terms. Subsequently his reputation was much damaged by Lord Dudley's disclosure of his vain attempts to obtain a pension.

lurch, and did not speak to any of them the other day when he
held a Chapter of the Garter . . .

Broadlands Papers

*(Taken from a copy made by the late Lord Mount Temple. The original
cannot be traced.)*

Towards the end of May, Emily went down to Panshanger to fetch
Minny who was 'ruralizing' after the chicken pox. On the 28th she
wrote to Frederick of all the beauties of the place, the rhododendrons
and lilacs in full bloom 'and everything so green and fresh'. Fordwich,
too, who was stationed at Windsor, was 'quite enchanted with the
merry bustling life they lead, and all the good-humoured, chattering
officers'. Then she turned to public affairs and to William's and
George's activities.

Pans[hange]r Monday 28th May [1827]
. . . W[illia]m talks of going to Ireland as soon as Par[liamen]t
is up, and that people talk of now [as being] in six weeks from
this time. He talked to me the other day of taking Augustus with
him, which seems to me little short of madness. Somebody was
there so I could say nothing, but I intend to speak to him seriously
about it, but you have no idea of the difficulty of getting at him
now, all the afternoon he is at the House, and all morning at his
Office. Brother George is getting quite stout again, all the political
arrangements do very well, and the Governm[en]t in all probability likely to last a great while. There was a strong majority of
57 in the Lords on the Corn question,[52] and it is thought there
will be no more difficulty about the Bill. Ld Egre[mon]t is very
silent. It is thought that he does not like the present arrangements,
but he says nothing . . .

Broadlands Papers
Canning's Ministry, p. 232

[52] The vote was taken on May 25th which carried an amendment of Wellington's to the Corn Bill. The figures were: for, 120; against, 63.

It was about a fortnight before Emily wrote to Frederick again,[53] and then she was busy speculating on the allocation of offices. She also deplored the 'childish and foolish' behaviour of the Duke of Wellington, 'producing Huskisson's private letter without leave was a wrong thing to do, and then reading only part of it, and as people say putting a different construction on it from the true one . . . all this is so unlike his general character and acting in this manner from private pique, and in fact so absurd since he looks to a return, to shut the doors against himself'.[54] So she concluded that there was no chance of the Duke regaining his command for the present. Then she turned to lighter matters. She and Lord Cowper were bidden to the King's Lodge to meet the Duke and Duchess of Clarence, when the Cannings and the Lievens were also to be of the party. This was pleasant for Lord Cowper remained 'hand and heart' with the present Government, though recent events had shattered many friendships. 'There is nothing more comical than to see the loosening of some friendships and the tightening up of others,' Lady Cowper told Frederick Lamb, 'it makes me laugh when I am alone to think of the events of this year, and its effects upon private society much more than any other political revolution could have done, because it's not measures or principles so much as pique and personal likings and dislikings which influence people . . .'

On the 2nd of July Parliament was prorogued. But Canning's difficulties remained. Three Whigs, Lansdowne, Carlisle and Tierney, entered the Cabinet; and the Premier secured the services of Lord William Bentinck[55] as Governor-General of India. But Wellington remained hostile and aloof, and all the King's blandishments failed to persuade him to resume his command.

Meanwhile, the Prime Minister's health was failing. On the 18th of July Huskisson, still unwell himself and on the point of going abroad, paid a last visit to his old friend. He found him looking pale and ill, but to his anxious inquiries Canning courageously pretended that his bad colour was only the reflection of the yellow lining of his curtains. Others knew better, and the ever-kindly Devonshire offered him his

[53] Lady Cowper to Frederick Lamb, London, June 12th [1827]. Broadlands Papers. Printed in *Canning's Ministry*, pp. 241-3.

[54] For Mrs Arbuthnot's version see *Mrs Arbuthnot*, II, pp. 123-4.

[55] Lord William Henry Bentinck (1774-1839), second son of the 3rd Duke of Portland.

house at Chiswick as a place of rest. 'Do not go there,' said the blunt Lady Holland, 'I have a presentiment; you know Mr Fox died there.' Canning merely laughed at her fears, but Lady Holland could never recall the incident without emotion.[56]

On the 20th of July the Cannings went to Chiswick; ten days later the Premier visited Windsor where he had his last audience with the King. He returned to Chiswick on the following day. On the 2nd of August he dealt with official business and signed his name to a number of documents. Then he tried to revise a despatch; but he was too weak and ill to work and in the evening he was seized with violent pain. However, news of the Prime Minister's serious state was not generally known. The popular view was that he was gradually recovering; and as late as the 3rd of August Emily was still writing of Canning as 'so unwell—not I hope seriously', and that what he needed was 'quiet of mind and brisk air'.[57] But of course the Prime Minister's state was far more serious than any one imagined, and only a few days later Emily wrote to Frederick to announce his death. The magnitude of the loss she fully realized, but they must hope for the best and the best would be, she felt, 'the continuation of the present Government with some Whig additions', and Wellington of course as Commander-in-Chief.[58]

Friday, Augt. 10th [1827]

... I hope there is every prospect of things being settled rightly. The King sent for Goderich and Sturges Bourne,[59] and propo[se]d to the former to be 1st Ld of the Treasury, and to the other to be leader in the H[ouse] of Commons;[60] this of course he

[56] Temperley, *Canning*, p. 443. Mrs Arbuthnot took much the same view. *Mrs Arbuthnot*, II, p. 134.

[57] Lady Cowper to Frederick Lamb, begun August 3rd 1827. Broadlands Papers. Lady Airlie, *Lady Palmerston*, I, pp. 138–9.

[58] Lady Cowper to Frederick Lamb, August 7th, 1827. Broadlands Papers. The letter is so dated, but Canning died at dawn on August 8th. Lady Airlie, *Lady Palmerston*, I, pp. 140–1, where the letter is inaccurately dated August 9th. Canning died in the very same room at Chiswick in which his early friend Fox had died twenty-one years previously.

[59] William Sturges-Bourne (1769–1845); Home Secretary, 1827.

[60] The King offered the Premiership to Goderich and urged Sturges-Bourne to become Chancellor of the Exchequer. *Letters of George IV*, III, No. 1375, pp. 275–6; No. 1378, pp. 276–8.

will decline, not feeling himself fit for it, but the former will do very well, and Ld L[ansdowne] and our friends are willing to act with him. There is still more discussion about [the] Catholic question, but this I *hope* will be managed and end favourably. The other arrangements of Office are not likely to produce any quarrels and they say no Cabinet was ever more cordial than this one, or more free from jealousies, and ill blood. The K[ing] told Ld Goderich that he felt no doubt now but that Duke W[ellington] would take the Army. If they could now get Hol[lan]d in as Privy Seal, and Carlisle, President of the Council, all would do well. I should imagine Dudley would remain in, and I think it would be desirable, to show the powers that the same system is to be acted upon.[61] Harrowby[62] has resign'd. He says his wish has long been retirement and quiet, and that he mainly kept Office on C[annin]g's account to show that he approved of his Govern-m[en]t, and did not approve of the conduct of his former Col-leagues. This will make him stand very high in public opinion. You never saw such regrets as poor C[anning]'s death has prod[uce]d, all Brooks's are in mourning, all former animosities are completely obliterated; Ld C[owper] surprized me just now by telling me that he had mentioned to Dudley that if any (except his private friends) attended the funeral, that he wished to do so. Esterhazy and others were in great joy for two days, but this sending for Goderich has damped their hopes; it shows also to our Whig malcontents that the idea of the K[ing] sending to the Whigs was always absurd and that he would rather do anything else. He sends to Goderich because he is unobjectionable and because he belonged to Canning, but I am quite sure that though out of the question, he would rather have the old Tories back than take the Whigs in a *body*, and forget and forgive. He seems to be determined to take a line of his own, and to say like George 2nd: 'Am I king, or am I not King?' His proposals to the Cabinet were in writing as he said to avoid all misconception, or idea of

---

[61] The main Cabinet appointments were: Lord Goderich, First Lord of the Treasury; Charles Grant, President of the Board of Trade; Lord Dudley and Ward, Foreign Secretary; William Huskisson, Colonial Secretary, Lord Lansdowne, Home Secretary; J. C. Herries, Chancellor of the Exchequer.

[62] Dudley Ryder, 1st Earl of Harrowby (1762–1847): President of Council, 1812–27.

intrigue, which he said had been imputed to his former arrangements. I suppose K[nighto]n is at his back, for I believe he has seen nobody else. Lauderdale[63] [is] fortunately away in Scotland and Eldon away. I hope the Cabinet may keep together and there seems every prospect of it, as they are all rational reasonable people, and pleased with each other, honest naturally, and their interest now [is] to be honest. They say nobody can behave better than Ld Anglesey, very straight forward, and very sincere for the Catholics, and very easy and accommodating about everything. If they continue and the Duke takes the Army, it will be a very strong Governm[en]t. I suppose Huskisson would be Chancellor of the Exchequer, if he returns well, as we hope . . .

Tomorrow I go down to Richmond to pass the day with la triste Lieven, she is really and very *sincerely* unhappy. There must have been something very intrinsically amiable about C[annin]g notwithstanding his manner and temper, for all those who have been near him lately and have acted with him were so completely devoted to him and so taken by his *straight forward* and candid way of acting and speaking; it is really very extraordinary, after all the tricks and double dealing one has always had imputed to him, and I assure you I have not seen the *trial* fail in any one instance. W[illia]m was completely devoted to him; Ld P[almersto]n the same, and the latter was quite a late convert, —Ld Lansdowne also quite come round. Ld Anglesey (after calling him always at first that Gentleman), our brother George, the Duke of D[evonshire], in short all who got within the circle of his influence. Ld C[owper] himself quite a follower, and Whiggism a secondary consideration . . .

Broadlands Papers

Later in the month Lord and Lady Cowper were bidden to Windsor, with Minny and Fordwich; 'a great favour', as Emily told her brother.[64]

[63] James Maitland, 8th Earl of Lauderdale (1759–1839): he had recently gone over to the Tory Party.
[64] Lady Cowper to Frederick Lamb, London, Tuesday, Augt. 21st [1827]. Broadlands Papers.

London Augt. 28th [1827]

We are just returned from the King's Lodge, and I am happy to say our political prospects look well, much better than I expected when I went down. Some of our Whig friends had persuaded me that they fancied that this business of Herries[65] was only a pretence, but that the real object was to disgust the Whigs and get rid of them. This, I am now convinced, is not the case. The K[ing] is as bitter as ever against the Tories, and has not at all forgiven the D[uke] of W[ellingto]n. He looks forward most anxiously to Huskisson's arrival,[66] and is always talking of him so that everything now depends on him, and as Mde Lieven says, '*on l'attend de tous les côtés comme un nouveau Messie*'!! for the general salvation. He must take the office of Chancellor of the Exchequer (with the lead), and so settle that very arkward subject . . . The K[ing] has a mind to show his power and so forth but I am sure he has no mind to get rid of the present Govern-[men]t, and that he thinks *tout s'arrangera*, as he said to somebody. He never ceases in his regrets and praises of C[annin]g and says he never had any Minister he liked half so well. He was par-[ticular]ly civil to Dudley when he came down and in my opinion every thing looks well, if Huskisson *is* but well and strong . . . Goderich is a poor creature and not up to the situation, but he is very cordial and honest and sincere. Huskisson is expected today, and the K[ing] has written to him with his own hand to desire he will come down as soon as he arrives . . .

Fordwich and Minny were at the Lodge with us, and the latter highly amused, so much that it drove away her shyness . . . The K[ing] told me you was coming home, but said he had still better news for you; what he meant I don't know, and I could not at that moment ask. He also praised W[illia]m to Mde L[ieven]. By the way, we hear on all sides of W[illia]m's popularity at Dublin . . .

Broadlands Papers

[65] John Charles Herries (1778–1855), Chancellor of the Exchequer in Goderich ministry from August 8, 1827 to January 8, 1828; wrote statement of events that led to dissolution of the ministry.

[66] Huskisson was on the Continent, and a courier had been sent to fetch him back with all possible speed. He became Colonial Secretary and Leader of the House of Commons.

George IV had indeed good news for Frederick Lamb on his return from Spain in September. In December he was dubbed a Knight Grand Cross of the Order of the Bath. Shortly afterwards he was sent to Portugal with the rank of Ambassador. His ambition had been realized at last!

Emily Cowper's views on the apparent strength and stability of the new Government proved singularly inept. Within the next few weeks there were bickerings and quarrels amongst the members of the Government, notably Herries and Huskisson, which the Prime Minister was quite unable to control; and in January 1828 the feeble Goderich resigned. To the intriguing wife of the Russian Ambassador, who had for long been labouring to gain an influence over Canning and his Ministers, the fall of the Whig-Tory coalition was a sorry blow. 'Quelle épouvantable catastrophe!' declared Princess Lieven to Lady Cowper, on hearing of the resignation of Lord Goderich. Posterity has certainly not echoed that cri du cœur.

Lord Ashley's Wooing

WHILST WILLIAM LAMB had been discharging the duties of his office in Ireland, his wife and Augustus had been living quietly at Brocket. Lady Caroline was only forty-two, but in October 1827 the doctors pronounced her dangerously ill of dropsy and it was soon clear that she would only live for a very short time. A few weeks later she was removed to London. Soon after her arrival at Melbourne House she became partly insensible and by mid-January it was evident that the end was near. Fully aware of her plight, the invalid longed only for one last sight of the husband she loved but whose life she had ruined. 'Send for William', she whispered, 'he is the only person who has never failed me.' He did not fail her now. He hurried over from Dublin and the last sad interview took place behind closed doors. For this she had been waiting; now she was content, and a few days later she died, her sister-in-law, the other Caroline, holding her hand. 'She only fetched one sigh and she was gone', reported Emily to Frederick, 'Mrs Lamb could hardly believe she was really dead, and only felt she was so by the placid look her features assumed.'[1]

In July of this same year old Lord Melbourne's 'unimpressive life' came to an end at last, and William succeeded to his father's peerage and the headship of the family. One of his first acts was to sell Melbourne House as far too large for his needs. In its place he took a more modest house in South Street, Mayfair.[2]

Meanwhile Sir Frederick Lamb had gone to Lisbon to take up his post of Ambassador to Portugal. No sooner had he assumed his new duties than he was faced with a crisis. On the 6th of March, 1826, John VI had been taken suddenly ill and within four days had succumbed to what many suspected to be poison. Immediately the Infanta Isabel Maria had been nominated Regent, and she had at once acknow-

[1] Lady Cowper to Sir Frederick Lamb [January] 1828. Lady Airlie, *Lady Palmerston*, I, p. 129; Cecil, *Melbourne*, 198–204.
[2] Cecil, *Lord M.*, pp. 29–30.

ledged Dom Pedro, the late King's elder son, as King Pedro IV. But Dom Pedro was already Emperor of Brazil and, as a recent treaty had provided that one person could not be both Emperor of Brazil and King of Portugal, Pedro was expected to abdicate in favour of his brother. This course, however, did not commend itself to him, though he was eventually persuaded to abdicate the throne in favour of his own seven-year-old daughter, Dona Maria da Gloria. This formality being completed, Dom Pedro's younger brother, Dom Miguel, who had been long resident in Vienna, was recognized as Regent on condition that he should marry his niece, the little Queen, who was some seventeen years his junior. Dom Miguel's prompt acceptance of his brother's conditions removed all obstacles to his return to Portugal, where he took an oath of loyalty, though with a secret reservation as to his legitimate rights. He landed at Lisbon on the 22nd of February, 1828, almost exactly at the time that Sir Frederick Lamb took up his duties as British Ambassador. The Wellington Ministry had arranged for the British army of occupation to leave Portugal early in April, and Miguel planned to seize the throne by a *coup d'état* immediately the troops had been evacuated. Lamb got wind of the plot and on his own responsibility countermanded the evacuation. He also returned £50,000 which Dom Miguel had borrowed from Rothschild's.[3] At Cabinet meetings held on the night of the 18th of March and on the afternoons of the 19th and 24th of March the Government approved the prompt action of their Ambassador; nevertheless, it was felt that we should not interfere in the internal affairs of a friendly country, and that the troops must be withdrawn.[4] Sir Frederick made no secret of his disapproval of the Government's action,[5] the inevitable result of which was, as he foresaw, that Miguel promptly proclaimed himself King; whereupon Lamb and other diplomatic representatives left Lisbon. The child-Queen was of course forced to quit Portugal, and she finally came to England where she was a source of much embarrassment to diplomats and statesmen for several years.[6]

Emily was of course delighted with her brother's success.

---

[3] *Wellington Despatches*, IV, pp. 321–3.
[4] Ashley, *Palmerston*, I, pp. 130–2.   [5] *Greville Memoirs* (1874), I, 137.
[6] Princess Lieven to Lady Cowper, Richmond, September 24th, 1828. *Lieven-Palmerston Correspondence*, p. 2.

I got a very good account yesterday from For[dwich] of all your proceedings, and I feel so glad he should see it all, but what a provoking turn for affairs to have taken, and what anxiety and responsibility for you. However one comfort is that everybody here praises you ... Before your last despatch (I have not seen them since) Palmella[7] and Ld *Heytesbury*[8] both expected the thing would be stopped and that your decided line would have saved a revolution. I am afraid there is less chance of this now, but still the strong remonstrance of our Gov[ern]m[en]t has not yet been received. I am sorry for the worry you must have, but still more pleased at the credit and praise you get from all, and the opportunity of distinguishing yourself ...

... W[illia]m goes to Ireland the 1st of April ... The K[ing] has a Levee Thursday, and they talk of a Drawing-Room for the 16th. I hope there is no chance of a quarrel with Russia, but [Madame] L[ieven] will not paper her rooms, which she was going to do, for the chance of it. How mischief seems to be brewing up in all parts ...

Broadlands Papers

The withdrawal of the British troops from Portugal made resistance to Miguel and his followers hopeless. In May he summoned the Cortes, which with acclamation offered him the Crown. Only in Oporto, where Palmella and others returned from exile and formed a Junta, was any opposition offered to the new régime; but the resistance was short-lived and on the 3rd July Palmella and others fled to London.

George Street, Wednesday July 2nd [1828]

... People say you are coming home; I should be very glad to see you, but sorry for the poor Patriots. We are all anxious

[7] Pedro de Sonza Holstein, Duke of Palmella, Portuguese statesman, who had been banished from Portugal by Dom Miguel in 1824, was responsible for the army of occupation in Lisbon and was therefore highly unpopular with Dom Miguel and his followers.

[8] Sir William A'Court, 1st Baron Heytesbury (1779–1860); Ambassador to Portugal 1824, to Russia 1828–32; created a peer 1828.

to hear of poor Palmella and whether he has got safe. This blockade of Oporto makes one anxious . . . The Merchants here have done much for him, report says he has a hundred thousand pounds in hand. Madame P[almella] is quite a heroine. I go to see her and comfort her. The Refugees who came after Fordwich are gone off after Palmella. There never was anything like their *Reconnaissance* to you. They say that they owe you everything and are quite pathetic. A Deputation of them came to call on me to express their feelings . . .

Broadlands Papers

Later in July Sir Frederick Lamb returned to England for a protracted stay; and passed most of his time at Brighton. In December the Cowpers had a large party at Panshanger, with the Lievens, the Huskissons, the Granvilles, Melbourne, and Frederick Lamb up from Brighton among their guests—at least one of whom did not find things very comfortable. 'I am, at near two, returned to my room,' wrote Lady Granville to her sister, Lady Carlisle, 'fire out, no housemaid having been near it, not a single morsel of writing-paper in either of our rooms, one bad pen and a drop of ink . . .' [9] In January Emily and her husband went on a round of visits; and it was from stately Cashiobury that she wrote to her old friend Lady Burrell,[10] 'My dearest Fanny', of Knepp Castle in Sussex.

Cashiobury Jany. 19th 1829

I have been always on the trot, or I should have written to you before. We have been to Ld Jersey's for a few days, and are now come here to Ld Essex's[11] in our way home . . . We met Ld and Ly King[12] at Middleton.[13] She talked to me about you, and seems to like you very much. They are now gone to Town . . .

[9] Lady Granville to Lady Carlisle, Panshanger, December 13 1828, *Lady Granville Letters*, II, pp. 38–9. Lady Granville was not the only one to find Panshanger uncomfortably cold. *Greville Memoirs* (1874), II, p. 104.

[10] Frances, sister of the 1st Lord Leconfield, of Petworth, and wife of Sir Charles Merrick Burrell, third baronet.

[11] Cashiobury, seat of the Earls of Essex, now demolished. Lady Cowper's host was George Capell, 5th Earl of Essex (1757–1839).

[12] Peter King, 7th Baron King of Ockham (1776–1833).

[13] Lord Jersey's seat.

The little rake Minny has been passing her time in London while I have been away, and amusing Papa ...

Broadlands Papers

The 'little rake Minny' was now grown up and must claim a little of our attention.

From the prominent position that Lady Emily held in her Mother's letters one would hardly be surprised if she were a precocious child, and Lady Cowper herself seems to have seen the danger of spoiling her. Indeed, she dealt with this very point in a letter to Lady Burrell at about this time.

George St., Thursday [1829 ?]

Many thanks for your account of Minny, and for your care of her. She arrived here last night, very much delighted with her little *séjour* with you, and I was really happy to have her again for I am so accustomed to having her with me that I feel quite low and solitary when she is away. She seems to have play'd a pretty prank on the night of the Ball, but she is none the worse for it, and I think it a good thing for children to sow their wild oats early, one may hope they will be the steadier afterwards. I however took occasion to tell her how little I felt she was to be trusted; she is charming, but as you truly say, she *must not* be spoilt. ...

Broadlands Papers

But whether Minny Cowper was or was not a spoilt child, she was by 1829 a beautiful young woman with whom, as Lady Granville told her brother, all the men were 'more or less in love'.[14] But though no doubt there were many suitors, her heart does not seem to have been touched until the appearance on the scene of a very remarkable young man, Lord Ashley, eldest son of the 6th Earl of Shaftesbury.

Lord Ashley, serious minded and intensely religious, had had an

[14] Lady Granville to Devonshire, Bruton Street, June 22nd 1829. *Lady Granville Letters*, II, p. 42. Only Creevey found her disappointing. *Creevey Papers*, II, p. 198.

unhappy childhood. Neglected by a father immersed in public affairs and by a vain, fashionable, pleasure-loving mother, daughter of the 4th Duke of Marlborough, the boy together with his brothers and sisters had suffered a miserable upbringing, made tolerable only by the loving care of a faithful old family servant, Maria Millis, a former maid to their mother when a girl at Blenheim, who in 1829 had been promoted to housekeeper at St Giles's House, Lord Shaftesbury's home in Dorset. At the age of seven, young Ashley had been sent to the Manor House School at Chiswick, an odious establishment not unlike Dotheboys Hall[15] presided over by a certain Dr Thomas Horne, no pale shadow, it seems, of the immortal Wackford Squeers himself. In this atmosphere of cruelty and neglect, Ashley suffered exquisite misery; and in the midst of his griefs Maria Millis died. It was an overwhelming blow to the lonely boy. She left him a handsome gold watch. 'That was given to me by the best friend I ever had in the world,' he was fond of saying, and to the day of his death he never wore any other. At the age of twelve Ashley was sent to Harrow, and at the school on the hill he experienced his first true happiness. At Harrow, too, when in his fifteenth year, he had a horrible experience which profoundly influenced his after-life. One day, walking alone down Harrow Hill, he heard a great shouting and yelling coming from a side street and the singing of a low drunken song. Presently the roystering party turned the corner and came into view; and to his horror young Ashley saw four or five drunken men carrying a roughly hewn coffin in which they were conveying one of their fellows to his burial. Swaying and staggering as they turned the corner, the men let fall their burden and then broke into foul and blasphemous oaths unfit for human ear. The solitary witness of this sickening spectacle stood rooted to the spot. 'Good heavens!' he exclaimed. 'Can this be permitted, simply because the man was poor and friendless!' Before the songs had died away in the distance, the young Harrovian had determined with God's help to devote his life henceforth to the cause of the poor and lonely.[16]

That was in 1815. Since that day fourteen years had rolled away, and Lord Ashley was sadly conscious of the fact that he had done little or nothing to fulfil his vow. The reason was clear to him: if he could but find the woman of his dreams and make her his wife, all would be

[15] In later life Lord Shaftesbury himself compared the school at Chiswick to Dotheboys Hall. Hodder, *Shaftesbury*, I, p. 51.
[16] Hodder, *Shaftesbury*, I, pp. 35 *et seq.*

well. 'If I could find the creature I have invented,' he wrote, 'I would love her with a tenderness and truth unprecedented in the history of wedlock. I pray for her abundantly. God grant me this purest of blessings!' When in 1829 Lord Ashley became acquainted with Lady Emily Cowper, he believed that he had found the answer to his prayer.

In August of that year Lady Granville, who was staying at Tunbridge Wells, had several meals with Prince and Princess Lieven, who were also visiting the famous spa; and she records meeting the Cowper family and Lord Ashley under the Russians' hospitable roof. 'We have had most agreeable, delicious little repasts at the Lievens,' she told her sister. 'The first day Cowpers and Lord Ashley . . . Emily was in the most captivating beauty. Lady Cowper very much in love with Lord Ashley and I too, we agreed, much more than the girl. However, I think her pleased with him and that she will like and marry him. He is quite willing to wait and hope and try everything to gain her affections.' [17] However, every one did not approve the match. 'Lord Ashley is thinking of marrying Lady Emily Cowper, who belongs to one of the most profligate families in the Kingdom, he being really as moral and religious a man as exists,' wrote Mrs Arbuthnot unkindly. 'I hope he will be able to give her good principles or she will make him very wretched.' [18] 'You really are very provoking about Ashley . . .' wrote Lady Harriet Leveson Gower to Charles Arbuthnot. 'What is there extraordinary or absurd in a man falling in a [sic] love with the prettiest and most fascinating girl in London? . . . With Ly E[mily] he is desperately in love, and thank Heaven Ly Cowper's politics[19] do not and ought not to interfere in an affair of her daughter. . . . Politics and political animosities are bad enough in themselves, Heaven knows. I am glad Ashley is not at any rate fool enough to allow them to interfere in his private happiness. Really, you never lose an opportunity of saying something against Ashley, wh[ich] is not right or kind. I like him excessively. I think he has a thousand excellent and valuable qualities and two or three failings, of which I think falling in love with Ly E. Cowper not one: on the contrary a proof of great good

[17] Lady Granville to Lady Carlisle, Tunbridge Wells, August 23rd, 1829. *Lady Granville Letters*, II, pp. 142–3. See also *Lieven-Palmerston Correspondence*, pp. 8–9. Lieven had recently been given the title of Prince.

[18] *Mrs Arbuthnot*, II, p. 306.

[19] Lady Cowper was a Whig and the Shaftesburys were Tories.

taste . . .' [20] 'You have now stated the case y[ou]rself and 3,000 a year
whereof the third comes from a place which he will probably lose very
shortly and which you and I both devoutly hope he may,' wrote Sir
Frederick Lamb to his sister, 'an odious Father, and four beggarly
brothers. What has poor Min done to deserve to be linked to such a
fate, and in a family generally disliked, reported mad, and of feelings,
opinions and connections directly the reverse of all of ours? Do you
know what 3,000 a year or *probably two* can furnish to a couple and a
family? . . .' [21] and much more in that strain.

For some months all was uncertain as to Ashley's suit, for Lady
Emily was quite unable to make up her mind. 'I received a letter from
Lady Cowper,' wrote Lady Granville to Lady Carlisle, 'she says "we
are still in a great state of irresolution about Lord Ashley. You cannot
think how much anxiety I feel, and indeed so does she from the
difficulty of making up her mind." I shall really break my heart for
him if she decides against, yet I should break a dozen, if I had them,
for him if she marries him without loving him. So I am glad to have
no voice in the affair and to have always advised, as she always con-
sults, leaving the Girl to her own decision.' And again a few days
later: 'I hear Emily says she is not in love, never was, and never shall
be . . . Lord A[shley] knows this, and Lady Cowper begged him
to consider how much his love and grief would be augmented by
coming to Panshanger, but he persists. He does not care what risk he
runs for the slightest hope . . .' [22] And to Mrs Huskisson the worried
Mother wrote in much the same strain.

Panshanger, Wednesday [1829]
I am anxious to say as little as possible about Ld Ashley as I
can say nothing quite positive, therefore pray don't quote me.
But this is the real state of the case. He proposed to her at Ton-
bridge when she knew him very little, and she of course refused.

[20] Lady Harriet Leveson Gower to Charles Arbuthnot, Shannon, Monday
night [14th September, 1829]. *Arbuthnot Correspondence*, pp. 119–20.

[21] Sir Frederick Lamb to Lady Cowper, Drummond Castle, 22nd [?] 1819.
The whole letter is quoted by Lady Airlie in *Lady Palmerston*, I, pp. 146–9; but
she does not appear to realize that Lord Ashley is the suitor referred to.

[22] Lady Granville to Lady Carlisle, Brighton, August 27, 1829; London,
September 2, 1829. *Lady Granville Letters*, II, 43–4, 45.

He then intreated her to take time to know him and to allow him as a common acquaintance the oppor[tunit]y of making himself agreeable to her, and so it now stands but of course she must soon make up her mind finally and decidedly and this we of course leave entirely to herself because if she likes him he is a very suitable match for her, and if not she will find somebody else she likes better, but he has many very agreeable and good qualities and he certainly improves very much upon acquaintance and I find him which I did not expect very accommodating and tractable and reasonable. But still on the whole I believe it would be as well for Min to refuse him and so I imagine will be the result, but there is no knowing. We are now preparing to go to Chatsworth where I expect there will be a large party,[23] and where she will have plenty of oppor[tuni]ty of seeing other people and deciding by comparison whether she prefers him to all the world. I am so far easy in my own mind on the subject that I feel sure if she chuses him that he will make a very good husband for I never saw anybody so in love and so devoted as he is and I think it is in his character to be partially [sic] fond of everything he likes. I thought him odd at first, but this I have ascertained is only manner and I never saw any body more rational or open to reason which he owns was not always the case with him, and he has given many a bad opinion of his candour. Pray say if you are asked that I have not written or say that you believe it is not to be a marriage. It is impossible to tell this story about and I had rather it was believed that it was over for it seems strange without the details to be so long giving an answer, and I don't wish people to think now that she is under any sort of engagement part[icular]ly as the probabilities are that she will refuse him at last . . .

Huskisson Papers
B.M. Add. MSS. 39949 (b), f. 124

For Christmas that year the Cowpers had a large party at Panshanger. We do not know if Lord Ashley was there, but the Lievens, Lord John Russell, Charles Greville and Fred Lamb were among the guests. And the Princess introduced them to an attractive German

[23] For particulars, see *Greville Memoirs* (1874), I, pp. 237-8.

custom for Christmas-tide. Three trees in large pots, each lighted with three circular tiers of blue, green, red and white wax candles, were placed upon a large table. Each child was allotted one of the trees and in front of each tree were placed a quantity of toys and other articles, presents to the owner of the tree. In Germany the custom extended, we are told, to the grown-ups also; but at Panshanger it was confined to the children.[24]

It seems to have been a merry Christmas, and we must hope that Lady Emily Cowper was not so harassed by her personal problems as to be unable to join in the fun. Yet early in the new year she was still in doubts about her suitor, as Lady Granville, who met them both at a ball, recorded. 'Lord Ashley behaved most beautifully last night,' she told her sister. 'How that girl can help liking him, seeing his devotion for her with something so noble, so manly in his whole manner and conduct! He danced all night with the girls, did not follow her at all, and his spirits appeared good without being forced, though I, who know, could have cried for him.[25] But fortunately, Lady Granville's tears were not needed; Minny, it seems, could not help liking her devoted suitor and Ashley's wooing prospered. In April, Princess Lieven wrote to Minny's mother that her daughter's engagement to Ashley was 'so well known that everyone takes me for a fool when I deny the rumours'.[26] The Princess did not need to deny the rumours for much longer, for soon the engagement was announced, and on the 10th of June, 1830, the wedding took place.

But this chapter cannot end with wedding bells. It opened with two deaths; it must close with two more.

Exactly sixteen days after the Ashley wedding, George IV died, to be succeeded by his eccentric brother, Clarence, as William IV. Some three months later occurred a far more tragic passing. William Huskisson was run over by a train at the opening of the Liverpool and Manchester railway. Naturally the widest sympathy was extended to his widow, and Lady Cowper was not slow in expressing condolences with her cousin.

[24] *Greville Memoirs* (1874), I, p. 259.
[25] Lady Granville to Lady Carlisle, London, February 1830. *Lady Granville Letters*, II, pp. 59.
[26] Princess Lieven to Lady Cowper, Wednesday, April 14th [1830]. *Lieven-Palmerston Correspondence*, p. 17.

Panshanger Sepr. 17th [1830]

We are all in the deepest affliction; and in the greatest anxiety about you. What a dreadful, what a cruel event, and how will it ever be possible to think of it calmly? I cannot express all I feel for you, nor how wretched we all are, indeed I would wish to speak words of comfort but in such a dreadful misfortune what comfort is there to give, what consolation, unless it is indeed that all the world share it with you and all acknowledge that the country could not have sustained a greater, or a more irreparable loss . . .

God bless you, my dearest Mrs H. and give you strength under this severe trial.

Huskisson Papers
B.M. Add. MSS. 37048, ff. 16–19[27]

[27] See also B.M. Add. MSS. 37048, ff. 102–3, 128.

Reform

FOR SOME TIME before the death of George IV it had become ever increasingly clear that the demand for reform in England was becoming more insistent; and, according to Greville, Lady Cowper had told him that the previous summer the Duke of Wellington had made some sort of approach to her brother William and to Palmerston on this very subject.[1] Nothing, however, had come of this, and now the reactionary attitude displayed by the great Duke towards reform made a change in Government inevitable. In fact, the Ministry resigned during the autumn of 1830 to be succeeded by Lord Grey, in whose Cabinet were Lady Cowper's brother, Melbourne, at the Home Office, and her friend, Palmerston, at the Foreign Office. Palmerston was one of the first people Grey saw after the King had summoned him to form a Government on the 16th of November.[2] At first he suggested that he should be Home Secretary but, as neither Lansdowne nor Holland was willing or able to take the Foreign Office, it was eventually offered to Palmerston, who thus obtained the post he had been anxiously seeking for the last two years.[3]

The new Prime Minister and his colleagues set about their task with a will, and between March 1831 and June 1832 three Reform Bills were introduced into the House of Commons. The first Bill, introduced by Lord John Russell, was outvoted in committee, whereupon the Premier appealed to the country and obtained a large majority in favour of reform. 'The bill, the whole bill, and nothing but the bill,' became the cry throughout the land. The new bill, which differed little from the old, was passed by the Commons but rejected by the Lords. There

[1] Ashley, *Palmerston*, I, pp. 211–13. It is only fair to add that the Duke, or at least some of his friends, denied that any approach had been made. *Greville Memoirs* (1874), II, pp. 94, 104.

[2] Ashley, *Palmerston*, I, p. 213. Trevelyan, *Grey*, p. 241. Webster, *Palmerston*, I, p. 21.

[3] Butler, *Reform Bill*, pp. 140–52. Trevelyan, *Grey*, Appendix D. Webster, *Palmerston*, I, p. 21.

thus started a direct struggle between the two houses. At first William IV refused Lord Grey's plea that he should create enough Whig peers to force the Bill through the Upper House; but, after an abortive request to Wellington to form a Tory Government, the King had to yield and promised Grey that he would create the necessary peers. But this was not needed. Wellington and many of his supporters realized that further resistance to Parliamentary reform would be useless and unreasonable. So they withdrew their opposition and allowed the Bill to pass.

Early in the new year 1832, Greville was much at Panshanger where he discussed affairs with Melbourne, Palmerston and Frederick Lamb; and he reported Lady Cowper to be 'a furious anti-Reformer'.[4] Though admittedly Emily was alarmed at the possible results of reform, Greville's dictum is hardly borne out by the letters she wrote to Frederick on his return to Vienna. To this Embassy he had been appointed through the influence of Palmerston, who was anxious to have there his own nominee and friend, 'the most capable of the professional diplomats except the great Stratford Canning himself'.[5] His sister's letters convey to us some of the excitement and confusion of those anxious days.

George St., Wednesday May 16 [1832]

It is very difficult to write my dearest Fred in the midst of all sorts of reports, expecting every moment to hear something certain. The K[ing] sent for the Duke upon our friends giving in their alternative of Peers and [or?] resignation. The Duke accepted the offer, and said he would bring in the bill himself, that some alterations would make it better, that he should concede Schedule A.[6] and Weymouth besides, to shew he did not stand about numbers—and then he went to all the Peers, and, wonderful to say, I believe they all agreed to turn round with him and take the bill nearly as it is, franchise and all. The D[uke] of Cumberland and all but 2 or 3 ultra Tories gave in their adhesion, and they were in spirits and praising each other for the sacrifices

---

[4] *Greville Memoirs* (1874), II, pp. 229–30, 231–3, 242–3, 244–5, 277–8.

[5] Webster, *Palmerston*, I, pp. 68, 224.

[6] In the Reform Bill, Schedule A contained the list of boroughs to be wholly defranchised, Schedule B those to be semi-defranchised.

they had made of their own opinions to the safety of the State and Crown. All this would at least have been tried if Peele [*sic*] would have come to them, but he could not or durst not in the face of the H[ouse] of Commons.[7] Goulburn,[8] Croker,[9] and others stood with him and the debate in the House on Tuesday frightened out of their wits those who had agreed to follow the Duke, and they backed out of it. The feeling of the House was expressed so strongly, the astonishment at the wheeling round of the Tory party produced such expressions of feeling even from independent persons and from their friends, that they were forced to give it up. Baring[10] said he hoped the quarrel between Ministers and the Govern[men]t might be made up, and this opinion was hailed on all sides as a wonderful Discovery, and so the Duke of W[ellington] threw up his Commission next morning. All his Party's enthusiasm and joy was turned to mourning and the K[ing] sent for Ld Grey and there they have been negotiating for the last 2 days; but this result I will keep for my letter tomorrow which is post day. Sugden[11] said in his speech in the H[ouse] of Commons that the Duke's conduct was either the basest direlection of principle or the highest and most patriotic instance of self devotion on record. The answer to this was if the D[uke] thinks the bill must be granted and that alterations can improve it, and make it safe, why would he never negotiate with the Waverers, why on the contrary drive them from him, and say he would never have anything to do with the bill, or any part of it? To be sure he is a wonderful bold man ever to have thought of such a course, and it certainly does damage him very considerably in public estimation, for it seems as if his objections were

[7] The attitudes of Wellington and Peel were in marked contrast. The Duke regarded it as his duty to carry on the King's Government. For Peel's view, see Parker, *Peel*, II, p. 206; Lever, *Peel*, p. 149.

[8] Henry Goulburn (1784–1856); Chancellor of the Exchequer, 1828–30; Home Secretary, 1834–5, Chancellor of the Exchequer, 1841–6.

[9] John Wilson Croker (1780–1857); spoke against Reform Bill, 1831; retired from Parliament, 1832. Supposed to be the origin of Rigby in Disraeli's *Coningsby*.

[10] Alexander Baring, 1st Baron Ashburton (1774–1848): M.P. for Thetford, 1831–2; President of the Board of Trade and Master of the Mint, 1834; raised to peerage, 1835.

[11] Edward Burtenshaw Sugden, 1st Baron St Leonards (1781–1875); Tory M.P. for Weymouth and Melcombe Regis, 1828–30; St Mawes, 1831–2; Ripon 1837; Solicitor-General 1829–30; Lord Chancellor and raised to peerage, 1852.

only to not carrying it himself and that office was more his object, than real objections to the Reform Bill. The K[ing] meanwhile had most imprudently given way to the expressions of his joy at getting rid of our friends, and now of course feels very awkward at being obliged to come to them again. On the whole it is certainly an unfortunate occurrence. The King's own weakness of character has been shown by it, and the power of the radicals and the violent language which has been used both outside and inside the House is a very bad example for the future . . .

. . . I am very glad Ld P[almerston] remains in Office, and so is he himself; some of the Courts will be glad but the greater number I believe sorry . . .

Thursday . . . The Duke is to state in the House today that he and others withdraw their opposition.

Friday—They made a very good explanation in the House yesterday. The Duke's speech *particularly* good, but no positive promise of letting the Bill pass, so nothing is yet quite settled, but I suppose it must be any moment. The K[ing] will not have Peers. I hear our friends are not very unreasonable now, they say the Bill must pass to stop the danger of a rising, and perhaps they are right . . . but there it is, radicalism has made a frightful stride the last three days and a most dangerous state of things it is for the radicals to see no Governm[en]t can be formed in spite of them, and that they have forced back Ld Grey on the King. Ld P[almerston] says as soon as this thing is settled he shall send you a Courier.

George Street, Friday—a great Ball at Court today, and I am going to it . . .

Broadlands Papers

George Street, Thursday May 17th [1832]

Nieumann tells me he has an opportunity of sending tomorrow, so I write tho I sent you a long letter by post today. I know how much you must wish to know all the details of the extraordinary events here, and yet how difficult it will be for you to understand them entirely. I am myself puzzled where to begin, the reports succeed each other so rapidly. One thing only is clear, that we are in a most ticklish state and that the events of the last few days have done more to produce revolution than one could have thought possible in so short a time. The King's popularity is gone, and the Queen is the object of general mob indignation, tho I believe perfectly innocent of anything else but having an opinion. The Duke and the Tories have lost character by their attempt to form a Governm[en]t with the Reform Bill, and the House of Commons and the Radicals have learnt to know their strength, and that they have only to persevere to carry any point they wish. They have forced back Ld Grey upon the K[ing] and the Aristocracy, and they feel that it is they who have done so. The Discussion in the Lords last night was very striking but very violent and if I was Ld Grey and had pursued the conduct he has done, I should have sunk into the earth at the hard things that were said to him. Ld Carnavon[12] told him that he had begun as a Necker, and would end by being a Robespierre.[13] The Duke made a very good straight forward speech and every body's feelings went with him. He quite cleared himself for his conduct, that is to say not the wisdom of it, but as to the integrity of his intentions, and clearly showed that there was no concert in the large majority who had beat Ministers. Oh, it's a sad piece of business altogether, and I do not think our friends have behaved well, but who can behave well when they are a small party dragged on by a violent and unreasonable one? Ld Grey should never have resigned, or asked for the creation of Peers, he should have waited to see what came next, and have been prepared to make concessions to conciliate the adverse Peers. I have just heard from P[almerston] that he sends a Courier off at 12 tonight, so the thing is settled, and I trust it may all turn out for the best. Birmingham is in a dreadful state of excitement and the bill seems now our only resource. So we must hope it may not turn out as bad as we have feared. I don't exactly know the terms our friends have made, but I suppose you will hear this from him. My letter of today by Post will be after this one ... Friday night—I am going off to the Court Ball.

Broadlands Papers

[12] Henry George Herbert, 2nd Earl of Carnarvon (1772–1833).

[13] Jacques Necker was the Minister who tried to reform the French finances before the revolution. Had he succeeded, he might have saved the Monarchy. Maximilian Robespierre was, of course, the leading revolutionary who destroyed it.

Meanwhile Lady Cowper's younger daughter, Fanny, had been ill; and, as the air of London was thought to be bad for her, the Cowpers were in treaty for 'a beautiful villa on Putney Heath . . . the Villa in which Mr Pitt died . . .'[14] she told her brother on the 18th of May. Then she turned to other topics. She and Minny had attended on the previous evening the Court Ball for the Duke of Orleans, who had been well received; and the following night Lord Palmerston was giving a Foreign Office dinner for him, from which Emily excused herself, 'wishing to avoid as many of the hot dinners as I could'. Among the entertainments for the Duke of Orleans was a Ball given by Lady Cadogan that did not go with a swing!

George St. May 18th [1832]

. . . Think of Ly Cadogan's bad luck. When she has a party something else turns up. When she has a dinner, 8 people send excuses from being kept at the H[ouse] of Commons, but to crown all, she gave a ball to the D[uke] of Orleans Friday, when a pipe burst, and the smell so horrid that they were all obliged to dance holding their Noses. What a contretemps. The Girls in despair of course, and next Morning Fordwich having heard nothing of the Ball met Noney [?] Cadogan, and said by way of a civility, I was so sorry I could not go to your Ball last night!! I hear I missed a great deal!! upon which she looked highly disgusted taking it for a *mauvaise plaisanterie*, and turned up her Nose . . .

Broadlands Papers

In her next letter Lady Cowper returned to the exciting topic of the Reform Bill debates, on which of course all England was talking.

George St. May 31st [1832]

. . . The Bill will probably pass through its last reading on Monday next, and this in all its original odiousness, or with such *very small* change as to be not worth mentioning. The fact is that those untoward events gave us up to the Radicals, and there is no help for it. Many of our friends are very unhappy about it. . . . They did not exert themselves, when they could have done so,

[14] The Younger Pitt died at Bowling Green House on Putney Heath on January 23rd, 1806.

let slip by opportunities, and now they repent of it, and will do so I fear more and more every day. The whole is a great speculation, and therefore all one has to hope now is that things may not turn out as bad as we *expect* . . .

. . . Next Tuesday the Reform Bill will pass and the Tory Peers will all then put forward a protest to record their opinions, while the bill men are all beginning to look very blue and now I believe for the *first* time look with some alarm at their own folly, and quake at the aspect of their own Frankenstein.[15] The D[uke] of Richmond[16] looks ill and wretched, and even little John[17] I am sure is frightened, but the effect with all these is to make them dreadfully out of temper, and irritable just like spoilt children, when they have everything their own way. They feel now that, let it be good or evil, the whole responsibility must lie on their Shoulders, and instead of being angry with themselves as they ought to be, they are angry with those whom they think blame them . . .

Broadlands Papers

A week later, on the 7th of June, the Bill received the royal assent. Many people, including Lady Cowper, as is shown by her next letter to her brother, thought that the consequences would be a coalition of the Whigs and Tories to withstand the onslaught of radicalism.

Thursday, June 14th, 1832

. . . It seems to me quite clear that [if] the radicals act in that manner, that it will force the Whigs and Tories together and this result of their conduct is so far good. This was the case last night in the Commons about the Irish Reform bill, and in fact the Tories are so frightened now at the state of affairs, that they are quite willing to support the Governm[en]t, and anxious to do so. Everything depends on the turn of the Elections and this nobody

[15] Lady Cowper makes the usual mistake. Frankenstein was not the name of the monster, but the name of its maker.

[16] Charles Gordon Lennox, 5th Duke of Richmond (1791–1860); Postmaster-General in the Grey Government.

[17] Lord John Russell, who introduced all three Reform Bills in the House of Commons.

can prophecy about but in a great many places where one could hardly expect it there is a great anxiety to have Gentlemen . . . The Counties of Eng[lan]d will be mostly respectable. Ashley[18] is safer than before and expects to have no contest. I was glad of what you said that Ld C[owper] ought this time to support no radical; it strengthened my endeavours. He will certainly not support Duncombe, but I want him to go *against* him and also to propose a compromise for the County that is that Grimston should be one, and then the other two might be Tom Brand and Hale, or Plumer Ward,[19] or one of the old Members. Fordwich and Watson will I think stand at Canterbury, and have no contest, but they do talk of a Tory standing, or perhaps a radical, as some people at Canterbury think Watson too conservative.

We have been staying a week at Richmond, and had various Society. One day Peele [*sic*] dined with us . . . he did not seem very desponding at the state of affairs, said nobody could tell how things would turn, they might be better than he expected, or much worse than he feared. He said like the child[20] that the present Governm[en]t must stay in, and that if they tried to resist the radicals, they should have his support. One thing he said must be done, without which *no* Governm[en]t could stand, and that was to curb the licence of the Press. These events in Paris are certainly a turn in our favour, and a check to the radicals.[21]

. . . Ld P[almerston] has been shamefully attacked lately in the Papers for his Tory Appointm[en]ts, he don't care much for it, but it has a bad effect for the whole party, he strongly suspects Durham and Bear Ellis [*sic*][22] . . . Bagot[23] has refused to go to

[18] Lord Ashley was M.P. for Dorset at this time.

[19] Robert Plumer Ward (1765–1846); M.P. Cockermouth, 1802–6; Haslemere, 1807–23; Under-Secretary for Foreign Affairs, 1805–6; a Commissioner of the Admiralty, 1807–11; Clerk of the Ordnance, 1811–23; High Sheriff of Hertford-shire, 1830.

[20] Presumably Wellington.

[21] On June 5th, the day of the funeral of the republican General Lamarque, who had died of cholera, his party had stirred up the people of Paris to revolt. At first things looked ugly; but Louis-Philippe soon appeared with troops and their success was short-lived.

[22] Edward Ellice (1781–1863): Secretary to the Treasury, 1830–2; Secretary at War, 1832–4.

[23] Sir Charles Bagot (1781–1843); Ambassador to St Petersburg, 1820; The Hague, 1824; Governor-General of Canada, 1841.

Petersburgh, and it is very difficult to find anyone suited, as they will not hear of S[tratford] Canning.[24] ... We have been staying a week at Richmond[25] during the Whitsuntide holidays. ... We went tonight to H[ollan]d House and find H[ollan]d foolish as usual. He cannot find fault with Louis Philippe and yet they have not sense enough to approve the measure of Severity he has been obliged to take. The Martial Law is a bitter pill, and the stopping the papers (both events being great nuts to me). I am sure that before long there will be only two parties in England, the Conservative and the Destructive and the sooner this line is drawn the better. The Viscount[26] is a little cured of his radical propensities, but still he has more leaning that way than I think right in these times; formerly it was all very well, but the times are changed and what was safe formerly is dangerous now, and so I am always working at him for his own good and to prevent his being spoilt by the company he keeps ...

Broadlands Papers

But if things were not as bad as many feared, nevertheless the country was in an unsettled state, as evidenced by stones thrown at William IV and the famous attack on Wellington on the anniversary of Waterloo.

Tuesday June 19th and 20th, 21 and 22nd [1832]
... This prospect of a dissolution in Nov[embe]r is a hindrance to every body and every thing. I wish they might put it off till Febr[uar]y. There must be a new Parliament before next April or March, I forget which, on account of the Mutiny Bill.[27] In some respects our Home Affairs look well, and in others badly. Contrary to expectation many of the new Towns want Gentlemen, and men of property, and they say the same of London districts

---

[24] Stratford Canning, 1st Viscount Stratford de Redcliffe (1786–1880); 'The Great Elchi': he was nominated Ambassador to St Petersburg in 1833, but the Czar refused to receive him.

[25] With the Lievens.   [26] Palmerston.

[27] Parliament was prorogued until October 16th and further prorogued until December 3rd, when it was finally dissolved.

... The Duke of W[ellingto]n has invited us to a great Ball on the 26th which their Majesties are to grace. He has put iron blinds to his windows, instead of the wooden shutters, made like the old green wooden ones at Whitehall. There was a shameful attack made upon him by the mob yesterday, the Anniversary of Waterloo!! somewhere in the City, but the police were on the alert and soon set it right, but such things are abominable in a civilized Country. There never was such a good invention as that new Police. Peele [*sic*] ought to have a statue raised to him if for nothing else. The Lieven is looking so well since she has been quiet at Richmond, and is really grown fat. The Duke W[ellington] is to dine with her Thursday, and she wanted me to come down, but I did not much fancy it. One may have too much of a good thing, and one may get tired even of Richmond road if one travels it every other day. She is in great tribulation to think whom they will have sent as Ambassador to Petersburg, and would like to have you, anybody but Canning ...

Thursday 21st
... The attack of the D[uke] of W[ellingto]n by the Mob has produced general indignation, and an address from leading people in the City to him sign'd by 20,000 people ...

22nd The Courier not gone yet, and will not go till tomorrow, as there has been no time for Ld P[almerston] to write. They all have such a deal of business ... You will see in the papers about the Stones thrown at the King, and the mob attack on the Duke. These things do I think good, it frightens the thoughtless, and makes our friends think what they are about, when they excite the ignorant. They were a good deal [illegible] about this in the H[ouse] of Commons, and I think the Whigs cut a ridiculous figure ... with their fine expressions of loyalty, after all they have said and done.

Broadlands Papers

In July the Cowpers again visited Princess Lieven at Richmond to escape the cholera which once more had appeared in London. However, this attack seems to have been far milder than the epidemic of

1849, so, though cases of the disease had been reported in Hertford-shire, Lady Cowper was able to go to Panshanger on the 1st of August, whence a few days later she reported to Mrs Huskisson that the neighbourhood was now 'very healthy'.[28]

A fortnight later the Cowpers were back at Richmond, where Prince and Princess Lieven had a political and diplomatic house-party. Apart from the Prime Minister and Lady Grey, and Lord Palmerston, the Foreign Secretary, the Russian Ambassador's guests included Madame Palmella, wife of the Portuguese Ambassador in London, Matuscewitz [29] who, according to Mrs Arbuthnot, had been sent over from Russia 'to spy on the Lievens',[30] and Flahault with his Scottish wife.[31] Other visitors included the Duke of Wellington, under whom Palmella had served in Portugal, the George Lambs, and that society toady Mr Mottaux. They had plenty to talk about.

In August 1831, Dom Pedro, who had been living in exile in England with his daughter, the little Queen Maria II, determined once more to enter the lists on his daughter's behalf and to attack his brother Miguel. With that object in view, he crossed with her to France, where since the July revolution Louis-Philippe had been reigning in place of Charles X. Palmella was left in England with the task of raising funds. He was so far successful that two East-Indiamen, the *Rainha* and *Dona Maria II*, were bought and transformed into frigates. The crews were English and were placed under the command of a certain Captain Sartorius, a British naval officer who was given the rank of Admiral. Some 300 mercenaries, enlisted in London, were placed on board the frigates, and these formed the nucleus of the army of liberation.

On the 10th of February, 1832, the frigate *Rainha* with Dom Pedro on board, on which Sartorius had hoisted his flag, the frigate *Dona Maria* and other craft sailed from Belle-Isle. In the *Rainha* was also Palmella, who had come over from England with other chiefs of the party. On their arrival at the Azores at the end of the month, Dom

[28] Lady Cowper to Mrs Huskisson, Panshanger, Sunday, 5 Aug. [1832]. Huskisson Papers, B.M. Add. MSS. 37048, f. 132.

[29] Count André Joseph Matuscewitz (d. 1842); Russian Envoy Extraordinary at London, 1829-35.

[30] *Mrs Arbuthnot*, II, p. 239.

[31] Auguste Charles Joseph, Comte de Flahault-de-la-Billardrie (1785-1870); son of Adelaide Marie Emilie Filleul, Comtesse de Flahault and mistress of Talleyrand, who was almost certainly the younger Flahault's father.

Pedro assumed all the powers of government. The English troops were here joined by some 500 French mercenaries, and these and the English were reckoned to be reliable soldiers. The rest of the army, which in total numbered no more than some 6,500 men, was not highly rated. It therefore seemed an act of the greatest rashness to attempt an invasion with so insignificant a force; but Dom Pedro, blinded to the realities that faced him, was deluded into thinking that he had but to show himself on Portuguese soil for the whole population to flock to his standard. Very different in fact was his reception. By the 9th of July he had possession of Oporto; on the 10th of July Sartorius' fleet entered the river; but it was at once clear that the inhabitants, far from regarding Dom Pedro as a liberator, looked upon him as an enemy. Nor did the Miguelist troops come over to him: quite the contrary, for he soon found himself blockaded within the walls of Oporto by vastly superior forces. The position of the besieged army was critical, and Palmella was sent over to England again to entreat our Government for help. It was perhaps to assist him that the Lievens had organized their party at Richmond. Be that as it may, the cause of Dom Pedro and his daughter was not likely to receive much encouragement from the Whig Ministry of Lord Grey.

Richmond, Aug. 20th, [1832]

... Poor Palmella is very anxious and going back directly. He came here to see if he could get the Govern[men]t to do anything for him, but they cannot serve him beyond *good wishes*. He says that nothing can be more courageous than their little Army, and that if they keep their position for a month longer, they are safe, but they may be crushed before. He says they have under their banner 400 English and 500 French, fighting side by side, a thing which has not happened since the time of the Crusades. Miguel's Fleet was gone out of Port and Sartorius after them, but they had heard nothing of them since. The former is the strongest in numbers, but *not well* disciplined, so if Sartorius is not a Taylor as his name seems to indicate he ought to blow them out of the water, and if the Fleet is destroyed, D[uke] of W[ellingto]n says the *moral* effect would be such that Miguel must be blown after them. This prognostick he utters with many sighs, and a look of deep feeling which would touch one if it did not make one laugh, but such sympathy for Miguel one cannot go with . . . People are astonished that Ld Grey should venture to go off to Howick for six weeks in the present state of Europe, but however I believe he really means it. All the other Ministers are also gone different ways and W[illia]m and Ld P[almerston] will be the only two left in town . . .

Broadlands Papers

A week later the Cowpers were back at Panshanger, where they prepared to stay for some time because of the cholera.

Panshanger, Monday, Augt. 27th, [1832]

. . . The Tories are in general in spirits about the Elections but nobody can say beforehand how they will turn out. The Press and the Unions do all the mischief they can and there seems to have been so many people disfranchised with this bill by non-payment of rates, that I dont see how Governm[en]t can dissolve without giving more time. I fancy the bill turns out even more absurd, and ill-managed than every body thought it, and there will be no end to the difficulties of setting it going; how could people be such idiots!! It is painful to think that our friends should be party to such a thing.

. . . Poor Palmella is I believe gone. One feels for him *very* much, and the whole concern is a bad job. Ad[mira]l Sartorious has no strength, or he would settle the whole thing. Miguel has the largest force both at sea and land, but they are not courageous, and so Pedro may be able to defend Oporto, but a protracted Civil War is the worst thing. One had hoped that the whole thing would have been settled one way or the other directly. Now I think single Combat would be the most theatrical way of terminating the affair. Pedro and Miguel to enter the lists as two Knights of old . . .

Broadlands Papers

In consequence of the cholera, the Cowpers determined to remain in Hertfordshire 'the whole season', as Emily told her brother; and so it was that we find them still there in October, when Lady Cowper was urging Mrs Huskisson, who had never recovered from the shock of her husband's death, to pay them a visit.[32]

Panshanger, Thursday [1832]

... I think a little change might do you good, and you know it would delight us so much to have you, and you could remain in your own room and do just as you liked ... The Cholera has not been bad at Hertford and we have not had any immediately in this neighbourhood ... I have ceased to be much alarmed about the Complaint myself, but it is a very horrid disorder and one cannot be too much on one's guard against it ... A new and mortal disorder will henceforward increase the uncertainty of life tenfold and, as for People's minds, I don't think they have the least chance of ever being quiet again. The *bill* might not turn out so bad as people thought in the first instance, but I think its bad effects are equally certain in the course of time.

My brother W[illia]m came here yesterday, he is quite well again and seems in tolerably good spirits. Lord Palmerston I expect on Sat[urda]y. He has still hopes of Pedro's success and thinks that the Belgian business is likely to be settled at last but to be sure it has been a long and very disheartening job.[33] A person of a less sanguine disposition than his would have been quite worn out long ago. Frederick writes to me very often. He is well in health but rather tired of his situation, the fact is that he likes nothing but being in Eng[land] ...

Huskisson Papers
B.M. Add. MSS. 37048, f. 139

In fact, nearly a decade was to pass before Sir Frederick Lamb was destined to retire from the diplomatic service and to settle in England for the remaining twelve years of his life.

[32] Lady Cowper to Mrs Huskisson, Panshanger, Tuesday [October, 1832]. Huskisson Papers, B.M. Add. MSS. 37048, f. 137.
[33] Lady Cowper told Greville, who stayed at Panshanger for the night of October 5th, that Palmerston attributed all the trouble over the Belgian question to Matuscewitz, 'who was insolent and obstinate, and astute in making objections ...' *Greville Memoirs* (1874), II, pp. 324-5.

CHAPTER XII

Widowhood

IN OCTOBER 1832 the Cowpers had a house-party at Panshanger for Talleyrand, the French Ambassador.

> Pans[hange]r Thursday, Nov. 1 [1832]
>
> ... Taley[1] was been [*sic*] here quite young and frisky—I never saw him in better spirits, convinced now that things will go on well in France. He talked and chatted all day, and was so agreable and we had just a party that suited him ... Ashley and Minny, I expect next week. They have made a long stay in Dorsetshire, and she is bored to death, but he is pretty near certain of having no contest,[2] which is comfortable ...
>
> Broadlands Papers

It is a curious fact that the Reform Bill of 1832 did little to cure the evil of bribery or to break the influence of the landlords. What it did, however, was to promote the cause of the radicals, some of whom were expected to be successful in the forthcoming General Election; and in a letter that has not been found Emily Cowper, it seems, had alarmed her brother with an exaggerated forecast of radical successes. About the middle of November the Cowpers went up to London for a short stay before going to Petworth and Brighton; and it was from the Capital that Emily wrote on the 19th to calm her brother's anxiety about the election.

> London Nov. 19th, 1832, Monday
>
> I dont wonder I alarmed you with 250 radicals. I cant think

[1] Lady Cowper's usual name for Talleyrand.
[2] For Dorset. He was re-elected and was M.P. there from 1831 to 1846.

what I had heard, but I suppose this number must have meant Members unknown as well as Radicals. I had a talk some days ago with Johnny[3] and he told me he had seen a list drawn out very exactly of all the probable results, and that *40* radicals was what they expected to have and he thought that more than he liked . . . I assure you the Governm[en]t is grown wonderfully Conservative, and I believe they will keep in their followers if they can . . . Ld H[ollan]d[4] has a much quieter tone, and generally the tone everywhere is much more moderate and rational than I have known it for a great while. The fact is people are getting alarmed of what may be the consequences of their folly, and I hope it may be in time . . . I think affairs would appear to you under a better aspect if you was here than they now do from a distance. We are going off today to Petworth . . .

. . . Ld P[almerston] says he is going to send you a Courier in a day or two. Emilie[5] is a dear good soul, but very like a Spoilt Child, cannot bear contradiction and has not temper to stand things turning out differently from her wishes. They live on the hopes of revolution in France, and say we do all sorts of things to bolster up a state of things there, which cannot last. The fact is that they are in a very uncomfortable position. They act from the Orders of their Court, and are therefore not responsible, but by refusing to join in any Hostile measures against H[ollan]d they have made themselves of no importance and they have *forced* us into a close alliance with France, which it has always been their object to prevent.[6] With respect to the very sore subject of Stratford C[annin]g she has determined to say no more about it; she has left the subject to her Court to object or accede to, as they think proper but she will say no more. It is an unlucky circumstance just now . . .

[3] Lord John Russell.

[4] Chancellor of the Duchy of Lancaster in the first reform ministry and under Melbourne.   [5] Code name for Princess Lieven.

[6] When Louis-Philippe came to the throne of France in 1830, he made advances to the Czar which were tardily and coldly received; and when it was clear that Russia was anxious to form a coalition of Great Powers against revolutionary Belgium, Louis-Philippe turned to England. It was in order to effect an understanding with England that he had sent over as Ambassador Talleyrand, the man who at the Congress of Vienna had opposed this ambitious project of Russia and Prussia.

... The Tories are in great spirits about the Dutch War, and in great hopes that Prussia will march and that there will be a general confusion. How strange it is that whoever is in opposition gets such a party spirit, that their own interest with that of the Country is all to be sacrificed to spite. Johnny ... has a sharp contest in Devonshire, and is very anxious about it. What he said there about the ballot was a fit of temper, and he is quite ashamed of it, and he has been lectured about [it] by the higher powers. The fact is that Hustings are dangerous places—bullied and bated on one side, and ragged on by the other, but he is come to his senses and will I hope now be more prudent; instead of being Cock-a-hoop with his bill, I think he is now rather ashamed at the details and working of it being so imperfect. However the Barristers have been very impartial in all cases and the Counties will do well ...

Broadlands Papers

The Cowpers stayed with Lord Egremont from the 19th until the 23rd of November when they left Petworth for Brighton. Two days later they dined at the Pavilion.[7] They again stayed at Petworth after their return to London in December.[8]

In Emily's next letter to her brother, written from Brighton, she returns to the subject touched on in her previous letter of the affair of Stratford Canning. Lord Heytesbury, our Ambassador at St Petersburg, had recently intimated his wish to retire; whereupon Palmerston, with the full approval of the Prime Minister, had designated Stratford Canning for the post, and for some time had been insisting on the appointment in spite of the violent protests of the Czar. Palmerston's motives were plain; Canning was the ablest diplomat we had, and as cousin of the great Canning, he had to be provided with a suitable post. Palmerston was, therefore, not disposed to give way to unjustified protests. Unfortunately, the whole affair had been complicated by the intrigues of the Russian ambassadress,[9] who insisted that the Foreign

[7] Princess Lieven to Grey, Brighton, Tuesday, Nov. 20th, Friday, Nov. 23rd, Sunday, Nov. 26th [error for 25th, 1832]. *Lieven-Grey Correspondence*, II, pp. 414, 416, 418. *Greville Memoirs* (1874), II, p. 334.

[8] *Greville Memoirs* (1874), II, pp. 336-7.

[9] Some said that Madame de Lieven, offended at some real or fancied grievance, had taken her revenge on Canning by intriguing against his reception at St. Petersburg. Lane-Poole, *Canning*, II, p. 18.

Secretary had promised her not to press this appointment. This Palmerston strenuously denied; whereupon the Princess fell back upon the extraordinary story that she had planned with her friend Lady Cowper for Sir Frederick Lamb to exchange the Vienna Embassy for that at St Petersburg.[10] The absurdity of this is clear for, as Emily knew perfectly well, Fred's one object was to return to England; so she would surely not have associated herself with a suggestion which he was certain to refuse.

On the 30th of October there appeared in the *London Gazette* the official notice of the appointment of Sir Stratford Canning to the Embassy at St Petersburg.

Brighton Dec. 6th [1832]

... your answer to our plan of a change with S[tratford] C[anning] is just what I expected ... It is a bad appointment, but I really believe it could not be avoided, and at any rate, as you say, it was no business of Emilie's.[11] The fact is that she really behaved very ill about this ... she has no temper and cannot bear to be thwarted ...

Broadlands Papers

Towards the end of January 1833, whilst on a visit at Panshanger, Princess Lieven received a statement from Nesselrode[12] that in no circumstances would Stratford Canning be received at St Petersburg.[13] It was clear that matters were becoming serious and that the deadlock might well put an end to the Lievens' embassy in London. The Princess wrote in great distress to Palmerston from Panshanger what can only be described as a 'pitiful appeal'.[14] The terrible prospect of having to leave England loomed before her; and what made matters worse was that this possibility was brought about by those she had considered her friends, of whom the Foreign Secretary had been foremost. Could he not even at this late hour do something to extricate

[10] Princess Lieven to Nesselrode, October 28, 29, 1832. Lieven MSS. Webster, *Palmerston*, I, p. 323.　　　　　　[11] Princess Lieven.

[12] Charles Robert, Count von Nesselrode, Russian Foreign Minister.

[13] Lane-Poole, *Canning*, II, pp. 18–23.

[14] Webster, *Palmerston*, I, p. 326.

her from her difficulties? She begged him on his honour to keep absolutely secret her letter which was known only to one *seule et unique* person who would transmit it to Palmerston; and we may be sure that Lady Cowper added her entreaties to those of her friend.[15] No answer in writing appears to have been sent to the appeal, but that he was not entirely insensible to it is shown by the Foreign Secretary's subsequent actions. But things had gone too far, and neither the King, who was strongly in favour of the appointment, nor Canning himself was willing to give way at the bidding of the Czar. Nearly four years later, writing from Paris, Madame de Lieven recalled that letter. 'How prophetic were my words to Lord Palmerston,' she reminded Lady Cowper, 'when I said, and repeated to him by letter from Panshanger in 1833, on the subject of Stratford Canning: "Remember, my Lord, that you are about to destroy and overturn my whole existence!" I will add no more, dearest, for it is a dreadful thing for me to look back into the past.'[16]

In her next letter Lady Cowper gave her brother an unflattering picture of the reformed House of Commons.[17] Early in June she had the satisfaction of recording that her old friend Lord Palmerston had been down to Windsor, where the King 'insisted out of his especial Grace and Favour to give him the Civil Grand Cross of the Bath'.[18]

In July things seemed to be calmer, but the Canning affair was no nearer solution. Palmerston did what he could to ease the situation by promising that, if the Ambassador designate were received at St Petersburg, he would find means of replacing him in a very short time. This was a considerable concession, and for a time it looked as if the Russian Foreign Minister would give way. But, according to Bligh, our Chargé d'Affaires in St Petersburg, the 'Russian' party led by Orlov persuaded the Czar not to yield. If that was so, the refusal to make any concession may have been aimed, not at Canning, but at the Lievens, for it seems that they had many enemies at St Petersburg as well as in London.[19]

Be that as it may, the Czar recalled the Princess to St Petersburg

[15] Princess Lieven to Palmerston, Jan. 26, 1833. Broadlands Papers.

[16] Princess Lieven to Lady Cowper, Paris, Sunday, 18th December, 1836. *Lieven-Palmerston Correspondence*, p. 132. Webster, *Palmerston*, I, p. 326.

[17] Lady Cowper to Sir Frederick Lamb, George Street, Feb. 26th, 1833. Broadlands Papers.

[18] Lady Cowper to Sir Frederick Lamb, George St., June 5th [1833]. Broadlands Papers.   [19] Webster, *Palmerston*, I, p. 328.

this summer, where she tried—unsuccessfully it would seem—to enlist the Empress's support against the machinations, real or supposed, of Orlov and his party.

George St. Monday July 2nd[20] [1833]

... I assure you that the very different tone of people in the last three weeks is very curious, all violence has disappeared and those who were most wrong headed begin to entertain doubts of the wisdom of their own proceedings ... The Elections will I really believe turn out better than one could have anticipated (in England) but Ireland is I fear a bad piece of business.

The Vis[coun]t[21] had a grand dinner yesterday for Prince Adalbert, a very handsome thing. We dined there and sat by the Duke of Richmond who sees the state of affairs just in the same light we do. (I shall try to find opportunities of cultivating him) ... Ld P[almerston] set off last night after his dinner to Cambridge for Commencement to consult his friends and see what chance he has of his Election.[22] It would be such a great thing if he could come in there. I am afraid Falmouth and Penrhyn will not answer,—at the latter place they want 5 a piece for their votes, so much for bribery being put down by the Bill.

Broadlands Papers

On her return to England, Madame de Lieven resumed her outwardly friendly relations with Palmerston, who visited her at Richmond and entertained her at Broadlands, though she wrote acidly about him both to her brother and to Nesselrode.[23] She also met him frequently with the Cowpers. Thus she was at Panshanger in September to celebrate Lord Fordwich's engagement to Lady Anne Robinson,[24] 'a fine young woman, very pleasant and very rich', as the

---

[20] So written, but July 2nd, 1833, was a Tuesday.   [21] Lord Palmerston.
[22] Having lost his Cambridge seat in 1831 through his support of parliamentary reform, Palmerston was not re-elected. He was however elected for Tiverton in 1835 and remained M.P. for the constituency until his death thirty years later.
[23] Webster, *Palmerston*, I, p. 329.
[24] Elder daughter of Thomas Philip, 2nd Earl de Grey. Lady Anne in 1859 succeeded her father in the Barony of Lucas.

Princess informed Lord Grey.[25] Lady Cowper was delighted at the match, and announced the news joyously to Mrs Huskisson.[26] On the 1st of October the Lievens gave a great dinner for the young couple 'ten members of the Cowper family and of the Lambs, and six of the De Greys', as well as Palmerston, Melbourne, Lady Jersey and other friends.[27] On the 7th of October Fordwich and Lady Anne were married, when, if we may credit Madame de Lieven, the bridegroom was suffering from a stomach ache! Nor on this occasion did the bride find favour with her captious critic. 'Heavens! What a size she is, and so far from pretty.' [28]

A few days later the Cowpers and the Ashleys with the Ashleys' little boy—'Sir Babkins', they called him—set forth on a six months' tour abroad. Towards the end of the year they were in Rome, and two days after Christmas Lord and Lady Ashley attended Mrs Montague's Ball, which was 'lively and pleasant'. 'Minny looked heavenly,' noted a delighted husband, 'and a foreigner requested to be introduced to "Mademoiselle Ashley!" Is it wrong to be so entirely proud of, and happy in, one's wife's beauty? But surely there is nothing so pretty and fascinating as my Min.' [29]

But soon Emily Cowper's life was saddened by news of the unexpected loss of her youngest brother; George Lamb died on the 2nd of January, 1834.[30] Mrs Huskisson, who was also in Italy, wrote to condole, and Emily replied from Nice in the middle of February.[31]

In the spring of 1834 the travellers returned to England. That summer, the blow that Madame de Lieven had been dreading for so long at last fell. The news that Czar Nicholas had decided to withdraw his Ambassador from London was brought on the 20th of May by

[25] Princess Lieven to Grey, Panshanger, Wednesday, Sept. 11th, 1833. *Lieven-Grey Correspondence*, II, p. 462.

[26] Lady Cowper to Mrs Huskisson, Panshanger, Wednesday [September 4th 1833]. Huskisson Papers, B.M. Add. MSS. 39949, p. 145.

[27] Princess Lieven to Grey, Richmond, Wednesday, Oct. 2nd, 1833. *Lieven-Grey Correspondence*, II, p. 473.

[28] Princess Lieven to Grey, Richmond, Oct. 8th [1833]. *Lieven-Grey Correspondence*, II, p. 478.

[29] Hodder, *Shaftesbury*, I, p. 184.

[30] Grey to Princess Lieven, Downing Street, Jan. 1st, 1834. *Lieven-Grey Correspondence*, II, pp. 494–5, 496.

[31] Lady Cowper to Mrs Huskisson, Nice, Feby. 15th, 1834. Huskisson Papers, B.M. Add. MSS. 39949, f. 146.

Benckhausen, the Consul-General.[32] Though long expected, this was a cruel shock to the intriguing Princess, who aired her grievances far and wide. But she won but scant sympathy from many of her friends, who felt that she had received no more than her officious conduct deserved. Indeed, Lady Cowper told Charles Greville that in her view Princess Lieven was entirely to blame for the whole affair; and as she made no secret of the fact that her sympathies were wholeheartedly with Palmerston in this matter,[33] a coolness naturally sprang up between the two women.[34] Yet the pain at parting must have been assuaged somewhat for the Princess by the gift of a magnificent bracelet from the noble ladies who had been her friends and associates for so long, many of whom, it must be admitted, gave a sigh of relief at the prospect of her imminent departure!

In November the death of Lord Spencer and the consequent elevation of his son Althorp to the House of Lords gave William IV the opportunity he had long been anxious for of ridding himself of the Melbourne Ministry and Peel was hastily summoned from Rome to form a government.[35] But it was soon apparent that the new administration was too weak to last long, and in fact in April of the following year, 1835, Sir Robert Peel resigned. William IV, after vainly trying to arrange a coalition between Melbourne and Wellington, Peel and Stanley, was reluctantly compelled to recall Lord Melbourne and ask him to form a government.[36]

Lady Cowper, delighted of course at her brother's return to power, wrote regularly to Princess Lieven in Russia; but she was careful to see that her old friend could garner little information from her letters! This discretion disgusted the intriguing Princess.[37] But Emily's reaction to the policy of the Melbourne Government tickled Lord Grey.

---

[32] For a detailed discussion of the whole question of the recall of the Lievens, see Webster, *Palmerston*, I, pp. 320–32.

[33] *Greville Memoirs* (1874), II, p. 358.

[34] Princess Lieven to Lady Cowper, London, Friday, 27th [June, 1834]. *Lieven-Palmerston Correspondence*, p. 50.

[35] For Lady Cowper's version of these exciting events, see *Lieven-Palmerston Correspondence*, pp. 61–70.

[36] *Melbourne Papers*, pp. 332–65; Walpole, *Russell*, I, pp. 219–29. For details of attempts to keep Palmerston from returning to the Foreign Office, see Webster, *Palmerston*, I, pp. 416–21.

[37] Princess Lieven to Grey, St. Petersburg, Aug. 24th/Sept. 5th, 1834, and Nov. 9th/21st, 1834. *Lieven-Grey Correspondence*, III, pp. 12–13, 50.

'I am often amused when I recollect her horror of my own Liberal principles,' he told his Russian friend, 'and see her now so anxious for a Ministry whose great merit, as proclaimed by their supporters, is that they were inclined to go greater lengths in the work of reform than I was.'[38]

In October the Cowpers were back at Panshanger,[39] planning visits later in the month to Petworth and Brighton. In November they were at Brighton, when Melbourne and his colleagues came and were better received by the old King. On their return, Lord and Lady Cowper stayed with the Burrells at Knepp Castle and with Lord Egremont at Petworth. From Knepp Emily wrote to Mrs Huskisson.

Knepp Wed[nesda]y Novr. 25 [1835]

... We are going to Petworth today and intend staying three or four days or a week according as we find Lord Egremont ... Brighton I thought delightful, a great many people there and the Court very amusing. Nothing could be more generous than the King was to me. I dined there several times and he made very particular inquiries about you.

The Ministers all came down last Friday and were received as well as possible. W[illia]m is in high favour, and the little ill humours which the King had on their first return to office seem to be entirely vanished and the whole thing going on as smoothly as possible, even the Prince and Princess seem reconciled to them and cordial ...

Huskisson Papers
B.M. Add. MSS. 39949, f. 151

Whilst these events were taking place Lord Cowper's health was beginning to fail. By Christmas 1835 he and his wife were back at Panshanger, whence Emily reported to Mrs Huskisson that her husband was 'pretty well';[40] but early in the new year she was showing

[38] Grey to Princess Lieven, Dec. 15th, 1834. *Lieven-Grey Correspondence*, III, p. 56.

[39] Lady Cowper to Mrs Huskisson, Panshanger, Sunday, Oct. 18th [1835] Huskisson Papers, B.M. Add. MSS. 39949, f. 155.

[40] Lady Cowper to Mrs Huskisson, Sunday, Panshanger [Dec. 20th, 1835] Huskisson Papers, B.M. Add. MSS. 39949, f. 159.

increased anxiety. Nevertheless, the letter she wrote to Mrs Huskisson in January was full of topical events in the political world.

Panshanger Tuesday 5 Jany. [1836]

. . . Politics look favourably and the result of three Corporation elections is a good pull in our favour. Indeed we want something for I hear the Tories were in great spirits at the late Elections and thought it proved the certainty of success if a dissolution was to take place. Now this motion either true or false was a dangerous one for them to house and therefore I hope the Corporation results will have damped their ardour.

I suppose you have read the portfolio.[41] It is a most curious exposure and puts all the Diplomatists in a dreadful taking, as they are in agony to know what will cause a heat. The disclosure of Russian prospects is a great point gained and will I hope open the eye of Europe to their common danger. Lieven and Matuschiovey[42] will be very much annoy'd at the candid and unflatter'd characters of the D[uke] of W[ellington] par[ticularl]y the latter who amongst his friends has always professed such profound admiration for him. Pozzo[43] is I hear in a very great fright, and nobody knows how these papers have been obtained, or by whom. It is a curious subject altogether.[44]

Huskisson Papers
B.M. Add. MSS. 39949, f. 160

Unfortunately, Lord Cowper's health did not improve and in July his wife took him abroad. They started on a tour up the Rhine to

[41] The *Portfolio* was a collection of diplomatic correspondence between the Russian Government and its agents, published at this time, which purported to throw light on the secret aims of the Government. It included copies of letters sent to Russia by Prince Lieven and other diplomats. Princess Lieven reported from Paris that it had no influence there. Princess Lieven to Lady Cowper, Paris, January 15th, 1836. *Lieven-Palmerston Correspondence*, pp. 109–10.

[42] Presumably Matuscewitz is intended.

[43] Charles André, Comte Pozzo di Borgo, who had succeeded Lieven as Russian Ambassador in London.

[44] For the whole matter discussed, see Webster, *Palmerston*, II, pp. 558-9.

Baden to see Madame Lieven. In August they were at Brussels, whence Lady Cowper reported to her eldest son.

> Brussels, August 8 [1836]
>
> We have got so far on our Journey, tolerably prosperous—the weather beautiful and I hope Lord C[owper] a little better, but still he does not sleep well. But I think he will improve more as he gets into the way of travelling and accustomed to the early dinner etc.
>
> We have been today to Waterloo and tomorrow we are off again expecting to be at Wisbaden [*sic*] in about six days, so direct there to the poste restante . . . I have had no letters yet and am very anxious for news of you all, par[ticular]ly of your measley Children . . .
>
> Panshanger Papers

In October Princess Lieven wrote from Paris to Lord Grey that the Cowpers were expected shortly 'if poor Lord Cowper's condition allows of his being brought to Paris alive'.[45] Whether or not he was 'brought to Paris alive' does not appear; all we know is that for another nine months he lingered on, and then at last on the 21st of June, 1837, Lord Cowper died. On the previous day, very early in the morning, the old King had died at Windsor, to be succeeded by his niece as Queen Victoria.

For a time the widow retired to Broadstairs, where on the 1st of August she was visited by Princess Lieven, who was staying with the Sutherlands at Stafford House.[46] In the autumn she was at Brighton, where the Duke of Devonshire lent her 'his pretty house'.[47] From there she wrote to her old friend, Lord Palmerston, who was paying Emily marked attention in her widowhood.

[45] Princess Lieven to Grey, Paris, Oct. 8th, 1836. *Lieven-Grey Correspondence*, III, p. 210.

[46] Princess Lieven to Grey, Stafford House, July 29th, 1837. *Lieven-Grey Correspondence*, III, p. 241.

[47] Lady Cowper to Princess Lieven, George Street, Sept. 28th, [1837]. *Lieven-Grey Correspondence*, III, pp. 136–7.

Brighton Sunday [*c.* September–October 1837]
Here I am in the Duke's House, which is most comfortable
and like an enchanted Palace, with all its beauties and nick
Nacks [*sic*]. Birds flying on India Papers, curiosities of all sorts,
a clock with two Birds that sing a duet, Pastiles kept burning by
invisible hands—in short it is just the thing for Fanny and she is
charmed with it . . .

Broadlands Papers

But these airy nothings were not what the Foreign Secretary wanted
in the least, for he was pressing the friend of his childhood to become
his wife. What precisely he wrote to her at this time we do not know;
but from Emily's reply to her 'dear Harry', we have a good idea of its
trend.

Kemp Town Wednesday (11 Oct. 1837)[48]
Your statement today is completely and entirely true. I wish to
say no more on this subject now, but this I will say, that there is
not another person *in the world* of whom I should ever think of
for one moment in that light, and that I am quite sure there
exists *No other person* with whom I could ever have the least
prospect of happiness. Now *pray pray* do me justice, look into
my heart, and cease your suspicions . . .

Broadlands Papers

It seems clear that Palmerston was pressing her to come nearer to
London, so that he could see her more easily. But this she was not
anxious to do, so there was no alternative; he must go down to
Brighton!

Kemp Town Sunday 15 (Oct. 1837)[49]
It is a pity you should not have known of this arrangement
before, but I am very glad *you are coming*, and I think you might

[48] Date added by Lord Palmerston.
[49] Date added by Lord Palmerston.

manage to go from here to Broadlands without going back to Town; from the 26th to the 9th of Nov[embe]r would be a good spell and I dont see that you should be in town before, unless there is some necessity, which I am not aware of . . .

Broadlands Papers

When Palmerston next heard from Lady Cowper she was on a short visit to London, but on the point of returning to Kemp Town.

George Street, Tuesday night [*c*. October–November 1837]
I am very much disappointed not to see you today as I had hoped part[i]c[ular]ly as I could have explained my position to you so much better than by letter. Had I only myself to consult, I would make any sacrifice however inconvenient to meet your wishes, but I cannot without sacrificing Fanny's health as well as my own leave Brighton at this moment . . . London has been so dreary these four days that we find it quite impossible to stay here. I have *no* Country House and where then would you wish me to go? Mrs Lamb is coming into my House at Brighton and I have all the comforts there which my situation admits of, fresh air, quiet and privacy, for Kemp Town is quiet and free from all the bustle of Brighton . . . [rest of letter missing]

Broadlands Papers

In November, however, Emily came to a momentous decision; she would set up house at Brocket, where her brother William would join her whenever he was able. The suggestion no doubt came from him, and it seemed attractive to the homeless widow. 'This arrangement,' she told Madame de Lieven, 'suits me in every way, Panshanger would be too painful at the moment.' [50] In June of the following year we catch glimpses of Emily at the Duke of Devonshire's villa at Chiswick and staying with the Hollands at Holland House. In August she dined with the young Queen, who received her with much kindness.[51] In the

[50] Lady Cowper to Princess Lieven, Brighton, November 13th [1837]. *Lieven-Grey Correspondence*, III, pp. 139–40.
[51] Lady Cowper to Princess Lieven, George St., Saturday and Monday [August 7th, 1838]. *Lieven-Palmerston Correspondence*, p. 153.

autumn she and her unmarried daughter Fanny paid a round of visits in Scotland and the north of England, from which she reported regularly to her eldest son, now Lord Cowper. Late in September they were staying with Lord and Lady Willoughby de Eresby[52] in Perthshire.

Drummond Castle, Crieff, September 24th [1838]

... we are altogether very much pleased with our tour and particularly charmed with this place and with its flower garden which is quite a Masterpiece in that way. The House itself is curious from its position, but otherwise bad—very comfortable however ... It is a fine place for sport, and I dont wonder Men like Scotland so much ... Next Tuesday we are going to Lord Kinnaird's for two days and to see Taymouth and Dunkeld and the pass of Killicrankie ... and then go to Tulliallan. This is for the present, after that we shall take Edinburgh and its Neighbourhood, and get to Chillingham I reckon about the middle of October ...

Panshanger Papers

At Tullyallan,[53] Lady Cowper heard from her son and daughter-in-law of a visit they had paid to Windsor.

Tullyallan, Kincardine, Friday 28 September [1838]

I was delighted to get your account of Windsor, and I long to see it in all its splendour. The Queen is as great a wonder in her way as Fair Star or any other enchanted Princess, and has the good fortune to be peculiarly gifted by the Fairies with *Le don de Plaisir*. What luck it is for this Country to have such a Jewel, to raise the Character of Royalty.

We came here on Wednesday, a pretty drive of thirty miles from Drummond Castle, over wild Hills and by a fine Cascade ...

[52] Peter Robert, 21st Baron Willoughby de Eresby, and Clementine Sarah, daughter of James Drummond, 1st Lord Perth.

[53] In Clackmannanshire. The property belonged to the Comtesse de Flahault, now in her own right Baroness Keith and Nairne.

This House is a little bit like Panshanger, but less so than Lord
Dunmore's, four miles off...

Panshanger Papers

Three weeks later, Lady Cowper and her daughter were at Chillingham in Northumberland, on a visit to the Tankervilles. Previously, it
seems, the Cawdors' son Lord Emlyn had been paying Lady Fanny
Cowper marked attention, so that Lord Grey reported, 'a match is
expected to be the consequence'.[54] But at Chillingham there was a
decided *contretemps*, for young Lord Ossulston showed signs of
falling in love with her, and she would have none of him.

Chillingham Castle, Belford, Northumberland, Oct. 18 [1838]
Did I write to you or to Anne last? I cannot remember but I
well know that I had to thank you each for a letter of amusing
details about Windsor. What a Jewel of a Woman that little Queen
is! I was very glad Minny went to you first, to season herself for
the greater exertion...
...I like being here, and should willingly stay some time but
for one little incident that may shorten my visit—and this is, but
dont repeat it, that Ossulston shows an evident wish to marry
Fanny, and as she cannot fancy him, but constantly snubs him I
fear that this may fall like an Apple of discord between us. It is a
pity that she should not like him, for he would be an excellent
match and Ld and Ly T[ankerville] would like nothing so well.
However as she will not, there is no more to be said about it. I
hope Ossulston will see that it is useless and give up the notion,
but if he does not, or it makes any awkwardness, I shall then
move off...

Panshanger Papers

Three days later Lady Cowper, still at Chillingham, wrote to her
son proposing to meet him and Anne at Brighton on her return in

[54] Grey to Princess Lieven, Howick, Oct. 15th, 1838. *Lieven-Grey Corre-*
spondence, III, p. 278.

the autumn.[55] In early November the travellers were at Howick on a visit to Lord and Lady Grey;[56] and later in the month in Staffordshire, guests of the Angleseys at Beaudesert.

Beaudesert   Monday   November   12   [1838]

... We go on Wed[nesda]y to Rowton and I suppose on the Monday after to Leamington a day or two there will bring me to London about the 23rd ...

This place is delightful and magnificent as you described it. We have been driving in an open Carriage round the Park and Chace, Lord Anglesey showing off all its beauties (and himself) on a Prancing Horse a la Portiere—and to be sure he is a wonderful Man of his age or of any age even putting aside the consideration of all he has gone through—such a figure and such a graceful seat ...

The Q[ueen] I hear still talks of Brighton but not before the end of this month or beginning of the next. My love to Anne and the Children. I hope you will all like Brighton and stay on. In this case, I shall come down first to a hotel, unless you write me word of any nice House near you ...

Panshanger Papers

And so after a visit to Colonel and Lady Charlotte Lyster at Rowton Castle, near Shrewsbury, the travellers returned to London early in December. For the next few months we do not hear a great deal of Lady Cowper, though she was doubtless gratified by the elevation in April 1839 of Sir Frederick Lamb to the peerage with the title of Beauvale. In February, with Lady Fanny Cowper, Spencer and William Cowper and Lady Ashley, she dined with the Queen at Buckingham Palace. Quite a family party! 'Coopers enough to mend all the butts and hogsheads in the world!' wrote Lady Lyttelton, who was in waiting; adding unkindly, 'The consequence was a very dull dinner.' But she took pleasure in looking at Minny, 'before whom all

[55] Lady Cowper to Lord Cowper, Chillingham, Sunday, 21st [October, 1838]. Panshanger Papers.
[56] Princess Lieven to Grey, Paris, Nov. 15th [1838]; Grey to Princess Lieven, Howick, Nov. 22nd, 1823. *Lieven-Grey Correspondence*, III, pp. 283, 285.

other women look mouldy and dirty and old . . .'[57] In May Emily attended a State Ball, when the young Queen reported her to be 'particularly kind'.[58]

In September we find Lady Cowper at Windsor Castle, whence she went to Chatsworth for a prolonged visit to the kindly Duke.[59] In November she was back again in London; and the letter she wrote to Mrs Huskisson makes it clear that she was beginning to tire of her widowhood. It was now more than two years since Lord Cowper had died, and she seemed to be asking herself for how much longer she must endure her loneliness.

George St. Nov. 6 and 7 [1839]

. . . We are just now returned from Windsor where I left W[illia]m looking par[ticularl]y well, and grown fatter, which I was glad for, for he had certainly fallen away a great deal during the session of Par[liamen]t. He is coming to town for a fortnight of Cabinets the middle of Nov[embe]r and I suppose Par[liamen]t will meet at the usual time, certainly not till after Christmas. P[rince] Albert of Coburg of whom there is so much talk is a very charming young man, very well manner'd, and handsome, and gay, and said to be very well informed and sensible, so that I don't think she can find a better person to marry; tho there is nothing declared or I believe settled at present, and he is going abroad again with his brother on the 14th—still I think it will be sooner or later.

Before the Windsor visit, we took a long tour to Newby,[60] Castle Howard and Chatsworth, which were all very agreeable, and the last particularly gay . . . We are now going to H[ollan]d House for a few days as London fogs are quite intolerable, and afterwards I have some thoughts of Brighton as For[dwich] and

[57] Lady Lyttelton to Sarah Lyttelton, Buckingham Palace, February 28, 1839. *Lady Lyttelton Correspondence*, p. 285.

[58] Queen Victoria to Melbourne, Buckingham Palace, 11th May 1839. *Queen Victoria's Letters*, 1st Series, I, p. 217.

[59] Lady Cowper to Princess Lieven, Chatsworth, Sunday, 22nd [September, 1839] October 27th [1839]. *Lieven-Palmerston Correspondence*, pp. 170–2, 173–5.

[60] Newby Park, near Ripon, belonged to Sir W. Robinson; Newby Hall, also in Yorkshire, to William Weddell. Which place is referred to is uncertain.

Anne are settled there. In short as you see by my constantly moving about my life is very unsettled and very uncomfortable tho I try to make the best of it, and not to repine at what is inevitable but it is a great trial for any woman after having enjoy'd every comfort and a happy Home for two and thirty years to find it all gone at the time of life when she naturally feels the most want of it, and when a Country Home in which she can receive her Children is the greatest pleasure one can have. For[dwich] is very kind and so is Anne, but still it cannot be the same thing, nor can I ever feel there either happy or at home, tho I bear it occasionally as a duty. The grief and regret of my heart nothing can alter, but I believe my worldly position might be improved, and some day I may perhaps take courage! You are always so kind to me, that I am sure you would be glad to hear of anything that would make me more comfortable now, and leave me less desolate for the future when I must naturally expect to lose Fanny.

Huskisson Papers
B.M. Add. MSS. 39949, f. 165

'. . . I believe my worldly position might be improved, and some day I may perhaps take courage!' So she was deciding to take the plunge! She had already told her suitor that there was no one else. Now she was trying to summon the resolution to say 'Yes'. It had been known for some time how things stood between these two people; indeed, they were both far too well-known for such matters to remain secret; and in April of the previous year Princess Lieven, hearing rumours, had enquired of her old friend, Lord Grey, whether Emily was contemplating re-marriage.[61]

The Queen, too, knew what was contemplated; and she was all in favour of the match. 'They are, both of them, about fifty,' she wrote, announcing the engagement to Prince Albert, 'and I think that they are quite right so to act, because Palmerston, since the death of his sisters,[62] is quite alone in the world, and *Lady* C[owper] is a very clever woman, and *much* attached to him; still, I feel sure it will make

[61] Princess Lieven to Grey, Paris, April 23rd, 1838. *Lieven-Grey Correspondence*, III, p. 266.
[62] Palmerston's last surviving sister, Mrs Bowles, had died in November 1838.

you smile.' [63] Whether or no in distant Coburg a solemn Albert smiled cannot be told; all that is certain is that just over a week later Emily plucked up courage. On the 16th of December, 1839, at St George's, Hanover Square, she and Palmerston were wed. 'A beautiful day,' noted the bride, 'which I accept as a good omen, and I trust the event of the day will contribute to our mutual happiness.' A good omen indeed it was to prove, for this radiant day was the first of many years of happiness for them both, terminated only by the death of Lord Palmerston a quarter of a century later.[64]

[63] Queen Victoria to Prince Albert, Windsor Castle, 8th December, 1839. *Queen Victoria's Letters*, 1st Series, I, p. 255.

[64] Bell, *Palmerston*, I, p. 259.

Book Two

VISCOUNTESS PALMERSTON

CHAPTER I

The New Life

'WHAT DO YOU THINK of the marriage of our dear Lady Cowper?' asked Princess Lieven of her friend, Lord Grey. 'She wrote to me on the subject, and such a simple, natural, good letter, so full of yearning for that happiness and comfort and support which every woman needs, that I am quite convinced she is right in what she does. I hope she will find the happiness she seeks, and I look forward to it as more than probable. What do you hear is going to be done with the children? They tell me the Ashleys refused to go to the wedding. Is this true?' [1] Whatever doubts or misgivings her children may have entertained of the wisdom of their mother's marriage to Lord Palmerston, they were rapidly dispelled.

The newly-weds were at Broadlands for Christmas,[2] but public affairs allowed them little privacy for a honeymoon. Lord Palmerston was immersed in his negotiations for the coercion of Mohammed Ali, for which strong action was needed; but France was far from being wholeheartedly with him and would have preferred to have the ambitious Viceroy as sovereign in Syria and Egypt. Thus the negotiations dragged on, and within a few days of his marriage, Palmerston invited Brunnow and Neumann to spend Christmas with him and his bride and to discuss the situation over the holiday. On the 23rd and the 24th of December the Foreign Secretary had long talks with Brunnow, and afterwards with Neumann, and most of the first Christmas Day of his married life was passed in going over the whole question with both of them together.[3]

[1] Princess Lieven to Grey, Paris, December 22nd, 1839. *Lieven-Grey Correspondence*, III, p. 308.

[2] This is believed to be Emily's first visit to her husband's home. The present building was remodelled in 1766-7 by Lancelot Brown (1716-83) with a further alteration in 1788 by his partner and assistant Henry Holland (1745-1806). Colvin, *Biographical Dictionary of English Architects* (ed. 1944), p. 102; Dorothy Stroud, *Capability Brown* (ed. 1950), pp. 122-3.

[3] Webster, *Palmerston*, II, 661.

Whilst the statesmen were immersed in their work, Emily found time to write to Mrs Huskisson in Rome about the happy promise of her new life.

Broadlands, Decr. 26, '39

. . . I am very comfortable here, and much happier than I thought I ever could be again in this world. I should hate myself if I could ever cease to regret what I have lost (the kindest hearted man that ever breathed); but except for *this regret* and all the past recollections of all the misery I have gone through, I have every thing else to make me happy. L[o]rd P[almerston] is utterly and entirely devoted to me, and so completely happy that it is quite a pleasure to look at him. This place is very beautiful and comfortable,[4] and I feel like a spoilt child that has only to express a wish to have it gratified. My children too are all pleased at the step I have taken, and at the prospect of domestic comfort and happiness which is open to me. Had any of them been annoy'd or made the least objection I could not have done it, nor would not; but their liking and approving has made every thing easy for me. I am glad also to find that Minny is my near neighbour, only 26 miles off and a beautiful drive through the new Forest. They were here for two days the beginning of this week. L[o]rd Shaftesbury has turned out the best of Fathers strange to say, and they are now established at St Giles's![5] We have taken L[o]rd Caledon's House in Carlton Terrace, and I have let my own to Lady Tankerville, so when you return to Eng[lan]d you will find me a neighbour, and very comfortably established, for it is a beautiful house and will do well for reception, should the Govern[men]t remain in, as I believe there is every chance, notwithstanding all the talk and crowing of the Tory papers . . .

. . . The Queen's marriage will be in Feb[ruar]y and rather on

[4] Lady Palmerston always loved Broadlands, of which she wrote nine years later: '. . . Nothing can be more comfortable than this House. It is magnificent when we have company, and when alone, it seems to be only a Cottage in a beautiful garden. I dine, and breakfast, and sit, all in my own sitting room, and it's most comfortable . . .' Lady Palmerston to Palmerston, Broadlands, Thursday, [1848]. *Melbourne Papers*, B.M. Add. MSS. 45546-7.

[5] Lord Ashley had for long been estranged from his father and had not visited his old home for some ten years.

a small scale as the Chapel Royal is the only suitable place for the Ceremony, and its size does not admit of much display or many spectators. The Q[ueen] will however have 10 Brides Maids of which Fanny is to be one. W[illia]m is pretty well but all these Ceremonials give him additional trouble which is unfortunate for one who has already such a load of public business; every thing however looks well for us, par[ticularl]y every thing connected with Foreign Affairs . . .

Huskisson Papers
B.M. Add. MSS. 39949, f. 170

Another old friend to congratulate the new Lady Palmerston was the late Princess Charlotte's intimate friend, Margaret Mercer Elphinstone, now the wife of the Comte de Flahault.[6] She wrote from Rome, and Lady Palmerston's letter in March 1840 is full of interest.

Carlton Terrace March 15 [1840]

. . . I am perfectly comfortable in my new situation, and very much happier than I ever expected to be again . . . My House is so beautiful and so suited to reception that I have taken advantage of it to gratify all the Corps Diplomatique, to give our party advantages in many ways, and to amuse Fanny. So this is all very well, and their *many* objects have all been successful . . .

The Queen and P[rince] Albert are very happy in their marriage, and there is no truth in any of the foolish stories that have been invented to the contrary. He is very good looking and amiable and charming, and pleases every body that approaches him. Even the mob, who are much taken with his looks and agreeable expression, so that I hope they will now become quite popular! The Queen has a dinner and Dance afterwards, every Monday which is charming and as she changes her guests many

---

[6] The Hon. Margaret Mercer Elphinstone (1788–1867) married in 1817 Auguste Charles Joseph, Comte de Flahault-de-la-Billardrie (1785–1870). In 1823 she succeeded her father as Baroness Keith and in 1827 her cousin as Baroness Nairne. They had (with three daughters who died unmarried) a daughter who married the 4th Marquess of Lansdowne, and another who married the Marquis de Lavalette. Both these married sisters are buried in the Mausoleum at Bowood.

have been gratified by invitations, altho' each party was not large.

Our political prospects are good and I hear of no threatening Hairs breadth escapes such as we had last year. Indeed the failure of the vote of want of confidence has placed us in a fortress. It was a great fault on the Tory side, but not S[i]r R. Peel's, for his judgment was always against the motion, and he was forcibly driven into it by his Tail.

Brunow and Nieuman are at a stand still, and no way can be made in settling the Turkish affair till Thiers is well in his stir-rups,[7] or till we see whether he can go on at all. Guizot has been well received,[8] his manner is now very quiet and conciliatory, and he seems very anxious to please, and to court all the Ministers. If he is a Tory in his heart, he keeps it to himself, and none of the opposition have found it out, but rather *frondé* him from believing that he is of the new French school. His work on the English Revolution has been a passport to favour with the book people, as it is reckoned the most impartial and best account published. (It seems odd that we should go to the Foreigners for this.)[9] Sebastiani was very angry and vexed at his recal [*sic*] and went off furious, but it seems he has calmed down since. We were sorry to lose him for I believe he is honest and behaved very well towards us—besides a change always stops the march of affairs . . .

Bowood Papers

Four days later Lady Palmerston wrote to Mrs Huskisson, and in much the same strain.

Carlton Terrace, March 19th/40

. . . We are all charmed also with this House which is one of the best I ever saw for receptions, and the situation is I think all

[7] Thiers had recently become Prime Minister of France.

[8] Guizot had just been appointed French Ambassador in succession to Sebastiani. Webster, *Palmerston*, II, pp. 666–7, 669, 673–4.

[9] Guizot was an eminent historian as well as a statesman. 'His work on the English Revolution is regarded as the best and most impartial account written on this subject. So that is one reason for his popularity.' Lady Palmerston to Princess Lieven, Carlton Terrace, Tuesday [*c*. March 24th, 1840]. *Lieven-Palmerston Correspondence*, p. 182, where, however, the date of this letter is given as February, though Guizot did not reach London until the middle of March.

one can desire. I have had one Ball and a great many dinners and parties, which have been very agreeable and have done much good politically, for a House open on our side was just the one thing wanted; and the Corps Diplomatique are as you may suppose much pleased at this improvement in their position, part[icularl]y as all the chief Embassys are at this moment only tenanted by Attachés. Brunow and Nieuman represent their Chiefs and live in Hotels and Mr Guizot [has] only just arrived. This last pleases us very much by his manner and appearance which is more of the old school than the new and he promises to be very friendly, so that I hope he may in time suit as well as Sebastiani.[10]

W[illia]m is overworked in mind and body but otherwise in good health and I am sure it is a very great relief to his mind to have the Q[ueen] so happily married, and that she should have found so charming a Mate, and one who in all respects suits her so well, for all the gossiping stories you may have heard of her marriage are perfectly untrue and I believe it is quite impossible for any two people to be more happy. P[rince] Albert is already very popular, and all who approach him sing his praises. The fact is that he is very handsome, and beauty tells upon every body. The public say 'he looks so pleasant' . . .

. . . Duke W[ellingto]n will not I think last long,[11] but he goes about again now . . .

Huskisson Papers
B.M. Add. MSS. 39949, f. 172

Some two months later Emily wrote to her husband's brother, William Temple, our Minister at Naples, with home news and gossip.

Carlton Terrace, May 13th [1840]

. . . We had a beautiful Ball at the Palace on Monday. The Q[ueen] danced two or three Quadrilles (which is little more

[10] It was wished in London to show Guizot every honour, and two days after his arrival he was received in audience by Queen Victoria; the same evening he dined with the Palmerstons, who had a party of twenty-six to meet the Duke of Sussex. Lady Palmerston to Princess Lieven, Carlton Terrace, Tuesday [c. March 24th, 1840]. *Lieven-Palmerston Correspondence*, p. 182.

[11] He lasted until 1852.

exertion than walking) but avoided all the more active dances. She has given up riding and takes great care of herself, so that I believe there is no doubt of our hopes being realised, tho I think she will not announce the event till her time is more advanced.[12]

Your brother is over worked, but otherwise well and in spirits —and I hope there is no doubt of his getting triumphantly over all his difficulties[13] . . .

Broadlands Papers

During the summer Princess Lieven paid a visit to England, and stayed for several weeks with the Duke and Duchess of Sutherland at Stafford House. In view of her notorious relations with Guizot, the new French Ambassador, many people questioned the wisdom of her coming to London at this time, and Queen Victoria received her coldly. Furthermore, Neumann writing home to Metternich dilated with the utmost bitterness on the Princess's supposed activities. 'Madame de Lieven a dans les derniers jours redoublé ses importunités pour tâcher de pénétrer ce que nous ferions, elle a poussé la témérité jusqu'à dire à M. de Brunow que Lady Palmerston lui avait avoué que le conseil avait adopté les propositions de son mari – espérant par ce mensonge (car c'en était un) faire tomber M. de Brunow dans un piège; il n'y donna pas, mais rendit le propos de Madame de Lieven à Lady Palmerston; celle-ci, piquée au dernier degré, fit à son amie un sermon très sec, lui conseilla de s'en aller pour ne pas accréditer l'opinion, qu'on avait, qu'elle avait été envoyée par M. Thiers pour aider M. Guizot à entraver l'affaire orientale.

'Telle est la fin de Madame de Lieven, qui après avoir occupé ici la première position sociale est déchue au point de n'être plus que la complaisante et l'entremetteuse d'un folliculaire et d'un professeur d'histoire, tellement épris des charmes surannés et déséchés de la Sybille ambulante, qu'il est devenu un objet d'amusement pour les salons, où l'on épie les regards doux et peu lettrés qu'il lui lance; il ne se doute pas que nous venons d'accomplir ce que son prédécesseur avait su empêcher et que celui-ci saura faire valoir.' [14]

[12] Queen Victoria's first child, afterwards the Empress Frederick, was born on November 21st, 1840.

[13] For Cabinet differences over the Eastern Question, and Palmerston's triumph, see Webster, *Palmerston*, II, pp. 688–94.

[14] Neumann to Metternich, Londres, 16 Juillet, 1840. Vienna, *Haus Hof und Staatsarchiv, England*, p. 295; Webster, *Palmerston*, II, Appendix D, pp. 884–5.

VISCOUNTESS PALMERSTON

aged about fifty-three

From the portrait by John Lucas at Broadlands

Nevertheless, as appears from the next two letters to Madame de Flahault, Lady Palmerston and other friends did what they could to make the Princess's visit congenial; and the Palmerstons gave at least one dinner party at which Guizot and the Princess were guests.[15]

Carlton Terrace, July 17th/40

... We dined yesterday at the Palace with the Duc and Duchesse de Nemours. She is improved by growing fatter, and he has more talk and manner than he had. The Granvilles go back to Paris early in the next week. Lord P[almerston] continues very busy and over worked, but his health stands it—and the interest of his department is so great that it carries him through. We are all in great kindness and affection with P[rince]ss Lieven, and I believe she is much pleased with her reception here, and the Corps Diplomatique are beginning to recover [from] all the alarm and agitation they were in at the thoughts of her arrival. Her manner with Guizot is very good and friendly without being particular, and he is very popular with every body ...

Bowood Papers

Carlton Terrace, Tuesday, 11th Aug. [1840]

... Parliament was prorogued today with a *beautiful* speech and very beautifully delivered. The King and Queen of Belgium below the Throne and P[rince] Albert in a chair to the left of it. Altogether it was a very touching and striking scene, and I should have been very sorry to have missed it.

P[rince]ss Lieven intends returning to Paris for the beginning of Sept[ember]. We have done all we could to make her comfortable from our old intimacy and affection, but it was an unlucky moment for her to come over! ! Tho I really believe she has kept from meddling in Politicks in any way, yet here every body abuses her for being *French* in her feelings, and having left all her Russian interests to adopt those of France. The Corps diplomatique has very much avoided her. The Russian, Prussian

[15] The information comes from Neumann, who was also present. Webster, *Palmerston*, II, p. 700.

and Austrian at open enmity with her, and there is no end to all the stories they tell of all she has said or done in this interest. They have gravely asserted to me that they *knew* she was sent over by M. Thiers at this crisis to aid and abet M. Guizot, and Brunow says 'est il possible qu'une Russe peu ainsi ramier sa Patrie'. And then as a sequel and companion to all this folly, I find she is accused in France of the very reverse, and that she is abused and reviled for being a complete Russian. Does not this cross fire give one the measure and value of these absurd reports and of all those who make them?

It is a great thing for my comfort to have Par[liamen]t up, and I am going out of town tomorrow. All our affairs look well, and we hope soon to hear that France has recovered from her war-like fever, as it would be too absurd to go to war with the whole of Europe for nothing or something very like it . . .

Bowood Papers

Nevertheless, things were not too easy with Princess Lieven, for unkind people had been saying that Lady Palmerston valued her as a friend so long as she was the wife of the Russian Ambassador, but had been far less interested in her since; whereas the truth was that Lord Palmerston, knowing the Russian's passion for intrigue, had discouraged his wife from seeing too much of her. This is made clear from Emily's letter to her 'dear love' early in September when it looked as if ill-health would delay the Princess's departure from England.

Broadlands Wednesday [Sept. 2 1840]

. . . Mde Lieven has been ill and unable to go off to Paris. She tells me in her letter today that she intends to go Sat[urda]y but if she would not and [*sic*] will express a wish to come here, I hope you will kindly not object, for I find myself in a very awkward position with her, and Minny tells me that *the world* abuse me and say I have been very unkind to her this time. That while she was Ambassadress I liked her very much but that now her evil day is come, like other false friends, I have changed towards her, and have not shewn her that support and affection which it was now in my power to afford her. Nothing can be more untrue or unjust, but Minny has had to defend me against this charge. The World is so ill natured . . .

Melbourne Papers
B.M. Add. MSS. 45546–7

However, later in the month Princess Lieven, though still unwell, was able to return to Paris.[16]

In the autumn we find more of Emily Palmerston's letters to Frederick, letters of considerable interest and importance, dealing, as they do, with her husband's foreign policy.

Palmerston's eastern policy, particularly his support of Turkey and his hostility to France, has been much discussed and criticized. But the Foreign Secretary, together with other experienced observers, did not share the popular view that the Ottoman Empire was done for; indeed, he firmly believed that, given a decade of peace under the enlightened rule of the courageous sultan Mahmud II, she might, as he told the Secretary of the Embassy at Constantinople, be regenerated once more into a 'respectable power'.[17] The unpopularity of this policy in France, which was pro-Egyptian and anti-English,[18] encouraged Russia to bid for the confidence of our Government;[19] and in order to forward this policy, Count Brunow was in September 1839 sent to London as Russian Ambassador. Palmerston, however, was anxious to set up a barrier between Russia and the Mediterranean. But Russia was not the only danger. The whole question was complicated by the hostility shown by Mohammed Ali, the pasha of Egypt, towards Turkey; this forced the Turks, lacking English or French support, to look for aid to Russia. Russia, only too ready to assist, extracted her recompense in the famous treaty of Unkiar Skelesi. These events showed clearly the dangers to be apprehended from Russia. Nevertheless, Palmerston, on

[16] Lady Palmerston to Comtesse de Flahault, Carlton Terrace, Sept. 22nd [1840]. Bowood Papers.

[17] Palmerston to Bulwer, Sept. 22, 1838, and Sept. 1, 1839. Ashley, *Palmerston*, I, pp. 354–5, 360–1.

[18] Princess Lieven to Lady Palmerston, Paris, April 5th, 1840. *Lieven-Palmerston Correspondence*, p. 185.

[19] Palmerston to Bulwer, Windsor, Sept. 24, 1839. Ashley, *Palmerston*, I, pp. 361–3.

his return to power under Melbourne in 1835, had been forced to enter into an alliance with the very power he most mistrusted.

The chief trouble was the foreign policy of France under Louis-Philippe and his minister Thiers, who had declined to respond to the English Foreign Secretary's suggestion that France should join England in a joint undertaking to defend Turkey against aggression. This refusal had a profound effect on Palmerston, who henceforth showed the utmost distrust of Louis-Philippe and his advisers. In consequence, when Egypt, having overwhelmed the Turks at the Battle of Nezib in June 1839, and, thanks to the treachery of the Turkish Grand Admiral, Achmet Pasha, captured the Ottoman Fleet, proceeded to attack Syria, Palmerston at once opened negotiations with Russia. This being very much to the taste of Czar Nicholas, who was of course only too anxious to steal Great Britain from France, a quadrilateral treaty was speedily concluded on the 15th of July, 1840, by which England, Russia, Austria and Prussia agreed with Turkey, at the mercy of her foes, to drive out the Egyptians and to bring peace to the stricken Levant.

Unfortunately, Palmerston had not achieved these results without considerable opposition from his Cabinet colleagues, and the pro-French Clarendon, Holland and John Russell were particularly hostile. The attack of Lord Holland was especially galling to the Palmerstons, for he insisted that the Foreign Secretary's approach to Russia would seriously weaken our ties with France. Lady Palmerston had strong views on this subject, as she wrote to her 'dearest Harry' at about this time.

St. Leonards, Thursday [c. July–August 1840]

. . . Ld Holland says the Russians have yielded *solely* in hopes of weakening and breaking up the Anglo French Alliance. Holland adds that our only *dependance* is the Emperor of the French, and that all about him long to throw themselves into the Arms of Russia.

What villains they are! The Ligitionists (*sic*) shew unbounded joy at the Peace, as they believe it will sever the Entente Cordiale, and will weaken the internal Government of the Emperor and soon make him unpopular with the Army.

I believe your *Lucky Star* and your Honest straightforward

course will bring us safely through all these difficulties and anxieties . . .

Melbourne Papers
B.M. Add. MSS. 45546–7

In spite of this irritating attitude of Lord Holland and others of his colleagues, the Foreign Secretary, who throughout insisted that there was not the remotest prospect of France resorting to war,[20] stood firm, and even went to the extreme of threatening resignation from his brother-in-law's government, if his policy was rejected.[21] The confusion among the members of the Cabinet was not helped by the pusillanimity of Melbourne, who was at his wits' end how to reconcile his warring colleagues. At length Lord John Russell determined to bring matters to a head at a Cabinet meeting by suggesting a solution of their differences on the basis of concessions on both sides, he being willing to accept the terms recently offered by the Pasha in co-operation with France. If Palmerston refused, as was expected, Russell was resolved to ask for the support from his other colleagues and, if that was not forthcoming, to resign, and to take an active part in Parliament against the foreign policy of Palmerston. Late in September Charles Greville met the Palmerstons at dinner at Holland House. When he asked Lady Palmerston what prospects there were of a compromise, any hopes he may have had for such a settlement were speedily dashed; for she spoke with the utmost bitterness and contempt of the Pasha's proposals, which she deemed not worth a moment's attention. They had, it seems, a long talk, which Greville regarded as principally of importance as showing the state of her husband's mind;[22] and, three days later, when the Clarendons were dining with the Palmerstons at Carlton Terrace, Lady Palmerston repeated to Clarendon what she had said to Greville.[23] It was perfectly clear that Palmerston had not the slightest intention of yielding: and how right he was soon proved to be! Success was complete. Between

[20] Palmerston to Bulwer, Carlton Terrace, July 21, 1840. Ashley, *Palmerston*, I, pp. 376–7.

[21] Palmerston to Melbourne, Carlton Terrace, July 5th, 1840. Ashley, *Palmerston*, I, pp. 370–3; *Greville Memoirs* (1885), I, p. 308.

[22] *Greville Memoirs* (1885), I, pp. 314–15.

[23] Palmerston to Bulwer, Carlton Terrace, Sept. 22nd, 1840. Ashley, *Palmerston*, I, pp. 379–82.

September and November 1840 Beyrout, Sidon and St Jean d'Acre were successively taken by the British fleet; and on the 11th of January, 1841, Mohammed Ali was forced to accept the hereditary pashaship of Egypt without Syria, and to return their captured fleet to the Turks. The only French reaction was an ominous strengthening of their fleet at Toulon, which called forth from the British Foreign Secretary instructions to Bulwer,[24] Chargé d'affaires in Paris, to tell Thiers 'in the most friendly and inoffensive manner possible, that if France throws down the gauntlet, we shall not refuse to pick it up'. As for Mohammed Ali, he added in true Palmerstonian style, 'he would just be chucked into the Nile'.[25] This homely language caused Louis-Philippe to act. In October he dismissed Thiers and formed a new ministry under Marshal Soult. Furthermore, he recalled his Ambassador in London to be Minister for Foreign Affairs in the new Government. It was generally anticipated that under his guidance England and France would gradually come together again.

It was with these momentous events that Lady Palmerston dealt in her next few letters to Lord Beauvale.

Carlton Terrace, Oct. 12/40
... We only came today from Panshanger and are off to-morrow to Windsor for a few days.[26] Your last letter I mentioned to nobody, for I think you had miscalculated the difficulties of this Turkish affair, and when your letter arrived, it found us under a great prospect of arrangement and success. When I asked you before whether you did not think it would be better for the V[is]c[oun]t[27] to give in a little, it was under a fit of depression and anxiety of my own, for in truth I have found him all through very calm and dispassionate and with no unwillingness to con-

[24] William Henry Lytton Earle Bulwer, Baron Dalling and Bulwer (1801–72), better known as Sir Henry Bulwer; Chargé d'affaires at Brussels, 1835; secretary of Embassy at Constantinople, 1837; Chargé d'affaires at Paris, 1839; Ambassador at Washington, 1849; Minister at Florence, 1852; Ambassador at Constantinople, 1858–65, peerage, 1871.

[25] Palmerston to Bulwer, Carlton Terrace, Sept. 22nd, 1840. Ashley, *Palmerston*, I, pp. 379–82.

[26] See Lady Lyttelton to Caroline Lyttelton, Windsor Castle, October 14 [1840]. *Lady Lyttelton Correspondence*, p. 305. [27] Palmerston.

ciliate and even to give up what he did not think absolutely necessary, [and] anxious to preserve Peace, as much as anybody could; but feeling what a great many of our own private reports stated, that any mean concession would be ruin to us part[i]c[u-lar]ly after the absurd and insolent tone the French had taken, and that if they thought we were afraid of War, and such ridiculous bullying was to succeed, we never again could object to any encroachment.[28] If on this occasion surrounded by Allies, we were to be driven from our rights by a *threat* of War, how could they even think we should stand up against them on any other occasion, and on many points too vastly important to us, which might arise any day, but on which probably we might have no sympathy from any other Countries.[29] He has had a hard battle to fight with some of his Colleagues, H[ollan]d really quite foolish and superannuated, but with a name, and following, and dinners, and activity of proselitism that was quite extraordinary, very good friends in the main with P[almerston] but thinking it quite fair to have all this cabal against him, and underhand work, and putting all springs in motion *not* to get him out, but to make him yield his opinions; in short friendly, but acting just as he would have done in opposition, and more vicious, and kicking and biting, because he found P[almerston]'s course was approved of by the Tories, Duke W[ellington], Peele [*sic*] and Aberdeen. There never was such an old fool, and all this very much caused by Allen,[30] who has a Physician friend with M[ohammed] Ali, one Clot Bey a French Turk. Ld Clarendon was less active, but I think more to blame because he had not the same excuse of old prejudice and folly. Other people of our Party, old Whigs and underlings, who understood nothing at all about the question,

---

[28] Beauvale had sent a despatch from Vienna stating that Metternich was seriously alarmed, and suggesting prompt action to diminish the effect the measures were likely to have on France. Melbourne to Queen Victoria, Downing Street, 2nd October, 1840. *Queen Victoria's Letters*, 1st Series, I, p. 293.

[29] 'The French have behaved like children, it must be confessed; but then French people are children; and that is all the more reason for treating them as such at the present time. They will be satisfied with very little, but they must be given something otherwise these children will ruin the world.' Princess Lieven to Lady Palmerston, Paris, Oct. 8th, 1840. *Lieven-Palmerston Correspondence*, p. 191.

[30] Librarian at Holland House.

but said what is Syria to us, that we should quarrel with France about it, and if we go to War the Tories will trip us up, and take our places and the H[ouse] of Commons will be against us. However, I hope all this is weathered. The French Public Papers and proposals look well, and our private accounts from France are very satisfactory. The King decidedly against War. The last violent proposals and outbreak of Thiers in the Council, a mere trick; a great desire for Peace in the Country, and their Marine, Army and Finance by no means in the state of preparation they pretend it to be, so that we have every fair prospect of having the whole thing settled amicably, and a great help to this would be the continuation of our successes in Syria, which we hope every day to hear. L[ouis] P[hillippe] will have gained three points, by all this turmoil, and may therefore consent to some sacrifice of M[ohammed] Ali. He will have got the fortification of Paris against internal comotions [*sic*], the increase of his Army, which he thought too weak, and an accession of popularity to himself and Thiers by all the spirit they have shown, and the big words they have used . . .

P[almerston]'s letter to Bulwer[31] had a wonderful effect in making the subject clear to all understandings, but I suppose the very awkward position of the French has obliged them now to frame a sort of special pleading answer. I am sorry for this, as it will force P[almerston] again to make a rejoinder and in some instances to explain and shew their false statements; however he will say as little as he can, as all his object now is to conciliate, but what tricky ungentlemenlike people they are. They date this letter the 3rd of Oct[ober]. Guizot brings it to P[almerston] and reads it to him yesterday evening, the 12th,[32] and this Morning it is in the Times—so that if anything had prevented him seeing Guizot yesterday, he would have seen it first in the Times and then ante-dated ten days. What a way of doing business.[33]

Broadlands Papers

---

[31] Dated Carlton Terrace, Sept. 22, 1840. Ashley, *Palmerston*, I, pp. 379–82.

[32] Lady Palmerston dated her letter October 12th, but she was always careless of dates.

[33] Lady Palmerston made the same complaint to Princess Lieven, but in rather more moderate terms. Lady Palmerston to Princess Lieven, Windsor, October 15th [1840]. *Lieven-Palmerston Correspondence*, pp. 192–3.

Ten days later Lord Holland died suddenly. Though his attitude over the Eastern Question had intensely annoyed Lord and Lady Palmerston, and though the constant intriguing that was known to go on at Holland House, where Guizot was a frequent guest, had for long been an embarrassment to the Foreign Secretary, who had complained to Melbourne only to be told that the Prime Minister could do nothing about it,[34] the unexpected and untimely passing of this fundamentally good man much affected his colleagues. But the death of Holland had a more profound effect on his party than at first appeared; for the consequent closing of Holland House deprived the Whigs of their accustomed meeting-place.[35] Henceforth, something of the *rôle* hitherto assumed by Lady Holland was sustained by Lady Palmerston.

C[arlton] Terrace, Oct. 23rd [1840]
A Courier is going tonight so I will not let it go empty handed. However my time is short, as I expect Alava, Niemann and Guizot to dinner. The latter one is off Sunday to Paris, and there is a report tonight that Thiers Governm[en]t is out and the King waiting for Guizot . . . but now my dear Fred for the painful part of my letter, the death of poor Ld H[ollan]d which took place yesterday morning. We are all deeply grieved as I am sure you will be, for with all his faults we shall hardly see his like again, that overflowing good-humour, and amicability and affection for his friends. That he was not a wise Man one must acknowledge, and that he has done much mischief lately, but still he is a great loss privately and publickly, for his House kept the Party together, and was of much use as a place of meeting, and had great effect upon literary people, and the second class of politicians . . . He had worked himself into such a state of agitation and fever about Egypt and Syria, and France ever since last June, that I think it must have done him harm, tho indeed his conduct on that

[34] *Chronicles of Holland House*, p. 282. Webster, *Palmerston*, II, p. 710.

[35] It is true that Charles Greville records dining at Holland House some three months after Lord Holland's death, when Macaulay was the lion of the evening, and he rather unfairly says that everything was as before 'excepting only the person of Lord Holland, who seems to be pretty well forgotten', but Lady Holland soon moved out of Holland House and few dinners were given there during her widowhood. *Greville Memoirs* (1885), I, p. 367.

subject and his conversation and views lead me almost to believe that his head was beginning to fail. Indeed the last few hours that he lived he was quite delirious and even then his raving was all about Egypt and Syria. It seemed to have altered his natural Character the last two months, he was unceasing in trying to make Converts and yet without any fixed object, and when he spoke on the subject he could hardly keep his temper or talk about it with any sense or moderation; he was for sacrificing everything to France, and thought Thiers quite right in his special pleading that the integrity of the Turkish Empire was only intended as against Russia; however now it is all over, poor fellow, and we have only to regret him with all his faults. Melbourne is, I am sure, deeply grieved for he really liked him. He is however at Windsor, and I have not seen him, tho Palmerston has . . .[36]

We have just heard from Paris that Thiers has resigned, and now if the Doctrinaires and the King can make a stronger Party all will be well.[37] The Chambres are said to be much for Peace; if so they will throw over Thiers, and his conduct must (I should hope) have lost him many supporters . . .

Broadlands Papers

Lady Palmerston wrote in similar strain to the Comtesse de Flahault, to whom the death of Lord Holland must have come as a particular shock as her husband and her daughter Emily had only recently been paying a visit to Holland House. Then she turned to other topics.

Tuesday [October 1840]
. . . London is very melancholy under these circumstances but here I am fixed with very little chance of moving even for a day. Fanny at Panshanger and all my other children away so that for society I am obliged to follow Palm[erston]'s example and bury myself in Red Boxes. We are very anxious for news from Paris,

[36] See also Lady Palmerston to Princess Lieven, Carlton Terrace, Friday, October 23rd [1840]. *Lieven-Palmerston Correspondence*, pp. 193-4.
[37] Webster, *Palmerston*, II, p. 722.

and to hear that this Ministerial Crisis has passed off safely, and a new Ministry established on solid foundations ...

Bowood Papers

'A new ministry established on solid foundations.' Lady Palmerston was destined to see a swift fulfilment of her hopes. Late in October Louis-Philippe dismissed Thiers and summoned Guizot from London to be Foreign Minister in a new government under Marshal Soult. No doubt was entertained that Guizot would accept office; indeed, he was delighted at his new appointment, and he called in high spirits on the Palmerstons to take his leave.[38] Within a very short time, on the retirement of Soult, he assumed the ostensible rank of Prime Minister. Thus began the notable administration of which Guizot remained the master spirit for nearly eight years.

[38] *Greville Memoirs* (1885), I, p. 343.

Two Romances in the Family

WE NOW COME to perhaps the strangest event in the life of Frederick Lamb, his romance at the age of about sixty with a girl of twenty-four. Her name was Alexandrine Julia Mahltzahn—Adine to her friends—and her father, Count Mahltzahn, a widower, was Prussian Ambassador at Vienna, where the extremely handsome Lord Beauvale had been our representative for nearly ten years. From an early age, it seems, Adine had been captivated by the good looks and charm of the English Ambassador who was a frequent visitor to her father's home; and though failing health was soon to force him to give up his post, she yearned only for the opportunity of tending and serving him. Unfortunately, Adine was unable to hide her feelings, so that before long she was suffering acutely from the cruel comments made by her friends in the small and highly critical society of Vienna. Faced with this dilemma, and with no mother to advise her, Adine resolved on desperate action; she would write to Lord Beauvale and propose what he would doubtless think himself too old to suggest.[1] Fred as usual consulted his sister. 'Read the inclosed if you can, D[eare]st Em, and tell me if I shall marry that Girl. Never mind a little Germanism in her letter. She is a straightforward laughing thing enough . . . She has made to herself a sort of vocation of charity and devotion to others, and seems to want an old husband to take care of. Shall I bring her to you? It would be a little interest and how such things turn out heaven only knows . . .'[2] and again nine days later— '. . . I wish I could show you this girl now as she stands, for I know you would love her—not a bit a romantic thing but more like Minny in disposition than any thing else I know'—a cunning thrust that was sure to reach his sister's heart!—'just as ready to laugh or to cry, just

---

[1] For Adine's charming letter and Beauvale's no less charming reply, see Lady Airlie, *Lady Palmerston*, II, pp. 53–6.

[2] Beauvale to Lady Palmerston, 21 [November 1840]. Lady Airlie, *Lady Palmerston*, II, pp. 57–8.

as devoted and as ignorant of interest or calculation. She has no money but I don't care a straw about that, for whenever I quit this Embassy all I want is a quiet life, and for that I shall be able to do very well . . .'[3]

Emily's reply to the first of her brother's appeals came promptly from Brighton.

Brighton, Nov. 30 [1840]

I will return your inclosure the first opportunity. I think you must have nearly made up your mind by your asking my opinion, and, if so, I am all for it. Henriette's brother[4] is not happy as he is, and if this is likely to make him so I should advise him to do it at once, and without hesitation. If she wishes it, and he thinks it would add to his comfort, there can be no possible objection. I know who it is—two or three people have mentioned the subject to me—and I have been very near asking you about it in my last letters, but something always put it off . . .

I am come to Brighton for a week with Fanny to get a little sea breeze, London was become so foggy and smokey; and now Acre is taken[5] and people all coming round to P[almerston] *since his success*, I thought I could be spared for a little while, having remain'd there two months doggedly to help fight his battles.

W[illia]m was not very well the last few days. He complains of feeling so weak on his legs, but I think this may come from Holland over physicing him. He told him his illness arose from a long course of over-eating, and I daresay it does; but still it does not do to lower some people. I have written now to try and persuade him to come down here, but I daresay he won't, he is so difficult to get at. I had looked forward to your being in the House with him to look after him, and now the only objection

[3] Beauvale to Lady Palmerston, 30th [November, 1840]. Lady Airlie, *Lady Palmerston*, II, pp. 59.

[4] That is, her brother Frederick.

[5] Following the convention of July 1840 Palmerston had acted vigorously. A British, Austrian and Turkish squadron united under the command of Admiral Stopford bombarded Beyrout on September 7th, 1840, and heavily defeated Ibrahim Pasha. On November 3rd the same force captured Acre with a loss of only sixty-six killed and wounded. The French were made to feel very foolish at this after the remark of Marshal Soult the previous year that there was no power in Europe capable of taking the town!

I feel to the event I anticipate is that this will be impossible, and if you are under another roof it is so difficult to get hold of him. Would it be possible for you to come over here first? or afterwards alone? He and you have not met for so long, and he is so anxious to have you again with him. Perhaps I am foolish at feeling so uncomfortable about him as I often do, for he has no complaint, but feeling languid; but his appetite often fails, and sometimes he says he sleeps ill, and then he leads a life of worry and anxiety and has neither time to take care of himself, nor does he understand his own management, and then he cannot resist the exigence of his little Governor.[6]

Now I have told you all the facts, do as you think best, and if you bring the friend over, why I daresay we shall all do very well . . .

What an absurd figure Thiers cuts,[7] one hardly knows whether he is most fool or rogue; and the revelations and declarations he makes completely throw on their backs all who advocated his cause or that of France in the late transactions. This is of course Nuts to us, and a great lift to P[almerston], for certainly but for him we should certainly have play'd Thiers' game, and accordingly now they all try to throw him over. I wish poor Lord Holland had remained here, to see and feel how completely wrong he was in all his views and opinions . . .

Broadlands Papers

What Emily wrote about William's health no doubt prompted the unromantic letter which Fred wrote to him a fortnight later. 'Dear Will, Em tells me you are not very well. At this time of year We with gout in us are often amiss, but I wish you would tell y[ou]r Doctor that strong physicking never did for you from a Boy. Business is coming to an end, I hope, and, whether or no, if you feel solitary and would like to see me, say so and I will come to you instantly. You will think me a consummate old fool but it's not unlikely I may marry a girl here. Emily knows who—but I would rather come to you if you wanted me.' [8]

[6] Queen Victoria.   [7] He had resigned a month previously.
[8] Beauvale to Melbourne, 15 Dec., 1840. Lady Airlie, *Lady Palmerston*, II, p. 57.

Meanwhile, Lady Palmerston at Brighton continued to fulminate to her 'dearest love' against the French and especially against Thiers.

Brighton, Tuesday 1st Dec. 1840
... What people they are, and what revelations they make. Thiers cuts a wretched figure; is it possible that there can be any party in France willing to acknowledge such a disreputable villain as their leader? Guizot stands a little awkwardly on two or three points, but where he was wrong he was evidently misled by Holland and Clarendon &c. and thought their strength would over bear yours in the Cabinet. These revelations are ruin to the reputation of that Cabal and everything that comes out only places you on a higher pinnacle of Glory. I wonder Clarendon's not ashamed to shew his face when he sees how Guizot built on dissentions in the Cabinet and did not therefore urge Thiers as he would otherwise have done. And is it right or proper that the discussions of the Cabinet (and what was at that moment going on there) should be revealed to the Enemy? There never was such Treachery. ...

Melbourne Papers
B.M. Add. MSS. 45546-7

Brighton, Thursday 3 Decr. 1840
... I wish John[9] could be kept off meeting till Feb[ruar]y. It is so foolish. I bullied him before I went about the meeting last year on the 15th Jan[uar]y, and showed him the little use of it in shortening the Session. Perhaps if it had not been for this, he might have proposed a yet earlier day. I feel like you very strongly that there is something miraculous in the course of late events. It *cannot* be accident that all these things should have so turned out! My impression is that it is the restoration of the Jews and fulfilment of the Prophecies. But we shall see what comes next, and I have long been thinking of this, even before your letter and all the circumstances you mention, some of which had escaped me. It is certainly very curious and Acre seems to have

[9] Lord John Russell.

243

fallen down like the walls of Jericho, and Ibrahim's army dispersed like the countless hosts that were enemies of the Jews, as we see in the Old Testament . . .

Melbourne Papers
B.M. Add. MSS. 45546–7

In her next letter to her brother, written a fortnight later, Lady Palmerston referred to an ugly intrigue that was rumoured to be afoot to bring about her husband's retirement from her brother's government, an intrigue that was supposed to involve Queen Victoria's officious Uncle Leopold, now King of the Belgians. There is no doubt that many people seriously apprehended that Palmerston's policy would inevitably lead to war with France, and no one could be more distressed than Leopold was at the thought of a conflict between one country ruled by his niece and another by his father-in-law. It is not impossible, then, that he had lent his aid to those who were not unwilling to replace the fiery Palmerston with some more pliable minister, such as Clarendon. Fred, at his vantage-point in Vienna, had soon been apprised of these stories, and he wasted no time in passing them on to his sister, who promptly forwarded his letter to William, the Prime Minister, whose reply she sent back to Beauvale.[10] Melbourne's letter was all that a colleague could wish for; but what a pity he had not been more decisive in the first place, when the ugly rumours might so easily have been smothered at birth!

Carlton Terrace, Dec. 17/40

Your letter is very curious, I mean of the 30th, in which you state the Story of *the Intrigue*. I do believe it was Leopold's plan, and some others might have given partially into it, but I will extract what W[illia]m says, for I sent your letter to him at Brocket, as I thought the account was useful to him. I had told him of this plan before, but he is too honest himself to suspect others. Your letter however I knew would be a strong corroberation. This is what he says.

I believe that they have been playing the Game Fred[eric]k

[10] Beauvale to Melbourne, 15 Dec., 1840. Lady Airlie, *Lady Palmerston*, II, p. 57.

'ADINE'. LADY BEAUVALE

(afterwards last Viscountess Melbourne
and subsequently Lady Forester)

From the portrait by Sir Francis Grant at Willey Park

describes, and I have thought so ever since I learned that my decisive letter to L[eopold] had produced so great and so sudden an effect. It could only do so by shewing them that they were upon a wrong tack, and must change it directly; but I do not think that the affair had proceeded so far as Fred[eric]k is informed. I daresay they said 'If we can get Melbourne, we shall have no difficulty with the Q[ueen],' but I do not think that they had opened the matter to the Q[ueen] or that she had said, 'If you can persuade Mel[bourne] I have no objection to get rid of P[almerston].'

I daresay also they designated Clarendon as P[almerston]'s successor. But he has (at least) too much sense to have thought of that himself. Why, consider what it was to abandon the Convention and change the Policy of the Country at the dictation of France, and upon that ground to take Office. Why he would have been torn to pieces, his life would not have been worth half an hour's purchase, and he must have known that.

Yrs affectly.

What a characteristic letter! The truth is that the moment W[illia]m declared himself strongly, Leopold gave the thing up, and his expressions were *so strong* that L[eopold] shiver'd in his shoes. 'I tell you what, Sir, I shall not stand that, and by God, if the French go on arming. . . .' I wish I could remember all the letter, but Bulow to whom it was shown repeated it to me, and I forgot the rest. I suppose he had got into a passion at all these tricks; and then he writes very sharply.

In truth his fault was being very shilly-shally at first. He thought the Treaty a strong step, and his plan is always to put off everything, (not thinking much of foreign questions, or understanding them well; he is so influenced by all people say to him). He never would speak out openly in Cabinet or take an active part, and the impression therefore of the Cabal was that he was *in heart* with them, hated the thing, and let himself be dragged on by P[almerston]. Had he shewn a little more spirit at first, I have no doubt the intrigue would never have taken place. He is easy, and candid, and not easily roused, and this emboldened the French party, who thought they should have no difficulty with him. When L[eopold] got this violent letter he was perfectly astounded, felt it was no joke, sent off an express to L[ouis] P[hilippe] who got this letter just before Thiers came to him to increase the Armaments. He felt this would never do and he got rid of him . . .

P[almerston] has done all he could to enlighten the Q[ueen] all along, and wrote one very strong letter to Leopold only a week or so before W[illia]m wrote his, saying that his interests were now mixed up with those of France, and that his object therefore was to bring the Countries together and to make England yield to unjust demands that all this was very natural in his position, but that P[almerston] himself had no mixed motives to sway him, and therefore could only consider the honour of the Country, and the interests of the Queen. This letter was very well written and worked up, and full of truths; and he sent a copy of it to the Q[ueen] that she might see what he had written.

She did not make any objection, but said it was a little hard upon her Uncle, and she feared it would vex him, which I have no doubt it did; but still it was a right thing to do, and he richly deserved it for he was always playing on her feelings, writing himself, getting his Wife to do so and the D[uche]sse de Nemours, and sending letters of L[ouis] P[hilippe]'s writing to him, saying, he should lose his life, his Crown, be shot at and deposed, if the Q[ueen] would not come forward and insist on helping him.

All that has since turned out must have shewn her the folly and deceit they practised on her, and the wretched figure she and Eng[lan]d would have cut if Leopold had carried his points, and I hope this will not be lost on her. Albert had I believe been more worked upon than her, but he wrote a very handsome letter to P[almerston] on his success, when all this turned out so well. And those fortunate exposures in the Chambers leave those who had taken up the French cause without a leg to stand upon . . .

Cla[ren]don takes the line of great satisfaction at this success, and praises P[almerston] up to the skies, right and left. This is well, and we take this for what it is worth, doing all the harm he could when he was wanted, and now only following the Cry, to try and identify himself with it, and let his conduct be forgotten.

We are going to get some Holidays tho P[almerston] is very busy still with the remains of the Eastern Questions. But I start

246

Sat[ur]d[a]y with Fanny for St Giles's, and then return Monday or Tuesday to Broadlands to meet Palmerston and pass a fortnight. I have invited everybody I can think of to make a gay party for Minny and Fanny, and we are determined to enjoy ourselves a little after so much labour and no play; but his success has been very gratifying to us and the quantity of letters of Congratulations which we receive every day even from the quarters one least expected . . .

Broadlands Papers

In the Queen's speech at the opening of Parliament in January, France was not mentioned. This, as Lady Palmerston rather anticipated in the letter she wrote to Frederick on her return from the House of Lords, might offend 'that spoilt child'.[11] But in a letter to Princess Lieven two days later, she expressed the hope that France would be satisfied with the friendly speeches in the House, '. . . and that they will realize that this is a greater compliment than if France had been mentioned in the Queen's Speech, for this would have been very difficult, indeed impossible, considering the state of the two countries. I do not know if France (that spoiled Child) will now take up a more agreeable attitude towards us, but she *must feel* that there is a great difference between our expressions of friendship for her and her attitude towards us. . . .'[12]

Meanwhile, an unhappy incident almost led to war with America. An American steamer, the *Caroline*, carrying arms to the rebels during the Canadian rebellion, was boarded under cover of darkness by a party of Royalists, set ablaze, and driven over Niagara Falls. In this affray an American citizen lost his life. In January 1841 a British subject, Alexander McLeod, who was alleged to have been concerned in the attack, was arrested in New York State and charged with murder. The British Government demanded McLeod's release on the grounds that he was acting under orders. The American Secretary of State replied that the matter was the concern of the State of New York, within whose territory the *Caroline* had been lying at the time of the

[11] Lady Palmerston to Beauvale, Carlton Terrace, Jan. 26th [1841]. Broadlands Papers.
[12] Lady Palmerston to Princess Lieven, Carlton Terrace, January 28th [1841]. *Lieven-Palmerston Correspondence*, p. 202.

incident, and that the American Government could not interfere. Lord Palmerston at once instructed our Minister at Washington to inform the United States Cabinet that the execution of McLeod would bring about a war 'immediate and frightful in its character, because it would be a war of retaliation and vengeance'.[13]

Lady Palmerston, writing to her brother, reported her husband's conviction that war would be averted. And how right he was, for McLeod was tried in October and fortunately acquitted.

C[arlton] Gardens Friday [c. February 5th or 12th 1841]

... The American affair is disagreeable, and most abominable on their part. But they say the Government there is pushed on unwillingly by its tail. However P[almerston] says he thinks it will be all settled quietly, and that the Americans have no wish for War. McCleod was certainly not implicated in the destruction of the *Caroline*, so if there is any fair play and not false swearing, he will get off on that. But we of course maintain that the affair was perfectly justifiable, and no individual accountable for it. P[almerston] was very much cheered when he stated this in the House, perhaps people thought he would not have given so bold and decided an opinion, but he is backed by the law opinions; as well might the Duke of W[ellingto]n be tried for Murder after the Battle of Waterloo.

Everything goes prosperously with our Governm[en]t (except Elections) which is very provoking ... The tide against us was despairing until St Albans, and now we hope there may be a turn. There was no doubt Bribery on both sides, but not more on ours than on theirs; so we think they will not venture a petition. These Election Successes had emboldened the Tories, and they say they were only looking for some great question to divide upon.[14] Meanwhile Peel wished for delay, and tho he bids for popularity in all his Speeches he disobliges his followers thereby. They do not like his fulsome Speech about France (which pleased much at Paris) nor a Speech he made at Tamworth at some

[13] Palmerston to Fox, Foreign Office, February 9th, 1841. Ashley, *Palmerston*, I, p. 408.

[14] Emily was echoing her husband's views. See Palmerston to William Temple C[arlton] T[errace] Friday 9, 1841. Ashley, *Palmerston*, I, p. 407.

Literary Meeting, in which he said all classes were alike and that education should not be merely confined to the Church of England (very displeasing to his bigot followers) and then to add to his Total misdeeds he says he *will* make changes in the Corn Laws, and will not take Office without this understanding; all very Liberal, but displeasing to his followers. Morpeth and our side have made a great hit in their Irish Bill, about settling the right of Voting by the payment to the poor, instead of rent qualification. This is thought to be the fairest qualification and a great discovery. Ld Stanley is very angry part[i]c[u]l[arl]y as he drove in his bill by a trick;[15] and now they say his party is sorry to be committed to it, and that ours is sure to prevail now or in future . . .

Broadlands Papers

In her next few letters Lady Palmerston reverted to family and personal matters.

C[arlton] Terrace, Feby. 25th, [1841]

I am quite charmed with Adine's letter, and so is W[illia]m. I am sure she must be a charming person from everything I hear of her, and I hope you have now got the Settlement, and that the Ceremony is over—the more I think of it the more I feel confident that this event will answer to you. All those who know Adine or have seen her praise her looks and manners and everything, and now I hope you will settle to come over and see us as soon as you can . . .

Jocelyn is returned here the Lion of the day, with all his accounts of Chusan and India and Arabia, and Syria and Bombay and Mehemet Ali and very much improved himself in all ways by his two years absence. With all this flourish, and a devoted attachment to Fanny, which began three years ago, how is it possible that any girl could resist, so it certainly will be, tho not quite yet, for his Father is at Naples, and cannot be home before the 10th of April, so it is useless to announce the event before it is

[15] Lord Stanley had compelled the Government to modify its Irish disendowment proposals, which naturally annoyed Lady Palmerston.

necessary ... I send you Night and Morning, a very pretty Novel of Bulwer's ...

Broadlands Papers

Beauvale and Adine were married in Vienna on the 25th of February, the very day this last letter was written. Emily wrote delightedly to Mrs Huskisson and also to her brother.

C[arlton] Terrace March 1st /41

I am delighted at Fred's marriage.[16] He seems delighted himself and to anticipate much happiness ... Fred disliked the *fuss* of marrying and being talked over beforehand so much that he enjoined strict secrecy till the deed was done, otherwise I should certainly have written to you to announce it, knowing the affectionate interest that you always take in every thing that concerns him ...

Ld Jocelyn is come back from Chusan and India full of interesting details, and as much devoted to Fanny as he was two years ago when he started in despair at her coldness. He is a very nice open hearted person and I can hardly think she will be so hard hearted as to remain insensible to such constancey ...

Huskisson Papers
B.M. Add. MSS. 39949, f. 174

C[arlton] Terrace Thursday [March 1841]

... I am charmed to hear your Marriage is over, and that you seem so happy. I have no doubts myself that you have taken the very wisest step, and one that will add to your comfort in every way. I am charmed with all I hear of my sister-in-law. There never was a person who had collected so many golden opinions and, strange to say, not one word to be heard against her in any shape from any body. I quite long to see her, and so we all do.

[16] Lady Palmerston wrote the same day in similar tone to Princess Lieven. Lady Palmerston to Princess Lieven, Carlton Terrace, March 1st [1841]. *Lieven-Palmerston Correspondence*, p. 205.

Fanny's Marriage is settled. Jocelyn came over, saw and conquer'd. She is very much in love with him, and he doats on her. He is very much improved by his two years in India and China and altogether a charming person, and we are all delighted with him . . .

I believe we are quite safe in Office for this year, Foreign Affairs have placed us on a pinacle [*sic*] of Glory, and Morpeth's bill is a great hit . . .

Broadlands Papers

Lady Palmerston's daughter's engagement was formally announced to Queen Victoria[17] to whom Lady Fanny had acted as bridesmaid at her wedding a year previously; and on the wedding day, the 27th of April, a brooch with the Queen's portrait inset arrived with a letter from Buckingham Palace. The young bride wrote her thanks to her Majesty within an hour of the completion of the marriage ceremony.[18]

Lady Palmerston's forecast that her brother's ministry was safe to last throughout 1841 proved singularly wrong. On their proposals about the sugar duties, they were defeated by a majority of ten. They then had to determine whether or not they should dissolve. Lord Melbourne, it seems, foreseeing that this would be followed by a crushing defeat, was against dissolution; but there was much difference of opinion in the Cabinet. Something of the confusion among Ministers is conveyed in the letter which Lady Palmerston wrote to her brother on the 12th of May.

C[arlton] Terrace, Tuesday 12 May [1841][19]

A Courier just going off, so I have only time to say we are in a great quandary here sure to be beat on the budget. Some say by 30, some even more, and then the question is resignation or dissolution. I am for the latter, if as I believe there is a good

[17] Lady Palmerston to Queen Victoria, Saturday morn[in]g [April 1841]. Windsor Castle Papers, M. 50, 23.

[18] Lady Jocelyn to Queen Victoria, Tuesday morning [April 27th, 1841]. Windsor Castle Papers, M. 50, 24. The Queen also gave the Jocelyns as a wedding present the use of the Lodge in Richmond Park. Melbourne to Queen Victoria, 3rd May, 1841. *Queen Victoria's Letters*, 1st Series, I, pp. 334-5.

[19] So written, but May 12th, 1841, was a Wednesday.

chance of a Majority. I think a great question should not have been put forward without we were prepared to carry it through, or at least to try if the Country is with us. To throw it out, and then run from your post is in my opinion cowardly, will dishearten your friends and break up the Whig party for many years to come, and seems to be unworthy of the people who do it. The Cabinet are much divided in opinion and W[illia]m, always feeling as he does when two lines are open to him, rather desirous to take the one of least responsibility, and the most inactive. He says he should not like to dissolve with the chance of being in a Minority in a new Par[liament] which would be awkward for the Queen; awkward no doubt but not more awkward, I think, than turning her over now into hands she is known to hate without making an attempt to learn the feeling of the Country.

I believe the principle of the budget is a good one, to increase revenue by taking off taxes but the putting Corn with it has been the stumbling block, tho in some parts our strength. It is this corn which will make our Minority at the end of this long discussion; so many of our best friends are ordered by their constituents to vote against us on this one point. If we could settle this difficult point of the Sugar duties which expire before the new Par[liamen]t could meet again, then I am quite sure dissolution would be the best plan, but this is a difficulty, tho it is said there are some means of getting over it. This discussion will last 2 or 3 days longer we suppose as we like it to do, to make it well understood; (the Tories wished to have had as little debate as possible and only a vote). The Queen is very unhappy at the thoughts of a change and would willingly do anything to prevent it.

The question of resignation or dissolution is still quite unsettled, the Cabinet very much divided. The Chancellor, Palmerston, Minto, Hobhouse, Duncannon very much for dissolution; W[illia]m rather against, J[ohn] Russell, Lansdowne uncertain; Morpeth against because he fears Yorkshire, and Macauley [sic][20] because he fears Edinburgh.[21] The calculation made by 6 wise heads on our side is that we should lose some Counties,

[20] Thomas Babington Macaulay, Lord Macaulay (1800–59): historian; he was M.P. for Edinburgh at this time.
[21] Bell, *Palmerston*, I, pp. 323–4.

but gain on the whole election 11 seats, 22 Majority more than we have now. *If* this is correct, there can, I think, be no doubt that we should try it. I have been out of town two days to see Fanny, so I do not know everything that has passed the last few hours in town. However between ourselves I think it is a stupid thing to have got into this *Galére* and without more consideration of probable results. Before such a measure was put forward they should have weighed all the consequences and have made up their minds what they should do—certainly have passed some sugar bill which would have allowed them time to dissolve without difficulty . . .

Broadlands Papers

In the event, when on the 27th of May the Melbourne government found themselves in a minority of one on a vote of confidence, the Prime Minister at once announced the dissolution of Parliament.

At the end of July Queen Victoria and Prince Albert honoured the Cowpers with a visit to Panshanger, whence they went to Lord Melbourne at Brocket. Lady Palmerston thus described the royal visits to Mrs Huskisson.

Carlton Terrace Wednesday [July 28th, 1841]

. . . We returned to Town Saturday after a charming and interesting week. The Queen's reception was everywhere enthusiastic, and nothing could go off better than the party at Panshanger and Brocket; even the weather was fortunate for the sun shone whenever it was wanted, and we had the most brilliant day at Brocket. I wish you could have seen W[illia]m with his grey hair floating in the wind and the Queen on his arm as he walked her round the lawn to show her to the multitude assembled against the rails, and all up the Hill, so that it looked like an amphitheatre of heads. We all walked in procession behind, the Welwyn band playing and all Pens old Yeomanry flags brought out on the occasion and waving on the hill. It really was a beautiful sight!—and I had made poor dear old Brocket so smart with red cloth and carpets, and ornaments and flowers, that you would hardly have known it again. Dawson[22] was in exticies, and all the people frantic with delight and enthusiasm.

The banquet was laid out for 36 in the Ball room, and very handsome; the centre of the table filled up by the three beautiful pieces of Plate given to Melbourne by the Queen and Albert on their marriage. She then went over the House, admired every thing with a curious eye, and then took the round of the lawn I before described, and so on to the Shrubbery, Green House, Hot House, Melon Ground to the Shrubbery again and round by the Water house. She had long wished to see Brocket, and it was evidently a very great pleasure and interest to her.

Panshanger too was beautiful and every thing went off well. We dined every day in the Gallery and Albert is a connoisseur and great admirer of pictures.

Fordwich felt very shy but acquitted himself extremely well —he is such a dear creature. The road from Cole Green to Panshanger House was like a race course, carts, carriages, Horsemen, Waggons and people all drawn up on each side of the road. Here too we had music and flags and yeomanry and everything to enliven the scene, and nothing could do better than the whole thing. The Queen's own manner to everybody was charming, and Albert is like the Prince of a fairy Tale, all perfection.

They walked out every morning alone between 8 and 9 oclock —and on one of these strolls got down to the keeper, who did not know the high quality of his guests but called them Mylord and milady when they questioned him about the rearing of Pheasants and other rural knowledge.

But all this fine Pageant is now over, and here I am again established till the meeting of Parliament. Palmerston is so busy wiping off old scores that he has hardly time to eat or sleep . . . We hear of great dissentions in the Tory camp about the Speaker. Peel, the Duke and Stanley want to keep Lefevre, the high Tory party wants one of their own. We shall see which gets the better . . .

Huskisson Papers
B.M. Add. MSS. 39949, ff. 190–5

[22] The Brocket agent.

254

'We were quite delighted with Panshanger,' the Queen told Fanny
Jocelyn, 'wh[i]ch is a lovely place, and your Brother and Lady Cowper
were all kindness and civility to us. I was so sorry you were not there.
We were likewise much pleased with Brocket, the grounds of w[hi]ch
are beautiful, and w[hi]ch I had so long wished to see. Lord Melbourne
did the honours of his House exceedingly well.[23] 'We enjoyed Panshanger still more than Woburn,'[24] the Queen told her Uncle Leopold,
'the country's quite beautiful, and the house so pretty and *wohnlich*;
the picture gallery and pictures very splendid. The Cowpers are such
good people too. The visit to Brocket naturally interested me very
much for our excellent Lord Melbourne's sake. The park and grounds
are beautiful.'[25] So the royal visit was pronounced a great success,[26] in
spite of the woeful unpunctuality of the hostess and her mother-in-
law! 'The visit is very agreeable, surprising from absence of formality,
contrived by Lady Palmerston and her daughter-in-law,' recorded Lady
Lyttelton, a fellow guest. 'The only fault is that they are immensely
unpunctual, and make the poor Queen wait for dinner and drives till
anybody but herself would be furious.'[27] Indeed, it was very soon to be
a jest in London that when the Palmerstons dined out they never saw
the soup served![28]

At the General Election in August the Government were badly
defeated, and four days later Melbourne resigned. Lady Palmerston
thus explained events to Mrs Huskisson.

C[arlton] Terrace, Augt. 28th [1841]

Our career ended yesterday with a most excellent speech of
John Russell's. The number was greater than we thought, but
our people were away and disheartened—a few more or less
does not signify. It is to a change in public opinion that we must
look. People were tired of a Govern[men]t that had lasted

[23] Queen Victoria to Lady Jocelyn, Windsor Castle, Aug. 8, 1841. Windsor
Papers, Add. MSS. U.
[24] The royal party had come to Panshanger from a visit to the Duke of Bedford
at Woburn.
[25] Queen Victoria to King of the Belgians, Windsor Castle, 3rd August, 1841.
Queen Victoria's Letters, 1st Series, I, p. 372.
[26] Bell, *Palmerston*, I, p. 319.
[27] Lady Lyttelton to Caroline Lyttelton, Panshanger, Thursday, July 29, 1841.
Lady Lyttelton Correspondence, pp. 315–16.   [28] Bell, *Palmerston*, I, p. 259.

10 years and was always struggling, and then as John Russell says so grossly misrepresented. It is perhaps better the Tory party should be so large, with so many internal dissentions they must split and fall to pieces; and will do so the more readily from having less to fear from the Whig Party. Our tactics must be to be quiet and give them rope.

The beginning of Peel's speech about France and Germany was a great rigmarole. I felt astonished he could go through such foolish stuff. The end was in parts good for his purpose, but it was all evasive and clap trap, and his followers are so well trained to cheer that they applaud all the greatest platitudes. O'Connell's[29] was quite excellent and very effective, his comparisons of the Whig and Tory very true, and wormwood to the latter. Pal[mersto]n says he thinks it almost the best speech he ever heard him make, his manner so dignified and impressive and in parts so touching. John Russell's speech was all one could wish, and I hope he will have it printed, for it must do a great deal of good. Ld Francis Egerton's was a dull sort of grumble without any point.

The Queen is very much annoy'd as you may suppose, but she has wonderful courage and firmness and will bear it all with composure. It is impossible that Melbourne should not be also very much vexed; he is too devoted not to feel *deeply* all her vexations, but he shews it very little to those who know him, and not at all to common observers. Altogether it is provoking to everybody, feeling too how well the country has been governed and how every thing has prospered at home and abroad. People on the continent cannot understand that with much success, and so much merit due to the Govern[men]t it should yet be rejected instead of applauded . . .

Huskisson Papers
B.M. Add. MSS. 39949, ff. 196–7

And to her husband she expressed much the same sentiments.

Wednesday [August 1841]
. . . Poor dear little Queen, I feel so sorry for her! The fact is our party in Govern[men]t and in the Country were grown

[29] Daniel O'Connell (1775–1847), Irish politician, called the 'Liberator'.

256

supine and tired, but I think this change will now alter the whole character of the party and that we shall before long prove stronger than ever. It is a bore to have to passer par là, but it could not be helped, and it will be pleasant to start up like a Giant refreshed . . .

Melbourne Papers
B.M. Add. MSS. 45546–7

Nearly five years were to pass before the 'giant refreshed' returned to office; meanwhile there was no alternative for the 'poor dear little Queen' to turning to the somewhat forbidding figure of Sir Robert Peel.

CHAPTER III

Lady Palmerston and the Peel Ministry

WHEN SIR ROBERT PEEL took office in 1841 many urgent problems faced the new government. We were at war with China; our relations with both France and America were strained; in India and Afghanistan trouble was brewing. At home, there were problems no less pressing. In Ireland the agitation for repeal of the union verged on rebellion; in Scotland there was a religious crisis that bade fair to disrupt the Church; and in England, in consequence of bad trade, there was the most appalling misery among the labouring classes throughout the land. Peel's remedies for these evils were three-fold: a modification of the Corn Law; the imposition of an income tax, never previously imposed in peace time, of 7d. in the £ on incomes of £150 and more; and drastic tariff reforms by removing some duties and reducing others, particularly the raw materials for manufacture and the most necessary articles of food. The consequence of Peel's enlightened policy was the conversion of a two million deficit into a five million surplus within some three years. Furthermore, the improvements in the country's finances permitted a reduction of the interest on a portion of the National Debt, which gave an immediate saving of £625,000 and ultimately of some million and a quarter a year. Towards Ireland, although O'Connell and others were prosecuted for conspiracy and sedition, the hand of toleration was extended. The Charitable Bequests Act, the increased allowance to Maynooth, the foundation of the three Queen's colleges for the higher education of the youth of Ireland without distinction of religion, and the removal from the statute book of the last of the penal laws are examples of the healing policy of the government of Sir Robert Peel. Abroad, too, success attended the efforts of the new ministry. It brought to a close the disastrous war in Afghanistan; outstanding questions with France, touching the right of search, the Morocco war and the Tahiti affair, were settled by negotiation; and the dispute with the United States on the vexed boundary question was settled by the sending of Lord

Ashburton, the husband of an American and a man with many ties in the States, to negotiate on the spot.

Soon after the Election, the Palmerstons set forth on a round of visits. First they went to inspect Lord Palmerston's Irish property, where Emily was struck with 'the candid warmth and vehement demonstration of feeling' of the people.[1] They stopped on the way for a few hours in Liverpool to see the memorial that had been erected there to the memory of William Huskisson, who had been killed so tragically in 1830. From Dublin Emily wrote to the widow.

Dublin, Oct. 18th/41

We arrived here Saturday morning after a very rough and stormy passage of fourteen hours, but I have not much reason to complain since in spite of the weather I was not sick, which I ascribe to the steamer's being such a magnificent and steady boat, 270 Horse Power and built on purpose for the Channel. But this is not the object of my writing, but to tell you that we staid a day at Liverpool, on purpose to have the melancholy satisfaction of going to see your dear Husband's Monument which is indeed a beautiful building, so classical and so simple and the statue a very fine one . . .

Huskisson Papers
B.M. Add. MSS. 39949, ff. 200-3

From Dublin the Palmerstons went to Powerscourt where they saw the famous cascade 'in one of the heaviest snowstorms I can remember'. They returned, re-visited the Huskisson memorial, and then went on to Wales. They passed a day at Powis Castle where they found Lord Powis 'in high force'. Thence they went to Aldenham, near Bridgenorth, to visit the Levesons; and so to Beaudesert to shoot with Lord Anglesey, the one-legged Waterloo veteran, who, though rising seventy-four, 'rides a pony and kills everything that gets up within reach of his gun, either before or behind him'. From Beaudesert, the travellers went to Hatherton's at Teddesley, and so to the Duke of Sutherland's at Trentham; thence for a day to Melbourne and so to

[1] Melbourne to Queen Victoria, South Street, 4th November, 1841. *Queen Victoria's Letters*, 1st Series, I, p. 449. Bell, *Palmerston*, I, pp. 325-6.

London, 'where we shall stay a week or ten days, and then go and settle at Broadlands till Parliament meets; and I look forward with great pleasure to hunting, shooting and thinning plantations as in the olden times. . . .'[2] Unfortunately, things did not quite work out like that. 'Our weather has been chiefly frosty, so that I have had no hunting; and the game this year has not been abundant, so that the shooting has been less good than usual; but still we have had game enough to afford good amusement, and an excuse for exercise,' Palmerston reported to his brother in January from Broadlands. 'But then, after what may be called an absence of ten or eleven years, one finds plenty to do in the place, and the mere marking young trees for thinning the plantations has given me many days' employment . . .' As for politics —'. . . The Government is, I conceive, secure for two or three years to come, and it is better for everybody that they should remain in that time. The country will then understand what they are, and find out the difference between them and us . . .'[3] And Lady Palmerston wrote much the same sentiments to Madame de Lieven. 'Our party is very patient and not at all discouraged,' she told the princess. 'People are betting that my husband will be back in the Foreign Office by the end of the year. Personally, I do not believe it, and do not want it. His position is excellent, and I would much prefer to stay as we are for a year or two, or even longer. All parties praise him, this is better than slavery and toil . . .'[4] How genuine these sentiments were is difficult to say, but Lady Palmerston professed to think that Peel's position was far from secure. 'Sir Robert Peel has great difficulties with his Tariff and Income Tax. . . . But I think all the same that his Budget will pass, because his majority will support him, and because party spirit is at this moment stronger than any other consideration. But I think his power and the devotion of his party will be very strained as a result, and that he will feel the effect of it sooner or later.'[5] To the Princess this seemed like wishful thinking. 'Judging from a distance,' she wrote, 'one would say from the enormous majorities he enjoys that

[2] Palmerston to William Temple, Beaudesert, November 26, 1841. Ashley, *Palmerston*, I, pp. 438-9.

[3] Palmerston to William Temple, Broadlands, January 19, 1842. Ashley, *Palmerston*, I, p. 441.

[4] Lady Palmerston to Princess Lieven, Carlton Terrace, 5th February [1842]. *Lieven-Palmerston Correspondence*, p. 223.

[5] Lady Palmerston to Princess Lieven, Carlton Terrace, 24th March [1842]. *Lieven-Palmerston Correspondence*, p. 223.

his position was sound and very lasting. What can upset him if both Houses are on his side?' [6] 'The Income Tax pleased all those who have less than £150 a year—also the Irish whom he has exempted from these taxes.' [7] Emily told Dorothea Lieven a few weeks later, 'We are opposed to them because Peel has not been able to show the need for them, and because in spite of all argument, it is obvious that there is no need for them at the moment. At the same time we are not sorry that this tax should have been imposed by Peel, and that he should have to support all the unpopularity of the measure; this cannot fail to have its effect so soon as the details are known. No doubt it is good for the country to have in hand a large surplus sum in case of an emergency, that is to say if the people are willing to advance the money (and we hold no responsibility for having imposed this tax without proving the need for it).' And thus Emily closed the argument, as if indeed there was nothing further to be said on the subject! 'Dearest, there you have a *résumé* of the state of affairs over here, and I do not think this will bore you, because the speeches and the newspapers are so dreadfully muddled about the whole affair that it's impossible to obtain a clear view.' [8]

At the time of his wedding, Lord Beauvale was suffering from a severe attack of gout. In consequence, he and Adine had been touring in Italy, where the mild climate was considered beneficial for this complaint. In the spring of 1842, however, the thoughts of the travellers turned towards England, and Fred wrote to his sister from Naples about a house near London. In her reply, Emily told him of a number of houses that might be available; but conveyed a general invitation from Melbourne to the Beauvales to stay at Brocket as long as they liked. Then she turned to political affairs.

London April 12–13, [1842]

. . . It was *impudent* of me to hold your knowledge of affairs here cheap, and I will not deny your assertions of having been

[6] Princess Lieven to Lady Palmerston, Paris, March 10th, 1842. *Lieven-Palmerston Correspondence*, p. 227.

[7] To compensate for this exemption, however, the duty on Irish spirits was increased by 1s. a gallon, thus equalling it with that on Scottish spirits.

[8] Lady Palmerston to Princess Lieven, Carlton Terrace, April 22nd [1842]. *Lieven-Palmerston Correspondence*, p. 229.

at least many times right. Still I think when you do come, that you will find many things here different from what they appear at a distance and I believe myself to be impartial, because I live quite as much with Tories as with Whigs, and read the Times every day, as well as the Morning Chronicle ... Peel's Tariffe [*sic*] is full of faults and errors, and will it is supposed be much altered. The Income Tax is sure to pass, tho, in the discussion, Peel has completely failed in proving any necessity for it at present. To make the deficiency greater Peel proposes to give up £600,000 of Duty upon Timber, which nobody had objected to —and all his pretences have been overthrown in turn. Afghanistan was dragged in and China as reasons for the tax, tho the first disaster was not known when he proposed the Income Tax, and both will probably be paid for without any charge on our Revenue. We have already got from the Ransom of Canton £1,500,000 in Specie towards the expenses of the Chinese War, and the other will no doubt be paid for entirely by the East India Company who are at this moment negotiating at Calcutta a most advantageous Loan, and without our security or help ...

Peel is so dishonest and tricky that he makes use of every advantage, and does not shrink from any statement that will serve his purpose. People are beginning to feel this very strongly and consequently it lowers his general Character, tho the Votes still remain, and there is a great fancy for the Income Tax amongst those who have no property. The Chartists particularly like its falling on the rich, and this prevents many public meetings, but I think these feelings will alter in a great measure, after the Tax has been felt. The Shopkeepers all dislike it very much, and professional Men, but the Irish are pleased at escaping, which indeed they ought not, for their paying no assessed Taxes is a strange reason for their paying no Income Tax either. So a hard working Lawyer of 200 a Year must pay his *Quota* whilst the Duke of Leinster and Lord Downshire escape all charge.

This is Peel's Art, he sets one party against another, and tries to please the strongest, and so get their support. The Sugar People, the Irish, and the Corn People, by raising the averages, (from taking in more Towns) so that the appearance of lowering the price of Corn may be a mere pretence, and so by double dealing to satisfy the Corn growers and Corn eaters ...

Fanny is now in Waiting[9] . . . The Q[ueen] looks very well, and is very amiable and Charming. We dined there Monday. Her plan is now to mix up parties in her dinners, which I think quite right, and very much wiser than having Tories one day and Whigs another. (A Q[ueen] should know no distinction of parties.) She is going to have a Fancy Dress Ball, which will be brilliant.[10] . . . [end of the letter missing]

Broadlands Papers

In a few weeks' time the Beauvales left Naples for Genoa on the first stage of their journey home.

May 6th/42

. . . I hope you will come home by the Corniche. There is nothing in Nature so beautiful as all that road . . . Paris you will like a look at, but not more, I believe. The French are so irritated, so jealous, so spiteful, that it cannot be a pleasant *séjour* to the English; and accordingly (as Mde de Lieven complains) they have all left off going there, and the Tradespeople, instead of being angry with themselves for driving us away, are only the more angry with us for not spending our money there as we did before.

Aberdeen[11] is always trying to plaster and conciliate, but only meets with the more insolence, and arrogant pretensions and in his private *abandon*, he complains bitterly of France, and above all of L[ouis] P[hilippe], whom he finds at the bottom of every intrigue.

When the Tories came in, I believe in their ignorance they blamed Pal[mersto]n for being unconciliatory, but now they acknowledge how right he was, but try to hide this from the public, as well as to conceal the way France bullies them, and tries

[9] As Extra Woman of the Bedchamber to Queen Victoria. Queen Victoria to King of the Belgians, Windsor Castle, 8th February, 1842. *Queen Victoria's Letters*, 1st Series, I, p. 477.

[10] Queen Victoria to King of the Belgians, Buckingham Palace, 19th April, 1842. *Queen Victoria's Letters*, 1st Series, I, p. 493.

[11] The Foreign Secretary.

to impose on their weakness. We don't *want* a Cobourg to marry the Q[ueen] of Spain, but it was insolence in Paget's instructions that he should have to say that it would be war with France if we did. A[berdee]n wishes to act boldly, but has not courage [to] cope with him, and that is why he always gets the better of us.

Since writing the above, I have received Adine's Picture, and am quite charmed with it. I am sure it must be like, for it is just what I fancied her, so interesting, such a pleasant, agreeable, nice countenance, and such really prettyly cut features, in short just what I expected, and what I wished her to be. W[illia]m has seen it also, and quite agrees with me . . .

The news from India and China is good. Sir R. Sale[12] quite safe, and Pottinger[13] going to attack Pekin. Elphinstone[14] was quite an old Woman . . . no precautions or prudence in their arrangements very bad. Everything neglected, and the troops cowardly and mutinous. Great blame attaches to the Horse Guards here, Hobhouse objected to Elphinstone's Appointm[en]t, thinking him not up to it, either in mind or body, but Fitzroy Somerset insisted because he was a friend of his, and the Duke of W[ellingto]n would not support Hobhouse in his objections. It is shocking to think of such loss of life, all owing to a job, for there is no doubt they might be still safe in Cabul, had the Troops behaved as they ought. The accounts from other parts of India are good . . .

Broadlands Papers

Carlton Terrace May 20th, [1842]
. . . It is expected that our Session will be a long one, there are so many things to settle . . . Peel is a poor creature, on all these things he has no spirit and is always trying to make fair weather with all parties, explaining and argueing like Joseph Surface[15] till

---

[12] Sir Robert Henry Sale (1782–1845). He defended Jalalabad from October 1841 till April 1842, when he defeated Akbar Khan, who fled to Kabul.
[13] Eldred Pottinger (1811–1843) succeeded Sir William Macnaghten as Resident in Kabul.
[14] William George Keith Elphinstone (1782–1842), Major-General, in command of the troops at Kabul, when in poor health and unequal to the work, 1841; died just before the final catastrophe.   [15] In Sheridan's *School for Scandal.*

you get quite puzzled and lose the real facts of the case. The Tariffe [sic] will certainly pass, but 70 or more of his people go against it, and so he will be obliged to depend on us for support. Some of our people would like to withdraw this on the plea that it is not *our* Tariffe [sic] and that we disagree in a great many of his details, and part[i]c[u]l[arl]y leaving out Sugar, but our chief people are too honest to give in to this crooked course, and so he will be supported in what is right . . .

Broadlands Papers

In a few weeks' time the Beauvales at last returned to England; and there were parties to welcome home the retired Ambassador and his young bride at Brocket and Panshanger. 'Melbourne, the Beauvales, the Cowpers, the Ashleys, Milbanke, the Jocelyns, and all the Ashley and Cowper children,' as Palmerston told his brother.[16] The new member of the family made a favourable impression on them all. 'Adine is very sweet and charming,' Emily told Princess Lieven, 'and her only object is to please her husband, she thinks of nothing else— I really have never seen such devotion!' Then she added charmingly, 'No, I am wrong, there's one *exception*, and that is the devotion of my husband to myself—but I discount this, and have never seen anything to equal it.' [17]

In September the Palmerstons had a house-party at Broadlands, and Charles Greville was one of the guests. To the Clerk of the Council the statesman out of office spoke freely; our foreign affairs mismanaged, Lord Ashburton the wrong man to have been sent to the States to settle the Boundary Question, the State treaty with the King of Hanover unreasonable,[18] Elphinstone's order to retreat from Kabul monstrous: everywhere there were concessions and disasters. Lady Palmerston spoke in similar terms, and she averred that Palmerston was happy out of office and by no means in want of occupation. But Greville was not deceived by Emily's pretence. Palmerston's abuse of the Government,

[16] Palmerston to William Temple, C[arlton] T[errace], September 1, 1842. Ashley, *Palmerston*, I, p. 451. Melbourne to Queen Victoria, South Street, 17th August, 1842. *Queen Victoria's Letters*, 1st Series, I, p. 532.

[17] Lady Palmerston to Princess Lieven, Carlton Terrace, September 28th and 29th [1842]. *Lieven-Palmerston Correspondence*, p. 236.

[18] This treaty between Great Britain and Hanover for the regulation of the State Tolls was not, however, signed until July, 1844.

though by no means impartial, was always expressed with gaiety and good humour so that social intercourse between him and his opponents was never interrupted; but beneath this gay exterior, Greville detected a fixed hostility and a determination to attack at every point; and never, he added, did a more unscrupulous assailant take the field. The loquacious Lady Palmerston, on the other hand, was less subtle than her husband, 'and it is easy to see, through her graceful, easy manner and habitual urbanity', recorded Greville, 'how impatient they are of exclusion from office, and how intolerant of any dissent from or opposition to his policy and opinions.' [19] And when he met the Palmerstons again in November at dinner at Lady Holland's they both seemed 'provoked', so Greville tells us, at our successes in India and the victory of the English troops against China in the war just satisfactorily concluded by the Treaty of Nanking. [20] Princess Lieven was tactless enough to congratulate Emily 'as an Englishwoman'. 'Peel has certainly been lucky . . .' she added, 'everyone has the greatest respect for him, for it's a long while since Europe has seen so firm and powerful a Minister at the head of affairs.' [21] Alas, we have not Lady Palmerston's reply to this sally; but she obviously wrote trenchantly! 'Your letter of the 1st shows me that I made a very great blunder, and I now ask your forgiveness for it,' wrote the Princess in mock contrition. 'It is obvious from what you say that the credit for your glorious successes in China is due entirely to Lord Palmerston, and I can only say in my defense that when I attributed the credit to Sir Robert Peel, I had completely forgotten your husband's speech and was only following the general opinion . . .' [22] Thus argued the two friends, 'dear friends who hate one another cordially', as Greville wrote. [23] It was all very human and feminine!

But Emily had her domestic worries at this time, for William's health was beginning to fail. In October 1842, Melbourne had an attack of the palsy; not serious, and he thought it was lumbago, but sufficient to alarm his family. [24] The Palmerstons were consequently

[19] *Greville Memoirs* (1885), II, pp. 104–6.
[20] *Greville Memoirs* (1885), II, pp. 125.
[21] Princess Lieven to Lady Palmerston, Paris, November 27th, 1842. *Lieven-Palmerston Correspondence*, p. 238.
[22] Princess Lieven to Lady Palmerston, Paris, December 5th, 1842. *Lieven-Palmerston Correspondence*, p. 240.
[23] *Greville Memoirs* (1885), II, p. 130.
[24] *Greville Memoirs* (1885), II, p. 116. Lady Lyttelton to Caroline Lyttelton,

much at Brocket for many months to come. 'I and my lady are both very well and prosperous, and we enjoy being out of office greatly,' Palmerston wrote to his brother in May 1843, adding, 'though this last year we have been much shackled by being obliged to spend a great deal of time at Brocket in consequence of Melbourne's illness'. [25] A few days later Emily reported to Mrs Huskisson in Paris that her brother was very much better. 'So well that nobody could tell now on seeing him that he had been ill . . .' Then she turned to public affairs.

Broadlands June 2nd '43

. . . So much for private affairs. The public ones are in a terrible state, and it is quite inconceivable how Peel and the Tories in two years of office have managed to bring every thing into such a state of confusion. The disturbances in Ireland are very serious and get every day more alarming. Scotland is very angry, Wales even [more] disturbed. The manufacturing towns disconcerted, and all Peel's plans of finance unsuccessful. The Agriculturists furious, the Canada Corn bill the most foolish mistake ever made by any Govern[men]t. Ld Ellenborough mad and either recalled or such a message gone out to him that they think he must resign upon it. It is curious to compare the position of this Govern[men]t and the last. The last succeeded in everything at home and abroad, but had not votes enough to carry out the Government. This Ministry fails in everything, is abused by everybody, but yet keeps their majority because people don't like to turn their coats, even tho they are betrayed. It is a strange state of affairs, and the late debates have been full of curious speeches. Peel looks miserable and must feel so, for he is in a very false position, and has lost Character and reputation to an inconceivable degree. The[y] came in on the cry of the Agriculturists, and should have acted true to them whatever it might cost him . . .

Huskisson Papers
B.M. Add. MSS. 39949, ff. 209–12

Windsor Castle, October 25, 1842. *Lady Lyttelton Correspondence*, p. 332. Queen *Victoria's Letters*, 1st Series, I, p. 549.

[25] Palmerston to William Temple, C[arlton] T[errace], May 29, 1843. Ashley, *Palmerston*, I, p. 458.

At the same time, Sebastiani, the French Ambassador, was trying to persuade the British Government that the troubles in Spain over the Spanish marriage question were not due to French intrigues. This was not likely to deceive Lord Palmerston, who knew full well how anxious Louis-Philippe was to marry his son Montpensier to the Infanta, nor was it likely to deceive his lady who thus wrote on the subject to her dear Harry.

C[arlton] Terrace Thursday [August 24 1843]
... Ld Clarendon told me also that he had had a visit from Sebastiani which surprized him at first as he hardly knew him, and that Sebastiani said he had come to him at the King's request to say that he was concerned to hear that he had said publickly and in many places that he believed all the disturbances in Spain had arisen from French intrigue, and that the King could assure him this was not the case. Clarendon said to me he was as sure of its being so as he could feel of anything, but I did not quite make out whether he said this to Sebastiani or only insinuated so and palaver'd. I think he acknowledged having expressed this opinion, but said he was glad to hear that the King said it was not so.

It is curious that Sebastiani should be charged with all these messages. It looks as if L[ouis] P[hillippe] was alarmed at what he had done and was making fair weather ...

Melbourne Papers
B.M. Add. MSS. 45546–7

But to return to Lord Melbourne. In December he was at Windsor, when the Queen thought him better, and Lady Beauvale 'a very, very charming person, and so attentive and kind to both her husband and Lord Melbourne';[26] but Greville, who met him dining with Lady Holland about the same time, reported him looking tolerably well but seeming out of spirits, and anxious to get away as soon as dinner was over.[27] Later in the month the diarist stayed at Broadlands, where he

[26] Queen Victoria to the King of the Belgians, Windsor Castle, 19th December, 1843. *Queen Victoria's Letters*, 1st Series, I, pp. 640–1.
[27] *Greville Memoirs* (1881), II, p. 214.

found Melbourne and the Beauvales his only fellow-guests, 'the former in pretty good form, more grave, more silent than formerly, but with intervals of talkativeness in his usual tone and manner'.[28] In February 1844 he met him yet again, this time dining with the Palmerstons, when the aged statesman clearly revealed that he had not given up all hope of some day returning to office;[29] and in August they were together again at Broadlands with Lady Holland, the Clanricardes and the Beauvales also in the party. This time Greville reported Melbourne very well; but 'he seems to have on his face a perpetual consciousness of his glory obscured, and looks grave and stern, while he sits for hours in silence . . .' and 'he never can speak of the Queen without tears coming into his eyes; he is however, in a very nervous, lachrymose state'.[30] But he was certainly recovering, and we catch a glimpse of him attending a performance of Ben Jonson's *Every Man in his Humour* at the St James's Theatre, on the 15th of November, 1845, when Dickens played *Bobadil* and Douglas Jerrold *Master Stephen*. Before the curtain rose the old statesman assured all and sundry that it was a very dull play; and between the acts he was heard to exclaim in a stentorian voice that reached right across the pit: 'I knew this play would be dull, but that it would be so damnably dull as this I did not suppose!' Lord Melbourne seemed almost his old self again!

In August 1844 the Palmerstons set out on a continental tour. They travelled by Dover, Brussels and Cologne, took the cure at Wiesbaden, and thence proceeded to Frankfort, Dresden and Berlin. But the waters of Wiesbaden had, Palmerston thought, been too much for them; and both he and his wife were thankful to be back home again before the end of the year.[31]

During the early part of 1845 the Peel government seemed as secure as it could possibly be. That Lady Palmerston recognized this is made clear by the letter she wrote to Mrs Huskisson in February.

C[arlton] Terrace, Sunday evening [late February, 1845]
. . . Politicks are not very active, for as Peel has '*stolen our Cloathes*' and put them on, it is not easy to get them off his back.

[28] *Greville Memoirs* (1885), II, p. 217.
[29] *Greville Memoirs* (1885), II, p. 233.
[30] *Greville Memoirs* (1885), II, pp. 289, 292.
[31] Bell, *Palmerston*, I, pp. 327-8.

I hope you read d'Israeli's[32] excellent speech last Friday; it kept the House in a roar of laughter and I am sure you will not have been sorry to see the severe truths that he inflicted on Peel, and how he turned his quotation of the *Candid friend*, and how he complimented him on his Courageous Conscience in having made such a quotation from Mr Canning.[33]

I had a party on Sat[urda]y which was very brilliant, the first I have had this year. My next and last before Easter will be on the 15th . . .

Huskisson Papers
B.M. Add. MSS. 39949, ff. 204–17

Towards the end of the year, however, the political scene was changed by Peel's conversion to the principle of free trade in corn, a question on which his Cabinet was hopelessly divided. The consequence was the resignation of the Government and a royal summons on the 11th of October to Lord John Russell to form a Ministry. This, however, proved impossible, owing apparently to an unfortunate misunderstanding. According to what Lady Palmerston told Princess Lieven, it seems that the ever-intriguing 'Bear' Ellice had persuaded Lord Grey that Palmerston could be induced to take the Colonial Office, thus leaving Grey to be Foreign Secretary. Acting on this assurance, Grey declined to serve with Palmerston at the Foreign Office, and as in fact Palmerston would accept no other post the negotiations came to an end. Had Grey been aware of this, so Emily told

---

[32] Benjamin Disraeli, Earl of Beaconsfield (1804–1881), M.P. for Maidstone at this time.

[33] On February 20th, 1845, in a speech in the House of Commons, Sir Robert Peel in reply to attacks from Disraeli had quoted the lines written by Canning:

> 'Give me the avowed, the erect, the manly foe;
> Bold I can meet, perhaps may turn, the blow,
> But of all plagues, Good Heaven, thy wrath can send,
> Save me, O save me, from the candid friend.'

The quotation gave Disraeli the opportunity of joining those who affected to believe that Peel had done Canning a grave injustice when early in 1827 he refused to serve under him because of divergence of opinion on the Catholic question. The attack came in Disraeli's famous speech on February 28th, 1845, in which was the well-known sally, 'The Right Honourable gentleman caught the Whigs bathing and walked away with their clothes.' For the whole matter discussed at length, see Lever, *Peel*, pp. 91 *et seq.*, pp. 249 *et seq.*

her friend, he would not have pressed the point.[34] As it was, the Whig leader had no alternative to giving up his attempt, and he, in Disraeli's famous phrase, 'handed back with courtesy the poisoned chalice to Sir Robert'.[35]

Sir Robert, so his enemies alleged, accepted the 'poisoned chalice' and undertook a shade too readily to do what the Whig leader had been unable to do, and much bad blood was engendered. 'Ma'am,' exclaimed the aged Melbourne at a Castle dinner, 'it is a damned dishonest act'; or words to that effect. The Queen laughed a trifle nervously at first; but eventually it required all her tact to calm him. 'My uncles came last night,' Lady Jocelyn, who was in waiting, told her Mother. 'Uncle W[illia]m got through the Evening very well and was not at all nervous. He took me into dinner and then sat by the Queen. The only thing that was rather distressing was that he would talk about the Corn Laws in a very loud voice in the middle of dinner, and say "it was the greatest piece of villany ever done"; and the Queen changed the subject as soon as she could. He did not go to Bed immediately after dinner, but sat at the round Table all the Evening . . .' [36] Whatever were Lord Melbourne's exact words, it was clear that he was no longer quite himself; it was all rather pathetic!

Meanwhile, brother Frederick, also at Windsor, reported Lord John Russell being seriously out of favour for his weakness and timidity. So, in the event of Peel's resignation: 'At Windsor there is every disposition, if the case sh[ou]ld occur, to send to some other Person than Johnny, but they do not see who.' It was of course Beauvale's object to make Her Majesty see that his brother-in-law was the only man fit to fill Lord John Russell's place, and that an invitation to Windsor before the opening of Parliament would do much to dispel false rumours of the Queen's reluctance to see Palmerston's return to the Foreign Office. This idea was delicately and tactfully insinuated by Lord and Lady Beauvale with the aid of the Prince's private secretary, George Anson, who, having previously been Melbourne's secretary, was a useful ally and friend to the visitors. 'The Queen asked me twice,' wrote Lady Beauvale, 'if you had been annoyed at Ld Grey's conduct

[34] Lady Palmerston to Princess Lieven, Broadlands, Friday, January 16th [1846]. *Lieven-Palmerston Correspondence*, p. 276.

[35] Disraeli, *Bentinck* (ed. 1905), p. 21.

[36] Lady Jocelyn to Lady Palmerston, undated [January 1846]. Broadlands Papers.

and how Ld P[almerston] seemed to take it, adding that the newspapers both here and in France were sure to put the most ill-natured
construction upon it which was exactly what I had said to that great
Man *Anson* attending to the *National* who said it was the Q[ueen] and
L[ouis] Ph[ilippe] who objected to Lord Palmerston and that Lord
Grey was only the instrument. I had said this to Anson in order to say
that it was these reports which would prove annoying to Ld P[almer-
ston] and make a public testimony of the Q[ueen]'s kind feelings
acceptable, and Her naming the newspapers allowed me to trace
Anson's interference. The Q[ueen] was also very anxious to know if
Lord M[elbourne] had not been hurt at Her sending to Lord John, if
he had approved Lord John's conduct, if his colleagues had kept him
au courant of what was going on, etc. etc. etc. In great haste, yrs.
affectly. A. Beauvale.' [37] So Adine played her part.

And when her husband turned to his brother-in-law's prospects, he
had encouraging news to convey to Emily. 'There has been much
political conversation here both with the Queen and Prince,' Beauvale
reported to Emily on the 5th of January, 'She evinces great consideration and regard for P[almerston] . . . In talking about Palmerston the
Queen said to me it was all in consequence of Syria and that the French
had hardly yet got over it; no, I said, nor never will, any more than
they have got over Waterloo, but that is no reason for us to regret
either one or the other, at which I had the satisfaction to see her
chuckle with hearty glee, and this gave me an opportunity to repeat
to her what Thiers had said "that He had no reason to be a friend to
P[almerston] by whom he had been worsted, but that that did not
prevent him from regarding him as the first Statesman of this age and
perhaps of any other". Surely I told you this before, but you may have
forgot, so I repeat. All this and much more in the same strain was
corresponded to with full harmony by the Queen. She spoke about
Ellice and asked if he was the cause of it all? I told her that in my
opinion He had been blowing up for years but that the explosion had
taken place against his will.' Fred's conclusion seems to make clear
what he and Emily had in mind. 'I sh[ou]ld have much more to say to
you if we were together but the above are the main points. Wild about
free trade and the whole Household talking nonsense in the same
direction. With this there is a great wish to undervalue the Aristoc-

[37] Beauvale and Lady Beauvale to Lady Palmerston, undated [*c.* 1st–4th
January, 1846]. Lady Airlie, *Lady Palmerston*, II, pp. 100–4.

racy and (I doubt not) a great willingness to see them lowered. If the Protectionists had but common sense we w[ou]ld yield what ought to be yielded, I firmly believe we sh[ou]ld beat Johnny, Peel and the League[38] united . . . I must add this whole affair[39] seems to me to have turned out a triumph for P[almerston] instead of a check . . .' [40] What the Queen thought of this, or what Palmerston knew or thought of the Beauvales' efforts on his behalf, we cannot say. But no royal invitation seems to have come at this time to Broadlands![41]

Parliament met in January 1846, and it was soon clear that the life of Sir Robert Peel's government was short, for on the Corn Bill all but some one hundred and twenty of his followers declared they would disown him. The Palmerstons had recently moved into a new London house, and under Emily's hospitable roof, where all parties met, there was much gossip and debate on political events and prospects, as she told Mrs Huskisson in March of this memorable year.

London March 19th '46

. . . The wonderful political events of the last few months have made everybody glad to have some talks, and this has answered particularly now, since all parties meet willingly in our House. I suppose the bill will be carried in the Lords as so many have turned round: but the numbers will be very near and after this bill is disposed of everybody expects Peel to be turned out on some motion made by the Whigs which the Protectionists out of revenge will join. That he does not intend to resign willingly seems now quite clear, tho such a report once spread, and some think now that his resource when best will be to dissolve; however one does not see much use in this, since a new parliament would probably be protectionists Whigs and radicals, and but very few Peelites. Altogether the state of affairs he has brought us to is in my opinion very disagreeable, so much ill blood and squabbling in families and all parties in confusion, a fixed duty the general wish of all but somehow affairs have got me entangled that this fixed duty which everybody would like, which would be a compromise between violent opinions and give us

[38] The Anti-Corn Law League.   [39] The crisis of December, 1845.
[40] Beauvale to Lady Palmerston, Jan. 5th and 9th, 1846. Lady Airlie, *Lady Palmerston*, II, pp. 104-9.   [41] Bell, *Palmerston*, pp. 363-5.

the advantage of revenue, is nevertheless now got to be almost impossible and the only possible chance would be the Lords throwing out the bill and so forcing a compromise, and this is a strong measure which many are afraid of, and I believe their Lordships not up to!

Mel[bourn]e does not like the bill at all but I believe he will vote for it out of regard to the Q[ueen]. We dined with her yesterday, she is very large and looks drawn, but is otherwise very well and in very good spirits ... Lord Grey is quite at a discount since his absurd outbreak we don't invite him here at present but he holds out a white flag, and thros [*sic*] all the blame on Ellice, who between our two parties is sent to Coventry and looks very glum. Pal[mersto]n might well afford to forgive them for he only stands the higher for the attack on him. We have some thoughts of going to Paris at Easter, the thing is not yet settled but [we] feel much disposed to do so, as the cordial invitation we have had from all parties there would I hope then set to rest for ever all such reports as Ld Grey puts about ...

Huskisson Papers
B.M. Add. MSS. 39949, ff. 223-5

A fortnight later the Palmerstons crossed to Paris. Though Lady Palmerston pretended to Princess Lieven that their visit had no political significance, it is evident that their object was to prepare the French for Lord Palmerston's return to the Foreign Office.[42] If only he could be shown to be less hostile to France than they supposed! The visit proved an unqualified success; everywhere they were received with kindness, and, as Emily proudly reported to Frederick, the great man was lionized wherever he went.

Hotel Clarendon 3 Rue Castiglione, Paris
Thursday [April 9th, 1846],

We got here yesterday from Abbeville, a long days Journey, but a lovely day, Spring much forwarder than in England. Nothing ever answer'd so well as our coming here, everybody charmed

[42] Bell, *Palmerston*, I, pp. 365-9. Lady Palmerston to Princess Lieven, Carlton Terrace, November 29th [1845]. *Lieven-Palmerston Correspondence*, pp. 274-5.

to see us, and courtesy on every side. Today we have been dining with Sebastiani,[43] a large party with some of the Ministers he had invited to meet us; afterwards we went to Mde de Lieven's early Soirée with Guizot and to Lady Sandwich's later Soirée with various French and English people. Saturday we dine with P[rince]ss Lieven and go afterwards to the Tuilleries with the Cowleys.[44] Monday we are to dine with the King and Wed[nesda]y with the Cowleys, and then Guizot and Duchatel give us dinners and Castellance and others, ask us to fix days; in short we are regular Lions and have not a moment to ourselves between visiting and receiving visits and all the sights we wish and hope to see. The Cowleys were very cordial and amiable and their feathers quite smoothed down the moment we asked them to present us, for what do you think Brougham had tried to persuade them, that we did not intend having anything to say to them but that we should get Sebastiani to take us to the King. Did you ever hear such folly? Brougham is so provoked at our coming and our good reception, that he has quite lost his head, and made himself the object of general ridicule.[45] He wrote two such abusive letters to Ly Tankerville, saying she had enter'd into a conspiracy to overturn Peel and Guizot's Govern[men]t by persuading us to come here that she wrote him word she should be obliged to send him a Straight Waistcoat and she afterwards sent his two letters to Mde Adelaide to shew her his excessive absurdity, and his jealousy at our coming here, and drawing some of the attention from himself. This is what Ly T[ankerville] stated, and is an excellent reason to account for his folly, but we who know better see very well that his real vexation arises from seeing that P[almerston] by coming here has thrown over the Horse which he and others were so fond of riding in Eng[lan]d and that after a brilliant

[43] He had been French Ambassador in London before Guizot.

[44] Henry Wellesley, 1st Baron Cowley (1773-1847), a younger brother of Wellington, British Ambassador in Paris 1841-6.

[45] Lady Palmerston to Princess Lieven, May 3rd and 4th [1846], and Carlton Terrace, May 10th [1846]. *Lieven-Palmerston Correspondence*, pp. 278-81. Greville says much the same about the success of Palmerston's visit and also about the animosity of Brougham. *Memoirs* (1885), II, pp. 383-4. For the secret correspondence that went on between Guizot, Princess Lieven, Aberdeen and the British and French Ambassadors, which shows the other side of the picture, see *Correspondence of 4th Earl of Aberdeen* (1845-7), pp. 151-2, 155, 151-86.

reception here it will be utterly impossible for them to talk any longer of the *violent* feeling here against him, or of Brougham's *own*, as he used to say, unsuccessful attempts to defend him. The fact is I am told that the King has begun to find him out and does not talk to him as much as he used to do, and this makes him rabid, and ready to quarrel with any body, and then this violent attack of his on Corise which she complained of to Guizot made him, I believe, not ask him to dinner when he had an English party two days ago, so that drove him frantic. However, I hate quarrels, so I have offer'd him an amnesty for the past if he will behave better for the future, and so I hope to bully him and keep him quiet. But he is like a vicious horse kicking at every body and they say since he has been here he wrote to Aberdeen to complain of William Hervey, saying that he spoke slightingly of the Govern[men]t.

The Champs Elysees looked beautiful today filled with people such a gay scene and Spring come out in all its beauty. The Town very much improved in all ways. We have not a very good apartment, but the rue Castiglione is a good situation, and we are lucky to get any lodging as every place is full, and many people running about distracted for a resting place.

It is the fashion now to be very devout so that nobody will dine at all tomorrow and it is even a stretch for Mde de Lieven to give us dinner Saturday and half her company will eat nothing but fish. There is a famous Preacher at Notre Dame who preaches for *Ouvriers* in the Morning, for Ladies at One and for Gentlemen in the Even'g, so that half Mde Lieven's Habitués were gone there tonight. What Children the French are, a few years ago believing *nothing*, and now believing everything, fasting, Miracles and all. They must always be in extremes.[46] . . .

Broadlands Papers

Paris April 15th [1846]
. . . We go on here most prosperously. There never was anything like Pal[mersto]n's success with everybody and our invita-

[46] Princess Lieven had expressed the same views some two years before. Princess Lieven to Lady Palmerston, Paris, Sunday, March 31st, 1844. *Lieven-Palmerston Correspondence*, p. 264.

tions and Visits still go on pouring like a Cascade and almost overwhelm us. We are fixed with dinners till Wednesday of next week, so up to that time, we must stay if possible. Delage and Dalmar want us Thursday, but that day I think we must go, and really I do not think my strength will hold out beyond that time. Nothing can be more flattering than all this empressment, but it is a Whirlwind, and I long for a little repose. Guizot's dinner yesterday was very handsome and agreable too, for I sat between him and Duchatel and we have all shaken together amazingly. Our Tuilerie dinner Monday went off as well as possible. The King and all the family most amiable, full of kind enquiries, and sending you many messages of interest and of great desire that you should come and see them, which I was to tell you. The King remarkably well, and as likely to live 20 years as anybody, which it is much to be hoped he may. Joinville was there, and almost all the other Princes and Princesses. Mde de Montjoye pretty well, only often suffering from *migraines*. There is an honest sincere way about her that pleased me much, and then she is so devoted to you. They are all gone today to Fontainebleau, to return Friday. About Monday or Tuesday we think of taking our Visit of leave. Rain is come on today and the Weather feels much colder, but I hope it is only temporary for the Summer before this seemed quite set in, and the profusion of flowers and holiday look of the Town was very delightful.

People talk here of les fatigues et les Veilles de Londres but their own way of rushing about all day, and all the Evening, is a great deal more trying and with all their high staircases to drag up and to add to the days work. After Guizot's yesterday we went to Molé's beautiful Hotel and then ended with Mde de Paix's. This morning by 11 we were off to Mon. Rambuteau who was to shew us the Hotel de Ville with all its ancient recollections, and modern restorations and a very grand display it certainly is, and so well done, but it is much easier to govern children than grown up people, and how should we stand having the food of the Town taxed to give the Corporation 400 Thousands pounds a year of pocket money to ornament the town with, and where should we find artists and mechanics ready to give their works at half price for the honor and glory of having them placed in such a fine situation, and how our Newspapers would attack all their *pensée intime* of keeping it in constant preparation as a Citadel and fortification, in case of *émeute*—however it is beautifully done, and wonderfully successful. It is here that the fêtes for our Queen's coming here will be given, and we shall have a little sample of its splendour Saturday, when Rambuteau gives a Ball on a very large scale.

Brougham is talking of going away Monday. He seems now pretty well resigned to his fate of our arrival having darken'd his Star, and is even content now to follow in our wake, and to borrow some of our light. However his quarrel with Corise is still open, she would forgive him if he made an apology for his injustice and rudeness, but he holds off. She is very amusing about all this, and she revenges herself for his rudeness by shewing his abusive and absurd letters, which have put everybody on her side. If he had *calculated* how to do us most good, it would certainly have been by getting up this little episode, which made his attempt ridiculous, and his jealousy a common topic of amusement. The Cowleys have taken advantage of his folly to slip away their own anxiety under his cover, and to laugh at him as if they had never shared in his feeling, but I am really glad we came, not merely as a childish triumph, but from the real advantage it will produce in the feeling of all sides. Whether we come into Office or remain out, I am sure it must have the best results. Mde Lieven has been most friendly, and so has Sebastiani, but indeed there are no exceptions. They have all been friendly and well disposed, and very glad to see us. Mde Lieven says there has been much curiosity in London about our reception and that she has had many letters of inquiry ... Tell Melbourne the King and Royal family were most kind in their message to him, and all full of enquiries ...

Broadlands Papers

Whilst the Palmerstons were in Paris King Louis-Philippe was fired upon by a man named Lecomte, who was ultimately executed for the crime. On hearing of the King's escape Palmerston wrote a letter of congratulation. This was thought by some to be an impertinence from an ex-Foreign Secretary out of office, though it was rumoured that he had received word privately from the French royal family that

such a letter from him would be welcome.[47] The accuracy of this
report is shown in Lady Palmerston's next letter to her brother.

Paris Sunday April 20th [1846][48]

This horrid *attentat* has made an enormous sensation. It is
quite miraculous that the King and all escaped, firing on a Chara-
ban[c] full of people and only a few yards off, and this by a Garde
Chasse knowing his gun, a very good shot, and accustomed to
kill *à chevreuil* at any distance. It does really seem to be an inter-
position of Providence, all the small details are curious. It seems
the carriage went nearer to the wall than he expected (for he fired
over the Wall, with the Wall for a rest). The bullets and shot for
them were both in the two Barrels, must have gone no more than
a foot over the heads of the party. After the first Barrel the King
said I am not hurt, don't be frightened. Then came the second.
An Equerry jumped over the wall and seized the Man, as he was
running away, who said: 'J'ai été bien maladroit.' He was an ill-
tempered, ill-conditioned fellow, but rather higher in position
than these people usually are; he was suspected of poaching and
discharged on that account. They hope there were no other people
in connection, but there are some suspicious circumstances, such
as a letter from Grenoble mentioning such an event, and if there
are others concerned, it is supposed that they have worked on this
Man's disposition and urged him on. Altogether it is a very
painful event and makes every body feel unhappy, and destroys
the confidence that was established from a cessation of five years.
The poor Q[ueen] and Mde looked very miserable last night
when we went to the Tuileries and the King too was low, and
worn with the excitement of his feelings. The wonderful escape
and the good feeling that had been shown by everybody. The
national Guard part[icular]ly on the King's arrival at the Tuileries,
asked to be marched there, and amongst the 6,000 men they said
there was not one who did not warmly cheer. The Deputies and
Peers too went en masse, and last night at the reception from
8 to 10 o'clock the crowd was so great you could hardly get up
to the door, and 800 persons must have passed through the room.

[47] *Greville Memoirs* (1885), II, p. 388.
[48] So written, but April 20th 1846 was a Monday.

It was very touching to see this fine old man and his family and to think what a scene of desolation it might have been! The whole family too so painfully affected, and yet so dignified. P[almerston] wrote a beautiful letter to the K[ing] on hearing of his escape, and he seemed much touched at this proof of interest, and wrote himself in return. He of course would have feared to do this of himself, as an assumption, had he not received a hint that it would be well taken; and then he was really very happy to be able to say what he felt. (The Q[ueen] and Made also spoke to me about the letter.) One thing alone surprizes me that the Legitimists gave no sign of regret and absented themselves from the Chamber when they went to congratulate. Now really this was very ill-judged, for on such an occasion they might so naturally have come forward to express their horror of Assassination, without doing anything contrary to their principles, and it is in my opinion even brutal to stay away and so appear to regret that the assassin should have failed.

From the Tuileries we went to a great Ball at the Hotel de Ville, given by Mons Rambuteau le Prefet de la Seine and Governor of this Hotel de Ville; a very fine spectacle, beautifully decorated and lighted, many great people there and others, being Deputys or Municipality, or Garde Nationale. Pal[mersto]n was as usual quite a Lion, every body gathering round to look at him, to hear him speak, or to be introduced to him, and as my ears were on the Watch I found the impression very favourable. The same took place at the Embassy Ball, and every place we go to, morn[in]g and even[in]g. I tell him that I am quite afraid he will get so elated with his success, that I shall hardly be able to bully him as usual. The Duc de Richelieu who is famous for always saying disagreeable things, chiefly, I believe, for fun, said to me, 'Ne croyez pas qu'on vous haïssait tant autrefois, ou qu'on vous aime autant à *present* qu'on voudrait vous faire croire' . . . This amused me as shewing at least the contrast in his mind and the intention to flatter us in the Public. I wonder what Brougham will say in Eng[lan]d? I wonder! because he cannot well deny our brilliant reception, and he certainly went off quite frantic at seeing it, whilst he was left quite in the background. Only imagine that he should start on the very morning of the King's return to Paris after the attempt, and not staying to express his congratulations on the escape, for he did not go off till 11 o'clock (after writing me two letters about the paragraph in the Herald accusing Corise of a political intrigue and denying his having anything to do with it). I answered him saying that I did not believe that Notion had enter'd any head but his, and therefore of course it was suspicious . . .

Monday

I missed the post yesterday, so inclose it now. The rain is gone and fine weather today; but I must be off. We had a great dinner at Thiers yes[terda]y, 25 people all grandees, which the Lieven did not like as she wanted to quiz it. From dinner we went to her party, which is always agreable, and then to Duchatel's. How my health stands the enormous dinners every day and the running about after all morning is to me surprizing. Excitement carries one on. We shall not be able to start homewards before Sat[urda]y or Sunday, and then leave many engagements declined. Thursday we are to have a diner en partie quarrée, at the Lievens, which will be repose and interest together. The K[ing] has had great comfort in finding the very good feeling manifested by all classes. I think you should write on this Event, the expressions of all the family are so kind and friendly about you and they gave me so many messages. P[almerston] was off before 8 today to go round the fortifications with Thiers. It is great fun to see the wheel of fortune turn round and produce such companionship.

Broadlands Papers

Some two months later, on the very night that the bill for the total repeal of the Corn Laws was passed in the Lords, the Government were defeated in the Commons on the first reading of the Irish bill by a combination of Whigs and Protectionists. Four days later, on the 29th of June, Sir Robert Peel resigned. The Queen summoned Lord John Russell to form a government; and Lord Grey now raising no difficulties, the Foreign Secretaryship was almost as a matter of course offered to Lord Palmerston.

CHAPTER IV

The Affairs of Spain and Portugal

WHEN ON THE 3RD OF JULY, 1846, Palmerston resumed his seat at the Foreign Office, many acute problems faced him. Perhaps the most pressing was that of the Spanish marriages.

For some years Aberdeen and Guizot had been labouring to find eligible marriage alliances for the young Queen of Spain and her sister, the Infanta. In September 1845, when Queen Victoria and Prince Albert visited Louis-Philippe at the Château d'Eu, they came to an understanding that Isabella of Spain should choose a husband from the members of the house of Bourbon, and that only after she had married and had children should the Duc de Montpensier, a younger son of Louis-Philippe, be free to marry the Infanta, Maria Louisa Fernanda. Unfortunately, no desirable suitor could be found among the Spanish Bourbons, and another candidate was in the field in the shape of Queen Victoria's and Prince Albert's cousin, Prince Leopold of Saxe-Coburg. The claims of this suitor were so actively pushed by Sir Henry Bulwer, British Minister at Madrid, that the French took alarm; and Guizot declared that if the marriage of either of the Spanish sisters became 'probable or imminent' the French Court were resolved to press the immediate marriage of Montpensier with the other. Thus matters stood when Palmerston returned to the Foreign Office.

He acted with the utmost vigour. On the 18th of July he sent to the Spanish Ministers a brusque despatch condemning their misgovernment; and at the same time he instructed Bulwer to press the candidature of Enrique, Duke of Seville, for the Queen's hand and to try for the immediate betrothal of the Infanta to Prince Leopold. This enraged Louis-Philippe, whose Ambassador in London announced on the 2nd of September the impending marriage of the Queen of Spain to the Duke of Cadiz, elder brother of the Duke of Seville, and that of the Infanta to Montpensier. On the 10th of October, the Queen's sixteenth birthday, both marriages were celebrated.[1]

Naturally this made a great stir in England, and the general indignation is reflected in several of Lady Palmerston's letters of this time.

In mid-October she wrote to Mrs. Huskisson:

Carlton Terrace, Octr. 15th [1846]

... This Spanish plot has given him [Palmerston] much work and it is very provoking to feel how much mischief may arise now, and in the future from one man's ambition. The Govern-[men]t of France and Louis Philippe have behaved as ill as possible and with the greatest duplicity in the whole affair. The only comfort we have is that all parties in England are united on this point, that the Queen and Prince are entirely of Palmerston's opinions upon everything and so I hear are Peel, Aberdeen and Graham. In fact the conduct of the French, after all our flattery and forbearance, only shows how right Palmerston has always been in mistrusting them, and that, if he had remained in Office, all this mess would probably not have occurr'd. However, all this will end in coolness, but certainly in no war at present, and all we must hope is that however improbable, the Queen may have Children,[2] and so settle the question ...

I am going to Brocket tomorrow, and return Monday, for London is now my headquarters. We found it quite impossible to continue at Broadlands while Palmerston had so much business, and our Cabinets are to begin on the 28th, tho I hope no chance of Parliament meeting. My accounts are very good both of Melbourne and Frederick ...

Huskisson Papers
B.M. Add. MSS. 39949, ff. 226–9

In December, Charles Greville was staying at Broadlands, where his fellow-guest was the Prime Minister, Lord John Russell. From a conversation he had with Lady Palmerston he became convinced that

[1] Perhaps the most impartial account of this affair is that given by Lord Stanmore in his *Life of Aberdeen*, pp. 162 *et seq*. See also Bell, *Palmerston*, I, pp. 373 *et seq*.

[2] It was generally believed that the Duke of Cadiz was impotent.

her husband's one object was to 'humble France and to make her feel her humiliation', and with that in view to try to form some sort of league against her. He expressed the utmost alarm at the outlook and fully expected that eventually we should 'get into some scrape'.[3] But in spite of the hostile Greville's fears, it is abundantly clear that the Foreign Secretary had the support of the Prime Minister, as well as of the Queen and Prince Albert, for his handling of the Spanish marriages problem, if not for his intervention in the affairs of Portugal, of which some mention must now be made.

Maria, Queen of Portugal, married since 1836 to Victoria's and Albert's cousin, Ferdinand of Coburg, had sadly disappointed the hopes of her more liberal subjects by behaving as despotically as her Uncle Miguel, who since his overthrow had been living in exile in London. The inevitable result was the formation at Oporto of a revolutionary junta bent on organizing armed resistance to the throne. The position of the British Foreign Secretary was awkward. He was repelled by the cruelty and bad faith of Queen Maria's government; at the same time, England's close ties with Portugal prevented him from doing anything calculated to bring about the fall of the erring Queen. Yet his protests, comparatively mild though they were, did not meet with the approval of Queen Victoria, who considered that tactful persuasion was as far as we could with propriety go. There thus arose one of many differences that separated the Sovereign and her Foreign Secretary.[4]

Emily's next letter to Beauvale was written towards the end of 1846.

C[arlton] Terrace, Saturday–Monday [1846]

P[almerston] says Jarnac[5] has had plenty of slaps in the face to mend his manners and he looked quite crestfallen yesterday at Ly John's party, and P[almerston] does not wish to get rid of him, because he would be afraid of their then getting the Flahaults[6] here, which would be worse.

[3] *Greville Memoirs* (1885), III, pp, 12, 14. For the intrigues of Greville and his young friend, Henry Reeve, who went to Paris and established intimate relations with Thiers and other French ministers, and with Princess Lieven, see Bell, *Palmerston*, I, pp. 305–7, and *Greville Memoirs* (1885), III, pp. 16 *et seq.*

[4] Bell, *Palmerston*, I, pp. 390–4.

[5] Count Jarnac, French Ambassador in London.

[6] Flahault had for some time been making efforts to be made French Ambassador.

John[7] wrote so strong an answer to Jarnac for Guizot, that P[almerston] was quite astonished, and he says if *he* had written anything so violent he should have been called a firebrand, and expect to have everybody on his back. He said he approved entirely of all P[almerston] had said and done, and that his forbearance and patience had astonished him, and that there was but one opinion here in the whole Country upon the conduct of the French. This spirited answer was highly extol'd and admired by the Q[ueen] and Prince, and praised to him.

Pal[mersto]n has also finished his answer to Guizot's letter to him, and that also was much admired. It goes into the whole transaction and all the circumstances, and the Prince said it was so clear and so conclusive that a child could not help understanding it, and feeling its truth. So all that's well. Howard[8] had a long talk with the P[rince] and was much pleased, he is as you say a lucky fellow to have come over just now. Wylde[9] goes off tonight, he is going to try exactly what you say to get Diez[10] sent off, and to try the part of mediator. This turn will astonish the Queen of Portugal, who has always, like the King, written to them to abuse Howard for being against Diez. The King and Queen are both now in a great fright, as great a fright as her Exultation was when she first made the blow up, thinking it was an amazing *coup*. She is said to be a very violent woman. Clarendon is very desponding about the thing, thinks the Spaniards will intervene, with the French behind them, and that the King and Queen will be at Windsor in a few months. Lionel Rothchild's correspondent says the Spaniards will *not* intervene, and he thinks the French are so sick of all the bother they have brought on themselves by the Montpensier marriage that they will try now to keep quiet. He says also that the Austrians hang back to see what advantage they can get for themselves, and that what they would like would be to see the two Liberal

[7] Lord John Russell.

[8] Lord Howard de Walden was Minister Plenipotentiary and Envoy Extraordinary to the Court of Lisbon, where his influence with the Queen and her advisers was said to be considerable.

[9] Colonel Wylde was sent on a secret mission to Oporto and Lisbon.

[10] Diez was a German tutor who had come to Portugal with Ferdinand. He was believed to be much in the Queen's confidence and to give her the worst possible advice.

Governm[en]ts of France and Eng[lan]d go on quarreling together *without* coming to blows.

Ly John had a nice little party last night, but people are flitting off today, to return for the Cabinet Monday. The Queen and P[rince] are very anxious about Portugal, glad our Parl[iamen]t dont meet now, and going off to Osborne for a month . . . I should like to get back to you at Brocket, but cannot just now, for poor P[almerston] is like a hunted hare; he has not even time to answer my small questions. It is such a bore! . . .

Broadlands Papers

From Lady Palmerston's next letter to her brother we get a vivid picture of the intrigues in the Paris of Louis-Philippe.

C[arlton] Terrace Monday [*c.* March, 1847]

. . . Palmerston says that he thinks Peel and Aberdeen did the Queen[11] harm by setting her against all Liberal Governm[en]t, and representing it as revolution, for instance her objection to Southern[12] for being a progressista is of that nature, and she mentions it as an objection, and in a bad sense.[13] Now Palmerston says we are all progressistas, Clarendon is one, and Espartero is the head of that party. We all want a strong fair and Liberal Governm[en]t, and the King of Portugal's quarrels with his people is [*sic*] all from the attempts he makes to get a more despotic Governm[en]t. However, it is clear that Southern can do no good if he is in their black books. Stockmar would be clearly the Man. P[almerston] is busy writing his answer to Guizot's letter, for which the Queen is impatient, so I can get nothing from him today, but he does not at this moment think of anybody better than Seymour.[14] . . .

[11] Queen Victoria.

[12] Henry Southern (1799–1853), British Chargé d'affaires at Lisbon, who on Palmerston's instructions delivered some sharp admonitions to the Portuguese Court. These were not entirely approved by Queen Victoria.

[13] See Queen Victoria to Disraeli, 14th March 1847. *Queen Victoria's Letters*, 1st Series, II, pp. 140–1.

[14] Sir George Hamilton Seymour (1797–1880); Envoy Extraordinary to Belgian Court, 1836–46; to Lisbon, 1846–51; to St. Petersburg, 1851–4; to Austria, 1855.

Louis Philippe took care not to know our opinion about the Montpensier Marriage, by keeping his plan so close, and mystifying us; but I believe with Cowley that if he had known we should all take it so seriously he might have hesitated. His trust was in the Queen and her weakness for him.[15] When one recollects that her first message to Pal[mersto]n on coming into Office was *not* to oppose French influence in Spain, and *not* to attempt to get up an English party there, *but this is profoundly secret*, one cannot wonder at Louis Philippe having some hopes of her. Then he thought the Radicals would stand by him, and the Tories, and that Pal[mersto]n standing alone might be got rid of. Now I have no doubt he is much disturbed, and would do anything to be well with us again; so P[almerston] says our line must be sulk, and then he hopes to have offers of Commercial advantages and other things. France, we hear, is very much disturbed at this break up of entente cordiale for no present advantage, and a very uncertain future one, and that there is much dissatisfaction a[t] this sacrifice merely for a Dotte. Guizot's position is said to be endangered and that L[ouis] P[hilippe] has seen Molé, and would throw over Guizot if he had any hopes of bringing things round by it. Guizot is, I believe, in a great fright, his Agents are always coming over here . . . and what looks like Guizot's leaving no stone unturned is a letter he has just now written to Lord John, a most artful thing, using flattery to him and trying to draw a comparison and to shew a difference between them and P[almerston]. In short, a most rascally attempt to sow division.[16] Somebody said of Guizot once: '*C'est un austère Intrigant*', but he is even worse than that for he lies and misrepresents without conscience. He has not succeeded and John sent P[almersto]n his letter, who luckily could blow it up, for it was all founded on misrepresentation of his or Jarnac's, or perhaps both. Guizot says that Pal[mersto]n was so *passioné* there was no hopes of him, that he had said to Jarnac, that the want of *égards* and *procèdes* of the French towards him on this Marriage, was so great that he could

[15] Queen Victoria was supposed to have a soft spot in her heart for Louis-Philippe and his wife, but she was certainly furious at what she regarded as his breach of the verbal promise he gave at the Château d'Eu and only forgave him when he was an exile in England after the revolution of 1848.

[16] *Greville Memoirs* (1885), III, p. 53.

not forgive it, and that he had added these words, 'and I shall resent it'. Now Pal[mersto]n recollects his conversation perfectly and says these words had nothing to do with the Marriage, nothing to do with *procèdes*, but that Jarnac either from himself or from reading some letter of Guizot's began to talk of Palmerston as acting from pique, and from personal feeling, and being different from his Colleagues and so forth. That upon this Pal[mersto]n stopped him short, said this was a style of attack that he would not stand, that he knew very well there were people in France and in England too who had endeavoured to run him down by saying that he acted from personal spite instead of the interest of the Country, that ascribed the worst motives to him, and that he was a lover of War, and hater of France, and endeavoured to draw a distinction between himself and his Colleagues; that the Charge was perfectly false, and groundless, and that by whomsoever it was made he should resent it . . . etc. etc. Is it not roguish after this to so misrepresent him and to work up this into a charge of unfair prejudice on Public Events and so continuing to work up the very same Attack, and even quoting his defence, as a proof of what they advanced? P[almerston] wrote this explanation to John, and will make Normanby go to Guizot about it. If the Lie is not Guizot's but Jarnac's Pal[mersto]n will refuse to have any more conversation with him except in writing. Perhaps he misrepresented a little and Guizot a little, but between them both it remains. I think Jarnac a Jack a Napes, and has misrepresented other things before; he is very anxious to be put forward and Aberdeen always talked to him instead of employing Cowley, who told P[almerston] he was kept quite ignorant of all that passed here. Jarnac got credit for his reports and probably seasoned them to please Louis P[hilippe] and Guizot, and now probably got vexed at finding that P[almerston] gave more into Normanby's hands and less into his, and so made up this falsehood.

Palmerston now thinks that he may have done the same about Aberdeen, who left in the Office his Statement of what had occurr'd about the Marriage, that he only said he should not put forward a Cobourg. Whilst Jarnac's despatch went to say that Ld A[berdeen] had promised to prevent a Cobourg coming forward. And he found him out before in another misstatement. I saw Dietrichstein[17] yest[er]d[a]y; he seems very anxious to find some means of shewing that they go hand in hand with us, tho they cannot protest on account of not having acknowledged, but he does not know what to do, and he wants P[almerston] to hit on some plan. He says if you was in town, he should consult you and shew you all his dispatches and letters. Brunow is also most cordial and quite with us in feeling (and very glad of the quarrel) but not knowing what to do . . .

Broadlands Papers

Nevertheless, there was much hostility to Palmerston's policy, and Aberdeen was particularly incensed at some violent attacks upon him in the *Morning Chronicle* which he attributed to the Foreign Secretary. Charles Greville sitting next to Palmerston at the Sheriff's dinner referred to these articles and to the harm they were doing. 'I dare say they attribute the articles to me,' was his neighbour's comment. Greville agreed that it was so and that Aberdeen thought the same. A few nights later, at a reception at Lady Palmerston's, Greville talked with Beauvale and reported him to be in accord with his views on the damage done by the articles; but he could do no good by talking, declared Beauvale, and therefore he held his tongue. Yet when the gossiping Clerk of the Council pumped Lady Palmerston she had assured him that her brother and her husband saw eye to eye on the whole affair! Some three weeks later, at a dinner given by the Palmerstons to Lord John Russell, Clarendon tackled Beauvale about the rupture in Anglo-French relations which had been worsened by the unfortunate conduct of our Ambassador at Paris. It appeared that Lord Normanby had got himself involved in the eternal squabbles between Thiers and Guizot, and that the Foreign Secretary was supporting his Ambassador. Indeed, if we can believe Greville, Palmerston, without reference to his colleagues, had announced that, unless Normanby received satisfactory reparation for the treatment that had been meted out to him, intercourse between the two countries should cease.[18] Lord John sought to intervene to give tempers time to cool; then Princess Lieven wrote to Lady Palmerston, hoping that peace could be made between the contending parties, which was taken

[17] Count Moritz Dietrichstein, Austrian Ambassador in London, 1846-8.
[18] *Greville Memoirs* (1885), III, pp. 52-3, 61-3.

to mean that Guizot would not reject any overture that was made to him: but the atmosphere was electric and our relations with France were at their lowest ebb. Less than a year later the Orleanist dynasty fell, and Louis-Philippe and his family were thankful to seek refuge in the country that they had done so much to alienate.

At the end of August Palmerston was due to accompany the Queen to Scotland as Minister in Attendance, and so Emily made plans with Fred for a holiday in the Isle of Wight.[19] Meanwhile she and her husband went to Broadlands, whence Emily wrote to her brother about the intrigues surrounding the young Queen of Spain.

Broadlands, Wedy. 18th [August 1847]

... Lord West[morlan]d[20] called on me yesterday Morning, as Pal[mersto]n was out, to say as how [sic] that Bresson[21] was come to London to look for Horses and so that he had got him to dinner. That was all right enough for him who knew him before and needed no explanation, but Rothschild[22] had been to Palmerston early in the morning to ask him to see Bresson, who wanted to see him. Palmerston made a civil excuse, said he was going out of town, and could not delay. Rothschild said he would wait for his return from Tiverton. (James [Rothschild] of Paris had written to Lionel [Rothschild] to ask him to manage an interview). Upon this Palm[ersto]n said he thought it better to tell Lionel the truth, and that he would not see him, that it could do no good to discuss things past, that he knew Bresson to be a great liar, and that if he saw him Bresson would misrepresent all he said, and therefore he should not give him an opportunity. The Horse buying is always a good pretence and Westmorland was quite taken in by it. It seems almost a *Mauvaise plaisanterie* that

[19] Lady Palmerston to Beauvale, Thursday [August 12th] C[arlton] Gardens, 1847. Broadlands Papers.

[20] John Fane, 11th Earl of Westmorland (1784–1859). Resident Minister at Berlin, 1841–51.

[21] Comte Charles de Bresson, French Ambassador to Spain.

[22] Lionel Nathan de Rothschild (1807–79): succeeded in 1836 to chief management of Rothschild banking house in England; in the recent General Election he had been elected Whig M.P. for the City of London, but not allowed to sit owing to refusal as a Jew of the required oath; finally allowed to sit, 1858; re-elected 1859, 1865, 1869. Original of Sidonia in Disraeli's *Coningsby*.

Bresson's object should be to come Ambassador here, but so it is, and P[almerston] knows from a former intercepted letter that it was the reward he asked for making the Spanish Marriages, that he should afterwards come Ambassador here—what a strange combination! And Westmorland told me yesterday that Bresson had asked him as a friend if he thought he could come here as Ambassador, and why as Palm[ersto]n received Isturitz so well he should not do the same by him.[23] ...

In Portugal, too, things were in a bad way, as Emily wrote to her brother some days later.

Broadlands Tuesday [August 24th or 31st 1847]
... Palmerston has been so driven from Pillar to Post, that we had no time for talk ... The Queen and Prince have now been doing all the good they can with the Queen of Portugal, urging her most strongly to be honest in her promises and to change the Cabral Govern[men]t at once. This was not their notion when P[almerston] arrived at Cowes, which shews the use of his seeing them often. When he arrived there, he found our Queen very anxious the Queen of Spain should not be *pressed* to make a change, but should be left to her *own time* for doing it. But however Palmerston's arguments and a letter he shewed them from Seymour made a complete change and Albert afterwards shewed P[almerston] a letter he had written to the Q[ueen] of Spain for our Queen to copy out to her using all Pal[mersto]n's arguements and telling her that everything now depended upon her shewing to her people that she was sincere in her intentions of keeping strictly to all her promises, that her people mistrusted her, and that she must try to re-establish their confidence. Her wish for delay was this, to get the Elections over with a Cabral Governm[en]t, who then by every means fair and unfair would then [*sic*] increase their party, and make elections in that sense, so that if they went out, no other Governm[en]t could stay in, a state of things that would probably bring on another revolution. Pal[mersto]n says nothing could be better or stronger than

[23] *Greville Memoirs* (1885), III, pp. 193-4.

291

Albert's letter, and he hopes it may have an effect. It is really fortunate that they should now have their eyes entirely open'd about Portugal, particularly the Prince, and the representations of Wylde and Mensdorff very luckily corroborates all that Seymour writes and Pal[mersto]n urges, but of course this is all quite secret.

Mde Lieven is going to Trouville a small bathing place near Havre,[24] as she says with no prospect of any company but Ly Sandwich's; however I believe there is no doubt that Guizot will somehow or other turn up there. We have heavy rain today and I fear the weather is dreadfully unsettled for the Queen's Voyage;[25] one comfort is that they put into harbour every night, so they may wait if the weather should be bad . . .

Broadlands Papers

With her beloved Pam off to Scotland in attendance on the Queen, Emily betook herself to the Ashleys' home in the Isle of Wight, whence within a day or so of her arrival she was writing anxiously to her 'dearest Love' that 'My great anxiety now is to hear of your safe arrival, and pray let me intreat of you not to let any circumstances persuade you to *sail* on Luggan Lake. Those lakes are all dangerous, and pray remember that you have promised me if you do bathe, not to go out of your depth . . .'[26] In a week Lady Palmerston was back at Brocket, writing urgently to her husband about the expected recall of the exiled former Spanish Regent, General Espartero, following the fall of Pacheco a few days previously.[27] Indeed, so worried was Emily at what she regarded as the supine attitude of the Spanish General that she called on him and his wife in order to encourage them to more forthright action. But, judging from her next letters to her absent lord, these well-meaning attentions were not particularly successful!

[24] Princess Lieven to Lady Palmerston, Paris, September 24th, 1847. *Lieven-Palmerston Correspondence*, p. 297.

[25] To Scotland, with Lord Palmerston as Minister in attendance.

[26] Lady Palmerston to Palmerston, Ryde, Friday (3rd Sept. 1847). Broadlands Papers. Date added by Lord Palmerston.

[27] Lady Palmerston to Palmerston, Brocket, Thursday [September 9th 1847]. Broadlands Papers. Espartero had been living in England since his overthrow in 1843. In fact he was not recalled to power.

FREDERICK LAMB, LORD BEAUVALE

From the portrait by John Partridge at the National Portrait Gallery

WILLIAM LAMB, VISCOUNT MELBOURNE

From the portrait by Sir Thomas Lawrence at Henfield Place

... On my way down here yesterday I bethought myself of going to call on the Esparteros, and there I found them at home in great joy at this Spanish news, but still I am afraid Supine. He had not received the regular notification of his Appointm[en]t tho he expected to do so today or tomorrow. However he knew it was coming and had seen the account in the Times. He said when it arrived he should send the Chevr. Gurseo [?] with a letter to the Queen and then he should wait to see you on your return. I ventured to say that, much as you would like to see him, I had no doubt you would much prefer to *hear* of his departure, that I thought he ought to be there to support the Queen and to give her courage, that she wanted good Counsellors to keep out bad ones, and that I felt very anxious to have him there, and that I was so afraid L[ouis] P[hilippe] if he had time, would bribe the Army and set bad engines at work. Oh, no, he said, that would not happen, that every thing depended on the Queen being stout, that if she was so, that all would do well and yet he seemed inclined to linger in the true Spanish way. He approves the Governm[en]t and all the measures they have yet pursued, and part[i]c[ular]ly the amnesty to everybody, and a paper one of his friends had sent him, he was delighted with, a paper given about in the streets stating his Appointm[en]t of Capt[ai]n General, and headed by a print of two couriers at full speed on horses racing with whips and spurs to carry him the news, and yet still the man hesitates about starting and says I must wait to see Lord Pal[mersto]n.

They were both very amiable and kind to me and happy to see me, and said they hoped I would give them a line to say when you was to come to town. I have written this account of Espartero to John Russell, in case he might like to see him and send him off. I may be wrong, but it seems to me so important that he should lose no time. In a crisis of this sort everything may depend on his being on the spot, and ready to take advantage of events or to command them. They say supineness and sleep was always his fault and that whenever he distinguished himself with any energy it was when Wylde was at his elbow. I wish you could put him there now. What a pity you should be so far off.[29]

[28] Date added by Lord Palmerston.
[29] See also Lady Palmerston to Palmerston, Brocket, Tuesday [21st] September, 1847. Lady Airlie, *Lady Palmerston*, II, p. 113.

I saw Clanricarde yesterday just before I left town, he had been dining with Sumner, an American just come from Paris. He says every thing tends there to a Republic, that people are so disgusted at late events and ill affected to the Governm[en]t, and that they the Governm[en]t are in a complete fix, that Guizot does not dare bring Beauvallon to trial as some of his friends have said, that if he does they will then denounce him Guizot and expose all his briberys with money and peerages, and that so he leaves the trial standing over and not knowing what to do . . .

Broadlands Papers

Brocket, Friday 17 [September 1847]
. . . You say nothing of Spain or Italy. Here Fred and I talk of nothing else, and we are so provoked with Espartero for his supineness. He has sent Gurreo with a letter of thanks to the Queen and he will not start till his return. What a thorough Spaniard waiting to see how affairs settle, instead of going off as an Englishman would do to settle them—and he says the Governm[en]t does not appear in its formation to be as liberal as he expected from the first accounts; I have no patience with him for sitting in his Abbey Lodge instead of going to take a post the moment he was named Captain General . . .

Melbourne Papers
B.M. Add. MSS. 45546–7

In her next two letters to Beauvale, Emily was still full of Spanish affairs.

1847, Broadlands Saturday Night [Sept. 25th]
. . . Bresson's impudence is inconceivable. Westmorland wrote Palmerston what he told him about Spanish Affairs and I should have liked to have sent you his letter, but it is gone to John.[30] Evidently Westmorland is a little staggered by his plausible statement, tho he don't really believe him. Bresson says there is no

[30] Lord John Russell.

truth in the Stories about the King, but that a Nun having told him that if he lived with the Queen she would put upon him Children that were not his own, he had determined to put a restraint upon himself, and hence the disagreements that had arisen between the Husband and Wife, that the object now should be to have a complete *Entente Cordiale* with France to quiet the King's suspicions, and to persuade him to live with his wife that she might have an Heir, that he Bresson and Louis P[hilippe] were most anxious for this result, as they were very much *afraid* that if these differences continued the Queen would insist on resigning her Crown as she had already shewn some wish of this sort, and therefore to prevent such a misfortune England and France should act cordially together . . .

Sunday

Bulwer writes that nothing is sure in Spain, but that he *hopes* there may be a change of Governm[en]t, and that Senaro[31] may come in with other new people and some Progresistes. He says he is not a Man of much knowledge or capacity, but well intentioned, honourable, and valiant and that it will be better for him to be in the Governm[en]t, than advising the Queen out of it, and that it would have a better effect with the Public, to be about her in a decided Character, than to be subject to so much misrepresentation.

The present Governm[en]t have been trying hard to bring the K[ing] and Q[ueen] into better terms, and it is the wish of all those who are not in the pay of France. Hitherto they have not managed it, but they still hope. He says the inventions made about the Queen are absurd and quite untrue, but he does not mention any prospect or thought of her resigning, so that also we hope are French inventions.

We got to Tiverton Wednesday and to town 31st . . .

Broadlands Papers

Towards the end of September the Palmerstons went down to Devonshire, so it was from Tiverton that Emily wrote her next letter to Fred, on the evening of their arrival.

[31] Marshal Serrano.

... I can understand that you should be puzzled with Spanish contradictions, because I tell you the reports I hear. It was Espartero who said Serrano was bought by Louis P[hilippe]. Bulwer does not believe this, but he finds him like the other Spaniards, changeable, weak and wavering. Bulwer does give all the good advice he can, but he is obliged to be careful of what he says, for Serrano is surrounded like the Queen by people he trusts, and who only seek to make use of him for their own purposes; therefore whatever Bulwer says to him goes to them.

Madrid is a nest of Intrigues, all wanting their own advantages so new plans succeed each other every day, and are again destroyed by others. Bulwer has a very good opinion of Serrano's honesty and good intentions, but he doubts his capacity. There is a very strong and good article in the *Times* today on Spanish Affairs and denouncing in strong terms the conduct of Louis P[hilippe]; his object is clearly by worry and vexation to drive her to resign. Palmerston thinks she has never had any real intention of doing this, tho she may have talked of it when she found herself so harassed or held it out as a threat. Thursday—Today P[almerston] has a dispatch from W[illia]m Hervey[32] who says Narvag[33] left Paris upon hearing by the French Telegraph that the Queen requested that he would instantly come to Madrid. He was much pleased with his order saying he should settle everything then; and *shoot Serrano*. Now if the Queen has sent for him in this manner, it must certainly be by Serrano's consent or advice. So that it is clear that he is deceiving somebody, but which party remains to be proved. At Paris they think him in their interests, and ready to act up to their views. On the other side, he has said that he is a true Spaniard, and that the thing he will do is to get the Queen a divorce and marry her to some Prince. Perhaps it may be in this view that he would shoot Serrano, to get him out of the way. It is all this double dealing and false confidences that make such contradictory reports, one does not know what to believe. W[illia]m Hervey says he doubts Narvag getting to Madrid, (supposing the Queen has sent for him without Serrano's approval, and that he will stop him at Bayonne) but I don't think

[32] William Hervey (1805–1850), son of Frederick William Hervey, 5th Earl and 1st Marquess of Bristol.　　[33] Narvaez.

it probable she would take such a step, without consulting Serrano[34] . . .

Broadlands Papers

Meanwhile, largely due to the vigorous policy of the Foreign Secretary, the Government of Lord John Russell looked stronger and more settled than ever, as Emily pointed out to Fred in October.

Wednesday Octr. 28th, [1847][35]

. . . Palmerston comes into town for a meeting tomorrow. We hear Ld Grey is very Couleur de Rose; that upon Miss Eden saying something of the Governm[en]t lasting, he said 'It will last for ever, I *wonder* what should break it up!' Lord Stanley is said to be well disposed and friendly towards this Governm[en]t, very spiteful and bitter only towards Peel and Graham, but he avoids talking politicks . . .

I dare say Pal[mersto]n will have some explanation with Aberdeen; but he never suspected Jarnac of lying till lately . . . This letter of Guizot's will be the 4th time that Pal[mersto]n has had to call him over the Coals, since he came into Office. The first time was his misrepresenting Pal[mersto]n to the D[uke] of Bedford, which I found out and for which P[almerston] hauled him up. The 2nd time he told John[36] that upon giving P[almerston] some letter of Guizot's he gave no answer, but merely said what a good hand M. Guizot writes. John thought this very strange and asked Pal[mersto]n, upon which he said it was a lie, and that he answered it fully, tho he did add upon giving back the letter a remark on the handwriting. Pal[mersto]n attacked Jarnac for this falsehood, who could not then deny it, but said he had forgotten what he had said, and then he went to John Russell to reproach him for having told Pal[mersto]n. Well then Palmerston said that he would not stand this *way* of going on, and these attempts to work at him through his colleagues, and that as a

---

[34] For Greville's account of these intrigues, see *Greville Memoirs* (1885), III, pp. 193-4.

[35] So written, but October 28th, 1847 was a Thursday.

[36] Lord John Russell.

Friend he gave him the advice to alter his course. This was surely clear enough, but what came next? Jarnac in talking himself to Pal[mersto]n said as you have desired me not to communicate with Ld John Russell, does not this seem like folly, as well as misrepresentation!

Thursday Morning

Here I found the Post gone, so I must finish today. P[almerston] is just come up breathless, and rushing off to the Cabinet. He is pleased with his Windsor Visit, and the great amiability of the Prince and Queen . . .

Broadlands Papers

Alas! The 'great amiability' of the Prince and Queen was to turn to indignant protests at the high-handed conduct of their Foreign Secretary before many months had passed.

CHAPTER V

'Civis Romanus Sum'

WITH ALL THE UNREST on the Continent of Europe in the Year of Revolution it is perhaps remarkable that in England there was nothing worse to be faced than the Chartist disturbances in April, led by the ineffectual Feargus O'Connor.[1] Yet even these mild affairs were taken seriously. Lady Palmerston, after walking out to see the sights, took refuge with her daughter, Lady Ashley, from whose house she sent an urgent appeal to her husband to allow her to return home. 'If all remains quiet, I am very anxious to return home in the Even[in]g. It will be much more comfortable and it seems perfectly safe, and besides if there is no danger, it would seem so foolish to go and *découcher* for nothing. Pray therefore give me leave to do so, if you see no objection and as we have now a good exit to our House above and below, there can be no danger. I await your orders . . .' The 'orders', it seems, were not to her taste, so she promptly ignored them. 'It seems ridiculous to be in fright about nothing, so I shall order W[illia]m's fly to take me home about ½ past 10. It is better than a shewing Carriage, so you will find us there quietly when you come home.'[2] A few days later she wrote to Mrs Huskisson a lengthy account of the precautions taken against this menace, vividly reminiscent of the enrolment of the Local Defence Volunteers in the terrible days of the late war.

C[arlton] Gardens, Friday, [April 14th, 1848]
    Your letter reminded me that I ought to have given you private details of *our revolution*, as the papers tho very full could only give the public ones.

[1] Feargus O'Connor (1794-1855). Chartist leader; pronounced insane, 1852.
[2] Lady Palmerston to Palmerston, Monday, 10th April, 1848. Lady Airlie, *Lady Palmerston*, II, p. 117; Bell, *Palmerston*, II, pp. 409-10.

Our Terrace was divided into districts, all the servants made special Constables. Ld Arundel commanded the other side of the Column and Mr Tomline with Ld Kildare this one. The arrangements were excellent everywhere, two thousand real police stationed in Trafalgar Square and Regent St. and Cockspur St., where it was thought there would be a fight.

The Admiralty and all the offices were garrisoned and provision'd as if for a siege, cannon placed on the Bridges and the Duke of Wellington's arrangements so beautifully made with Corps stationed, and pickets between, that they said a force of 10,000 could be collected at any given point in a few minutes. All these arrangements were his own, and everybody was in admiration of his clearness and judgment just as in the olden time when he got upon his old ground of glory. There certainly was great alarm in all quarters, the uncertainty of what number of disaffected might come in from the manufacturing districts, and the very great number of foreigners in the Country, French, Poles and Germans and the daily arrival of many more, known to be revolutionists from Paris of the very worst character.

This, with all that has occur'd lately in Europe made one of course anxious to avoid no precautions, that could be taken; and I am sure it is very fortunate that the whole thing has occur'd as it has shewn the good spirit of our middle classes, and almost one may say of the whole population of London, as well as the activity and courage of the aristocracy. 2 hundred Thousand were sworn in special Constables and all higgledy piggledy Peers and Commons, servants, workmen, and all kinds of people, all hale fellow well met, an example of union and loyalty and a determination to stand by our constitution which will have a great effect everywhere in England, in Ireland, and in Europe. Besides I think it a positive advantage to bring the higher classes in contact with the lower ones, to see them unite cordially and without pride and ready to stand out in the wet, and the rain, and to fight like Journeymen with no other arms than staffs.

Our Police too are highly gratified to find themselves supported, and to see these specials taking upon themselves as they did the whole police of the Town for 5 hours from 6 to 11 while all the real policeman went to their quarters to rest.

Palmerston went off at 11 to defend his office as it was thought the people from Kennington Common were to attack that part of the town, to force their way to the Houses of Parl[liamen]t and there were frightful reports about of a large number of these people being armed with guns and Pikes and Pistols and daggers and knives which was I believe to a certain degree true. But when the Chartists found their own numbers so very far short of what they expected, and no sympathy from the Middle Classes, or Soldiers, and the number of the well disposed so overwhelming, they gave up all hopes of revolution and therefore fighting or stabing [sic] would have been without an object and only dangerous to themselves. However this notion of Daggers and Cutlasses and pistols had frighten'd the Police a good deal, and therefore did this danger redound still more to their credit and shew the courage of our Aristocracy old and young, for the old went out like the young, Ld de Grey, the Duke of Norfolk, the D[uke] of Leeds, old Ld Strafford etc. etc. and I must say these pistols and daggers were *my terror*. I thought our Gentlemen would be a mark for the ill intention'd with special written on a white band on the left arm, and my two sons and Ashley and Jocelyn were on duty the whole day.

When Pal[mersto]n went off to his office I went to pass the day with Minny and we walked about in that neighbourhood at different times to see the state of affairs. The ill looking workmen and foreigners looking out for mischief, and the shoals of Special Constables, some two and two on guard at different corners, and then Patrols of 18 or 20 going their rounds all laughing and talking. These specials were all in sections, large numbers for each district and then subdivided again into parties of 20, a gentleman in command, then Tradesmen and servants and Journeymen.

Cantelupe we met with one of these parties, Frederick with another, and loads more of gentlemen whom we knew or did not know. It was certainly a proud day for England and it has I hope insur'd our safety for a long time to come. Our foreigners are in great admiration of all this display and Mde de Lieven says '*les laches Francais devraient mourir de honte de voir la différence entre les deux pays, l'esprit d'ordre, et le courage de cœur que le soutiennent*'.

Bunsen says London was a beautiful sight that day. It looked like a large ship cleared for action, everything so quiet, everybody in their place all anxious and ready to do their duty, and nobody saying any thing but when you looked behind the screen, all the means of defence ready.

The Parks shut up and deserted, no Carriages in the Streets, no omnibus's allowed, no soldiers to be seen, all the Troops shut up in Barracks and riding Horses and out of sight, so there was no hopes of fraternizing. I believe this circumstance awed the Foreigners more than all. It was so unusual a sight to them. Knowing they were all there, and yet seeing nothing of them or of the Cannon and Marines and Chelsea Pensioners, all of whom were known to be there.

If we can only get our bill through the House, and an Alien bill and an arms bill, *and Ireland safe*; then I hope we shall be very well, and have no more anxiety and alarm, but Ireland is the danger now!! Let us hope however that the failure here will have some effect, as well as Lamartine's answer, and the ridicule with which Fergus O'Connor has been cover'd by the discovery of the absurd exageration [*sic*] of his numbers and the ridiculous signatures to his monster petition, of which you see an account in the papers. The Duke of Wellington's name had been written down 17 times and Queen Victoria's and numbers of women and words without sense and all sorts of indecency's [*sic*] which shows the manner in which it was got up. Adieu dear Mrs H[uskisson]. This is a long letter but I think these details may amuse you . . .

Huskisson Papers
B.M. Add. MSS. 39949, ff. 233–40

Towards the end of the year there was bad news for Lady Palmerston, for it was apparent that her brother, Melbourne, was seriously ill. At first she had better accounts of the invalid, who was paying one of his rare visits to Melbourne Hall. He 'got down very comfortably, but with the luxury of four Horses instead of the odious Rail road and its dangers', Emily told Mrs. Huskisson. Furthermore, he had bought a Bath chair, which was a great success. Then she turned to public affairs, and her remarks show the disturbed state of Europe at this time.

Broadlands, Monday 11th [September 1848]

... Austria accepts our mediation, and we are in great hopes all those difficult affairs will be settled by negociation so that all chances of war may be avoided.

Palmerston believes that our joint mediation alone prevented the French from marching into Italy. This strengthened the hands of Cavagnac and enabl'd him to resist Lamoriciere and the war party. Mon[sieu]r de Beaumont says that but for us, their army of the Alps would now be there and there is no saying how soon this would have lighted up a general war.

We have tried all we could to prevent the King of Naples invading Sicily, but he is very obstinate, and we did not feel justified in ordering our fleet positively to interfere. Now we shall see what comes of it, and if any negociation can avert the bloodshed which is likely to ensue, if he tries to conquer Sicily.

Huskisson Papers
B.M. Add. MSS. 39949, ff. 246–9

The good news of her brother's health was shortlived, and some six weeks later she had a very different story to tell Mrs Huskisson. William was dangerously ill with jaundice and Frederick with the worst attack of gout and rheumatism she had ever known.[3] Less than a month later William was dead.

Brocket, Nov[embe]r 26 [18]48

... Poor dear William is now in heaven and one must not grieve too much that he is removed from this earth, and from all the worry, anxiety and pain and trouble from which he has suffered the last six years of his bad health ... Epileptic fits he had the last few days which were very painful to see, but I trust and believe to himself free from pain, as pressure on the brain destroys sensation.

Tho conscious to a certain degree up to the last day or two and knowing those around him, his mind was quite composed and peaceful, and I believe he felt no anxiety or painful thoughts now,

[3] Tuesday Morn[in]g [October 31st 1848]. Huskisson Papers B.M. Add. MSS. 39949, ff. 242–5.

tho he had no doubt long contemplated his own death, and his mind was quite prepared for the awful change.

At last, thank God, his end was peaceful and he only breathed one sigh . . .

Huskisson Papers
B.M. Add. MSS. 39949, ff. 250–2

Meanwhile throughout the year groups of refugees from France kept coming to England, ever the haven of the afflicted. Early in March, Louis Philippe 'disguised in a rough pea-jacket, enormous goggles, and a week-old beard, and escorting a heavily veiled consort', landed at Newhaven. Other members of the French royal family soon followed, and within a few days were all installed at King Leopold's dreary house at Claremont.[4] About the same time came Guizot, who settled in a small house in Brompton, where he set about writing his great history of his countrymen and of England's revolution of 1688; and Princess Lieven, who established herself first in Brighton and then in Richmond, there to re-open her once-famous *salon*. Before long, Prince and Princess Metternich arrived, and under the name of Herr and Frau von Meyer took up their residence at Brighton. The Palmerstons went out of their way to be friendly to the exiles, and they gave a special dinner-party in honour of Guizot, to which, almost as a matter of course, Princess Lieven was also invited. 'I thought Palmerston and Guizot would have shaken each other's arms off', recorded Charles Greville, a fellow guest, 'and nothing could exceed their cordiality or apparent ease with which they conversed. There was not the slightest symptom of embarrassment; and though Guizot's manner is always stiff, pedantic, and without the least approach to *abandon*, he seemed to me to exhibit less of these defects than usual . . .'[5]

The peaceful revolution of February 1848 was speedily followed by bloodshed and confusion. France, it seemed, demanded a Napoleon. Consequently, at the election for the presidency held in December, the

[4] Bell, *Palmerston*, I, p. 428. For an account of the King and Queen's escape, see Featherstonehaugh (British Consul at Havre) to Palmerston, Havre, 3rd March 1848. *Queen Victoria's Letters*, 1st Series, II, pp. 184–8.

[5] *Greville Memoirs* (1885), III, p. 157. For Palmerston's account of his dinner-party, see Palmerston to Normanby, F[oreign] O[ffice], April 4, 1848. Ashley, *Palmerston*, II, p. 77.

socialists adopted as their candidate Ledru-Rollin, the republicans Cavaignac, while the recently re-organized Imperialists chose as their champion Prince Louis Napoleon. The man with the magic name gained an overwhelming majority at the polls, where universal suffrage was adopted for the first time in France. With the new French Government Palmerston made every effort to agree, as his wife was careful to explain to her brother Beauvale[6] early in the new year.

Broadlands Janry. 21 [1849]

... I think the President[7] was very foolish to banish these people, and I dare say he has made other mistakes, but people who know him believe that when he can he will relax in his measures and give more liberty. It must be so difficult to settle a Constitution. Mrs Craven[8] has been here and Craven, both entirely with the President and quite in astonishment at the folly and nonsense talked by all their fashionable friends. She says that she knows what the State of Paris was before the *Coup d'Etat*, everybody crying out for it and so frightened at the prospect of The Rouge and Civil War during the time of dispute between the President and Chambers that her brother and others came to see her with their Money about their persons, thinking the danger so imminent that they might not have time to run home to get it. They came here from the Grange and before that were at Wrest; she told me it was quite a comfort there to get next to our Fordwich[9] at dinner, because he was so dispassionate and would listen, but most of them gabbled like Geese without any sense or reflection, following the *Times* and abusing the President, Anne[10] one of the most noisy. Pal[mersto]n is not surprized at Mde Lieven

6 Lord Beauvale had in fact succeeded his brother as Viscount Melbourne, but in order to avoid confusion I shall follow the example of Charles Greville and other of his friends and continue to refer to him as Beauvale for the last few years of his life.

7 Prince Louis Napoleon.

8 She was a Frenchwoman, Pauline Marie Armande Aglaé-Craven (1808-91), authoress, daughter of Comte Auguste Marie de la Ferronays; an emigrant in London, married Augustus Craven, a diplomatist, and lived in various continental towns where her husband was attached to the English Legations.

9 Since the death of his father, Lord Cowper, but still called Fordwich by his mother.

10 Presumably Lady Cowper, Fordwich's wife.

beginning to cavil at the Constitution, because what Russia and Austria wanted was that the President should govern solely as they do, by their Will and the Army, *any* Constitution is distasteful to them and the idea of universal Suffrage they of course detest. We are not surprized either at the French People bearing all these orders as they do, because they feel themselves now safe from the Rouge and Pillage, and Murder; before they were in momentary terror of what might happen any day. Mrs Craven says all her friends at Paris and all Society (all but the Intriguers banished) are thankful to be in safety and look upon the President with gratitude. She says the horrors committed in the departments by Socialists exceed all belief, but she has heard the accounts in many letters. One case she mentioned of some of these wretches having got into a Convent for Education of 42 Girls some of the first families of the place, and there they staid for three days, pleased to throw these insults upon des Aristocrats. Some had orders in their pockets '*Bon pour une femme*'. She says all this was known in the neighbourhood but attempted to be concealed and hushed up to save the names of the families. It certainly must be the dread of dangers escaped and this frightful state of things that make people now so contented in France, and so quiet, that you hear not a word of complaint . . .

Broadlands Papers

Three days later we find Lady Palmerston at her beloved Brighton, whence she wrote to her husband in London.

Brighton, Wednesday [Jan. 24, 1849]
. . . I have had an active day here being out incessantly since $\frac{1}{2}$ past 11 when I went to Mrs Lamb's where I found the Duke.[11] At 2 I went to lunch with them and Minny went with me, to admire the new furniture of his House, then she and I drove to see Princess Metternich, then up and down the cliffs, then to see Alvanley, and lastly I ended with Princess Lieven . . . The Lieven

[11] Of Devonshire.

was very kind and agreeable and very amicable in her enquiries after you. I thought her sincere . . .

Melbourne Papers
B.M. Add. MSS. 45546-7

In March of the previous year, Sir Henry Bulwer, our envoy at Madrid, had received from the Foreign Secretary a strongly worded despatch which he had foolishly allowed the Spanish Government to see and which he had permitted to be published in the opposition press. The result had been that the Spanish Government had ordered his prompt removal from Madrid. The Queen was furious with Bulwer for having got himself into such a false position; but Palmerston refused to sacrifice an agent he respected, and early in 1849 Bulwer was named Minister at Washington. During her stay at Brighton this spring he called to pay his respects on Lady Palmerston, who was sorry he was being 'thrown away on the stupid Americans'.[12]

In August, Kossuth and other defeated leaders of the unsuccessful revolution in Hungary, with some three thousand Hungarians and Polish refugees, took refuge in Turkey; whereupon both Austria and Russia promptly demanded their extradition. The Sultan, however, stood firm and resisted these extravagant claims, with the result that on the 4th of September Prince Michael Radzivil arrived at Constantinople with an ultimatum from the Czar announcing that the escape of a single refugee would result in war. The Turkish Government, greatly alarmed at this imperious declaration, sought counsel with Sir Stratford Canning, our envoy at Constantinople, who in conjunction with his French colleague urged resolute resistance, allowing the Porte to understand that in the event of war Turkey would have the support of England and France.[13] So when the imperial ambassadors broke off diplomatic relations with the Porte, Palmerston obtained Cabinet sanction to support being sent to Turkey, with the result that French and English squadrons were soon moving up to the Dardanelles with orders to aid the Sultan if called upon for assistance.[14] Palmerston's

[12] Lady Palmerston to Beauvale, Brighton, Thursday (19 Ap. 1849). Broadlands Papers. Date added by Lord Palmerston.

[13] Lane-Poole, *Stratford Canning*, II, p. 191.

[14] Palmerston to Normanby, Carlton Gardens, September 29 and October 2, 1849. Ashley, *Palmerston*, II, pp. 107-8, 110-11.

determined action brought the two Emperors to reason, and very shortly Austria was to intimate that she would not press her claims for the extradition of the refugees.

No wonder that Press and public were firmly in favour of the energetic Foreign Secretary!

Thursday [Oct. 4 1849]

Many thanks for your letter today, my dearest Harry, there never was such a Correspondent. It is a great thing that all the papers are so unanimous against the conduct of Russia. The article again yesterday of the *Times* was very good and so was the *Chronicle*, and when Neselrode's insolent letter is known it will tend more than ever to unite public feeling . . .

Mad[am]e Lieven again writes in great turmoil, blames the Emperor but says he will not go back. She thinks the Vanity of Success, and now sorrow for his Brother have turned his head . . .

Melbourne Papers
B.M. Add. MSS. 45546–7

No sooner had the question of the extradition of the Hungarian and Polish refugees been settled, than the Foreign Secretary was involved in a dispute with Greece. A British subject named George Finlay, long resident in Athens, had had his land seized to round off the gardens of the royal palace, and a Jewish native of Gibraltar, Don Pacifico, had suffered the pillaging of his house in broad daylight by a mob headed by the sons of the Greek Minister of War. For some time the British Government had been trying to get justice for their two nationals, but without success: the Greek Government repudiated their right to any compensation.[15] At last Lord Palmerston's patience was exhausted, and in December 1849 he told our Minister at Athens that Admiral Sir William Parker had been instructed to blockade the Piraeus.[16] In spite of vigorous French and Russian protests, this order was carried out in the early days of the next year and, after some ineffectual attempts by

[15] It must be admitted that Don Pacifico's claim was much inflated.
[16] Palmerston to Wyse, F[oreign] O[ffice] December 3, 1849. Ashley, *Palmerston*, II, pp. 135–6.

VISCOUNTESS PALMERSTON,

aged about eighty

Attributed to E. Butler Morris

Broadlands, on loan to the National Portrait Gallery

France to mediate, again in April, when the Greek Government was compelled to accept England's terms.

Palmerston as usual kept his wife fully informed of events, on which it is clear that both she and her brother had strong views.

Wednesday [January 1850]

Many thanks for your details, my dearest Harry. It is very *satisfactory* that the Cabinet should be so united on this point. If the Emperor is not mad, he will pause and our bold attitude will deter him.

I hope Sir W[illiam] Parker started directly, but it is a great comfort to hear the Turk has Troops and ships enough to repulse a surprise. Frederick thinks the Sultan should be advised to send off directly from his territory the refugee Poles because he would then have acted in accordance with his Russian Treaty and the Emperor could not find any reason to complain. His saying their departure was a cause of War could not be maintained and this might perhaps let him out of his difficulty, for I cannot but think he would like to slip out, tho he is so arrogant and proud, he would rather be cut in pieces than alter a determination.

What fools the Austrians are to have taken him on their shoulders, instead of trying consiliation [*sic*] with the Hungarians. Frederick says that he cannot believe the Austrians will really go with him on this occasion, so contrary to all their former policy; he says that he is quite sure Metternich would not.

Mad[am]e Lieven writes in great anxiety, but never contemplating the possibility that *her* Emperor should give way. She says if the Turk is obstinate *voilà la Guerre generale*, and she is in despair. Frederick has written to her what he thought would be good, that her Emperor had not a leg to stand upon and that in Eng[land] everybody would be united to support the Turk and that the Govern[men]t was all of that opinion. He shewed me this letter and I might see that he did not *Compromettre* you.

He has written also to Metternich to ask if it was possible that the Austrian Government should go with the Russian in such an outrageous proceeding . . .

Melbourne Papers
B.M. Add. MSS. 45546–7

The French Government, highly indignant at the renewed bombardment of the Piraeus, which they chose to regard as a breach of an agreement made between Palmerston and the French Ambassador, Drouyn de Lhuys, determined to seize the opportunity of fixing a quarrel upon England; they accordingly withdrew their envoy from London on the Queen's birthday, and in the Chambers openly accused us of duplicity. Palmerston, understanding tortuous French politics, did not deem it necessary to retaliate by withdrawing Normanby from Paris, and indeed did everything possible to conciliate French susceptibilities. Nevertheless, a motion of censure upon the Foreign Secretary was carried in the Lords, by a majority of thirty-seven. In the lower house, however, a vote of confidence in the Government introduced by Roebuck[17] was carried by a majority of forty-six.[18] The debate lasted four nights. On the second, Lord Palmerston rose to vindicate his foreign policy. His speech was his greatest masterpiece and closed with the famous peroration that included the familiar, noble words 'Civis Romanus Sum'. 'A most able and temperate speech,' declared Sir Robert Peel, generous to the last,[19] 'a speech that made us all proud of the man who delivered it.' Palmerston spoke for more than four hours and a half;[20] and his wife in the Gallery, whose eyes never left his face, thought it had lasted for just one hour.[21]

Immediately following the debate a hundred and twenty members of the House of Commons presented to Lady Palmerston a painting of her husband by John Partridge. On the 8th of July the Duke of Cambridge died, and shortly afterwards the Palmerstons acquired the lease of his house in Piccadilly, a residence eminently suitable for the great political receptions that Lady Palmerston was wont to give throughout her husband's public life. The portrait by Partridge was soon familiar to the many privileged to attend her routs, for it long hung over the staircase at Cambridge House.[22]

[17] John Arthur Roebuck (1801–79): M.P. for Sheffield at this time.
[18] For Palmerston's own account of the debate, see his letter to Normanby, F[oreign] O[ffice], June 29th, 1850, and to his brother, C[arlton] G[ardens], July 8, 1850. Ashley, *Palmerston*, II, pp. 161–2.
[19] The next day Peel suffered the riding accident that in a few days proved fatal.
[20] For Lord John Russell's account, see Russell to Queen Victoria, Chesham Place, 26th June, 1850. *Queen Victoria's Letters*, 2nd Series, II, pp. 299–300.
[21] Lady Palmerston to Clarendon, July 1st, 1850. Clarendon MSS.
[22] The portrait is now at Broadlands.

CHAPTER VI

'Tit-for-Tat'

A FEW MONTHS after the events recorded at the end of the last chapter, an Austrian general of the name of Haynau, who had won an odious reputation in the Hungarian war for various enormities, including the flogging of women, came to London and was unwise enough to visit the brewery of Barclay and Perkins, then one of the sights of the capital. On hearing of the identity of their visitor, a number of draymen suddenly emerged from the premises and with shouts of 'Down with the Austrian butcher!' proceeded to attack him; whereupon the General was forced to beat a hasty retreat to a neighbouring public-house, where he was at length rescued by the police.

Queen Victoria was shocked at this treatment of a foreign visitor, but Lord Palmerston remarked pointedly to the Austrian Ambassador that, if there were a prosecution, the defence would obviously be 'a minute recapitulation of all the barbarities committed by Haynau in Italy and Hungary, and that would be more injurious to him and to Austria than any verdict obtained against the draymen could be satisfactory'.[1] This warning had its effect, and there was no prosecution!

Lady Palmerston as usual agreed with the views of her lord, as can be seen by the following letter.

[c. October 1850]

... [I] admire the Feeling which was manifested by the Draymen of Bankside and I cannot be sorry that Haynau should carry back with him to Austria some slight tokens of what the People of England think of such Proceedings as his. Perhaps the best thing they could have done would have been to have tossed him

[1] Palmerston to Sir George Grey, the Home Secretary, Broadlands, October 1, 1850, where he used almost identical language to that of his wife in the next letter. Ashley, *Palmerston*, II, pp. 169–70.

in a Blanket and after rolling him in the Kennel to have sent him Home without further personal chastisement. But when a mob begins, it is difficult to put a precise limit to their actions . . .

Melbourne Papers

B.M. Add. MSS. 45546–7

In January 1851 we find Emily with the Ashleys in the Isle of Wight.[2] Two days later she was at Brighton again, but anxious to return to her lord. To this letter there was a postscript recording that 'Duke D[evonshire] is come down, and Mrs Lamb with him.' [3] In consequence, although Emily and the Ashleys were on holiday, appearances must be kept up. The Duke of Devonshire was coming to dinner, so the Palmerston butler must hasten from London to supervise arrangements!

Brighton Wednesday (22 Janry. 1851)[4]

. . . I have sent to Singleton to come down here tomorrow morning, for in a weak moment I asked Mrs. Lamb and the Duke to come and dine with us tomorrow, and afterwards when I came to consider our dinner arrangements, and the untidiness of Minny's footman and mine, I felt ashamed of my set out, and thought it better to have Singleton to put everything straight, and I know you don't want him so I thought it better to write and tell him to come down, and so I have done so . . . It will be only the additional expense of his journey up and down, and Minny's Footman who takes precedence of mine is such a Vulgar little fellow. I think he would surprize and shock the Duke's delicacy and tact.

Broadlands Papers

But, after all, Singleton's attendance was not required! The Duke

[2] Lady Palmerston to Palmerston, East Lodge, Friday (17 Jany., 1851). Broadlands Papers. Date added by Lord Palmerston.

[3] Lady Palmerston to Palmerston, Tuesday, 19 January, 1851. Broadlands Papers. So written, but January 19th, 1851, was a Sunday.

[4] Date added by Lord Palmerston.

had a cold, so he persuaded Emily and the Ashleys to dine instead with him.[5]

In another letter, written just over a week later, Emily turned to the activities of the Roman Catholics in England, a topic that was exercising many people's minds at this time.[6] Some, it is true, did not take things very seriously, and Charles Greville staying at Panshanger recorded that things were 'very merry'. 'The house and its Lord and Lady furiously Protestant and anti-Papal; so we had a great deal of wrangling and chaffing; all in good humour and amusing enough.'[7] Lady Palmerston, however, did not approve of such levity, as she wrote anxiously to her 'darling love'.

Friday Morning (31 Janry. 1851)[8]

... I hope you read the *Times* leading Article yesterday, on the dangers of Popery, so very true and all so well described. It is *impossible* for the well being of any Protestant Country to allow the System which the Pope is trying to introduce here. To have such a band of conspirators leagued together to overthrow Protestantism in Eng[lan]d and leaving no means untried to compass their ends, and to work on the Weak Minded by the most unscrupulous agents ...

Broadlands Papers

A fortnight later, on the 13th of February, the Russell Ministry, which for some time had been showing considerable weakness, had a majority of no more than eleven over a protectionist motion moved by Disraeli. A week later it was defeated on a motion for the extension of the county franchise; in consequence of which on the 22nd of February Lord John resigned. Greville, who was staying with the Beauvales at Brocket, recorded that 'the town was electrified by the news',[9] but it is difficult to say why the fall of so feeble a ministry

[5] Lady Palmerston to Palmerston, Thursday, 23 Jany., 1851. Broadlands Papers.
[6] For Lord Palmerston's views, see Palmerston to Temple, C[arlton] G[arden s], January 27, 1851. Ashley, *Palmerston*, II, pp. 172–5.
[7] *Greville Memoirs* (1885), III, p. 375.
[8] Date added by Lord Palmerston.
[9] *Greville Memoirs* (1885), III, p. 378.

should have caused much surprise. The Queen sent for Lord Stanley to form a government, and, if we can believe the ever-hostile Greville, Lady Palmerston was 'provoked' that her husband had not been thought of in that connection![10] However that may be, Stanley found himself unable to comply; so in the end the old Whig ministry came back to office, though only to survive for one more year.

At about this time Brunow, the Russian Ambassador in London, went back to St Petersburg, where he strove to give his Emperor some first-hand information about England 'which they understand no more than they do China', and about the true aims of Lord Palmerston. The envoy on his return to London made haste to call at the Foreign Office to recount the results of his mission, and Emily was at pains to pass on to her brother what his Excellency had said.

Carlton Gardens, Sunday [1851]

Brunow is come home very much elated at his favour with the Emperor and Empress (his Daughter is appointed one of her Demoiselles d'Honneur) and he is full of amusing details about the Court and the Russian notions about Engl[and], which he says they understand no more than they do China. He says they are quite ridiculous about Pal[mersto]n believing that he has all sorts of intentions and plans, one is that he wants to get Sicily for England and to give up Gibraltar in exchange to Spain. Brunow said *'Dittes* [sic] *tout ce que vous voudrez de Ld Palmerston, mais ne croyez pas qu'il a perdu son bon sens et son jugement'*!!! Brunow says that he thinks he has done a great deal of good by his Journey and all he has told them. He said that very far from Pal[mersto]n wanting to get Sicily in Exchange, that if it was offered to him he would not take it. He said to the Emperor that all he wished was that he could have two hours' conversation with Palmerston to see what he really was, and how different from the opinions that were ascribed to him. Brunow is amazingly pleased with his position at home, and quite renovated by his Journey; he came to Palmerston again this morning for two hours, discussing all the affairs of Europe, upon all of which they are very much agreed, and so Brunow ended his talk *'Je vois que sur toutes les grandes questions nous sommes bien d'accord, ainsi sur les petites*

[10] *Greville Memoirs* (1885), III, p. 386.

314

nuances où nous pourrions être de différents avis, passez je vous prie légèrement làdessus'. Brunow says the Emperor is amazingly pleased with Hamilton Seymour[11] likes his appointment very much and finds him particularly agreeable; he has a great deal of small talk conversation, which is much appreciated in Courts where so many more important subjects are taboo'd, and a courteous ingratiating way besides, which generally pleases most people, tho it utterly failed with you . . .

Broadlands Papers

With the conclusion of the Pacifico affair, Palmerston was at the very height of his power and at the summit of his popularity with the vast majority of his countrymen; but just at this moment, apparently so propitious for his future, an event happened which was not unforeseen by the most closely associated with the Court. For some time the Foreign Secretary had been allowed to do very much as he chose in his own department; indeed, as Charles Greville stated, he exerted 'an absolute despotism at the F[oreign] O[ffice] . . . without the slightest control, and scarcely any interference on the part of his colleagues'.[12] This was very little to the taste of Queen Victoria and her husband, who regarded foreign affairs as peculiarly their province, and they were driven to distraction by their truculent Foreign Secretary's inconvenient habit of despatching instructions involving important questions of policy without even notifying, let alone consulting, the Crown.

Lady Palmerston was sorry to notice the Queen's growing resentment, and as early as 1848 she had warned her husband. 'I am sure the Queen is very angry with you!!' she told him, 'I am afraid you contradict her notions too boldly. You fancy she will hear reason, when in fact all you say only proves to her that you are determined to act on the line she disapproves, and which she still thinks wrong. I am sure it would be better if you *said* less to her—even if you *act* as you think best. I often think there is too much knight-errantry in your Ways. You always think you can convince people by arguments, and she has not reflection or sense to feel the force of them—therefore the strength of your Arguments and all the explanations you give only

[11] He had just been appointed envoy extraordinary to St Petersburg.
[12] *Greville Memoirs* (1885), I, p. 298.

prove to her how deeply imbued you are with what she calls error, and how impossible it is for her to make any effect on you. I should treat what she says more lightly and courteously, and not enter into argument with her, but lead her on gently, by letting her believe you have both the same opinions in fact and the same wishes, but take sometimes different ways of carrying them out.' [13] Excellent advice, but not likely to be followed. The result of Palmerston's intractability was Queen Victoria's famous memorandum of the 12th of August, in which she informed the Prime Minister that she required that the Foreign Secretary should state distinctly what he proposes in a given case, so that she may know as distinctly to what she has consented, and that after she has given her sanction it shall not be arbitrarily altered by the Minister.[14] Palmerston affected to acquiesce in the Queen's requirements;[15] but it must be admitted that he was quite incorrigible, and that there were many instances after the memorandum of which Victoria had a right to complain. Probably by 1849 and certainly by 1850 the Court was extremely anxious to rid itself of the Foreign Secretary; but it was not until late in the latter year that Lord John Russell at last determined to exert his authority. Unfortunately, the pretext he chose was indeed flimsy. In the course of an unofficial conversation on the 3rd of December with Count Walewski, the French Ambassador, Palmerston had expressed approval of Louis Napoleon's *coup d'état* of the previous day,[16] and though Lord John himself and several other members of the Government had expressed similar opinions to the same person at about the same time, the Prime Minister took the view that the approval of the Foreign Secretary, even though privately and unofficially given, meant a great deal more than the approval of other ministers, and curtly dismissed him from his office.[17] He further insulted his colleague by, at the same time, offering him the Lord-Lieutenancy of Ireland.

[13] Lady Palmerston to Palmerston, Broadlands, Thursday [1848]. B.M. Add. MSS. 45546-7. Lady Airlie, *Lady Palmerston*, II, p. 22.

[14] Queen Victoria to Lord John Russell, Osborne, 12th August, 1850. *Queen Victoria's Letters*, 1st Series, II, p. 315.

[15] Palmerston to Russell, Foreign Office, 13th August, 1850. *Queen Victoria's Letters*, 1st Series, II, pp. 315-16.

[16] For Palmerston's views, see his *Memorandum of certain Circumstances connected with the Coup d'état* and his letter to Normanby, C[arlton] G[ardens], December 3rd, 1851. Ashley, *Palmerston*, II, pp. 200-2, 202-3.

[17] Lord John Russell to Palmerston, Woburn Abbey, Dec. 19, 1851. Ashley,

Lady Palmerston's indignation at this treatment of her husband can be well imagined, and Charles Greville, who was spending Christmas at Brocket, recorded in his Journal that Beauvale had had a long letter from his sister who was 'in a high state of indignation and resentment, and bitter against Lord John and the colleagues who did not support Palmerston . . .' [18] This is the letter to which he refers:

Broadlands Decr. 23, Tuesday [1851]

You will hardly believe all the anxiety and worry I have gone through the last few days, and it is from indignation and anger more than sorrow, that I have suffered. Will you believe it that John has behaved in the meanest and most treacherous manner and has got Pal[mersto]n out of Office. The Queen, I suppose, acted upon him and he has taken the most silly pretence to get him out. I believe because he feared that Pal[mersto]n was not favourable to his reform bill, and now he thinks probably to get in Graham[19] or some people of that sort who will help him to carry it through; this we surmise, but all we know for certain is that Pal[mersto]n is out. But I will begin from the beginning.

On the third of Dec[embe]r (before all the street shooting)[20] Pal[mersto]n had a private conversation with Walewsky who told him of all the intrigues that had assailed the President and the Intentions of all these Men to have shut him up at Vincennes etc. etc. Upon this Palmerston said that he thought the President was quite justified in what he had done. After this, Normanby, you know, pronounced himself very much against the President and even proposed to suspend all relations with him, in short to make almost a quarrel.[21] Palmerston then wrote him a very strong letter urging him to keep on the best terms with him, not to interfere in any way, but not to let the President believe that he was his

Palmerston, II, p. 211. For Palmerston's own account of his dismissal, see his letter to his brother, Broadlands, Jan. 22, 1852. Ashley, *Palmerston*, II, pp. 215–18.

[18] *Greville Memoirs* (1885), III, p. 428.

[19] Sir James Graham supported Lord John Russell against the Protectionists.

[20] On December 2nd, Louis Napoleon had seized the Government, arrested his chief opponents, ended the National Assembly and Council of State, and had declared Paris in a state of siege.

[21] One of Palmerston's difficulties was Normanby's evident hostility to the French President, which necessitated his recall shortly afterwards.

enemy, as he had received information that the President was thinking of asking for his recall.[22] The day that we came down here, John sent Pal[mersto]n a Minute from the Queen saying that she found great fault with what Pal[mersto]n had said to Walewsky, and that he ought not to have given any opinion without consulting the Cabinet,[23] and John added, that Walewsky had written this opinion of Palmerston to Mr Turgot, that Normanby complained of it, and also of Pal[mersto]n's letter to him, as very offensive; and John said he himself blamed it very much, and added that he was quite tired of all these complaints, and that he had shewn such a want of discretion that the Queen wished to withdraw the Seals from him and waited for an answer to all these charges, which John desired him to write and that he would send it to the Queen. Upon this Pal[mersto]n wrote nearly what follows, that he was quite ready to give up the Seals whenever he had a Successor appointed, but that the opinion which he had given to Walewsky was merely given as his own opinion, and from himself, and that it in no ways fether'd [sic] Her Majesty's Governm[en]t in any course which they might wish to pursue, that everybody knew the difference in diplomatic intercourse between conferences which were held by the Ambassador and the Secretary of State, and by which their respective Governm[en]ts became answerable, and the mere expressions of individual and personal opinion in a friendly intercourse, and that if there was not that acknowledge[d] difference that it would not be possible for the Secretary and Minister to discuss any thing of that sort, or maintain those habits of free intercourse which contributed so much to the good relations of the parties and of their Governments, and then he added that his letter to Normanby was written in haste, and that he expressed himself strongly because he felt how embarrassing it would be to this Country if the President was to ask for Normanby's recal[l], whether it was conceded or whether it was refused, and that he had not been mistaken in his expectation for that since writing to Normanby, the President had sent him a private Message to ask whether, in the event of his

[22] Palmerston to Normanby, Foreign Office, December 16, 1851. Ashley, *Palmerston*, II, pp. 206-7.
[23] Queen Victoria to Russell, Osborne, 13th December, 1851. *Queen Victoria's Letters*, 1st Series, II, p. 412.

making a demand for his recal[l], his demand would be granted, as he had reason to look upon Normanby as his personal Enemy.[24] I thought this explanation would have been satisfactory, as the only fault which could be then found with P[almerston] was that he had expressed a private opinion to Walewsky, that he thought the President was justified in what he had done—that is, putting into Vincennes those who wanted to put him there. Was there ever such a *querelle d'Allemand*, and such a contemptible foolish reason to give for parting with a Minister, that I am sure the Country will feel more than ever that it is the old Foreign Conspiracy over again, and that such a reason as that can be only a pretence. And so it is, for I have no doubt all her[25] foreign correspondents go on poisoning her mind against Pal[mersto]n and the Clermont party also,[26] and no doubt she is deeply vexed at seeing their plans all destroyed and their chance now so very remote. But what an effect all this will have on the President's mind, who had before said how anxious he felt to rely upon Eng[lan]d, but that he could have no confidence in any Members of the Cabinet except Pal[mersto]n and Lansdowne, and that the latter was very weak. When the Cabinet met yesterday I was in hopes some of them would have objected, and said the reason was too absurd, and that they could not give such a reason to the Public, but it seems they had no courage or that John so represented the case that they did not understand it and could not object, for he said the Cabinet had all agreed with him and so he was going down to the Queen. But we don't know what passed, for of course Palmerston did not go himself, and he has had no communication with any of the Members. This is dreadfully vexatious to find yourself in this manner sacrificed by all your friends and people upon whom you would have thought there might be some dependance. It is really too bad, and John's conduct there is no name low enough to characterise. This towards a Man too who would rather have cut off his right hand than have behaved so to one of them and John, I really believe, actuated in great measure by the

[24] Palmerston to Russell, Carlton Gardens, December 16, 1851. Ashley, *Palmerston*, II, pp. 207-11.   [25] The Queen's.

[26] Claremont, where the exiled Louis-Philippe and his family were living. It was believed by some that they were intriguing with the Queen and Prince Albert to regain the French throne.

mean jealosy which we have often seen proofs of, and I have no doubt too that Normanby will have been intriguing with Albert and the Queen through Phipps.[27] I see that four of the Cabinet were absent, Clanricarde, Minto, Hobhouse, all 3 Palmerston's friends, and Grenville. I write so much that *you* may understand the case, but pray do not mention it at present or anything about it. And poor dear Pal[mersto]n, even now tho dreadfully vexed, shows no change of manner, always kind and good humoured, so that none of the people here can perceive that he has any Annoyance. As for me, I can neither eat nor sleep and I feel quite frantic with rage.[28]

Broadlands Papers

Early in the new year, Lady Palmerston wrote to her old friend, the Comtesse de Flahault, who had written to sympathize with her at Palmerston's dismissal.

Broadlands, Janry. 3d. '52

. . . I have been very much vexed at this extraordinary business and more I can assure you on public grounds than private ones, because I feel that this sort of *esclandre* about nothing is very hurtful to Lord John and to the Whig party. I *know* that Palmerston is quite free from blame of any sort, and that therefore, whenever the Cabinet meets, he will prove himself to be perfectly free from the slightest [illegible] as he did on the Greek question; but that the triumph which one feels at defending oneself from enemys becomes a source of pain when one has to prove such an old friend as L[o]rd John to be entirely in the wrong. I must say that I never was more pained at any thing than at his conduct, and look upon it as one of the most rash and indiscreet acts I have ever known him to commit . . .

Bowood Papers

[27] Sir Charles Beaumont Phipps (1801-66), Keeper of Her Majesty's Privy Purse and Treasurer of the Household to Prince Albert. He was Normanby's younger brother, and Lady Normanby was in frequent correspondence with him at this time. See Lady Normanby to Phipps, Paris, 7th December, 1851, and 9th December 1851. *Queen Victoria's Letters*, 1st Series, II, pp. 406-8, 409-12.

[28] *Greville Memoirs* (1885), III, pp. 425-31.

Four days later Emily wrote to Frederick again, and it is clear that she had not recovered from her intense annoyance.

Broadlands, Janry. 7, [1852]

I know I have been an idle writer lately, so I am going to make up for it now, and first tell you of Walewsky's Visit here which was most satisfactory. One thing surprized us and that was to find that John had used exactly the same Expressions about the President's success as Palmerston on two several occasions, on Wed-[ne]s[da]y the 3rd at our House when he asked Walewsky to dine with him the Friday after and on that Friday when he dined with him and repeated very nearly the same things which Pal[mersto]n had, so that Walewsky wrote to Turgot of those two satisfactory interviews in much the same terms as he did of Pal[mersto]n's. He also met Ld Grey[29] riding, who said much the same things, and Wood[30] also on another occasion; therefore John must have forgotten all this when he accused Pal[mersto]n of approving the President without consulting the Cabinet, since he had done just the same thing, and so had Grey and Wood. In truth there was no reason why they should not, for the Cabinet never agreed not to give any opinion, nor was the subject ever brought forward in that shape. When the Cabinet met on the 4th it was upon the instructions to be given to Normanby (who had proposed to cease relations with the President) telling him to keep on the best terms he could, to show no coldness, and not to interfere in the internal affairs of France,[31] but nothing was said of the course they were themselves to follow. The whole of John's attack was done in such a hurried manner that Palmerston could not himself remember exactly all the circumstances, for he made no Memorandums and conversed every day with Walewsky, as at that time they met nearly every day, and he was glad to refresh his memory of what he had said by talking over the circumstances with

[29] Henry George Grey, 3rd Earl Grey (1802–94); Secretary for Colonies at this time, son of Lord Grey of the Reform Bill.

[30] Sir Charles Wood, 1st Viscount Halifax (1800–85); President of the Board of Control at this time, created Viscount Halifax 1866.

[31] Queen Victoria to Russell, Osborne, 4th December, 1851, Russell to Queen Victoria, Downing Street, 4th December, 1851 (6 p.m.). *Queen Victoria's Letters*, 1st Series, II, pp. 404–5.

Walewsky. He P[almerston] had said namely this, which Walewsky reported to Turgot—That as it appeared a rupture was imminent between the Parliament and President it was much better that the President should have succeeded, that it was better for the interests of France, as it would conduce more to a settled Govern[men]t, and that as it was better for France, it must also be so for the rest of Europe. How curious it is that out of this simple and incontrovertible Statement, so much mischief should have arisen; but it is clearly an intrigue of Normanby, Phipps, and the Prince, worked up by the deep disappoint[men]t of the Orleans overthrow, and the hopes which no doubt Normanby had helped to raise. I will inclose you a 2nd letter from Ly Clanr[icar]de[32] stating more of what passed in the Cabinet, and the Queen's determination. The beginning of the letter is about Howdens, which I sent her, the end about P[almerston]'s keeping her waiting[33] is all satisfactorily explained, but I hear fools in town have talked of this *impropriety*, as if he could have intended it. The mistake rose from Ld John sending a foolish message to Ld Stanley about the Seals, by which Pal[mersto]n understood that they did not wish him to go to Windsor, but that he was to send the Seals to John. However as soon as he found out the mistake, he wrote an ample apology and regrets for the Queen, so thats all right. Ly Clan[ricar]de's letter places John in a miserable light; to give way under such circumstances was a very great weakness and he had much better have resigned at once, and not sacrificed his Character. It is so mean to give up a colleague, and then to try and hang the excuse upon any pretext he could invent; besides if he had made a bold front they could not have ventured on such a desperate course, and I am sure things would never have come to this pass if John had acted honestly by P[almerston]. For a long time past I have suspected him that he thought it easier to throw all the blame on P[almerston] and that his small vanity and jealousy was gratified at feeling that he was liked and trusted while Pal[mersto]n was not. This is not mere surmise for I have a good proof to give of this. I hear he is now deeply annoyed and vexed, and mortified at the manner in which the event has been taken and at having raised up at his own expense of popularity, the person

---

[32] Lord Clanricarde was Postmaster-General at this time.
[33] For the giving up of his Seals of Office.

whom he meant to crush. No doubt he had little idea of the hub-
bub this event would make!! You cannot see one tenth part of all
the Newspapers with very good articles which are sent to Pal[mer-
ston] from all parts of the Country, nor the loads of anonymous
letters and others very well written which flow upon him, also
from all parts, full of praises and regrets. There never was such a
movement. Even Ballads and Printed Papers to sing or stick up
in the streets. I dont know whether all this reaches the Court, but
no doubt some of it does, and must, I have no doubt, annoy
them . . .

Broadlands Papers

Broadlands Wednesday[34] [January 8th 1852]

I believe I forgot to tell you in my letter yesterday that John
had offered to Palmerston to go Ld Lieut[enant] to Ireland with a
Peerage, which he refused at once. It was in the letter which I
mentioned yes[terda]y among the facts of the case; John has
behaved shamefully ill to Pal[mersto]n and I suppose there never
was such a case before of a Man throwing over a Colleague and a
Friend without the slightest reason to give for it. No doubt the
Queen and Prince wanted to get Palmerston out and Granville[35]
in because they thought he would be pliable and Subservient and
would let Albert manage the Foreign Affairs which is what he has
always wanted. One may think it lucky therefore that the dream
of United Germany and the Schleswig Holstein business are now
pretty nearly over. John has behaved like a little Blackguard giving in to their plans, and trying to put it upon a private opinion,
expressed to Walewsky (which bound the Govern[men]t to no
course, and left it quite unshackled). *The Times* article today is
full of false statements for there are no differences now between
Pal[mersto]n and any Governments, or any foreign Ministers,
nor are there any differences at home. We have often seen that
many of his colleagues were jealous of him, but apparently they
were all on the best possible terms, and there were no points in
dispute. I think the House of Commons will be very Angry at

[34] So written, but January 8th, 1852, was a Thursday.
[35] Granville George Leveson Gower, 2nd Earl Granville (1815-91),
Minister for Foreign Affairs until the fall of the Russell Government in February.

this Granville Appointm[en]t! a young Lordling who has done nothing but dance attendance on Albert and patch up differences amongst the Crystal Palace Commissioners, who has whispered a little speech or two about the Board of Trade, and the one at Paris, in which he put forward his having passed his holidays in his Father's House at Paris and having married a French woman.[36] He has a good deal of tact, and is very courteous, and those are his real merits, and that is what makes him so popular. I am still vexed and provoked at the whole thing but I take it much more calmly. It is so lucky for an Effervescing Woman to have such a calm and placid husband, which [sic] no events can irritate, or make him lose his temper, and this appointment will not do the same harm to our relations with the President, which I feared might arise if Normanby had been appointed, which I feared yesterday. It would have been such an insult to the President and we ought to try and get well with him, as his personal liking for Eng[lan]d is all we have to trust to. Normanby in a last Despatch said amongst the French Officers there was much talk of a descent upon Ireland, and making common cause with the Catholics, so if they want to do mischief at any time that will be their line. If you remember that was a plan of Ledru Rollin's when he first got power. However our best chance is the President's living, and our encouraging his good feelings and preference for us, and our Institutions, and it is the abuse of the *Times* and other papers that was very hurtful and dangerous, because it tended to make him doubt our honest and good intentions. Normanby and the *Times* have been equally mischievous and really forced Palmerston to speak out more openly than he would otherwise have done, to shew that he did not agree with them and wished to quiet the President's suspicions . . . The best thing now that can happen in my opinion would be the break up of this Governm[en]t and to let the Protectionists have a turn. We should then see whether the land can be relieved, whether there can be any duty on Corn, and what changes can be made; and I think it would be fair enough to see that side of the question tried. And from all I hear this result does not seem to me at all improbable, for John's difficulties will

[36] Lady Granville was Maria Louisa, only child of Emeric Joseph, Duc de Dalbert, and widow of Sir Ferdinand Acton, Bt. By her first husband she was the mother of Lord Acton, the great historian.

be very great, the feeling of the House very much against him, and then Reform and Income Tax, and many other difficulties might thus be got over. Don't you think so? Pal[mersto]n is very happy, very well contented, and very well satisfied to stay out of office[37] [end of letter missing].

Broadlands Papers

But however furious Lady Palmerston might be, appearances have to be maintained, and in a few weeks' time we find her paying a formal call on Lady John Russell 'with a view' so we are told, 'to a *personal—* not political—reconciliation . . .'[38] It must have been an awkward meeting for them both!

In January, Madame de Flahault wrote from Paris of the tactless indiscretions of Thiers, who was obviously trying to make political capital out of the French crisis. In England, meanwhile, a body of opinion led by *The Times* was abusing the French President in un-measured terms. This infuriated Lady Palmerston who replied pointedly that '... the French are certainly the best judges of their own affairs, and if 8 millions have approved his *Coup d'État* and have thought it necessary, I don't see what right we can have to make such a clatter . . .'[39]

Lady Palmerston's views on the instability of the Russell ministry after her husband's dismissal proved only too correct. Already the fallen hero was beginning to assume the air of a martyr, and within a week of Lord John's explanation to the House of his colleague's dismissal, Wellington, Gladstone, Disraeli and the Duchess of Bedford were all to be seen at one of Lady Palmerston's parties. That was indeed significant.[40] So, no doubt, thought Palmerston; and within a few weeks he had had his unexpected revenge on his former leader. The Government brought in a Militia Bill at which Lord Palmerston expressed his dissatisfaction; and, much to his surprise, he carried an amendment in committee by a majority of eleven. Lady Palmerston, a

[37] See also Lady Palmerston to Mrs Huskisson, Broadlands, Jany. 9th, 1852. Huskisson Papers, B.M. Add. MSS. 39949, ff. 266–70.

[38] *Greville Memoirs* (1885), III, p. 448.

[39] Lady Palmerston to Comtesse de Flahault, Broadlands, January 21 [1852]. Bowood Papers.

[40] Sir Henry Drummond Wolff, *Rambling Recollections*, I, p. 141. Bell, *Palmerston*, II, p. 58.

few days later, recorded these events for her brother-in-law, Sir William Temple:

Broadlands, March 5th [1852]

... How surprised you must have been at all that has occur'd here. P[almerston] did not intend to put out the Govern[men]t but merely to force L[or]d John's bill into a more reasonable and practical shape, but they took this opportunity of going out to fall easy, as they would no doubt have been beat on the Caffre Debate and that would have been a vote of censure. Ld Grey's odious despatch to Sir Harry Smith had produced such universal disgust, that even D[uke] of Well[ingto]n had threatened to resign, and they had much difficulty in persuading him to remain —and no doubt there would have been a very great indisposition in any of our people to support him.

The Govern[men]t of course deny that they slip'd out in this way to avoid the Caffre Debate and the Greys talk boldly of their *excellent* case, now the danger is past, but the Circumstantial evidence against them is very strong. Tho they had agreed to go out if they were beat, this was kept secret, and there were no treasury notes, and no attempts to get their supporters to attend. Ld J[ohn] need not have divided at that moment, and Hayter had told him that he would be beat if he did.

Whatever may have caused Ld John to resign, the scene was altogether a great triumph for Pal[mersto]n and one I shall never forget. Every word he said was applauded and the Cheers were quite deafening.

Everybody looked upon it as an act of retributive Justice that Lord John should fall by his hand, after the way in which he had treated him. However even in this Pal[mersto]n has had his revenge for amongst many motives for Lord John's conduct Jealousy was certainly one of them and this has been a signal failure, since that which was intended to lower him in public estimation has only served to raise him more and the Press and the Voice of the Country has been everywhere raised in his favour, and so generally by all parties as to be quite astonishing even to his greatest admirers, for it is seldom that all parties unite

to do justice to one public character!! and there was no exception
but an occasional bit of spite from the *Times* . . .

Broadlands Papers

Thus the enfeebled administration fell, much to the joy of Emily
who, after drinking in from the gallery the applause that greeted Russell's defeat, hurried home to receive the crowd of friends who thronged
her drawing-room to offer their felicitations to the fallen hero and his
loving wife. 'One would think,' wrote Lady Palmerston's son-in-law,
'that he had saved an empire, or that he was mounting a throne.' [41]
And to his brother Palmerston announced his triumph in familiar
words. 'I have had my tit-for-tat with John Russell, and I turned him
out on Friday last. . . .' [42]

[41] Hodder, *Shaftesbury*, II, p. 378.
[42] Palmerston to Temple, C[arlton] G[ardens], February 24, 1852. Ashley,
Palmerston, II, p. 230.

CHAPTER VII

Lord Palmerston at the Home Office

ON THE RESIGNATION of Lord John Russell in February 1852, Lord Derby—the former Lord Stanley, who had succeeded his father the previous summer—agreed to form a Government. He approached both Palmerston and Gladstone, but their refusal to co-operate compelled him to compose his ministry of mainly untried material. During the 305 days life of the Derby Government, Palmerston twice refused to join it: but he rendered cordial and much-appreciated assistance throughout to the new Foreign Secretary,[1] Lord Malmesbury,[2] grandson of the distinguished diplomatist who had helped to teach Palmerston his business nearly half a century earlier, and on at least one occasion he saved the Ministry from destruction. In late November, following the political truce imposed in some measure by the funeral of the Duke of Wellington,[3] Charles Villiers[4] attempted to commit the House to a definite policy of free trade and to the complete repeal of the Corn Laws by 1856. Palmerston saved the ministry with alternative resolutions attributing the country's prosperity in the main to Free Trade and declaring that this policy should be maintained and extended. Disraeli, the Chancellor of the Exchequer, and other protectionists, sagaciously realizing that a downright policy of protection would stand no chance at this time, accepted the amended resolutions, which were adopted by an immense majority. This, however, only postponed the evil day, for the Chancellor's budget proposals, which were severely handled by Gladstone, proved unacceptable to the House, and on December 18th, much to the disgust of Palmerston, the Derby Government resigned. Had Palmerston not been laid up and prevented from going

---

[1] Malmesbury, *Memoirs*, I, p. 317.

[2] James Howard Harris, 3rd Earl of Malmesbury (1807–89), Foreign Secretary, February–December 1852 and 1858–9.   [3] November 18th.

[4] Charles Pelham Villiers (1802–98) moved a resolution against the Corn Laws in 1838 and repeated it annually until their abolition in 1846.

to the House, Beauvale claimed that this would never have happened: furthermore he said he was pretty sure that his brother-in-law would never take office under Aberdeen.[5]

In this, however, he was mistaken, for when Aberdeen was called upon to form a government he at once went to Palmerston, who received him cordially,[6] and soon, much to the surprise of many of his friends, accepted the office of Home Secretary.[7] The news was thus conveyed by his wife to Mrs Huskisson.

C[arlton] Gardens, Wednesday December 22 [1852]
... We intend going down Friday to Brocket to eat our Xmas dinner with Frederick and to return on Monday for the announcement of the new Ministry.

Shall you be surprised if I tell you that after many negociations and many refusals from Palmerston he has at last been prevailed upon by L[o]rd Lansdowne to form part of the new Govern-[men]t and that he has consented to take the Home Office?

He was offered a choice of all places even including the Foreign Office—but do not repeat this—he refused at first because he feared that his motives might be misconstrued in taking office under L[o]rd Aberdeen, that instead of its being looked upon as proceeding from high motives and the feeling that in these times all public men should give up party spirit and devote themselves for the public good, people might say he was mean spirited and forget Ld John's conduct to him and Ld Aberdeen's long difference of opinion upon Foreign Affairs. Indeed he was unwilling to take office on this account and required a great deal of pressing, but I am very glad he gave way and I cannot but think he is right and that with so many clever men put together it may turn out a

[5] *Greville Memoirs* (1887), I, pp. 16–17.
[6] *Greville Memoirs* (1887), I, p. 21.
[7] For Palmerston's own reasons for accepting this office, see his letters to his brother, C[arlton] G[ardens] December 22nd, 1852, to his brother-in-law, Sulivan, Carlton Gardens, Dec. 24th, 1852, and to his brother, Carlton Gardens, January 31, 1853, and C[arlton] G[ardens] April 3, 1853. Ashley, *Palmerston*, II, pp. 258–9; 259–60, 261, 263–5. See also his letter to his brother-in-law of December 31, 1852. Lady Airlie, *Lady Palmerston*, II, pp. 151–3 and Prince Albert's memorandum, Windsor Castle, 22nd December, 1852. *Queen Victoria's Letters*, 1st Series, II, pp. 510–12.

good and lasting Govern[men]t, and that Palmerston instead of standing lower will stand the higher in public estimation for having consented to take office and forgeting [*sic*] all old grievances and resentments . . .

Huskisson Papers
B.M. Add. MSS. 39949, ff. 271–4

Early in the new year there was bad news for the Palmerstons; Lord Beauvale was seriously ill and anxiously calling for his sister. On the 14th Emily hastened to Brocket. 'I have got down safe, dearest, but find things in a sad way,' she wrote to her husband, who was at Tiverton for the General Election, 'poor Adine wretched and crying and Fred[eric]k very suffering . . .' The Gout was taking a grip of his whole body. His young wife was quite distracted. 'It's so hard for her, poor thing, in her nervous frightened state to have nobody to look to . . .'[8] A few days later Emily heard from her beloved Harry in Devonshire. How sorry she was that she could not go there to help in his fight, but she sent encouragement and love to the veteran campaigner.

Brocket Hall, Tuesday [January 18th 1853]
Your letter has made me very happy, it arrived here by the afternoon post, but I had the satisfaction of seeing the *Times* early this morning which gave the report of your excellent speech at Tiverton Election. So I saw that everything had gone off well. Nothing can be better than your speech, so candid and so true in all the statements, and even the *Times* in its leading article says it contrasts favourably with the boasting of L[o]rd John's. It will be agreeable to the late Govern[men]t because it gives a fair statement of their merits and does not deal in misrepresentation like most of the speeches of other Election Candidates, and I am very glad also that it gave you an opportunity of fairly stating your motives and conduct on the occasion of your amendment on Villier's [*sic*] motion, because that some people may not have quite understood . . .

Melbourne Papers
B.M. Add. MSS. 45546–7
Lady Airlie, *Lady Palmerston*, II, p. 154.

Eleven days later Beauvale died. 'Frederick is gone, I have lost almost the best friend I ever had,'[9] recorded his sorrowing sister. And his poor young widow was inconsolable,[10] as Emily reported to Mrs Huskisson some two months later.

Broadlands, March 28 [1853]

... Poor Adine is also I think a little better. Her utter state of despair was at first very dreadful to see, and after she came to town I used to pass every afternoon with her, so that I had no chance of being able to calm down my own feelings, but she is certainly now more calm and resigned and I left her in London under the care of Minny and Miss Cuyler. She talks of going soon to Hastings, and she is expecting her Brother to come over to her, and one of her sisters, and they will no doubt persuade her to take a Tour abroad which would certainly be the best thing for her, and w[oul]d help to restore her health which is a good deal deranged.

I am happy to say she is very well off, indeed very rich, so that she never need think of money, but can do whatever suits her best.

I feel a great blank in my existence from the loss of poor Fred[eric]k with whom I lived in such close intimacy *all* my life, and there is something very painful in the idea of surviving all one's family and standing alone! after having had so many brothers and one sister, however such is the common lot of age. And I have so much to be thankful for in what remains to me. Such a husband! and such Children, that I must be very ungrateful if I repined, and did not acknowledge how much more happiness remains to me than what so many others enjoy ...

Palmerston gets golden opinions from all the Country gentlemen and the public, and is much more appreciated than when he was Minister for Foreign Affairs, which the public in England

[9] Lady Airlie, *Lady Palmerston*, II, p. 155.
[10] 'Lady Palmerston is deeply afflicted by the loss of her last surviving Brother to whom through life she has been most warmly attached; and Lady Melbourne is entirely overwhelmed by the Calamity she has sustained.' Palmerston to Queen Victoria, Home Office, 31 January, 1853. Royal Archives, Windsor Castle, 13.12.15.

never will try even to understand, and he employs himself very warmly in all the national defences which gives them great confidence . . .

Huskisson Papers
B.M. Add. MSS. 39949, ff. 275–8

The utter misery and despair showed by Adine in her elderly husband's death is sad to contemplate;[11] but it is satisfactory to know that she found in due course a new happiness. In 1856 she married the 2nd Lord Forester with whom she lived contentedly until his death in 1874.[12] Then almost twenty years of widowhood lay before her, for Adine Forester survived until the summer of 1894.

In June 1853 Lady Palmerston went to join her son-in-law and daughter, Lord and Lady Jocelyn, at St Leonards, where they had a house. Emily reported to her lord her safe arrival.

10 Eversfield Place, St. Leonards
Monday (20th June 1853)[13]

I am arrived quite safe and had a very pleasant journey as all the Country after Brighton was quite new to me, and I had never seen before all the Martello Towers which cross all the flat land about Pevensey, and have a curious effect from being so numerous all along the coast. Poor dear Fanny looks better than I expected and I found her waiting for me at the Station in a little Donkey Chaise . . .

Broadlands Papers

Some two months later Emily paid one of her very rare visits to Melbourne Hall, which together with the estate of Brocket had now passed to Lady Palmerston on Frederick's death.

---

[11] For Charles Greville's elaborate character-study of the husband and his account of the utter desolation of the widow, see *Greville Memoirs* (1887), I, pp. 34–7.

[12] She seems to have had an attraction for elderly men, for Lord Forester was fifty-five at the time of their marriage and had not been married previously. The widow was about thirty-five.   [13] Date added by Lord Palmerston.

Melbourne Monday [August 1853]

... Really this place is quite lovely and the more I see of it, the more I admire it.

I have been round with Fox[14] this mor[nin]g calling on people of the town and seeing every thing; now I have had some lunch and am going out driving with Anne ...

... The weather is very hot and very delicious. We expect Mrs Lamb this afternoon ...

Melbourne Papers
B.M. Add. MSS. 45546–7

In September, through the insistence of Aberdeen, who feared that Palmerston, if slighted, might go over to the Opposition and become its leader,[15] the Home Secretary was invited to the recently built Balmoral Castle, as Minister in attendance on the Queen. He left Emily in the care of his brother Sir William Temple at Broadlands whence she reported to her 'dearest Love'.

Broadlands, Friday, (17 Sept. 1853)[16]

... I have put off going till Monday, and then I shall go through to Panshanger without stoping [sic] in town. I have no object in sleeping in that cold comfortless House, and this place tho shorn of its beams by your departure, is still lovely and sunny, and so I think it better to remain here, and I think your Brother prefers to remain. So on Monday we shall move off and not before and then I shall meet you in town on your return, or I may come up a day or two sooner, if I hear of Minny's arrival. It is a long time to be without you in whatever way I spend it. I shall be anxious to hear of your safe arrival at Balmoral ...

Broadlands Papers

[14] The estate agent at Melbourne Hall.

[15] *Greville Memoirs* (1887), I, pp. 82, 87–8; Aberdeen to Queen Victoria, London, 11th September, 1853. *Queen Victoria's Letters*, 1st Series, II, p. 548.

[16] Date added by Lord Palmerston, but it appears from the next letter that Lady Palmerston wrote this one on Friday, 16th September, 1853.

Broadlands Saturday, (17 Sept. 1853)[17]

I hope you got my letter Yes[terda]y, and I direct again today [to] Balmoral Aberdeenshire ... But I shall really go through to Panshanger Monday, as I find I can easily manage it, and as I wish to stay a few days with Fordwich and Anne ...

Broadlands Papers

Carlton G[arde]ns Monday (19 Sept. 1853)[18]

I am just arrived in town with your Brother, and I am going on in two hours to Panshanger, to stay till Saturday ... I am glad Balmoral is an improvement on Ardverikey and I hope you will *this time* be able to give some praise to Scotland. Your letter from Perth I found here with the one from Balmoral. Dont shut yourself up too much with your papers in your distant room, but remember you have only one week to remain there, so you should manage to make yourself agreable and to appear to enjoy the Society, and besides it will be very good for your health to be out in that bracing air. You see that I am always poking in my small advice, incidents which I fancy you may not think of amid all your greater and more important occupations ... How happy I shall be to have you again with me! These small absences make one feel still more keenly the happiness of being together ...

Broadlands Papers

While Lord Palmerston was in Scotland, we were on the eve of the Crimean War. In the spring of this year, 1853, the strong-willed Tsar Nicholas had had two momentous talks with Sir Hamilton Seymour, our Ambassador at St Petersburg, when he had virtually proposed the partition of the dominions of Turkey. Russell, alarmed at these suggestions, had in April sent out Lord Stratford de Redcliffe[19] to Constantinople. Meanwhile, Nicholas had despatched Prince Menshikov to enforce his demands which on the 5th of May were formulated in a peremptory note which gave the Porte only five days to comply with

17 Date added by Lord Palmerston.　　18 Date added by Lord Palmerston.
19 The former Sir Stratford Canning.

its terms: whereupon the French hurriedly despatched their fleet to Smyrna.

The Aberdeen Government was ill equipped to deal with a major European crisis, for whilst the Prime Minister himself and the majority of his Cabinet were anxious at almost all costs to keep the peace, there was in the Government a vigorous war party consisting of Palmerston, Russell and Newcastle. Between these two groups stood Clarendon, the Foreign Secretary, vainly trying to bridge the gap.

Lady Palmerston's views were, as usual, in accord with those of her husband.

Panshanger Friday 23 (Sept 1853)[20]

I think I shall stay here till Monday and then I shall wait in London till you come. I have told Singleton to come up Monday with a kitchen maid for I think you will like to stay *at least* one whole day in town, and you will like to find me there comfortably instead of hurrying to Broadlands. And I fancy you must have a Cabinet about Turkish affairs, which seem to look as ugly as possible. I really see no way out of the fix . . . I am afraid reliance on Austria is indeed a broken reed. It seems to me that there never was such a mess, and after so much shilly shally work, it is but too natural for France to lose patience and act by herself . . .

Broadlands Papers

Panshanger Sat[u]r[da]y 24 (Sept. 1853)[21]

. . . I have ordered Singleton and a Housemaid to meet me in town Monday . . .

Broadlands Papers

And so at last, husband and wife were united again!

Towards the end of the year, Palmerston resigned his office. The reason given to the public was the Government's too pacific attitude towards Russia;[22] but the real reason was on account of Reform. This is clear from a letter from Emily to her husband in mid-November:

[20] Date added by Lord Palmerston.   [21] Date added by Lord Palmerston.
[22] *Greville Memoirs* (1887), I, pp. 95, 109.

335

Broadlands, Friday, 11 Novr. 1853

How hateful it is to hear of John Russell beginning again with his Reform Bill, and all to indulge his wretched Vanity! However, *per contra* the news from the East is very satisfactory and agreeable . . .

Broadlands Papers

and from two entries in her Diary:

Palmerston sent in his resignation after receiving a letter from Aberdeen, in which he said that James Graham would make no alteration in their Reform Bill . . .

The Cabinet met on 22nd December, everybody was frantic to get Lord Palmerston back—the Cabinet sat 5 hours and a half, and the Duke of Newcastle was deputed to negotiate with him.[23]

Meanwhile, Charles Greville received the news of Palmerston's resignation on the 14th of December when he was staying with the Cowpers at Panshanger. He could hardly believe his ears, and as soon as he got to London he hurried round to Clarendon for confirmation of the report. The Foreign Secretary explained that when he had been invited to join the Aberdeen Government Palmerston had been careful to explain his views on reform and had warned both Aberdeen and Lansdowne that he feared that the Reform Bill would bring about a separation between them. His conduct therefore, as Greville was forced to admit, had been irreproachable. A few days later Greville received a friendly letter from Lady Palmerston, explaining that her husband would have accepted a Reform Bill, but had proposed to Aberdeen some amendments to Russell's Bill which had not been accepted. There had in consequence been no alternative left to the Home Secretary but to offer his resignation from the Government. The next day Greville called on Lady Palmerston and found her in excellent

[23] Lady Airlie, *Lady Palmerston*, II, pp. 158-9. See also Palmerston's letter to his brother-in-law, Sulivan, C[arlton] G[ardens], December 19, 1853. Ashley, *Palmerston*, II, pp. 269-70.

spirits, and of course much gratified by the many tributes that were being offered to her lord. 'He is always in the right in everything he does,' she avowed proudly, 'a position I could not confirm,' wrote Greville, 'and which I did not care to dispute.' Then, very much to Charles Greville's surprise, Emily suggested that even at this late hour compromise might be possible.[24] The truth was that both Palmerston himself and an important section of the Government were anxious to find a way out of the difficulty; this is clearly shown from a memorandum by Prince Albert on an audience which the Queen had given to the Premier on Christmas Eve.

Windsor Castle, 25th December 1853

... He [Aberdeen] reported that some of his colleagues, Sir C. Wood, the Duke of Newcastle and Mr Gladstone, had been very anxious that Lord Palmerston should be readmitted into the Cabinet; they had had interviews with him in which he had expressed his hope to be allowed to reconsider his step. Lady Palmerston had been most urgent upon this point with her husband. All the people best conversant with the House of Commons stated that the Government had no chance of going on with Lord Palmerston in opposition, and with the present temper of the public, which was quite mad about the Oriental Question and the disaster at Sinope.[25] Even Sir W. Molesworth[26] shared this opinion.

Lord Palmerston had written a letter to Lord Aberdeen, in which he begs to have his resignation considered as not having taken place, as it arose entirely from a misapprehension on his part ...[27]

In his letter to Aberdeen Palmerston had stated: 'I find ... that I was mistaken in inferring from your letter that the details of the intended

[24] *Greville Memoirs* (1887), I, pp. 111–18.
[25] On November 30th the Russian Black Sea Fleet had attacked and destroyed the Turkish squadron in the harbour of Sinope.
[26] Sir William Molesworth, eighth baronet (1810–1855), first Commissioner of the Board of Works in Lord Aberdeen's Government.
[27] *Queen Victoria's Letters*, 1st Series, II, pp. 573–4.

Reform Bill had been finally settled by the Government, and that no objection to any part of these details would be listened to'; and therefore he felt that he should comply with the wishes of many of his colleagues that he should withdraw his resignation.[28] So a compromise was reached and Lord Palmerston was still Home Secretary.[29]

Within a few weeks of Palmerston's return to the Government there descended upon the family a domestic tragedy that was as sad as it was unexpected. Only in September Lady Palmerston had written to her husband from Panshanger that the cholera did not seem to be spreading and that she felt no alarm about it. In the summer of 1854, however, there was an outbreak of the plague in the Tower of London, and soon the epidemic was to spread with alarming rapidity throughout England. Lady Palmerston's son-in-law, Jocelyn, had long pined to go to fight for Turkey, but had been restrained by the pleadings of his wife and her family; had he gone abroad, perhaps his life might have been spared. As it was, he had stayed at home, and had been quartered in the Tower. The scourge struck home. On the 11th of August, 1854, recorded his mother-in-law: 'At 1 o'clock Jocelyn rushed into my room ill of cholera! All the rest is too dreadful to write. There never was such a day of misery!!! After 12 hours of distress and agony we lost him. The cholera symptoms were all subdued, he was warm and calm and thought himself better when his strength failed and he expired.' [30] Lady Palmerston thus reported these terrible events to Mrs Huskisson.

[August 13th, 1854]

Fanny tries to be calm for the sake of her Children but she is quite overwhelmed at this sudden and awfully sudden calamity. We go to Gros[veno]r Square today to Ld Shaftesbury's House as they are gone to Ems.

Oh what a day we had yesterday!! Hopes and fears and Agony for 12 hours from the hour when he rushed into my rooms at 1 o'clock until we lost him in the night at 1.

[28] *Queen Victoria's Letters*, 1st Series, II, p. 575. For Palmerston's correspondence with Aberdeen, see *Quarterly Review*, CXLIII, pp. 370–9.

[29] For Palmerston's account, see his letter to Laurence Sulivan, C[arlton] G[ardens] December 25th, 1853. Ashley, *Palmerston*, II, pp. 270–1.

[30] Lady Airlie, *Lady Palmerston*, II, p. 162.

We got all the Doctors in London but to no avail.

That horrid atmosphere of the Tower killed him—and he stood there from a sense of duty.

Huskisson Papers
B.M. Add. MSS. 39949, ff. 280-1

Gros[venor] Sq[ua]re, Monday [August 14th 1854]

I well know all you feel for us. We are none of us ill, but worn with such a scene and so much sorrow. Her anxiety to preserve her own life for the sake of her children keeps her from despair, but poor dear Creature her profound grief is quite heart rending and you may think what I feel at seeing all her happiness destroy'd . . .

Huskisson Papers
B.M. Add. MSS. 39949, ff. 283-4

The Queen too sent her condolences and anxious enquiries about the poor widow, to which Lady Palmerston replied on Lady Jocelyn's behalf.[31]

In November, Lord and Lady Palmerston paid a visit to Paris with the object of having an interview with the Emperor. They were of course received with much courtesy. 'Yesterday Emily and I dined at St Cloud,' Palmerston told his brother. 'The dinner was very handsome, and our hosts very agreeable. The Empress was full of life, animation, and talk, and the more one looks at her the prettier one thinks her. I have found the Emperor and Drouyn de Lhuys in very good opinions on the subject of the war, and acting towards us with perfect fairness, openness, and good faith.' [32]

In the following January, Lord John Russell resigned office as Lord President of the Council. For some time now he had been anxious to see the War Minister in the Commons and the offices of Secretary for War and at War combined; furthermore, he was anxious for a stronger minister than the Duke of Newcastle. This of course pointed only in one direction, but Lord Aberdeen had declined to change his course.

[31] Lady Palmerston to Queen Victoria, Grosvenor Sq[uar]e, Sunday [August 13, 1854], Augt. 16th [1854]. Royal Archives, Windsor Castle, S.8.2.3.

[32] Ashley, *Palmerston*, II, p. 300.

The public dilemma was well expressed by Emily to her husband a few weeks before this time.

> Brocket Hall, Tuesday [1854]
>
> ... those people who rejected Horsman's[33] proposal of ejecting Aberdeen, evidently did so from the notion that the only alternative was Johnny[34] and the Whigs, and this they thought even worse than Aberdeen. This is their difficulty that they cannot in any way get hold of you. When they try to get you for War Minister, they catch Newcastle, and when they try to catch you for Prime Minister, they fall into Johnny's hands, which they dislike more than Aberdeen. It is altogether a provoking position!!!
>
> Broadlands Papers

When, however, Roebuck carried a motion in the House of Commons to inquire into the conduct of the War, Russell and Aberdeen resigned; whereupon Lord Derby and Lord John Russell both vainly tried to form an administration. In consequence of their failure the Queen was reluctantly compelled to turn to Palmerston. The event is thus chronicled by Emily in her Diary under date the 4th of February: 'Palmerston commissioned to form a government by a letter from the Queen at 6 o'clock.' It was the greatest moment of their lives.

[33] Edward Horsman (1807-76), a prominent Whig; junior lord of the Treasury, 1841; Chief Secretary for Ireland, 1855-7.
[34] Lord John Russell.

CHAPTER VIII

Prime Minister's Wife

THE SITUATION that faced Palmerston when he became Prime Minister for the first time at the age of seventy was no easy one, for the war in the Crimea had for some time been going badly and the fall of beleaguered Sebastopol seemed as far off as ever. The new government took prompt measures, however, to cope with this unsatisfactory state of affairs. These included the amalgamation of the offices of Secretary for and at War in the person of Lord Panmure, the enlistment of older men on short service, the establishment of a special Board to superintend the transport service, and the prompt despatch of a sanitary commission and a commissariat commission to the seat of the War.

Nevertheless, Parliament was querulous, and the Whigs in particular were dissatisfied with the share of power and place offered to them. In consequence, the Prime Minister, who had proposed to his wife's son-in-law the Duchy of Lancaster with a seat in the Cabinet, was obliged to withdraw the offer in order to give the post to one of the discontented Whigs; and Lady Palmerston was left to write to Lord Shaftesbury to explain: no wonder that she told him that 'Palmerston is distracted with all the worry he has to go through . . .'[1] Furthermore, in the Commons Layard[2] suggested that the House should send out some of its members to the Crimea to sit in judgment on the guilty; to which suggestion the Prime Minister riposted amidst laughter that the idea might be satisfactory to the House provided the honourable member went himself and provided further that he remained in the Crimea during the rest of the session! More formidable was the

---

[1] Palmerston to Shaftesbury, Piccadilly, 7th Feb. 1855 (two letters); Shaftesbury to Palmerston, Feb. 7th 1855 (two letters); Lady Palmerston to Shaftesbury, Thursday morning, Feb. 8th. [1855]. Hodder, *Shaftesbury*, II, pp. 490–4.

[2] Sir Austen Henry Layard (1817–1894), Excavator of Nineveh; published *Nineveh and its Remains*, 1848–9; *Nineveh and Babylon*, 1853; Liberal M.P. for Aylesbury, 1852–7.

attack of Roebuck who renewed his demand for the appointment of a Committee of inquiry into the conduct of the Crimean War. To this Palmerston reluctantly consented, whereupon the Peelites, Gladstone, Graham and Sidney Herbert,[3] who had only joined the new government some three weeks earlier, promptly resigned. Their places were filled by Sir Charles Wood, Sir George Cornewall Lewis[4] and Lord John Russell, the last named of whom was absent as English representative at the peace Conference which had been renewed at Vienna. The appointment of Russell to the conference was a master stroke; and old Lady Dufferin, attending a reception at Lady Palmerston's whilst Russell's reply to the invitation was in doubt, found 'all England sitting with its hair on end and its mouth open waiting for events'.[5]

At the same time the Queen received a visit from Louis Napoleon and his Empress, now almost our only friends in Europe, when the Prime Minister took the opportunity of remonstrating with the Emperor upon his desire for peace at any price.

Lady Palmerston's comments on public affairs at this time are given in a letter in April to Mrs Huskisson.

Broadlands Wedy. April 11th [1855]

... We came here Sat[urda]y only for six days as we have to go back on Friday, and yet Pal[mersto]n has been whisked off today for a Cabinet and only returns to dine.

There are so many things of importance now going on that he can hardly absent himself at all, par[ticularl]y as he takes such a lead on all Domestic [issues] and now in addition to his *Premier* duties has taken upon himself the management of the Colonial office till Ld John's return[6] ... Pal[mersto]n's health and strength

---

[3] Sidney Herbert, Lord Herbert of Lea (1810–1861): War Secretary 1845–6, 1852–5, 1859–60; primarily responsible for Florence Nightingale going to Crimea.

[4] Sir George Cornewall Lewis, second baronet (1806–63): M.P. for Radnor Boroughs at this time.

[5] Bell, *Palmerston*, II, p. 116. For the representative's instructions, see Palmerston to Russell, Piccadilly, March 28, 1855. Ashley, *Palmerston*, II, pp. 310–12.

[6] Lord John Russell was appointed Colonial Secretary to succeed the Peelite, Sidney Herbert. As he was absent at Vienna and the Home Secretary was ill, the Premier had to deputise for him until his return.

are wonderful; but it is bad luck to boast, so I will say no more of that. . . .

The War is now our great anxiety and engrosses every body's thoughts. Lord John's mission will I fear have little success, and in his disappointment I fear he will come home and perhaps prove very troublesome, but I think he will be afraid of shewing his Temper, as the newspapers have so constantly predicted that he would do so.[7]

The Emperor and Empress's Visit is a curious event. I believe the Queen is now very curious to see them and will do all she can to do them honour (including the gift of the Garter), such a good ally is not to be deflected when Austria, and Prussia particularly, have proved so unworthy. How curious it is to remember all the resentment the Q[ueen] shewed to P[almerston] only for advocating the French alliance at the Time of the Emperor's accession —and now he is the only Friend we have now to depend upon. However she is very friendly and courteous to P[almerston] as in olden Times, and he is to stay at Windsor all the Time the Emperor remains . . .

Huskisson Papers
B.M. Add. MSS. 39949, ff. 287–90

Early in June, Emily was at St Leonards, whence she wrote to bid her 'dearest' have the Coachmen at London Bridge tomorrow 'with the Barouche, if the day is fine, if not the Chariot', so that she could get to London in time to see him before he went out to attend a public dinner.[8] Later in the month she was at Brocket for a couple of days or so. 'We came down most pleasantly, not more than an hour on the road. . . .' The next day she would return. 'Leave me a line that I may find when I arrive to tell me any news or to leave me any orders and say I shall want a bit of dinner at 8 . . .'[9] She was back at Brocket in

[7] Russell had favoured the Austrian peace proposals, but on his return found his colleagues unwilling to accept them. He wished to resign immediately, but refrained until Sir Edward Bulwer-Lytton's motion directed at his conduct in Vienna compelled him to resign in July.

[8] Lady Palmerston to Palmerston, St Leonards, Tuesday (5 June, 1855). Broadlands Papers. Date added by Lord Palmerston.

[9] Lady Palmerston to Palmerston, Brocket, Monday (25 June 1855). Broadlands Papers. Date added by Lord Palmerston.

July '. . . I have been in such a racket ever since I came down here that I have not had a moment to write . . . I am very anxious about Ld John's explanation, but fear from W[illia]m's account that he will be obliged to go out'.[10]

Early in August, Emily was back with Fanny Jocelyn and her grandchildren at St Leonards. 'Fanny and all her Children with Minny's make an immense Squad, and they seemed all so happy and comfortable together on the beach'.[11]

Meanwhile, Lord John Russell was explaining his conduct at Vienna in the House of Commons.

Eversfield Place, St Leonards, Wednesday (8 Aug. 1855)[12]

A Beautiful day with Showers, My dearest Harry, I do so hope you have enjoy'd it in some way either on horseback or on foot. I have read of your House events as Fanny takes in the Morning Post, and Adine the Times, so don't take the trouble to send me any papers, as they are deliver'd here the same morn[in]g. What a folly John's Speech was!! As usual his restlessness must do something, but I think the Times Articles upon him will make him feel his folly. Your Speech was excellent, and all one could wish, so courteous, and so kind to that wayward Johnny, but one feels sorry for him, he *is* in an arkward position and instead of remaining quiet under it, he will always be doing something to provoke fresh criticisms . . .

Broadlands Papers

St. Leonards, Thursday (9 Aug. 1855)[13]

. . . I have been reading over again your Speech of Tuesday, and I admire it more and more. It was so cautiously and so

[10] Lady Palmerston to Palmerston, Brocket, (Thursday 12 July 1855). Broadlands Papers. Date added by Lord Palmerston. For Charles Greville's views on Lord John Russell's conduct at the conference, for Russell's explanations and for the resultant Cabinet confusion, see *Greville Memoirs* (1887), I, pp. 269-70, 273-9.

[11] Lady Palmerston to Palmerston, 26 Eversfield Place, St Leonards, (7 Augt. 1855, Tuesday). Broadlands Papers. Date added by Lord Palmerston.

[12] Date added by Lord Palmerston.

[13] Date added by Lord Palmerston.

cleverly managed on many very difficult points, and you so well expressed your opinion of Gladstone's conduct, without naming him. *The Times* cuts up Ld John again today, and he well deserves what the *Times* says. It was very reckless of him to stir up such difficult subjects, and all without reason and without any care of what mischief he might do . . .

Broadlands Papers

In September came the welcome news of the fall of Sebastopol: whereupon Austria redoubled her efforts to bring about a peace, and found France a far more accommodating subject than England. At the same time Lord Normanby, our former Ambassador in Paris, who had the previous year been transferred as Minister to Florence, was tactlessly inter-meddling in local politics and trying to gain sympathy for the Austrian peace party. In October, Emily wrote to her lord from Broadlands on this subject.

Piccadilly Friday (19th Oct. 1855)[14]

We are all comfortable, at least as much as we can be without you . . . I told you one day that Azeglio[15] was much disturbed by Normanby's conduct, and his always encouraging and taking part with the Austrias. Today he writes to say that the Minister for Foreign Affairs at Turin, Cibriario, writes and complains *amèrement* of Lord Normanby. I hope he will make a representation of this to Ld Clarendon, for in the present state of things Ld Normanby may do much mischief.

Broadlands Papers

Broadlands Sunday (21 Oct. 1855)[16]

How glad I am to see this new Victory at Kimburn, an important place from its situation and so easily taken. There is no end to your Glory and Success's—every day some new Victory,

---

[14] Date added by Lord Palmerston.

[15] Massimo Taparelli, Marquis d'Azeglio, chief Minister of Victor Emmanuel II of Italy, also a distinguished writer.

[16] Date added by Lord Palmerston.

345

but I long for you to come home. I have some hopes of you to-morrow, tho they are rather slender . . .

Broadlands Papers

Broadlands Monday [October, 1855]

Many thanks for all your details. I shall be charmed to see you tomorrow, and it was unreasonable of me to expect you any sooner, with all the work you have on your hands . . . Kimburn must be a great event, if one may judge from the papers. I have been looking for it on the Map . . .

Try and fix your Cabinet next Tuesday, so that you might go up that Morning, and remain here Monday. Why could you not fix your War Meeting here, Ld Panmure, Granville and Charles Wood. You see my proposals and inventions are many.

Broadlands Papers

Meanwhile, Austria strove to bring about a peace and joined with France in attempting to coerce us into the same frame of mind. But Palmerston was no Aberdeen, and the Prime Minister addressed a firm letter to the Comte de Persigny, the French Ambassador in London.[17] A few days later Persigny called at Downing Street to try to persuade our Government to consent to Count Buol's[18] proposal that the Black Sea question should be the subject of a separate treaty between Russia and Turkey.[19] He met with a blank refusal. 'We ought to stand firm', Palmerston wrote to his foreign secretary, 'as to having all the stipulations about the Black Sea made part of the Treaty between Russia and all the belligerents. I can fancy how I should be hooted in the House of Commons if I were to get up and say that we had agreed to an imperfect and unsatisfactory arrangement about one of the most important parts of the whole matter, as a personal favour to Count

[17] Palmerston to Persigny, Piccadilly, 21 November 1855. Ashley, *Palmerston*, II, pp. 322-3.

[18] Count Karl Ferdinand von Buol.

[19] The Austrian suggestion was that Russia and Turkey should agree that any addition to the Russian strength might be met by a corresponding addition to the Turkish fleet and the admission of some French and British men-of-war into the Euxine. In return, Buol undertook to form a triple alliance between Austria, France and Great Britain.

Buol, or to save the *amour-propre* of Russia. I had better beforehand take the Chiltern Hundreds.' [20]

At the very end of the year 1855, Count Buol put forward fresh peace proposals, which were on the 16th of January accepted by the Czar as a basis for negotiation. Relief was general, and Henry Reeve, meeting the Palmerstons at a party at the French Embassy, recorded: 'Palmerston in great spirits, and proud of the success of the firm and consistent language his Government has held. Persigny assured me that it was the energy and precision of the British Cabinet which had mainly, if not solely, brought about this result; for that Walewski and most of the Emperor's advisers in Paris would have given in half a dozen times over.' [21] Furthermore, Lady Palmerston's son-in-law, now Earl of Shaftesbury, wrote to her at St Leonards, where she was then staying: 'My dear Mum, Give my hearty congratulations to Palmerston on this opening success to all his vigour, principles, good sense and resolution. Under God we owe to him, and him only, this hope of a just and secure peace. But his troubles are only beginning. He must be as firm as ever; *ask no more* than he has done, but *take no less*. May God guide him . . .' [22] But Emily, like her husband, would have preferred the Russians to have suffered further punishment before the conclusion of peace, for as she told the Prime Minister, they 'are little to be trusted' and 'will somehow wriggle out of their conces-sions. . . .' [23] The next day she wrote to ask her husband whether he had decided who was to go to the Peace Conference. '. . . Panizzi says to me that everybody says there is nobody fit to go to the Conference but *yourself.* This is of course quite impossible, but ought not Lord Clarendon go there by some arrangement (as the next best hand) . . .' [24] In fact, Lord Clarendon went to Paris as plenipotentiary to act in concert with our Ambassador, Cowley; but Palmerston, the old, experienced Foreign Secretary, kept a firm hand on his representatives during the protracted negotiations,[25] until at length peace was signed

[20] Palmerston to Clarendon, November 26, 1855. Ashley, *Palmerston*, II, pp. 323–4.   [21] Reeve, *Memoirs*, I, p. 345; Bell, *Palmerston*, II, p. 140.

[22] Shaftesbury to Lady Palmerston, St Giles' House, Cranbourne, Salisbury, Jan. 19th, 1856. Lady Airlie, *Lady Palmerston*, II, p. 164.

[23] Lady Palmerston to Palmerston, St Leonards, Tuesday [January 22nd 1856]. Melbourne Papers, B.M. Add. MSS. 45546–7.

[24] Lady Palmerston to Palmerston, St Leonards, Wednesday [January 23rd 1856]. Melbourne Papers. B.M. Add. MSS. 45546–7.

[25] Bell, *Palmerston*, II, pp. 146–7.

on the 30th of March. Thus ended the terrible, ill-omened Crimean War. Palmerston's reward for his services was the Garter bestowed upon him in July 1856 as the expression of his Sovereign's well-deserved approbation. Queen Victoria had at last come to appreciate and to acknowledge the outstanding merits of the great statesman whom she had formerly distrusted.

In the spring of 1856 Lady Palmerston suffered a severe shock in the sudden death of her eldest son, Lord Cowper, the unexpectedness of whose end was reminiscent of the terrible last moments of her son-in-law, Jocelyn. 'Poor dear Fordwich!' noted Lord Shaftesbury in his Diary, 'He was with us well on Monday morning; he left London well on Tuesday morning for business at Maidstone:[26] at three o'clock he was taken ill in court, and at half past nine he was dead! The suddenness, the awfulness of it recalls forcibly the death of poor Jocelyn. Both mysterious, both inscrutable decrees of Providence; we have only to do as the children of Israel, "bow the head and worship". A more lovable man never lived; a good husband, and tenderly attached to his children.'[27] Some two months later we find Emily once again with the Jocelyn family at St Leonards, whence she wrote to her 'dearest Harry'.

St Leonards, Sunday (20 June 1856)[28]

I sent you a letter last night directed to Windsor to tell of my safe arrival, and today the weather is perfectly delicious so that I have been walking all day and have hardly a leg to stand upon ... Fanny looks very well, and the Children particularly so, and no wonder for they are constantly in the air either walking with us or disporting themselves on the beach and rocks.

Lady Elcho wrote Fanny word that she had met Sidney Herbert on the train and never saw anybody look so disappointed as he does at the Peace news, evidently quite disturbed by it. No doubt it is a great blow to all that party and shows up the extreme folly of their conduct. I dare say he feels it in too [sic] ways disappointment, for himself and party; and also as destroying the

[26] Lord Cowper was Lord-Lieutenant of Kent.
[27] Hodder, *Shaftesbury*, III, p. 37.
[28] So written, but 20 June 1856 has been added later and not by Lady Palmerston; it is not the correct date, as that was a Friday, not a Sunday.

power and prestige of Russia which is so dear to every Russian and therefore I have no doubt in the same way to this *half* Russian.[29]

The only thing that could have set them right with the public would have been the success of Russia and the next thing, what I believe they fully intended to say, that *you never would* would [*sic*] agree to any Peace with Russia. How all these points have finished, and they must go and hide their diminished heads . . .

Melbourne Papers
B.M. Add. MSS. 45546–7
Lady Airlie, *Lady Palmerston*, II, p. 165

All this, it must be admitted, is rather unfair, though Sidney Herbert and other Peelites like Gladstone and Graham had doubtless dubbed Palmerston a 'war-monger'! But the truth was that Emily Palmerston had never quite forgiven them for resigning from her husband's government rather than concede Roebuck's demand for an inquiry into the Crimean War.

In the autumn of 1856, war seemed impending in the East. In the previous year Palmerston had sent out Lord Canning, son of the great George Canning, to succeed Dalhousie as Governor-General of India. No sooner had he reached Calcutta than trouble seemed imminent, for Persia in defiance of treaties having seized Herat the English government was forced to declare war on the Shah. On these events Lady Palmerston wrote to her son William, who was staying with his brother Spencer at Sandringham, the estate in Norfolk which Spencer Cowper had inherited in 1843 from Lord Cowper's old crony Motteux.

Piccadilly, Ocr. 28 [1856]

I found your letter when we arrived today and was delighted to hear that you are both at Sandringham. The improvements you mention must be very great and give quite a new appearance to

[29] Sidney Herbert's mother was a Russian, Catherine, daughter of Simon, Count Woronzow, Russian Ambassador to Britain. She married, first, Prince Buttera de Rubari and, secondly, the 11th Earl of Pembroke.

the House, and I am very glad that it should have been done. Every body likes to improve and to alter. It gives a feeling of ownership, and an interest in your own possession. I think I could easily myself get very fond of Sandringham if I lived there. It is such a nice wild Country with all its sandy drives and extent of heath and gorse and firs and I hope now to see Spencer and Harriet[30] get very fond of the place. It would have been a great pity therefore if he had sold the place to the Duke of Wellington.[31]

Palmerston has got very much better of his Lumbago, but he does not look so well as he did before this attack . . . we have been a whole week at Broadlands quite alone and entirely intent on Doctoring. We were obliged to excuse ourselves from going to Windsor last Wednesday, and I suppose we shall now have to do so next Friday or Saturday. After this we shall go to Broadlands and return here to settle for two or three weeks about the 7th or 9th. There are so many subjects of importance to settle that we must have several consecutive Cabinets. But in truth the difficulties of India alone are enough and more than enough for one Govern[men]t and one Session.

I hope Canning has done well on the whole but he is supposed to be too much in the hands of his Council—inferior people brought up under the old system. Canning's Manifesto might have been useful later but it was ill timed at that moment, and tended to depress the zeal and energy of our Armies fighting for their lives by implying blame when they ought to have had every encouragement. The English feeling is never cruel. It is not in our nature, and I dont believe English Troops would ever kill a Woman or a Child. Elphenston[32] [sic] I hear much praised by everybody. He seems to have risen with the occasion and to have shown great Courage and Spirit and no fear of responsibility (the bugbear of many) . . . But what an awful state it is for those who command so far off, have to take the determination, and then to stand the brunt of Criticisms. People ought to be very careful

[30] Lady Cowper's third son, Charles Spencer Cowper, had married in 1852 Lady Harriett Anne, daughter of Charles John, Earl of Blessington, and widow of Alfred, Count d'Orsay.

[31] He did, however, subsequently sell the Sandringham estate to the Prince of Wales for £220,000.

[32] John Elphinstone, 13th Baron Elphinstone (1807–60), Governor of Bombay, 1853–9.

of blaming or finding fault with those who have the misfortune
of being in that painful position!!

Broadlands Papers

In January 1857 Princess Lieven died from bronchitis after a short
illness, but there is no echo of this in Emily's correspondence; the two
had drifted so far apart that Lady Palmerston probably felt little real
regret at the passing of her former friend. She no doubt felt much more
the death, a year later, of beloved Hart, the bachelor Duke of Devonshire, who had shown her unfailing kindness and goodwill throughout
her life.

In the summer of this year Emily was back at St Leonards, where
the French Ambassador and his wife were also staying. She gave her
husband a curious picture of his Excellency in one of his less-dignified
moments!

Wednesday St Leonards [26 August 1857]

I am perfectly well and had a nice journey and have had a walk
since I came down and saw the Persigneys coming home from
riding. She swims every day at 7 or 8 o'clock in the morning and
they say Persigny tucks up his Trowsers and goes into the sea
shrimping with a net—*est-il-possible?* ...

Melbourne Papers
B.M. Add. MSS. 45546–7

The first Palmerston Government fell in February 1858. The
details were curious. The Emperor of the French, when driving to the
Opera with the Empress, had narrowly escaped assassination at the
hands of a group of desperadoes headed by a man named Orsini. The
plot had been hatched in London, and England was much irritated by
the French threats of reprisals for our harbouring assassins. Accordingly, the Prime Minister determined to silence these complaints by
introducing a Bill to make conspiracy to murder, hitherto only a mis-
demeanour, a felony punishable with penal servitude, and empowering
the Government to expel, if they thought fit, any foreigner whom they
suspected of plotting against a foreign sovereign. This measure might

have sufficed and French threats been ignored but for the unhappy chance that some of the addresses congratulating the Emperor on his escape and ascribing the blame to England appeared in the *Moniteur*, the official organ of the French Government. This aroused the nation, and on the 19th of February the Tories, who had not opposed the first reading of Palmerston's bill, now turned round and voted for the amendment of Milner Gibson,[33] the Member for Ashton-under-Lyne, regretting that the Government, before inviting the House to amend the law of conspiracy, had not replied to the despatch dated the 20th of January, which Count Walewski, the French Foreign Minister, had sent to the Ambassador in London urging the British Government not to allow any abuse of the right of asylum. The defeat of the Ministry, which was largely due to bad management on the part of the Whips, came as a great surprise. Palmerston promptly resigned and the Queen sent for Lord Derby.

Lady Palmerston, who was with the Jocelyn family at St Leonards, was of course furious.

St. Leonards, 20 Feby. 1858

I am greatly provoked, my dear Harry, at this abominable Division, the extreme folly of the House of Commons and the low and mean spirits display'd by so many members, some acting from folly and so many from a vile and reckless desire to annoy the Government and to do mischief. I have not yet seen the names, but I see the speeches of those who spoke and they are enough to provoke a Saint . . . I hope you don't think of going out, but will go on with the bill.

Melbourne Papers
B.M. Add. MSS. 45546–7

And again, the next day, she wrote indignantly to her lord: 'I think you are all quite right. The House has behaved so abominably that I am glad they should find the difficultys of what they have done, and you go out on a subject to which no blame attaches, merely a sham reason and an excuse used by the Crafty to catch the fools. In my belief

[33] Thomas Milner-Gibson (1806–84), later became President of the Board of Trade in Palmerston's last Ministry, 1859–65, and in Russell's, 1865–8.

I think Derby will not be able to form a Government that will stand, and if they try a dissolution the cry will be Palmerston "and no base Coalitions" . . .' [34]

Meanwhile, as it seemed quite hopeless that Emily and her husband, even when he was out of office, would be able to find time to visit her Melbourne estates, she determined to let the property to a certain Captain Gooch, about whom Lady Palmerston wrote to her agent, Fox.

Piccadilly, April 18, 1858

. . . I don't think it much signifies his giving three or six months' notice and I should feel willing to accommodate him in small things if he is likely to be a good tenant and to keep up the gardens as they are. I should not like them to be spoilt or neglected. If he can make the expenses less, he may well try to do so, but the beauty of the gardens must not be spoilt, so as to be any permanent destruction to them.

I always thought that a Hunting Man might be tempted to take Melbourne Hall as it is so near several packs of Hounds. The little alterations he talks of in the Stables need not I think be much expense, and I hope he will not want to have a Laundry at home . . .

Melbourne Hall Papers

In November, Lord Palmerston visited the Emperor Napoleon at Compiègne, when he both shot and hunted the stag. 'They are all very civil and courteous', he told his brother-in-law, 'and the visits of the English to the Emperor serve as links to maintain and strengthen English alliance.' [35] May one detect some lack of enthusiasm in these words? Perhaps he was thinking of his Emily, whom he had left at Broadlands and who wrote of her anxieties for the safety of her 'dearest Harry'.

[34] Lady Palmerston to Palmerston, St Leonards, Sunday [February 21st 1858]. Lady Airlie, *Lady Palmerston*, II, pp. 169-70.
[35] Ashley, *Palmerston*, II, p. 359. For a description of the Emperor's party by Lord Clarendon, one of the guests, see Clarendon to Duchess of Manchester Nov. 18/58. *My Dear Duchess*, pp. 34-5.

Broadlands Sunday [Nov. 14 1858]

I feel very lonely without you and of course very anxious I must be, but I hope there is no reason for being so and that you will return quite well and safe on Saturday, and that you will write to me as soon as you get to Boulogne.

If you have crossed this afternoon I am afraid it will have been a rough passage for there is a high wind here this afternoon, and much rain all morning.

I shall be glad when I hear of your being arrived at Compiègne ... [and she concluded her letter with quite exceptional warmth], Ever most tenderly and affectionately yours, Emily.

Melbourne Papers
B.M. Add. MSS. 45546–7

But her anxieties were soon set at rest by a letter from her husband from Boulogne.

Broadlands, Wedy. 17th Nov. 1858

I was made very happy on Tuesday morn[in]g by your letter of Sunday night dated Boulogne. I had worked myself quite into a fright about you when I heard that horrid howling wind Sunday even[in]g and night and all Monday. It was really quite frightful here ... so I fancied you either at sea in a regular storm or coop'd up at Folkestone and unable to cross. So it was a great happiness when I got your letter dated Boulogne! So now I hope you are amusing yourself and passing your time well. But our weather is very cold here, so I fear it must be the same with you. I got your letter from Compiègne and it seemed so comfortable that I quite regretted not being with you, tho no doubt it was much more prudent for me to have remained here ...

Melbourne Papers
B.M. Add. MSS. 45546–7

Meanwhile, Lord Derby's government was running into difficulties. Emily's forecast was to prove not wide of the mark.[36] The new govern-

[36] See pp. 352–3.

ment was in a minority and early in the new year was beaten on a Reform Bill; whereupon Lord Derby dissolved Parliament. Whilst the General Election was in progress the Emperor of the French at the new year's reception of the diplomatic corps saw fit to address the Austrian Ambassador in terms reminiscent of those of his Uncle to our Envoy in 1803. The relations between Austria and Sardinia were strained because of Italian impatience at the continued predominance of Austria in the peninsula, so it was rapidly assumed that the words spoken at the Tuileries were to convey the meaning that France would come to Sardinia's aid if hostilities should break out. This proved correct. Sardinia refused to disarm at the imperious edict of Austria, who immediately declared war; whereupon French troops at once advanced into northern Italy to Victor Emmanuel's aid.

These disturbing events were naturally the subject of comment in several of Lady Palmerston's letters to her husband.

Thursday night [28 April 1859]
... Nothing has been heard of the advance of the Austrians so people think they have stopt or may not have crossed and Brunow says there is no Treaty between France and Russia only an understanding. One hears very little as there is nobody in town ...

Melbourne Papers
B.M. Add. MSS. 45546-7

Friday 29 April 1859
... It seems there is no regular treaty between France and Russia and that this is a Stock jobbing report set afloat by Rothschild to get back the loss he would have suffer'd from war breaking out. I think they ought to be hanged, I mean the Jews. 19 Stock jobbers broke yesterday in the City from this manœuvre, but in one way this move may be good [in] that I believe the fright of War is against the Govern[men]t Elections. They say the Govern[men]t people all look very low. Derby has much reason to be so, as well as Melinesky.

Melbourne Papers
B.M. Add. MSS. 45546-7

Piccadilly 11 o'clock [Sunday 22 May 1859]

. . . Azeglio had another Telegraph at 12 ok. last night with the account of another victory which seemed more important than the last. The Austrians attacked 15 thousand strong and were repulsed with much loss and were in full retreat. The Sardinian Horse attacked them six times, and the [illegible] Army had much success and took two hundred Prisoners. Of the Allied Army 500 were killed or wounded and a French General killed . . .

Melbourne Papers
B.M. Add. MSS. 45546-7

These happenings on the Continent had some effect on our General Election, because Lord Derby's government displayed clear leanings towards Austria, whilst public opinion in general favoured Italian independence. The result was that the Conservatives failed to gain their majority. The Prime Minister tried to strengthen his position by making yet another attempt to induce Lord Palmerston to join his administration with the leadership of the House of Commons; but such efforts were futile for Palmerston and Russell had come to an agreement that whichever of them should be invited to form a government should receive the assistance and support of the other. A great gathering of the Whig party, at which some Peelites were present, was held at Willis's Rooms, when it was arranged that a vote of confidence in ministers should be moved by Lord Hartington. The result of this was the defeat of the Government on the 10th of June by a majority of thirteen. Whereupon the Queen, professing herself as embarrassed at having to choose between the rival claims of Palmerston and Russell, to the astonishment of everybody sent for Lord Granville, under whom Palmerston generously consented to serve.[37] But Granville's efforts were vain; the nation looked to 'old Pam' and him only as its leader. So it was that on the 30th of June, 1859, at the age of seventy-five, Palmerston formed his second administration.

[37] Palmerston to Queen Victoria, 94 Piccadilly, June 11th, 1859. Ashley, *Palmerston*, II, pp. 363-4.

CHAPTER IX

Last Years

THE GOVERNMENT that Palmerston formed in the summer of 1859 was a very strong one, with Lord John Russell as Foreign Secretary, Sidney Herbert Secretary for War, and the rising Gladstone Chancellor of the Exchequer. It was hardly surprising, therefore, if his wife wrote exultantly to her agent at Melbourne.

> Piccadilly, Wednesday June 28, 1859[1]
>
> ... Lord Palmerston has been fortunate in having been able to form such a strong government and we hope it will be well supported—for himself it is very flattering to have so many talented and distinguished Individuals anxious to serve under him and making no difficulties, but in general all people have behaved well and shown much public spirit by giving up offices they might have liked for the purpose of forming a strong Government at a time when it seemed most necessary for the public good and when the late Govern[men]t had done so much to lower themselves in public estimation abroad and at home.
>
> Melbourne Hall Papers

But unfortunately the labours of office made a visit to distant Derbyshire seem as far off as ever! '. . . The idle workmen who are now striking for nine hours work instead of ten are little aware of the labour of being Prime Minister and having occupation all day and half the night beside . . .'[2]

In November, Emily went down to Brighton for a few days' change of air, whence she wrote to her 'dearest Love' to announce her safe

[1] So written, but June 28, 1859, was a Tuesday.

[2] Lady Palmerston to Fox, Piccadilly, Augt. 21st 1859. Melbourne Hall Papers.

arrival and the weather 'very sunny and bright, but very cold'.[3] She wrote again the next day.

> Monday (Brighton, 28 Novr. 1859)[4]
> I got no letter from you today, which I regret, but I received two Newspapers which shows you had not forgotten me, many thanks for them . . .
> Pray order the Chariot or Brougham at Pimlico Station at 5.30 as I shall return by that Train.
>
> Broadlands Papers

> Tunbridge Wells, Friday [1859]
> I got down here very well and am lodged in Mount Ephraim Hotel, with Shaftesbury and Minny, Conty and Cecil,[5] who have all begun their drinks this morning . . .
>
> Broadlands Papers

> East Lodge, Friday (9 Decr. 1859)[6]
> I hope that you really will come tomorrow. It would be pleasant to have some walks with you, in this fine Climate. I have been walking a great deal today, and I have taken another Bath today, as I would not have one tomorrow to prevent my walking with you. God bless you, dearest, come if you can . . .
>
> Broadlands Papers

During the closing years of Lord Palmerston's life there are not many of Emily's letters to be found, for the old Prime Minister's loyal, loving wife was constantly at his side. We get a glimpse of her in May,

---

[3] Lady Palmerston to Palmerston (Brighton, 27 Nov. 1859). Date added by Lord Palmerston.

[4] Date added by Lord Palmerston.

[5] Lady Constance Ashley-Cooper and Cecil Ashley-Cooper, a daughter and son of Lord and Lady Shaftesbury.

[6] Date added by Lord Palmerston.

1860, in the Gallery of the House of Commons during the debate on the Paper Duties[7] expressing her hopes for the heavy defeat of the Bill in terms sufficiently forceful to shock some of the more zealous Whigs who begged the Duke of Bedford to remonstrate with her upon her language. But the cautious Duke knew full well that Emily was only expressing her lord's views, though he could not avow his sentiments as openly as she did![8]

Other glimpses of Emily at this time we get, but they are no more than glimpses.

Wednesday (29 Aug. 1860)[9]

Thank you, my dearest Harry, for your letter and all your details about Evelyn.[10] It is quite extraordinary that in all your work and business you always find much more time than an idle Man does to do kind and good natured things, and to enter into all the minute details of affection and interest. There is *nobody* to compare with you on this subject! . . .

Broadlands Papers

In October the Palmerstons at last found a little time to spare and they went first on a visit to Lord Fitzwilliam at Wentworth Wood-house in Yorkshire, and thence to Melbourne. On the 28th Lady Palmerston wrote to Fox to advise him of their plans.[11]

In November, however, she was not well and had to excuse herself from accompanying the Prime Minister to Windsor, as she told Fox.

Piccadilly, Novr. 19 '60

. . . I am well now, but very much afraid of any exertion or cold that might give me a return of illness, so I sent an excuse to

[7] A Bill for abolishing the duty on paper was carried in the Commons but subsequently rejected in the Lords. The dispute was eventually settled by a resolution for removing so much of the duty on paper as exceeded the Excise Duty at home.   [8] *Greville Memoirs* (1887), II, pp. 310-11.

[9] Date added by Lord Palmerston.

[10] Evelyn Ashley, who was acting as Lord Palmerston's private secretary, and subsequently edited and in part re-wrote Lord Dalling's biography of his chief. He was the father of the late Lord Mount Temple, who was the father of Lady Mountbatten.

[11] Lady Palmerston to Fox, Octr. 28th '60. Melbourne Hall Papers.

Windsor on Saturday and Lord Palmerston went there without
me and returned today.

Melbourne Hall Papers

In the autumn of 1861 the Shaftesburys suffered a sad loss in the
death of their daughter Mary. In August the child had seemed somewhat better, as Emily wrote to Palmerston.

Friday (1861)[12]
I got here in a Jiffy, an Express Train took me to Hatfield in
20 Minutes and so I had a good long walk in the garden by a
bright sun, and before the rain came down. Minny came with her
child about Six, the poor thing seems a little better and more comfortable, and Minny ascribes this improvement to her inhaling the
Oxigen [*sic*].
I shall come up tomorrow by the 4.35 Train which reaches
London at half past five. Pray send the horses to meet my Carriage
at that time. God bless you, darling.

Broadlands Papers

But their hopes were short-lived, for on the 3rd of September the child
died. The distress of the Grandmother is vividly shown in her two next
letters to Fox at Melbourne.

Walmer Castle Monday Sepr. 2d 1861
. . . I wish very much to settle a time for going to Melbourne
and other places in that neighbourhood, but it is very difficult to
name a time as I have been so distressed every day at the thoughts
of losing my dear g[rand]daughter, Lady Mary Ashley [-Cooper].
She is now at Torquay and in such a precarious state that I feel
it possible that I may hear of her death any day and yet at the
same time we are not entirely without hope that her state might
improve tho I am afraid that the chance is very small . . .

[12] Year added by Lord Palmerston.

Ld Palmerston's Installation[13] at Dover was a splendid sight and most gratifying to him in every way. The Queen herself could not have been received with more enthusiasm. The Town was cover'd with Flags and Banners and Triumphal Arches ...

Melbourne Hall Papers

Piccadilly, Sepr. 23 '61

This great affliction of my dear Grand Daughter's death has quite overturned all our plans and intentions, and poor L[o]rd and Ly Shaftesbury have suffered so much in mind and body for their long attendance on this dear Child that we were obliged to go and stay with them at Walmer Castle to give them some comfort, and this has taken up all our time but I am happy to say that they are now better and going to remain on in that Healthy and beautiful Spot ...

Melbourne Hall Papers

And so the last few years of Lord Palmerston's life passed slowly by. In spite of his age and the anxieties of his office, he kept remarkably fit, and at Christmas 1862 Lord Clarendon told his friend the Duchess of Manchester of a visit his brother had just paid to Broadlands where the old man played at billiards all night and went out shooting in the morning 'just as he w[oul]d have done 50 y[ea]rs ago' adding pointedly that Lady Palmerston 'does all the same things (perhaps not *quite* all) as it was her wont to do at about the same period'.[14]

No wonder that Emily could write with such confidence to Fox at Melbourne Hall!

Piccadilly, Decr. 31, 1862

I am glad to say that Lord Palmerston has thrown off his gout entirely and is nearly as well as usual walking about without crutch or stick, and we are going to Broadlands next week ...

[13] As Lord Warden of the Cinque Ports in succession to Lord Dalhousie who had died in the spring.

[14] Clarendon to Duchess of Manchester, The Grove, Watford, Dec. 25/62. *My Dear Duchess*, p. 208.

The Queen's health is wonderfully good considering the over-whelming affliction she has suffered.[15]

Melbourne Hall Papers

Early in 1863 Lord Palmerston was installed as Rector of Glasgow University, and presented with the freedom of the city of Edinburgh. He was quite a wonder '. . . fancy going at 79 y[ea]rs old 400 miles to make speeches to Scotch crowds', commented Lord Clarendon, 'when most men at any time of life w[ou]ld perform double the distance *not* to make such speeches, but that one he made to the University was really admirable both as to the matter and its arrangement—it must have cost him a deal of thought and when he c[oul]d have found time for it one can't imagine'.[16] Nevertheless, his faithful Emily seldom left him now; and on the few occasions when they were parted, she was sad and ill at ease.

Brocket 3rd Morng. Augt. [1863]
Here I am very comfortable and the showers of rain have not interfered with my Journey, and the weather is warm enough. The only thing I am sorry for is that I shall not get your letter this Morning, unless they send it by a train . . . The flowers here are beautifully laid out in front of the house, and very much improved since we were here before. No Day can be more beauti-ful than this one, so brilliant and fresh from the rain of yesterday. I wish I could have enjoy'd these two days with you here, instead of your rushing over dangerous mountains and mines, and trains.

Broadlands Papers

Early in August 1864, the Palmerstons went to visit Emily's estates in Northamptonshire, and at Towcester she cut the first sod of a rail-way from Northampton to Stratford-upon-Avon. Later in the month, Lady Palmerston went to Brocket, whilst he went north for some meetings and then to Hereford to unveil a statue erected to the

[15] The death of the Prince Consort, December 14th, 1861.
[16] Clarendon to Duchess of Manchester, The Grove, Apr 1/63. *My Dear Duchess*, p. 221.

memory of Sir George Cornewall Lewis. In September, Palmerston visited Wilton, Lord Pembroke's seat and Sidney Herbert's old home, where he presided at a meeting of the Wiltshire Volunteers. From Brocket, Emily wrote to her absent lord.

Tuesday, Brocket (30 Aug. 1864)[17]

I got here yes[terda]y very comfortably . . . I trust you will have fine weather for all your various expeditions, and that you will find them useful and agreable . . . God bless you dearest.

Broadlands Papers

In July 1865, Parliament, having nearly run its full course, had been dissolved; and Palmerston, now over eighty, went down for the last time for the contest in his constituency. 'Once more he smiled on Tiverton and Tiverton smiled on him';[18] and he appealed to the electors in telling terms: 'The old Romans had a fable about one of their heroes, a great wrestler, who when they threw him upon the ground his mother earth gave him additional vigour, and he got up stronger than when he fell down. Now I think I shall receive renewed vigour by coming back to the good mother earth of Tiverton, and I hope mother earth will send me back stronger than when I came here.' [19] Of course they cheered him to the echo, and of course they re-elected him. Indeed, the elections throughout the country were very favourable to the Ministry, as Emily wrote to him from London at this time.

Piccadilly, Wedy. (11 July 1865)[20]

I was very happy yesterday morning to get your letter and to find everything so prosperous, as I had felt very anxious about the long Journey you had in prospect, but all's well that ends well, and I trust you will come back tomorrow or Friday. Our Election prospects seem to be bright everywhere, and we have

---

[17] Date added by Lord Palmerston.
[18] Bell, *Palmerston*, II, p. 415.
[19] *The Times*, July 12, 1865; Bell, *Palmerston*, II, pp. 415–16.
[20] Date added by Lord Palmerston, but July 11, 1865, was a Tuesday.

gained a great many [seats] . . . I am very flourishing, and went last night to a Ball with Alice at Stafford House.[21] Our weather is very fine and enjoyable, and people are very anxious for invitations to our party Saturday. The Queen and the P[rince] of Orange and Duke of Cambridge are all coming to dinner.

Broadlands Papers

Indeed, invitations to Lady Palmerston's parties were as highly prized as ever; nor were people in the slightest deterred by the incurable unpunctuality of both host and hostess—a Saxon diplomatist, Count Vitzthum, records how he arrived at 94 Piccadilly for a great dinner to find his host just mounting for a pre-prandial ride in Rotten Row. But like other guests he took this in good part; indeed, he could not afford to take offence, for in his view a call on Lady Palmerston was often more informative than studying the papers. That may well have been true, if it is rightly stated that Lady Palmerston copied such of her husband's papers as were too confidential to be shown to a Secretary.[22]

But this was the last of Lady Palmerston's great receptions. Shortly afterwards she and her husband went down to Brocket for rest and change. One day in mid-October, the Prime Minister caught a chill when driving with his wife. On his return he dawdled, taking an hour and a half to undress and insisting on having his usual bath.[23] The result was inflammation of the kidneys, and he almost died that night. By Sunday, however, he was better, and by Monday his anxious wife could write quite hopefully to her son, William.

Brocket, Monday 16 [October 1865]

. . . P[almerston] certainly looks better every day so there is no necessity for any change and the only thing is to be patient, meanwhile he improves his diet, and wonderful to say eat a Mutton Chop at Breakfast yesterday and another today and says he is only surprized that he should have lived so long without finding out what a good breakfast it is, and he took his half glass

[21] The Duchess of Sutherland's London house.
[22] Bell, *Palmerston*, II, pp. 252-3.
[23] Guedalla, *Palmerston*, p. 453.

of old Port besides, so he is quite a Convert to *Protham Smiths Theories* . . .

Clarendon called here yesterday from Hatfield and was surprized to see Pal[mersto]n looking so well, but he don't look very well himself, and I am sorry to hear from him that Ld Derby has a very bad fit of gout and pain all over him in every joint . . .

Broadlands Papers

But mutton chops and old port are no diet for elderly invalids; and on the next day the Prime Minister was decidedly weaker, though inquiries from Balmoral could still elicit a murmured: 'It is very kind of her Majesty: I am much better.' Brave words, but far from the truth; and on the morning of the following day, Wednesday, the 18th of October, 1865, he died, his devoted Emily, with Minny and Fanny near her, seated at his side.

Lord Palmerston had prepared for himself a resting-place in Romsey Cemetery; but, as he had left no positive directions for his burial, it was thought fitting to yield to the universal wish that he should be publicly interred. Accordingly, on the 28th of October, before a vast concourse of national leaders, the great Englishman was laid to rest in Westminster Abbey.[24]

During her few remaining years, Emily Palmerston divided her time between London, Broadlands and Brocket. Cambridge House was soon given up for a house of more modest size in Park Lane, as she wrote to Mr Fox early in 1866.

Jan. 29th '66

. . . I came up from Broadlands two days ago and I am going into my new House tomorrow, No. 21 Park Lane. It is a fine healthy situation looking over the Park and I shall be as comfortable there as I can be after suffering such an irreparable and overwhelming loss and all my happiness on earth. Fortunately the

[24] For Lord Shaftesbury's account of Palmerston's last hours and funeral, see Hodder, *Shaftesbury*, III, pp. 184 *et seq.*

comfort of my Children and the hopes of another life enable me
to bear this great affliction . . .

Nevertheless, in spite of her grief, Emily continued to take an in-
terest in public affairs. She also maintained her prejudices; and when in
February 1868 advancing age and failing health brought about the
retirement of Lord Derby and the succession of Disraeli to the
Premiership, she had the bad taste to write to Fox at Melbourne that
'We are all dreadfully disgusted at the prospect of having a Jew for our
Prime Minister'.[25] But of course nothing was the same now that her
dearest Pam was not there to direct the affairs of the nation!

Park Lane, June 13 [1868]
. . . there is much misery about in all quarters, and much dissatisfaction and our public prospects are very gloomy, with this
horrid Reform Bill and no Man living fit to be Minister of this
great Country. The whole world are regretting more and more
every day the loss of Lord Palmerston . . .

Melbourne Hall Papers

However, Disraeli's period of power was short and the General
Election in the autumn terminated his government. Lady Palmerston
took the greatest interest in the results, and during the campaign
wrote to her son William Cowper in anxious terms.

[25] Lady Palmerston to Fox, Park Lane, Feby. 25 [1868]. Melbourne Hall
Papers. On the other hand, some excuse may be found in Disraeli's description
of Palmerston in 1855, which may have come to Lady Palmerston's ears '. . .
Palmerston . . . is really an impostor, utterly exhausted, and at the least only
ginger-beer, and not champagne, and now an old pantaloon, very deaf, very
blind, and with false teeth, which would fall out of his mouth when speaking if
he did not hesitate and halt so much in his talk . . .' Monypenny and Buckle,
Disraeli, III, pp. 566-7. Quite apart from the fact that the description is absurdly
wide of the mark, the man who can write like that puts himself in a certain
category easily defined.

Broadlands, Wednesday [*c*. September–October 1868]
... Fox tells me there will be a sharp Contest for Derbyshire South. Evans and Colvile against two Tories and he is doubtful of the result; so I have written to him strongly in favour of these two, for he said many Liberals did not like Mr [name omitted from MS] and I thought *he* was a little shaky himself. So I wrote to him strongly about my anxiety for the two Sitting Members and the certainty I felt that Ld Melb[our]ne and Ld Palmerston would have supported the Liberal party now, against such a bad Govern[men]t as the present one and such a Minister as Disraeli.

It is Vexatious that Gladstone should make so many Enemies to himself ...

Broadlands Papers

As the autumn of 1868 passed to the summer of 1869 Lady Palmerston was visibly failing; and though she continued to attend to her affairs it was now with a very trembling hand that she wrote to Fox on estate matters.

Brocket Augt. 25th [1869]
... I dare say the Prices of these Houses are fair enough but I do not like House property for there is always so much expense in repairs and letting. I much prefer buying land. However as they are so near the House it may be well to have them, but dont buy any thing more. I hope there may be enough Trust Money in hand to pay for them but I was obliged to build a Farm House now that was burnt down a year ago ...

Melbourne Hall Papers

At about the time this letter was written, Lord and Lady Shaftesbury and their three daughters, one of whom, Lady Constance Ashley-Cooper, was ill, arrived at Homburg. They had not been there a fortnight before a letter reached them giving a disturbing account of Lady Palmerston's health. Next day there followed an alarming telegram, and preparations were made for Minny's immediate return, her husband to follow more slowly with their ailing daughter and the rest of the party. On the eve of his departure, Lord Shaftesbury received a further telegram which read: 'Sinking, no hope'; and indeed, Lady Palmerston died before Minny, whose return was delayed by contrary winds, could reach her. 'Poor, dear, kind Mum,' wrote Shaftesbury in his diary, 'How can I ever forget, nay, how can I ever *fully* remember —all her unbroken, invariable, tender, considerate goodness towards me? Turn her very inmost heart unto Thyself, O God, for Christ's blessed sake! . . .' [26]

They laid her to rest beside her husband in Westminster Abbey.

[26] Hodder, *Shaftesbury*, III, p. 231.

Some Abbreviations used
in the Notes

Arbuthnot Correspondence = *Correspondence of Charles Arbuthnot.* (1941 ed. Professor A. Aspinall)

Ashley, *Palmerston*   = Evelyn Ashley, *Life of Lord Palmerston.* (ed. 1879)

Aspinall, *Brougham*   = Professor A. Aspinall, *Lord Brougham and the Whig Party.* (ed. 1927)

Bell, *Palmerston*   = Herbert C. F. Bell, *Lord Palmerston.* (ed. 1936)

B.M.   = British Museum

Butler, *Reform Bill*   = J. R. M. Butler, *The Passing of the Great Reform Bill.* (ed. 1914)

Canning's Ministry   = *The Formation of Canning's Ministry, February to August 1827.* (1937 ed. Professor A. Aspinall)

Cecil, *Melbourne*   = Lord David Cecil, *The Young Melbourne.* (ed. 1954)

Cecil, *Lord M.*   = Lord David Cecil, *Lord M.* (ed. 1954)

Chronicles of
      Holland House = Earl of Ilchester, *Chronicles of Holland House, 1820–1900.* (ed. 1937)

Colchester Diary   = *The Diary and Correspondence of Charles Abbot, Lord Colchester.* (1861 ed. Lord Colchester)

Creevey Papers   = *The Creevey Papers, a selection from the Correspondence and Diaries of the late Thomas Creevey, M.P.* (1903–4 ed. Sir Herbert Maxwell)

Croker Papers   = *The Correspondence and Diaries of the late Rt. Hon. John Wilson Croker, Secretary to the Admiralty 1809 to 1830* (1884 ed. Louis J. Jennings)

Greville Memoirs (1874) = *A Journal of the Reigns of King George IV and King William IV* by Charles C. F. Greville. (1874 ed. Henry Reeve)

Greville Memoirs (1885)	= *A Journal of the Reign of Queen Victoria from 1837 to 1852* by Charles C. F. Greville (1885 ed. Henry Reeve)
Greville Memoirs (1887)	= *A Journal of the Reign of Queen Victoria from 1852 to 1860* by Charles C. F. Greville. (1887 ed. Henry Reeve)
Hary-O	= *Hary-O, Letters of Lady Harriet Cavendish.* (1940 ed. Sir George Leveson Gower and Iris Palmer)
H.M.C.	= Historical Manuscripts Commission
Hodder, *Shaftesbury*	= Edwin Hodder, *Life of the Seventh Earl of Shaftesbury.* (ed. 1836)
Ilchester, *Lady Holland*	= *Letters of Elizabeth Lady Holland to her Son, 1821–1845.* (1946 ed. Earl of Ilchester)
Lady Airlie, *Lady Palmerston*	= Mabell, Countess of Airlie, *Lady Palmerston and her Times.* (ed. 1922)
Lady Bessborough	= *Lady Bessborough and her Family Circle.* (1940 ed. Earl of Bessborough and Professor A. Aspinall)
Lady Granville Letters	= *Letters of Harriet, Countess Granville.* (1894 ed. the Hon. F. Leveson Gower)
Lady Lyttelton Correspondence	= *The Correspondence of Sarah Spencer, Lady Lyttelton, 1787–1879.* (1912 ed. Hon. Mrs Hugh Wyndham)
Lane-Poole, *Canning*	= Stanley Lane-Poole, *Life of Stratford Canning, Viscount Stratford de Redcliffe.* (ed. 1888)
Letters of George IV	= *The Letters of King George IV, 1812–1830.* (1938 ed. Professor A. Aspinall)
Lever, *Peel*	= Tresham Lever, *The Life and Times of Sir Robert Peel.* (ed. 1942)
Leveson Gower Correspondence	= *The Private Correspondence of Lord Granville Leveson Gower, First Earl Granville.* (1916 ed. Castalia Countess Granville)
Lieven-Grey Correspondence	= *Correspondence of Princess Lieven and Earl Grey* (1890 ed. Guy le Strange)
Lieven Letters	= *Letters of Dorothea Princess Lieven during her residence in London, 1812–34.* (1902 ed. Lionel G. Robinson)

Lieven-Metternich Letters	= *The Private Letters of Princess Lieven and Prince Metternich.* (1937 ed. Peter Quennell)
Lieven-Palmerston Correspondence	= *Lieven-Palmerston Correspondence, 1826–56.* (1943 ed. Lord Sudeley)
Melbourne Papers	= *Lord Melbourne's Papers.* (1889 ed. Lloyd C. Sandars)
Mrs Arbuthnot	= *The Journal of Mrs Arbuthnot.* (1950 ed. Francis Bamford and the Duke of Wellington)
Peel Papers	= *Sir Robert Peel from his private papers.* (1891 ed. Charles Stuart Parker)
Petrie, *Canning*	= Sir Charles Petrie, *George Canning.* (ed. 1946)
Queen Victoria's Letters	= *The Letters of Queen Victoria, a selection from her Majesty's Correspondence between 1837 and 1861.* (1907 ed. A. C. Benson and Viscount Esher)
Temperley, *Canning*	= Professor Harold Temperley, *The Foreign Policy of Canning 1822–7*
Torrens, *Melbourne*	= W. M. Torrens, *Memoirs of Viscount Melbourne.* (ed. 1878)
Trevelyan, *Grey*	= George Macaulay Trevelyan, *Lord Grey of the Reform Bill.* (ed. 1920)
Walpole, *Russell*	= Spencer Walpole, *Lord John Russell, first Earl Russell.* (ed. 1889)
Webster, *Palmerston*	= Sir Charles Webster, *The Foreign Policy of Palmerston.* (ed. 1951)
Wellesley Papers	= *The Wellesley Papers, the Life and Correspondence of Richard Colley Wellesley Marquess Wellesley, 1760–1842.* (ed. 1914)
Wellington Dispatches	= *Dispatches of Duke of Wellington.* (1844 ed. Colonel Garwood)

INDEX

*As Lady Palmerston appears throughout the book, it has not
been thought necessary to include her in the Index.*

375